Since 1980, energy scarcities have no longer been seen as a "crisis." Tax credits for solar, wind, and other energy conservation approaches have been eliminated. The emphasis of the 1970s on making the United States energy-independent dwindled and virtually disappeared. During the 1980s, the policy was to let the economic marketplace decide the nation's energy policy, a policy that continued into the 1990s. Nonetheless, the willingness of the United States to go to war against Iraq when it invaded Kuwait indicates American commitment to protect its oil resources. The recent collapse of the Asian economies led to a further drop in the demand for energy, and petroleum is at its lowest cost ever (when inflation is considered).

An emerging factor in energy policy has been the environment. Concerns about pollution and ozone depletion have led to automobile and industrial emissions regulation. Concern about environmental issues in general, however, has dropped at a time when oil seems once again plentiful and cheap.

A PROBLEM FOR THE GOVERNMENT OR THE MARKETPLACE?

In 1977, President Jimmy Carter (Democrat) described the energy problem as one that could only be "effectively addressed by a Government that accepts responsibility for dealing with it comprehensively and by a public that understands its seriousness and is ready to make necessary sacrifices." On the other hand, the Ronald Reagan Administration (Republican) downplayed the importance the Carter Administration had placed on government responsibility for dealing with the energy problem.

The Reagan Administration sharply cut federal programs for energy and opposed government intervention in energy markets (for example, the administration refused to tax energy imports). President Reagan believed that the expansion of the role of the federal government in energy policy was counterproductive and misguided. That adminis-

tration pursued a course of transferring the center of the decision-making process to the states, the private sector, and individuals. Reagan's decontrol of petroleum and natural gas reflected his commitment to reducing federal regulation.

The subsequent Republican administration of President George Bush continued the Reagan policy of limiting government regulation of the energy industry. In 1991, Bush unveiled a long-awaited energy policy that promised to reduce the U.S. dependence on foreign oil supplies by increasing domestic oil production and nuclear power. President Bush's aim was to rely on "the power of the marketplace, the common sense of the American people, and the responsible leadership of government and industry." He planned to achieve this by, among other proposals, producing additional oil from environmentally sensitive areas, encouraging pipeline construction, simplifying the construction permit process of nuclear power plants, and increasing competition in the production of electricity. His proposals did not include government-directed conservation efforts or tax incentives.

Conservationists objected to increased offshore drilling, especially in the coastal plain of the Arctic National Wildlife Refuge in Alaska. They also wanted to see automobile fuel mileage increased and conservation methods stressed, rather than increasing the use of nuclear power.

The Democratic Administration of Bill Clinton has sought to bring government involvement back into energy and environmental issues, such as proceeding with enforcement of emission standards to clean up the environment. At the same time, it has opened up several areas for oil exploration that had previously been out of bounds, such as in Alaska, and has backed off on raising CAFE standards (see Chapter X).

U.S. ENERGY PRODUCTION

American energy production has leveled off in recent years. Low oil prices have led to a situation

TABLE 1.1

Energy Production by Source, 1949-1997
(Quadrillion Btu)

Year	Fossil Fuels – Coal	Natural Gas (Dry)	Crude Oil [1]	Natural Gas Plant Liquids	Total Fossil Fuels	Nuclear Electric Power	Hydroelectric Pumped Storage [3]	Renewable Energy – Conventional Hydroelectric Power	Geothermal Energy	Biofuels [4]	Solar Energy	Wind Energy	Total Renewable Energy	Total
1949	11.974	5.377	10.683	0.714	28.748	0	(5)	1.425	0	0.006	0	0	1.431	30.179
1950	14.060	6.233	11.447	0.823	32.563	0	(5)	1.415	0	0.005	0	0	1.421	33.983
1951	14.419	7.416	13.037	0.920	35.792	0	(5)	1.424	0	0.005	0	0	1.429	37.221
1952	12.735	7.964	13.281	0.998	34.977	0	(5)	1.466	0	0.006	0	0	1.472	36.449
1953	12.278	8.339	13.671	1.062	35.349	0	(5)	1.413	0	0.005	0	0	1.418	36.767
1954	10.542	8.682	13.427	1.113	33.764	0	(5)	1.360	0	0.003	0	0	1.363	35.127
1955	12.370	9.345	14.410	1.240	37.364	0	(5)	1.360	0	0.003	0	0	1.363	38.727
1956	13.306	10.002	15.180	1.283	39.771	0	(5)	1.435	0	0.002	0	0	1.436	41.208
1957	13.061	10.605	15.178	1.289	40.133	(s)	(5)	1.516	0	0.002	0	0	1.518	41.651
1958	10.783	10.942	14.204	1.287	37.216	0.002	(5)	1.592	0	0.002	0	0	1.594	38.812
1959	10.778	11.952	14.933	1.383	39.045	0.002	(5)	1.548	0	0.002	0	0	1.550	40.598
1960	10.817	12.656	14.935	1.461	39.869	0.006	(5)	1.608	0.001	0.002	0	0	1.610	41.485
1961	10.447	13.105	15.206	1.549	40.307	0.020	(5)	1.656	0.002	0.001	0	0	1.660	41.987
1962	10.901	13.717	15.522	1.593	41.732	0.026	(5)	1.816	0.002	0.001	0	0	1.820	43.578
1963	11.849	14.513	15.966	1.709	44.037	0.038	(5)	1.771	0.004	0.001	0	0	1.776	45.852
1964	12.524	15.298	16.164	1.803	45.789	0.040	(5)	1.886	0.005	0.002	0	0	1.892	47.721
1965	13.055	15.775	16.521	1.883	47.235	0.043	(5)	2.059	0.004	0.003	0	0	2.066	49.344
1966	13.468	17.011	17.561	1.996	50.036	0.064	(5)	2.062	0.004	0.003	0	0	2.069	52.169
1967	13.826	17.943	18.651	2.177	52.597	0.088	(5)	2.347	0.007	0.003	0	0	2.357	55.043
1968	13.608	19.068	19.308	2.321	54.306	0.142	(5)	2.349	0.009	0.004	0	0	2.362	56.809
1969	13.864	20.446	19.556	2.420	56.286	0.154	(5)	2.648	0.013	0.004	0	0	2.665	59.104
1970	14.607	21.666	20.401	2.512	59.186	0.239	(5)	2.634	0.011	0.003	0	0	2.649	62.074
1971	13.185	22.280	20.033	2.544	58.041	0.413	(5)	2.824	0.012	0.003	0	0	2.839	61.294
1972	14.091	22.208	20.041	2.598	58.938	0.584	(5)	2.864	0.031	0.003	0	0	2.899	62.420
1973	13.993	22.187	19.493	2.569	58.242	0.910	(5)	2.861	0.043	0.003	0	0	2.907	62.060
1974	14.074	21.210	18.575	2.471	56.331	1.272	(5)	3.177	0.053	0.003	0	0	3.232	60.835
1975	14.990	19.640	17.729	2.374	54.734	1.900	(5)	3.155	0.070	0.002	0	0	3.227	59.860
1976	15.654	19.480	17.262	2.327	54.723	2.111	(5)	2.976	0.078	0.003	0	0	3.057	59.892
1977	15.755	19.565	17.454	2.327	55.101	2.702	(5)	2.333	0.077	0.005	0	0	2.416	60.219
1978	14.910	19.485	18.434	2.245	55.074	3.024	(5)	2.937	0.064	0.003	0	0	3.005	61.103
1979	17.539	20.076	18.104	2.286	58.005	2.776	(5)	2.931	0.084	0.005	0	0	3.020	63.801
1980	18.597	19.908	18.249	2.254	59.007	2.739	(5)	2.900	0.110	0.005	0	0	3.014	64.761
1981	18.376	19.699	18.146	2.307	58.529	3.008	(5)	2.758	0.123	0.004	0	0	2.885	64.421
1982	18.639	18.319	18.309	2.191	57.458	3.131	(5)	3.266	0.105	0.003	0	0	3.374	63.962
1983	17.246	16.593	18.392	2.184	54.416	3.203	(5)	3.527	0.129	0.004	0	0	3.661	61.279
1984	19.719	18.008	18.848	2.274	58.849	3.553	(5)	3.386	0.165	0.009	0	(s)	3.560	65.962
1985	19.325	16.980	18.992	2.241	57.539	4.149	(5)	2.970	0.198	0.014	0	(s)	3.183	64.871
1986	19.510	16.541	18.376	2.149	56.576	4.471	(5)	3.071	0.219	0.012	0	(s)	3.303	64.350
1987	20.142	17.136	17.675	2.215	57.167	4.906	(5)	2.635	0.229	0.015	0	(s)	2.879	64.952
1988	20.737	17.599	17.279	2.260	57.874	5.661	(5)	2.334	0.217	0.017	0	(s)	2.569	66.105
1989	21.345	17.847	16.117	2.158	57.468	5.677	(5)	R2.798	0.197	0.020	(s)	(s)	R3.015	R66.160
1990	22.456	18.362	15.571	2.175	58.564	6.161	-0.036	R,6 3.032	R,7 0.344	7 2.632	R,7 0.063	7 0.023	R,7 6.094	R,7 70.782
1991	21.594	18.229	15.701	2.306	57.829	6.579	-0.047	R3.005	R0.349	2.642	R0.066	0.027	R6.089	R70.450
1992	21.583	18.375	15.223	2.363	57.554	6.607	-0.043	R2.618	R0.361	2.788	0.068	0.030	R5.864	R69.983
1993	20.221	18.584	14.494	2.408	55.708	6.519	-0.042	R2.893	R0.375	2.784	0.071	0.031	R6.154	R68.339
1994	22.068	19.348	14.103	2.391	57.909	6.837	-0.035	R2.683	R0.370	2.838	0.072	0.036	R5.999	R70.711
1995	21.978	19.101	13.887	2.442	57.408	7.177	-0.028	3.206	R0.321	R2.846	0.072	0.033	R6.479	R71.035
1996	R22.646	R19.300	R13.723	2.530	R58.199	7.168	-0.032	3.594	0.339	R2.938	0.075	0.035	R6.981	R72.315
1997P	23.173	19.474	13.572	2.535	58.754	6.686	-0.042	3.723	0.366	2.723	0.075	0.039	6.925	72.324

[1] Includes lease condensate.
[3] Represents total pumped storage facility production minus energy used for pumping.
[4] Includes wood, wood waste, peat, wood liquors, railroad ties, pitch, wood sludge, municipal solid waste, agricultural waste, straw, tires, landfill gases, fish oil, and/or other waste.
[5] Through 1989, pumped storage is included in conventional hydroelectric power.
[6] There is a discontinuity in this time series between 1989 and 1990; beginning in 1990, pumped storage is removed and expanded coverage of industrial use of hydroelectric power is included.
[7] There is a discontinuity in this time series between 1989 and 1990 due to the expanded coverage of non-electric utility use of renewable energy beginning in 1990.
R=Revised. P=Preliminary. (s)=Less than 0.0005 quadrillion Btu.
Note: • Totals may not equal sum of components due to independent rounding.

Source: *Annual Energy Review 1997*, Energy Information Administration, Washington, DC, 1998

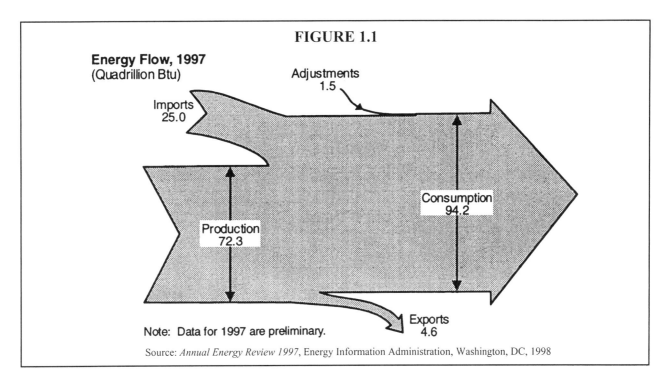

FIGURE 1.1

Energy Flow, 1997
(Quadrillion Btu)

Adjustments
1.5

Imports
25.0

Consumption
94.2

Production
72.3

Exports
4.6

Note: Data for 1997 are preliminary.

Source: *Annual Energy Review 1997*, Energy Information Administration, Washington, DC, 1998

where drilling costs can often be higher than potential returns. In fact, the drop in oil prices has contributed to a decline in the prices of other fossil fuels.

U.S. total energy production in 1997 reached 72.3 quadrillion Btu.* (See Table 1.1 and Figure 1.1.) Figure 1.2 shows that over the past 25 years, the energy production from coal has generally been increasing, the energy production from oil has generally been declining, and the energy from natural gas, after falling in the 1970s and early 1980s, has been increasing. Energy from nuclear power has grown until the last couple of years, and hydroelectric and biofuel power remains relatively steady.

U.S. ENERGY CONSUMPTION

Energy consumption more than doubled from 1949 to 1973, increasing from 30 quads to 74 quads. Meanwhile, the economy grew at about the same rate, so the increased consumption of energy reflected the growth in the economy — as the nation grew, it used more fuel, mainly more petroleum and natural gas. However, after the huge 1973 oil price increases, energy consumption fluctuated, eventually returning to 1973 levels by 1986. Following the drop in crude oil prices in 1986, U.S. imports of oil began to rise, and energy consumption increased, reaching an all time high of 94 quadrillion Btu in 1997. (See Figure 1.3.) While the U.S. population expanded by 79 percent from 1949 to 1997, energy consumption grew by 209 percent during the same period.

Unlike the 1949-1973 period, energy consumption since the 1973 oil crisis has not increased proportionately with the growth in the economy. Americans have been using less energy to accomplish more. Since 1973, energy consumption has shifted away from petroleum and natural gas toward electricity generated by other fuels. In 1973, petroleum and natural gas accounted for 77 per-

---

* One quadrillion Btu equals approximately the energy produced by 170 million barrels of crude oil. Production and consumption figures are given in "quads" to make it easier to compare the actual energy production and use of the various types of energy. If the figures were given in tons for coal, cubic feet for natural gas, and barrels for petroleum, only an expert could make comparisons between the sources.

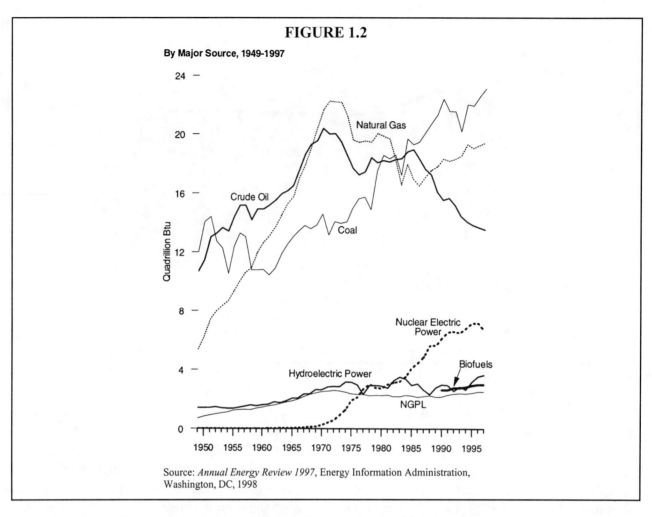

FIGURE 1.2

By Major Source, 1949-1997

Source: *Annual Energy Review 1997*, Energy Information Administration, Washington, DC, 1998

cent of total energy consumption; by 1997, their share had dropped to 63 percent (39 percent petroleum and 24 percent natural gas).

Coal, which in 1973 accounted for 17 percent of the energy consumed, accounted for 23 percent in 1997. Nuclear electric power, which produced barely 1 percent of the nation's consumption in 1973, accounted for 8 percent in 1995 and 7 percent in 1997. (See Figure 1.4 for energy production and consumption flows in 1997.) Renewable energy sources (hydroelectric, solar, biofuels, and wind energy) accounted for 8 percent of energy consumption. (See the separate chapters for further discussion of each energy source.)

FUEL IMPORTS AND EXPORTS

Since 1958, the United States has consumed more energy than it has produced and has made up the difference by importing energy. Imports (mainly oil) grew rapidly from 1953 through

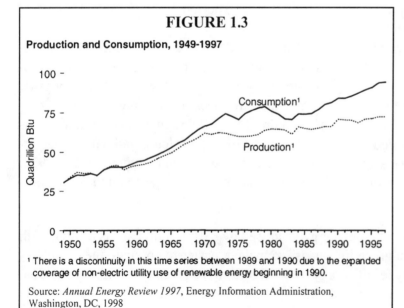

FIGURE 1.3

Production and Consumption, 1949-1997

¹ There is a discontinuity in this time series between 1989 and 1990 due to the expanded coverage of non-electric utility use of renewable energy beginning in 1990.

Source: *Annual Energy Review 1997*, Energy Information Administration, Washington, DC, 1998

FIGURE 1.4

Energy Flow, 1997
(Quadrillion Btu)

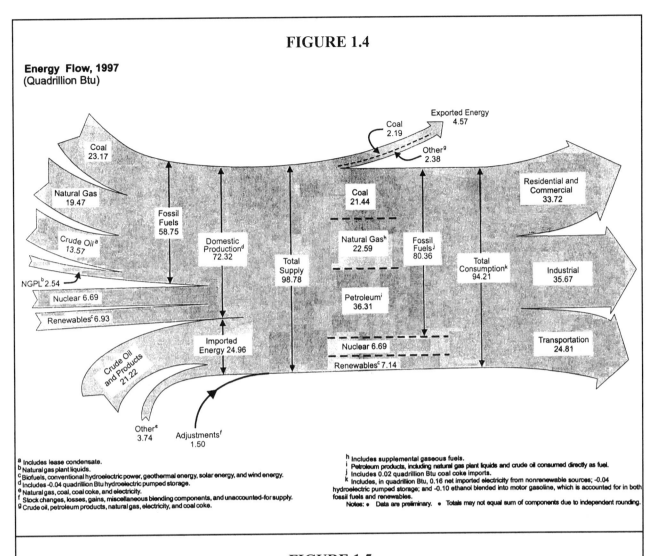

a Includes lease condensate.
b Natural gas plant liquids.
c Biofuels, conventional hydroelectric power, geothermal energy, solar energy, and wind energy.
d Includes -0.04 quadrillion Btu hydroelectric pumped storage.
e Natural gas, coal, coal coke, and electricity.
f Stock changes, losses, gains, miscellaneous blending components, and unaccounted-for supply.
g Crude oil, petroleum products, natural gas, electricity, and coal coke.

h Includes supplemental gaseous fuels.
i Petroleum products, including natural gas plant liquids and crude oil consumed directly as fuel.
j Includes 0.02 quadrillion Btu coal coke imports.
k Includes, in quadrillion Btu, 0.16 net imported electricity from nonrenewable sources; -0.04 hydroelectric pumped storage; and -0.10 ethanol blended into motor gasoline, which is accounted for in both fossil fuels and renewables.
Notes: • Data are preliminary. • Totals may not equal sum of components due to independent rounding.

FIGURE 1.5

Energy Exports

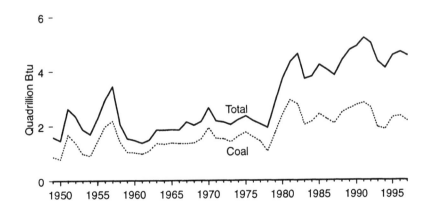

Source of both figures: *Annual Energy Review 1997*, Energy Information Administration, Washington, DC, 1998

TABLE 1.2

Energy Imports, Exports, and Net Imports, 1949-1997
(Quadrillion Btu)

Year	Imports Coal	Imports Natural Gas (Dry)	Imports Petroleum[2]	Imports Other[3]	Imports Total	Exports Coal	Exports Natural Gas (Dry)	Exports Petroleum	Exports Other[3]	Exports Total	Net Imports[1] Coal	Net Imports[1] Natural Gas (Dry)	Net Imports[1] Petroleum[2]	Net Imports[1] Other[3]	Net Imports[1] Total
1949	0.01	0.00	1.43	0.03	1.47	0.88	0.02	0.68	0.02	1.59	-0.87	-0.02	0.75	0.02	-0.13
1950	0.01	0.00	1.89	0.04	1.93	0.79	0.03	0.64	0.01	1.47	-0.78	-0.03	1.24	0.03	0.47
1951	0.01	0.00	1.87	0.04	1.92	1.68	0.03	0.89	0.03	2.62	-1.67	-0.03	0.98	0.01	-0.71
1952	0.01	0.01	2.11	0.04	2.17	1.40	0.03	0.91	0.02	2.37	-1.40	-0.02	1.20	0.02	-0.20
1953	0.01	0.01	2.28	0.04	2.34	0.98	0.03	0.84	0.02	1.87	-0.97	-0.02	1.44	0.02	0.47
1954	0.01	0.01	2.32	0.04	2.37	0.91	0.03	0.75	0.01	1.70	-0.91	-0.02	1.58	0.02	0.67
1955	0.01	0.01	2.75	0.06	2.83	1.46	0.03	0.77	0.02	2.29	-1.46	-0.02	1.98	0.04	0.54
1956	0.01	0.01	3.17	0.06	3.25	1.98	0.03	0.91	0.02	2.95	-1.98	-0.03	2.26	0.04	0.30
1957	0.01	0.04	3.46	0.06	3.57	2.17	0.04	1.20	0.03	3.45	-2.16	(s)	2.26	0.02	0.12
1958	0.01	0.14	3.72	0.05	3.92	1.42	0.04	0.58	0.02	2.06	-1.41	0.10	3.14	0.03	1.86
1959	0.01	0.14	3.91	0.05	4.11	1.05	0.02	0.45	0.02	1.54	-1.04	0.12	3.46	0.03	2.57
1960	0.01	0.16	4.00	0.06	4.23	1.02	0.01	0.43	0.02	1.48	-1.02	0.15	3.57	0.04	2.74
1961	(s)	0.23	4.19	0.04	4.46	0.98	0.01	0.37	0.02	1.38	-0.98	0.22	3.82	0.02	3.08
1962	0.01	0.42	4.56	0.03	5.01	1.08	0.02	0.36	0.03	1.48	-1.08	0.40	4.20	(s)	3.53
1963	0.01	0.42	4.65	0.03	5.10	1.36	0.02	0.44	0.03	1.85	-1.35	0.40	4.21	-0.01	3.25
1964	0.01	0.46	4.96	0.07	5.49	1.34	0.02	0.43	0.06	1.84	-1.33	0.44	4.53	0.01	3.65
1965	(s)	0.47	5.40	0.04	5.92	1.38	0.03	0.39	0.06	1.85	-1.37	0.44	5.01	-0.02	4.06
1966	(s)	0.50	5.63	0.05	6.18	1.35	0.03	0.41	0.06	1.85	-1.35	0.47	5.21	-0.01	4.32
1967	0.01	0.58	5.56	0.04	6.19	1.38	0.08	0.65	0.06	2.15	-1.37	0.50	4.91	-0.02	4.04
1968	(s)	0.67	6.21	0.04	6.93	1.38	0.10	0.49	0.06	2.03	-1.37	0.58	5.73	-0.02	4.90
1969	(s)	0.75	6.90	0.06	7.71	1.53	0.05	0.49	0.08	2.15	-1.53	0.70	6.42	-0.02	5.56
1970	(s)	0.85	7.47	0.07	8.39	1.94	0.07	0.55	0.11	2.66	-1.93	0.77	6.92	-0.04	5.72
1971	(s)	0.96	8.54	0.08	9.58	1.55	0.08	0.47	0.07	2.18	-1.54	0.88	8.07	(s)	7.41
1972	(s)	1.05	10.30	0.11	11.46	1.53	0.08	0.47	0.06	2.14	-1.53	0.97	9.83	0.05	9.32
1973	(s)	1.06	13.47	0.20	14.73	1.43	0.08	0.49	0.06	2.05	-1.42	0.98	12.98	0.14	12.68
1974	0.05	0.99	13.13	0.25	14.41	1.62	0.08	0.46	0.06	2.22	-1.57	0.91	12.66	0.19	12.19
1975	0.02	0.98	12.95	0.16	14.11	1.76	0.07	0.44	0.08	2.36	-1.74	0.90	12.51	0.08	11.75
1976	0.03	0.99	15.67	0.15	16.84	1.60	0.07	0.47	0.06	2.19	-1.57	0.92	15.20	0.09	14.65
1977	0.04	1.04	18.76	0.26	20.09	1.44	0.06	0.51	0.06	2.07	-1.40	0.98	18.24	0.20	18.02
1978	0.07	0.99	17.82	0.36	19.25	1.08	0.05	0.77	0.03	1.93	-1.00	0.94	17.06	0.33	17.32
1979	0.05	1.30	17.93	0.33	19.62	1.75	0.06	1.00	0.06	2.87	-1.70	1.24	16.93	0.27	16.75
1980	0.03	1.01	14.66	0.28	15.97	2.42	0.05	1.16	0.09	3.72	-2.39	0.96	13.50	0.18	12.25
1981	0.03	0.92	12.64	0.39	13.97	2.94	0.06	1.26	0.06	4.33	-2.92	0.86	11.38	0.33	9.65
1982	0.02	0.95	10.78	0.35	12.09	2.79	0.05	1.73	0.06	4.63	-2.77	0.90	9.05	0.28	7.46
1983	0.03	0.94	10.65	0.41	12.03	2.04	0.06	1.57	0.05	3.72	-2.01	0.89	9.08	0.36	8.31
1984	0.03	0.85	11.43	0.46	12.77	2.15	0.06	1.54	0.05	3.80	-2.12	0.79	9.89	0.40	8.96
1985	0.05	0.95	10.61	0.49	12.10	2.44	0.06	1.66	0.08	4.23	-2.39	0.90	8.95	0.41	7.87
1986	0.06	0.75	13.20	0.43	14.44	2.25	0.06	1.67	0.08	4.06	-2.19	0.69	11.53	0.36	10.38
1987	0.04	0.99	14.16	0.57	15.76	2.09	0.05	1.63	0.08	3.85	-2.05	0.94	12.53	0.49	11.91
1988	0.05	1.30	15.75	0.47	17.56	2.50	0.07	1.74	0.10	4.42	-2.45	1.22	14.01	0.37	13.15
1989	0.07	1.39	17.16	0.33	18.95	2.64	0.11	1.84	0.18	4.77	-2.57	1.28	15.33	0.14	14.18
1990	0.07	1.55	17.12	0.26	18.99	2.77	0.09	1.82	0.23	4.91	-2.70	1.46	15.29	0.03	14.08
1991	0.08	1.80	16.35	R0.36	R18.59	2.85	0.13	2.13	0.11	5.22	-2.77	1.67	14.22	0.25	R13.37
1992	0.10	2.16	16.97	0.44	19.66	2.68	0.22	2.01	0.11	5.02	-2.59	1.94	14.96	0.33	14.64
1993	0.18	2.40	18.51	0.45	21.54	1.96	0.14	2.12	0.13	4.35	-1.78	2.25	16.40	0.32	17.19
1994	0.19	2.68	19.25	0.59	22.71	1.88	0.16	1.99	0.09	R4.13	-1.69	2.52	17.26	0.50	18.58
1995	0.18	2.90	18.86	0.54	22.48	2.32	0.16	1.99	0.11	4.58	-2.14	2.74	16.87	0.43	17.90
1996	0.18	R3.00	R20.27	R0.52	R23.97	2.37	0.16	2.06	R0.12	R4.71	-2.19	R2.85	R18.21	R0.39	R19.26
1997 P	0.19	3.04	21.22	0.52	24.96	2.19	0.16	2.10	0.13	4.57	-2.00	2.88	19.12	0.39	20.39

[1] Net imports = imports minus exports.
[2] Includes imports into the Strategic Petroleum Reserve, which began in 1977.
[3] Coal coke and small amounts of electricity transmitted across U.S. borders with Canada and Mexico.
R=Revised. P=Preliminary. (s)=Less than 0.005 quadrillion Btu.

Notes: • Includes trade between the United States (50 States and the District of Columbia) and its territories and possessions. • Totals or net import items may not equal sum of components due to independent rounding.

Source: *Annual Energy Review 1997*, Energy Information Administration, Washington, DC, 1998

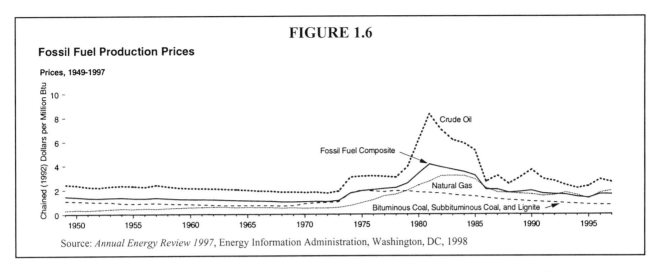

FIGURE 1.6

Fossil Fuel Production Prices

Prices, 1949-1997

Source: *Annual Energy Review 1997*, Energy Information Administration, Washington, DC, 1998

1973 as the United States built up its economy using inexpensive oil. In 1973, net imports of petroleum reached almost 13 quad Btu.

Although the Arab oil embargo of 1973-74, coupled with increased oil prices, momentarily slowed the growth in petroleum imports, the general increase continued, exceeding 18 quads in 1977. That year, U.S. dependence on petroleum imports rose to 46.5 percent of the nation's oil consumption, the highest as of that date. Despite the lesson of 1973, it took a second round of price increases in 1979-80, accompanied by lengthy and frustrating lines at the gas station, to convince Americans that they had to either become less dependent on imported oil or more conserving of resources, or both. Oil imports declined in 1985, and U.S. dependence on foreign oil decreased sharply to 27.3 percent of oil consumption.

Nonetheless, when the price of crude oil dropped, the demand returned, and U.S. dependence on foreign sources of oil increased. When Iraq invaded Kuwait and appeared to threaten the international flow of oil, the United States quickly showed that it intended to guarantee the flow of oil to America and the other industrialized nations. By 1997, imported oil accounted for a record 47.9 percent of U.S. oil use. (See Figure 2.11, Chapter II.) The idea of "energy independence," considered important

less than two decades ago, is hardly thought of today, and demand continues to grow.

Since 1950, the United States has produced more coal than it has consumed and has been an exporter of coal to other nations. In 1997, coal net exports totaled 2.19 quadrillion Btu, approximately half of U.S. energy exports. (See Figure 1.5 and Table 1.2.)

FOSSIL FUEL PRICES

Fossil fuel (crude oil, natural gas, and coal) production prices increased dramatically though the 1970s into the early 1980s. The prices began to level off in the mid-1980s, and in some instances, to drop very sharply, 36 percent in 1986 alone. Crude oil, the most expensive of the fossil fuels, tumbled (in constant dollars that account for inflation) from $8.30 per million Btu in 1981 to only $2.16 per million Btu in 1994 and $2.64 in 1997. The price of natural gas (in constant dollars) sank from $3.17 per million Btu in 1983 to only $1.30 per million Btu in 1995 and $1.94 in 1997. Soft coal dropped from $1.99 per million Btu in 1975 to 76 cents per million Btu in 1997, while anthracite (hard coal) fell from a high of $3.55 per million Btu in 1975 to $1.34 per million Btu in 1997.* (See Figure 1.6 and Table 1.3.)

---

* The measurements, in this case, prices, are given in common units (in this case, cents per million Btu) so that comparisons can be made more easily among the different types of fuel. For prices in dollars per ton, barrel, cubic foot, etc., see the separate chapters on each energy source.

TABLE 1.3

Fossil Fuel Production Prices, 1949-1997
(Dollars per Million Btu)

Year	Gross Domestic Product Implicit Price Deflator (1992 = 1.000)	Crude Oil [2] Nominal	Crude Oil [2] Real [7]	Natural Gas [3] Nominal	Natural Gas [3] Real [7]	Bituminous Coal, Subbituminous Coal, and Lignite [4] Nominal	Bituminous Coal, Subbituminous Coal, and Lignite [4] Real [7]	Anthracite [5] Nominal	Anthracite [5] Real [7]	Fossil Fuel Composite [6] Nominal	Fossil Fuel Composite [6] Real [7]	Percent Change [8]
1949	R0.181	0.44	R2.42	0.05	R0.30	0.20	R1.08	0.36	R2.01	0.26	R1.45	—
1950	R0.183	0.43	R2.37	0.06	R0.34	0.19	R1.06	0.38	R2.07	0.26	R1.40	R-3.4
1951	R0.196	0.44	R2.22	0.06	R0.32	0.20	R1.00	0.41	R2.08	0.26	R1.32	R-5.6
1952	R0.199	0.46	R2.19	0.07	R0.36	0.20	R0.98	0.39	R1.98	0.26	R1.31	R-0.7
1953	R0.202	0.48	R2.35	0.08	R0.40	0.20	R0.96	0.41	R2.02	0.27	R1.35	R3.0
1954	R0.204	0.48	R2.31	0.09	R0.44	0.18	R0.88	0.36	R1.77	0.28	R1.36	R0.5
1955	R0.207	0.48	R2.24	0.09	R0.43	0.18	R0.86	0.33	R1.60	0.27	R1.31	R-3.6
1956	R0.215	0.53	R2.40	0.10	R0.46	0.19	R0.89	0.35	R1.62	0.28	R1.29	R-1.2
1957	R0.222	0.52	R2.29	0.10	R0.45	0.20	R0.90	0.38	R1.72	0.30	R1.35	R4.2
1958	R0.227	0.50	R2.17	0.11	R0.48	0.19	R0.86	0.38	R1.67	0.29	R1.29	R-4.5
1959	R0.230	0.50	2.13	0.12	R0.51	0.19	R0.83	0.36	R1.56	0.29	R1.24	R-3.3
1960	R0.233	0.50	R2.12	0.13	0.54	0.18	0.81	0.34	1.45	0.28	1.22	R-2.3
1961	R0.235	0.50	2.10	0.14	R0.57	0.18	R0.78	0.35	R1.47	0.29	R1.22	0.2
1962	R0.238	0.50	R2.07	0.14	R0.61	0.18	R0.76	0.34	R1.41	0.29	R1.21	-0.6
1963	R0.241	0.50	2.03	0.14	R0.60	0.18	R0.73	0.37	R1.52	0.28	R1.17	R-3.0
1964	0.245	0.49	1.97	0.14	0.56	0.18	0.73	0.38	1.55	0.28	1.13	R-3.7
1965	0.250	0.50	1.93	0.14	0.58	0.18	0.72	0.36	1.45	0.28	1.11	-2.0
1966	0.257	0.50	1.90	0.14	0.56	0.18	0.72	0.35	1.35	0.28	1.09	-1.7
1967	R0.265	0.51	R1.84	0.14	0.55	0.19	0.71	0.36	1.36	0.28	1.07	-1.6
1968	R0.276	0.53	R1.84	0.15	R0.53	0.20	R0.71	0.39	R1.42	0.30	R1.03	R-3.6
1969	R0.289	0.55	R1.80	0.16	R0.50	0.26	R0.86	0.44	R1.52	0.32	R1.04	R0.4
1970	R0.305	0.58	R1.82	0.17	R0.51	0.30	R0.94	0.49	R1.60	0.34	R1.04	1.9
1971	R0.321	0.58	R1.75	0.20	R0.52	0.33	R0.98	0.53	R1.66	0.35	R1.06	-1.0
1972	R0.334	0.58	R1.75	0.27	R0.57	0.36	R1.03	0.55	R1.75	0.40	R1.05	R7.5
1973	R0.353	0.67	R1.90	0.40	0.71	0.36	1.77	0.62	2.66	0.40	1.13	R55.8
1974	R0.385	1.18	3.08	0.53	R0.96	0.68	R1.99	1.02	3.55	0.68	1.76	R11.0
1975	R0.421	1.32	R3.14	0.72	1.19	0.84	1.91	1.50	3.45	0.82	R1.95	R3.7
1976	0.446	1.41	3.17	0.84	1.52	0.85	1.85	1.54	3.24	0.90	2.02	5.2
1977	0.474	1.48	3.12	1.08	R1.64	0.88	R1.92	1.54	R3.00	1.01	2.13	R3.1
1978	R0.509	1.55	R3.05	1.45	R1.96	0.98	R1.91	1.53	R3.08	1.12	R2.57	R17.1
1979	R0.552	2.18	R3.95	1.80	R2.40	1.05	R1.81	1.77	R2.88	1.42	R3.39	R31.9
1980	R0.603	3.72	R6.17	2.22	R2.72	1.09	R1.79	1.86	R3.05	2.04	R4.16	R22.8
1981	R0.660	5.48	R8.30	2.32	R3.16	1.18	R1.74	1.90	R3.14	2.74	R3.93	-5.6
1982	R0.702	4.92	R7.00	2.40	R3.17	1.22	R1.60	2.14	2.75	2.76	R3.69	R-6.0
1983	R0.732	4.52	R6.17	2.26	3.16	1.17	1.53	2.30	R2.60	2.70	3.49	R-5.5
1984	R0.759	4.46	5.88	1.75	R2.88	1.16	R1.46	2.09	2.37	2.65	R3.20	R-8.2
1985	R0.785	4.15	R5.29	1.50	2.17	1.15	1.34	2.04	2.27	2.51	2.05	R-35.9
1986	0.806	2.16	2.68	1.53	1.81	1.08	1.26	1.91	2.20	1.65	2.05	-0.2
1987	0.831	2.66	3.20	1.55	1.77	1.05	1.12	1.89	2.05	1.70	1.78	-13.0
1988	0.861	2.17	2.52	1.48	1.70	1.01	1.06	1.90	R1.86	1.53	1.86	4.7
1989	0.897	2.73	3.05	1.57	1.65	1.00	1.02	1.84	1.66	1.67	1.97	5.7
1990	0.936	3.45	3.69	1.84	1.52	1.00	R0.97	1.74	1.52	1.84	1.72	-12.8
1991	0.973	2.85	2.93	1.67	1.57	0.99	0.90	1.61	R1.42	1.67	R1.66	R-3.3
1992	1.000	2.76	2.76	1.40	R1.80	0.97	R0.86	1.52	R1.52	1.66	R1.63	R-1.8
1993	R1.026	2.46	R2.40	1.96	R1.59	0.93	R0.82	1.46	R1.64	1.67	R1.46	R-10.7
1994	R1.051	2.27	R2.16	1.67	R1.30	0.91	R0.79	1.60	R1.48	1.53	R1.37	-6.0
1995	R1.078	2.52	R2.34	1.40	R1.30	0.88	R0.79	1.76	R1.48	1.47	R1.37	R21.0
1996	R1.102	3.18	R2.89	1.96	R1.78	0.87	0.76	1.63	R1.46	1.82	R1.65	-1.0
1997P	1.124	2.97	2.64	2.18	1.94	0.85	0.76	1.51	1.34	1.84	1.64	-1.0

[2] Domestic first purchase prices.
[3] Wellhead prices.
[4] Prices are based on the value of coal produced at free-on-board (f.o.b.) mines.
[5] Through 1978, prices are f.o.b. preparation plants; for 1979 forward, prices are f.o.b. mines.
[6] Derived by multiplying the price per Btu of each fossil fuel by the total Btu content of the production of each fossil fuel and dividing this accumulated value of total fossil fuel production by the accumulated Btu content of total fossil fuel production.
[7] In chained (1992) dollars, calculated by using gross domestic product implicit price deflators.
[8] Based on real values.
R=Revised. P=Preliminary. — = Not applicable.

Source: *Annual Energy Review 1997*, Energy Information Administration, Washington, DC, 1998

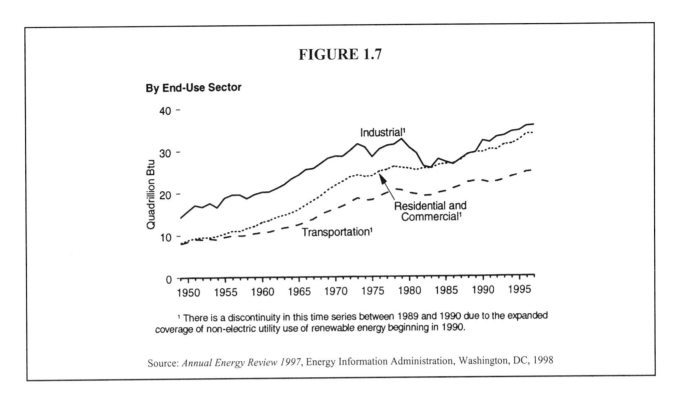

FIGURE 1.7

By End-Use Sector

¹ There is a discontinuity in this time series between 1989 and 1990 due to the expanded coverage of non-electric utility use of renewable energy beginning in 1990.

Source: *Annual Energy Review 1997*, Energy Information Administration, Washington, DC, 1998

To indicate how marked this decline in fuel prices was, the composite value of all fossil fuel prices (in constant dollars) dropped by two-thirds from $4.16 in 1981 to $1.64 in 1997. These huge drops meant economic problems in American states such as Texas, Louisiana, Oklahoma, Montana, West Virginia, and Ohio and in energy-exporting nations such as many of the Middle East nations, Nigeria, Indonesia, Venezuela, and Trinidad. On the other hand, they represented a windfall for industries that used a lot of energy, such as airlines, trucking companies, steel mills, and electric utilities.

ENERGY USE BY SECTOR

Consumers use energy in three main sectors: the residential and commercial sector, the industrial sector, and the transportation sector. Historically, industry has been the largest consuming sector of the economy, followed by the residential and commercial sector and transportation. In 1997, industry used 36 quadrillion Btu, compared to 34 quadrillion Btu in the residential and commercial sector and 25 quadrillion Btu in transportation (Figure 1.7).

Within the sectors, energy sources have changed dramatically over time. For example, in the residential and commercial sector, coal was the leading source until about 1951 but disappeared after that in favor of petroleum, then natural gas, and then electricity. In transportation, however, reliance on petroleum has been almost total since 1949. (See Table 1.4.)

WORLD ENERGY USE

World Energy Production

World production of primary energy rose from 247 quadrillion Btu in 1973 to 375 quadrillion Btu in 1996 (Table 1.5). The Energy Information Administration (EIA) of the U.S. Department of Energy reported that the world's total output of primary energy increased at an average annual rate of 1.8 percent since 1987. Petroleum has been the most heavily used type of energy, accounting for 37 percent of world energy production. Coal production contributed 25 percent; natural gas, 22 percent; hydroelectric, nuclear power, and renewables, the remainder.

11

TABLE 1.4

Energy Consumption by End-Use Sector, 1949-1997
(Quadrillion Btu)

Year	Residential and Commercial						Industrial						Transportation		Total[3]
	Coal	Natural Gas[1]	Petroleum	Electricity	Losses[2]	Total[3]	Coal	Natural Gas[1]	Petroleum	Electricity	Losses[2]	Total[3,4]	Petroleum	Total[5]	
1949	2.83	1.39	1.85	0.43	1.72	8.21	5.43	3.19	3.47	0.42	1.68	14.26	6.15	7.99	30.46
1950	2.80	1.64	2.20	0.47	1.76	8.87	5.78	3.55	3.95	0.50	1.86	15.71	6.69	8.49	33.08
1951	2.47	2.01	2.40	0.54	1.89	9.30	6.20	4.05	4.27	0.57	2.00	17.13	7.36	9.04	35.47
1952	2.25	2.21	2.46	0.59	2.02	9.54	5.52	4.18	4.36	0.60	2.05	16.76	7.71	9.00	35.30
1953	1.93	2.29	2.50	0.65	2.12	9.50	5.93	4.30	4.48	0.68	2.20	17.65	8.06	9.12	36.27
1954	1.68	2.57	2.87	0.72	2.15	9.78	4.73	4.32	4.63	0.71	2.14	16.58	8.12	8.90	35.27
1955	1.67	2.85	2.87	0.79	2.23	10.41	5.62	4.70	5.11	0.89	2.51	18.86	8.80	9.55	38.82
1956	1.55	3.15	3.00	0.87	2.39	10.96	5.67	4.87	5.34	0.98	2.68	19.55	9.15	9.86	40.38
1957	1.19	3.39	2.91	0.95	2.55	10.98	5.54	5.11	5.24	1.00	2.70	19.60	9.29	9.90	40.48
1958	1.16	3.71	3.12	1.01	2.64	11.65	4.53	5.21	5.41	0.98	2.54	18.70	9.51	10.00	40.35
1959	0.99	4.02	3.18	1.12	2.84	12.15	4.41	5.65	5.74	1.08	2.73	19.64	9.85	10.35	42.14
1960	0.99	4.27	3.49	1.23	3.06	13.04	4.54	5.97	5.75	1.11	2.76	20.16	10.13	10.60	43.60
1961	0.90	4.48	3.58	1.30	3.18	13.44	4.38	6.17	5.75	1.15	2.80	20.25	10.32	10.77	44.46
1962	0.88	4.85	3.72	1.41	3.40	14.27	4.35	6.45	6.00	1.23	2.95	21.04	10.77	11.23	46.53
1963	0.76	5.01	3.72	1.54	3.68	14.71	4.59	6.75	6.23	1.29	3.08	21.95	11.17	11.66	48.32
1964	0.65	5.33	3.62	1.67	3.96	15.23	4.91	7.11	6.55	1.38	3.29	23.27	11.50	12.00	50.50
1965	0.62	5.52	3.87	1.78	4.25	16.03	5.13	7.34	6.79	1.46	3.49	24.22	11.87	12.43	52.68
1966	0.61	5.95	3.91	1.94	4.65	17.06	5.21	7.80	7.11	1.58	3.79	25.50	12.50	13.10	55.66
1967	0.52	6.47	4.04	2.09	4.98	18.10	4.93	8.04	7.12	1.65	3.95	25.72	13.11	13.75	57.57
1968	0.47	6.73	4.20	2.32	5.52	19.23	4.85	8.63	7.39	1.78	4.24	26.90	14.21	14.86	61.00
1969	0.44	7.20	4.26	2.57	6.12	20.59	4.71	9.23	7.70	1.91	4.56	28.10	14.81	15.50	64.19
1970	0.37	7.46	4.31	2.79	6.78	21.71	4.66	9.54	7.79	1.95	4.72	28.63	15.31	16.09	66.43
1971	0.35	7.71	4.29	2.99	7.25	22.59	3.94	9.89	7.86	2.01	4.87	28.57	15.92	16.72	67.89
1972	0.27	7.94	4.43	3.25	7.80	23.69	3.99	9.88	8.53	2.19	5.25	29.86	16.89	17.71	71.26
1973	0.25	7.63	4.00	3.50	8.38	24.14	4.06	10.39	9.10	2.34	5.61	31.53	17.83	18.60	74.28
1974	0.26	7.52	4.00	3.47	8.48	23.72	3.87	10.00	8.69	2.34	5.70	30.70	17.40	18.12	72.54
1975	0.21	7.58	3.80	3.60	8.70	23.90	3.67	8.53	8.15	2.35	5.66	28.40	17.62	18.25	70.55
1976	0.20	7.87	4.18	3.75	9.02	25.02	3.66	8.76	9.01	2.57	6.20	30.24	18.51	19.10	74.36
1977	0.21	7.46	4.21	3.96	9.56	25.39	3.45	8.64	9.78	2.68	6.48	31.08	19.24	19.82	76.29
1978	0.21	7.62	4.07	4.12	10.07	26.09	3.31	8.54	9.87	2.76	6.75	31.39	20.04	20.61	78.09
1979	0.19	7.89	3.45	4.18	10.10	25.81	3.59	8.55	10.57	2.87	6.94	32.61	19.82	20.47	78.90
1980	0.15	7.54	3.04	4.35	10.58	25.65	3.16	8.39	9.53	2.78	6.76	30.61	19.01	19.69	75.96
1981	0.17	7.24	2.63	4.50	10.70	25.24	3.16	8.26	8.29	2.82	6.70	29.24	18.81	19.51	73.99
1982	0.19	7.43	2.45	4.57	11.00	25.63	2.55	7.12	7.80	2.54	6.12	26.14	18.42	19.07	70.85
1983	0.19	7.02	2.50	4.68	11.24	25.63	2.49	6.83	7.42	2.65	6.36	25.75	18.59	19.13	70.52
1984	0.21	7.29	2.54	4.93	11.51	26.48	2.84	7.45	8.01	2.86	6.68	27.86	19.22	19.80	74.14
1985	0.18	7.08	2.52	5.06	11.87	26.70	2.76	7.08	7.81	2.86	6.69	27.22	19.50	20.07	73.98
1986	0.18	6.82	2.56	5.24	12.06	26.85	2.64	6.69	7.92	2.83	6.53	26.63	20.27	20.81	74.30
1987	0.16	6.95	2.59	5.44	12.48	27.82	2.67	7.32	8.15	2.93	6.71	27.83	20.87	21.45	76.89
1988	0.17	7.51	2.60	5.72	12.92	28.92	2.83	7.70	8.43	3.06	6.90	28.99	21.63	22.30	80.22
1989	0.15	7.73	2.53	5.86	R13.16	R29.42	2.79	8.13	8.13	3.16	R7.09	R29.36	21.87	22.56	R81.35
1990	0.16	7.22	2.17	6.02	R13.24	R,6 29.45	2.76	8.50	8.06	3.23	R7.10	R32.12	21.81	6 22.54	R,6 84.12
1991	0.14	7.51	2.15	6.18	R13.46	30.12	2.60	8.62	8.06	3.23	R7.03	R31.78	21.46	22.12	R84.03
1992	0.14	7.73	2.13	6.10	R13.25	30.05	2.51	8.97	8.64	3.32	R7.21	R33.03	21.81	22.46	R85.55
1993	0.14	8.04	2.14	6.42	R13.77	R31.17	2.50	9.41	8.45	3.33	R7.16	R33.31	22.20	22.88	R87.37
1994	0.14	7.97	2.09	6.56	R14.00	R31.42	2.51	9.56	8.85	3.44	R7.34	R34.26	22.82	23.57	R89.25
1995	0.14	8.09	R2.08	6.81	R14.47	R32.30	2.49	10.06	8.62	3.46	R7.34	R34.48	23.31	24.07	R90.86
1996	0.14	R8.63	R2.18	7.04	R14.98	R33.69	R2.42	R10.39	R9.07	R3.52	R7.48	R35.51	R23.89	R24.66	R93.87
1997P	0.14	8.50	2.19	7.10	15.25	33.72	2.35	10.32	9.25	3.53	7.59	35.67	24.04	24.81	94.21

1 Includes supplemental natural gas.
2 Electrical system energy losses.
3 Beginning in 1990, includes renewable energy.
4 Also includes hydroelectric power and net imports of coal coke.
5 Also includes coal, natural gas, electricity, and electrical system energy losses.

Total losses are calculated as the sum of energy consumed at electric utilities to generate electricity, utility purchases of electricity from nonutility power producers, and imported electricity, minus exported electricity and electricity consumed by end users. Total losses are allocated to the end-use sectors in proportion to each sector's share of total electricity use.

6 There is a discontinuity in this time series between 1989 and 1990 due to the expanded coverage of non-electric utility use of renewable energy beginning in 1990.
R=Revised. P=Preliminary.
Note: Totals may not equal sum of components due to independent rounding.

Source: *Annual Energy Review 1997*, Energy Information Administration, Washington, DC, 1998

TABLE 1.5

World Primary Energy Production by Source, 1973-1996

(Quadrillion Btu)

Year	Coal	Natural Gas[1]	Crude Oil[2]	Natural Gas Plant Liquids	Nuclear Power[3]	Hydroelectric Power[3]	Geothermal Energy[3] and Other[4]	Total
1973	63.87	45.00	117.88	4.23	2.15	13.52	0.21	246.86
1974	63.79	45.82	117.82	4.22	2.87	14.84	0.22	249.57
1975	66.20	46.17	113.09	4.12	3.85	15.04	0.24	248.70
1976	67.33	48.14	122.92	4.24	4.52	15.08	0.26	262.49
1977	68.47	49.35	127.75	4.40	5.41	15.56	0.27	271.21
1978	69.55	50.79	128.51	4.55	6.43	16.80	0.28	276.91
1979	73.80	54.44	133.87	4.87	6.69	17.69	0.34	291.70
1980	72.94	R52.63	128.12	5.10	7.58	R18.07	R0.32	R284.76
1981	R73.07	R53.52	120.16	5.36	8.53	R18.36	R0.35	R279.35
1982	75.68	51.86	114.51	5.34	9.51	R18.83	R0.38	R276.11
1983	R75.92	R53.59	113.97	5.34	10.72	19.73	R0.43	R279.71
1984	R80.13	R58.91	116.86	5.71	12.99	R20.35	R0.49	R295.44
1985	R83.95	R61.56	115.40	5.82	15.37	R20.57	R0.54	R303.21
1986	R86.08	R62.55	120.24	6.12	16.34	21.04	R0.60	R312.98
1987	R87.89	R65.49	121.16	6.32	17.80	R21.12	R0.65	R320.42
1988	R89.62	R68.67	125.93	6.63	19.30	R21.92	R0.66	R332.73
1989	R91.08	R71.12	127.98	6.67	19.81	R21.72	R0.66	R339.05
1990	R92.38	R72.53	129.50	6.85	R20.37	R22.60	R3.54	R347.77
1991	R87.76	73.29	128.77	7.13	R21.29	R22.98	R3.58	R344.80
1992	R88.70	73.70	129.13	R7.38	R21.36	R22.98	R3.77	R347.02
1993	R86.85	75.18	R128.86	R7.67	R22.02	R24.36	R3.81	R348.74
1994	R88.87	76.01	R130.46	R7.84	R22.45	R24.37	R3.91	R353.91
1995	R92.41	R77.77	R133.32	R8.14	23.31	R25.80	R3.91	R364.67
1996P	93.34	81.67	137.39	8.30	24.10	26.25	4.06	375.11

[1] Dry production.
[2] Includes lease condensate.
[3] Net generation, i.e., gross generation less plant use.
[4] Includes net photovoltaic, solar, wind, and some biofuel electric power. Data for the United States also include biofuels for other than electric power generation.
[5] There is a discontinuity in the series between 1989 and 1990 due to the expanded coverage of U.S.

renewable energy beginning in 1990.
R=Revised. P=Preliminary.
Notes: • Totals may not equal sum of components due to independent rounding.

FIGURE 1.8

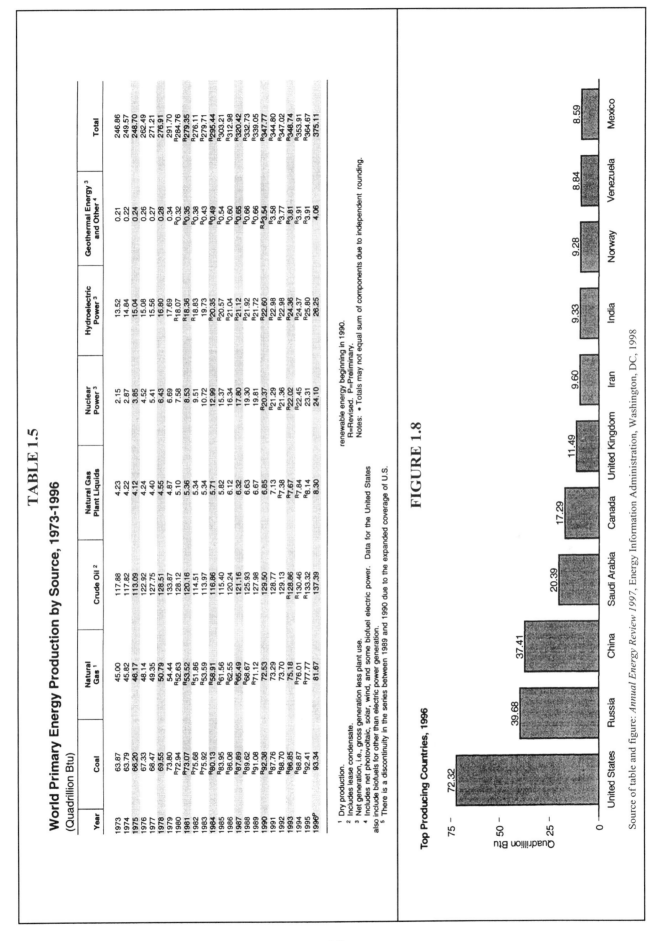

Top Producing Countries, 1996

United States 72.32
Russia 39.68
China 37.41
Saudi Arabia 20.39
Canada 17.29
United Kingdom 11.49
Iran 9.60
India 9.33
Norway 9.28
Venezuela 8.84
Mexico 8.59

Source of table and figure: *Annual Energy Review 1997*, Energy Information Administration, Washington, DC, 1998

TABLE 1.6

World Primary Energy Consumption (Btu), 1987 - 1996
(Quadrillion (10^{15}) Btu)

Region Country	1987	1988	1989	1990	1991	1992	1993	1994	1995	1996[1]
North America										
Canada	10.13	10.87	11.13	10.88	10.82	11.06	11.37	11.68	11.79	12.20
Mexico	4.50	4.67	4.83	4.89	5.15	5.30	5.35	5.41	5.46	5.62
United States	76.91	80.26	81.84	84.16	83.98	85.18	87.05	88.57	90.37	93.36
Other	0.01	0.01	0.02	0.01	0.01	0.02	0.01	0.01	0.01	0.01
Total	91.55	95.82	97.82	99.95	99.96	101.55	103.78	105.67	107.62	111.19
Central & South America										
Argentina	1.97	1.96	1.89	1.84	1.90	2.15	2.30	2.37	2.48	2.60
Brazil	5.25	5.45	5.62	5.66	5.90	5.95	6.20	6.50	6.76	7.24
Chile	0.41	0.45	0.50	0.56	0.56	0.61	0.66	0.71	0.76	0.79
Colombia	0.82	0.92	0.95	0.96	1.00	1.00	1.05	1.09	1.12	1.27
Cuba	0.48	0.49	0.50	0.49	0.45	0.40	0.40	0.40	0.41	0.41
Venezuela	1.89	1.91	2.03	2.09	2.22	2.23	2.30	2.44	2.53	2.57
Other	2.43	2.44	2.49	2.55	2.63	2.70	2.85	3.06	3.23	3.34
Total	13.26	13.61	13.97	14.14	14.67	15.05	15.76	16.57	17.29	18.22
Western Europe										
Austria	1.06	1.14	1.15	1.19	1.23	1.21	1.25	1.24	1.27	1.28
Belgium	2.05	2.05	2.09	2.16	2.26	2.25	2.24	2.30	2.34	2.51
Denmark	0.84	0.83	0.82	0.80	0.83	0.82	0.85	0.84	0.86	0.91
Finland	1.09	1.11	1.13	1.14	1.14	1.11	1.14	1.16	1.06	1.06
France	8.49	8.35	8.63	8.84	9.41	9.41	9.34	9.20	9.46	9.87
Germany	--	--	--	--	14.33	14.03	14.18	14.05	14.25	14.44
Germany, East	3.94	3.86	3.71	3.31	--	--	--	--	--	--
Germany, West	11.41	11.46	11.16	11.43	--	--	--	--	--	--
Greece	0.90	0.97	0.99	1.05	1.07	1.04	1.09	1.11	1.12	1.18
Ireland	0.32	0.33	0.35	0.37	0.39	0.40	0.40	0.42	0.45	0.46
Italy	6.66	6.78	7.03	7.02	7.14	7.18	7.00	6.93	7.51	7.63
Netherlands	3.24	3.24	3.25	3.36	3.55	3.51	3.57	3.56	3.66	3.76
Norway	1.59	1.55	1.56	1.58	1.59	1.65	1.65	1.66	1.72	1.74
Portugal	0.64	0.67	0.70	0.74	0.74	0.75	0.77	0.81	0.84	0.86
Spain	3.62	3.92	4.09	3.93	4.14	4.11	4.05	4.24	4.55	4.50
Sweden	2.23	2.22	2.18	2.15	2.15	2.15	2.15	2.13	2.31	2.27
Switzerland	1.10	1.12	1.13	1.17	1.20	1.21	1.19	1.19	1.17	1.21
Turkey	1.67	1.83	1.78	1.97	2.08	2.10	2.33	2.23	2.47	2.67
United Kingdom	9.09	9.13	9.38	9.48	9.61	9.35	9.60	9.54	9.43	10.05
Former Yugoslavia	2.23	2.23	2.24	2.10	1.85	--	--	--	--	--
Croatia	--	--	--	--	--	0.32	0.32	0.35	0.37	0.40
Serbia and Montenegro	--	--	--	--	--	0.70	0.55	0.58	0.46	0.54
Other	0.26	0.28	0.29	0.30	0.31	0.87	0.86	0.82	0.83	0.88
Total	62.45	63.06	63.67	64.11	65.01	64.15	64.55	64.37	66.13	68.23
Eastern Europe & Former U.S.S.R.										
Bulgaria	1.56	1.55	1.45	1.27	1.00	1.00	0.95	0.95	0.98	1.03
Former Czechoslovakia	4.39	4.30	4.20	3.92	3.57	3.22	--	--	--	--
Czech Republic	--	--	--	--	--	--	2.16	2.32	2.31	2.34
Slovakia	--	--	--	--	--	--	0.73	0.75	0.77	0.66
Hungary	1.43	1.43	1.41	1.25	1.16	1.07	1.09	1.08	1.11	1.14
Poland	5.24	5.17	4.96	3.91	3.85	3.84	3.98	3.78	3.80	3.77
Romania	3.14	3.11	3.25	2.88	2.14	1.97	1.95	1.86	2.07	2.10
Former U.S.S.R.	56.16	57.96	57.45	58.12	54.93	--	--	--	--	--
Azerbaijan	--	--	--	--	--	0.92	0.79	0.72	0.69	0.71
Belarus	--	--	--	--	--	1.50	1.28	1.09	1.01	1.03
Kazakhstan	--	--	--	--	--	3.36	2.76	2.04	2.05	2.07
Lithuania	--	--	--	--	--	0.43	0.36	0.35	0.35	0.35
Russia	--	--	--	--	--	33.75	31.09	28.22	26.84	25.98
Turkmenistan	--	--	--	--	--	0.27	0.25	0.25	0.27	0.26
Ukraine	--	--	--	--	--	8.50	8.23	7.02	6.49	6.25
Uzbekistan	--	--	--	--	--	1.61	1.99	1.73	1.79	1.86
Other	0.16	0.16	0.15	0.11	0.09	1.92	1.44	1.26	1.28	1.27
Total	72.08	73.69	72.87	71.47	66.75	63.35	59.04	53.41	51.81	50.81

See footnotes at end of table.

(continued)

TABLE 1.6 (Continued)

World Primary Energy Consumption (Btu), 1987 - 1996 (Continued)

(Quadrillion (10^{15}) Btu)

Region Country	1987	1988	1989	1990	1991	1992	1993	1994	1995	1996 [1]
Middle East										
Bahrain	0.27	0.23	0.24	0.27	0.30	0.25	0.31	0.32	0.30	0.31
Iran	2.53	2.70	2.97	3.10	3.24	3.35	3.47	3.66	3.81	4.03
Iraq	0.64	0.77	0.82	0.92	0.60	0.84	0.96	1.08	1.13	1.19
Israel	0.39	0.42	0.44	0.45	0.48	0.54	0.60	0.62	0.61	0.64
Kuwait	0.54	0.62	0.70	0.45	0.11	0.26	0.43	0.50	0.52	0.54
Oman	0.14	0.13	0.17	0.18	0.21	0.20	0.23	0.24	0.22	0.23
Qatar	0.27	0.27	0.29	0.36	0.42	0.49	0.57	0.57	0.57	0.58
Saudi Arabia	3.00	3.11	3.07	3.15	3.28	3.39	3.52	3.64	3.85	4.03
Syria	0.43	0.47	0.50	0.60	0.57	0.60	0.65	0.69	0.65	0.66
United Arab Emirates	1.07	1.17	1.26	1.23	1.49	1.55	1.48	1.49	1.60	1.79
Yemen	0.14	0.14	0.15	0.16	0.17	0.17	0.14	0.14	0.15	0.15
Other	0.30	0.29	0.28	0.29	0.33	0.36	0.40	0.45	0.47	0.48
Total	9.71	10.32	10.90	11.14	11.19	12.01	12.76	13.37	13.89	14.63
Africa										
Algeria	1.05	1.12	1.09	1.14	1.26	1.22	1.16	1.22	1.33	1.36
Angola	0.08	0.09	0.08	0.09	0.09	0.09	0.09	0.09	0.09	0.09
Egypt	1.29	1.30	1.35	1.44	1.43	1.43	1.51	1.55	1.58	1.64
Gabon	0.03	0.04	0.04	0.04	0.04	0.05	0.04	0.05	0.05	0.05
Libya	0.45	0.46	0.48	0.51	0.53	0.49	0.51	0.53	0.54	0.57
Morocco	0.25	0.27	0.30	0.31	0.32	0.33	0.36	0.41	0.37	0.38
Nigeria	0.62	0.66	0.71	0.70	0.77	0.79	0.80	0.67	0.83	0.86
South Africa	3.53	3.66	3.40	3.36	3.52	3.45	3.49	3.71	4.18	4.26
Zimbabwe	0.20	0.21	0.22	0.23	0.23	0.24	0.22	0.24	0.15	0.16
Other	1.24	1.32	1.40	1.44	1.45	1.51	1.55	1.65	1.60	1.67
Total	8.76	9.12	9.08	9.24	9.65	9.59	9.73	10.12	10.73	11.05
Far East & Oceania										
Australia	3.27	3.38	3.55	3.70	3.69	3.85	3.92	3.95	4.13	4.08
Bangladesh	0.21	0.23	0.25	0.25	0.26	0.29	0.30	0.33	0.36	0.37
Brunei	0.08	0.07	0.08	0.07	0.04	0.05	0.05	0.05	0.06	0.06
China	24.74	26.45	26.94	26.99	28.24	29.30	31.34	33.97	36.35	37.04
Hong Kong	0.43	0.48	0.50	0.48	0.46	0.50	0.55	0.59	0.64	0.61
India	6.36	6.89	7.24	7.74	8.01	8.65	9.04	9.62	11.11	11.55
Indonesia	1.82	1.86	2.07	2.18	2.29	2.49	2.80	2.97	3.31	3.51
Japan	15.98	16.93	17.53	18.11	18.82	19.08	19.26	20.12	20.76	21.37
Korea, North	1.91	1.98	2.04	2.10	2.13	2.02	2.08	2.07	2.10	2.15
Korea, South	2.74	3.05	3.29	3.68	4.19	4.65	5.39	5.90	6.53	7.16
Malaysia	0.75	0.80	0.86	0.98	1.09	1.13	1.29	1.43	1.48	1.66
New Zealand	0.65	0.68	0.71	0.73	0.73	0.74	0.77	0.80	0.87	0.88
Pakistan	1.00	1.08	1.13	1.18	1.25	1.29	1.41	1.50	1.58	1.68
Philippines	0.60	0.64	0.71	0.73	0.74	0.79	0.86	0.90	0.95	0.98
Singapore	0.63	0.68	0.73	0.80	0.86	0.96	1.08	1.19	1.18	1.22
Taiwan	1.68	1.81	1.93	2.04	2.10	2.21	2.44	2.62	2.87	3.11
Thailand	0.79	0.92	1.08	1.25	1.37	1.47	1.68	1.82	2.24	2.33
Vietnam	0.26	0.25	0.23	0.28	0.27	0.29	0.40	0.44	0.48	0.49
Other	0.57	0.62	0.62	0.64	0.59	0.56	0.60	0.64	0.66	0.68
Total	64.46	68.81	71.47	73.93	77.10	80.34	85.24	90.91	97.66	100.93
World Total	322.27	334.42	339.78	343.97	344.34	346.04	350.85	354.41	365.13	375.07

[1] Preliminary.
- -* Not applicable.
(s) = Value less than 5 trillion Btu.
Notes: Sum of components may not equal total due to independent rounding.
Primary energy consumption includes petroleum, natural gas, coal, and net hydroelectric, nuclear, geothermal, solar, and wind electric power. Data for United States include biofuels energy consumption and data for Brazil include consumption of biofuels electric power. United States apparent coal consumption is calculated as: production+imports-exports-stock builds.

Source: *International Energy Annual 1996*, Energy Information Administration, Washington, DC, 1998

In 1996, the United States, Russia, and China were, by far, the leading producers of energy, followed by Saudi Arabia, Canada, and the United Kingdom (Figure 1.8). Almost all the energy from the Middle East is in the form of oil or natural gas, while coal is particularly important in China. Most of Poland's energy production comes from coal mines, while a large part of French production flows from nuclear power plants. Canada is the leading producer of hydroelectric power and, alone, accounts for 14 percent of world production.

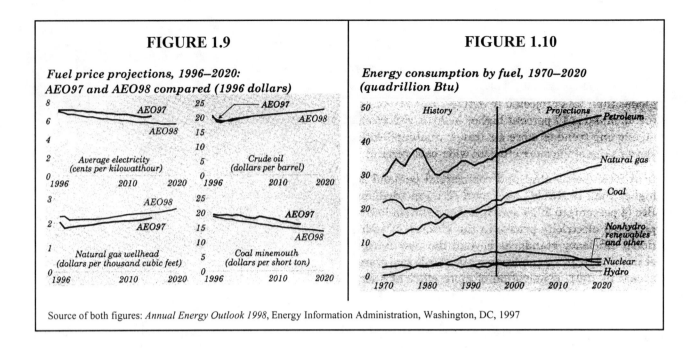

FIGURE 1.9

Fuel price projections, 1996–2020: AEO97 and AEO98 compared (1996 dollars)

FIGURE 1.10

Energy consumption by fuel, 1970–2020 (quadrillion Btu)

Source of both figures: *Annual Energy Outlook 1998*, Energy Information Administration, Washington, DC, 1997

Worldwide Consumption

Table 1.6 shows the world consumption of energy from 1987 to 1996. Five countries — the United States, Russia, China, Japan, and Germany — together consumed 51 percent of the world's total energy.

The United States accounted for 93.4 quadrillion Btu, more than two and one-half times that of China's 37 quadrillion Btu, while Russia consumed 26 quadrillion Btu. For the details of consumption of different types of fuel, see each relevant chapter.

PROJECTED ENERGY USE

Worldwide Energy Use

The Energy Information Administration (EIA) of the U.S. Department of Energy annually forecasts energy supply, demand, and prices. Its latest projections, through the year 2020, are based on U.S. laws in effect on July 1997 and are used by governments, trade associations, and decisionmakers in the public and private sectors. The EIA predicted that average crude oil prices will likely remain close to current rates through 2020, with demand reaching 116.6 million barrels per day in 2020 (Figure 1.9; AEO — Annual Energy Outlook). The EIA expects recent offshore discoveries in Nigeria and Algeria and expanded capacity in Venezuela will offset the declines in production by Persian Gulf countries. Much of the energy demand will come from developing countries, as they try to catch up with industrial nations. Energy consumption in the developing world will likely surpass usage in the industrial world.

Projections for the U.S. Energy Market

The EIA forecasts that U.S. energy consumption will increase from 94 quadrillion Btu in 1996 to 119 quadrillion Btu by 2020 (Figure 1.10 and Table 1.7). Transportation demand will likely grow at an average annual rate of 1.6 percent through 2020. In 1996, light vehicles accounted for 62 percent of energy use in the transportation sector (Figure 1.11). The agency expects increased light-vehicle travel and slower growth in efficiency of such vehicles because of continuing consumer preference for more horsepower and larger vehicles over efficiency. Jet fuel demand will increase due to the trend toward more jet travel as major airlines convert their feeder carriers to jet aircraft, combined with slower sales of more efficient wide-body aircraft.

TABLE 1.7

Summary of results for five cases

Sensitivity Factors	1995	1996	2020				
			Reference	Low Economic Growth	High Economic Growth	Low World Oil Price	High World Oil Price
Primary Production (quadrillion Btu)							
Petroleum.	16.26	16.17	13.71	13.13	14.28	11.47	16.03
Natural Gas.	19.12	19.55	28.21	25.65	30.12	27.28	28.62
Coal.	21.98	22.64	28.59	26.10	31.28	28.68	28.64
Nuclear Power	7.19	7.20	4.09	4.09	4.09	4.09	4.09
Renewable Energy	6.40	6.91	7.71	7.28	8.45	7.68	7.74
Other	1.36	1.33	0.47	0.46	0.51	0.46	0.48
Total Primary Production	**72.31**	**73.80**	**82.77**	**76.71**	**88.73**	**79.66**	**85.60**
Net Imports (quadrillion Btu)							
Petroleum (including SPR)	16.87	18.25	33.71	29.28	37.35	38.57	29.24
Natural Gas.	2.75	2.77	5.02	4.70	5.48	4.91	5.23
Coal/Other (-- indicates export).	-1.73	-1.80	-2.68	-2.71	-2.65	-2.68	-2.68
Total Net Imports	**17.89**	**19.22**	**36.06**	**31.26**	**40.19**	**40.80**	**31.79**
Discrepancy	0.66	0.99	-0.25	-0.24	0.18	-0.48	0.36
Consumption (quadrillion Btu)							
Petroleum Products.	34.74	36.01	47.64	42.65	52.31	50.02	46.12
Natural Gas.	22.18	22.60	33.06	30.19	35.43	32.00	33.69
Coal.	19.96	20.90	25.61	23.08	28.34	25.71	25.67
Nuclear Power	7.19	7.20	4.09	4.09	4.09	4.09	4.09
Renewable Energy	6.40	6.91	7.74	7.31	8.48	7.72	7.77
Other	0.39	0.39	0.43	0.42	0.45	0.44	0.42
Total Consumption	**90.86**	**94.01**	**118.58**	**107.74**	**129.10**	**119.98**	**117.75**
Prices (1996 dollars)							
World Oil Price (dollars per barrel).	17.58	20.48	22.32	21.24	23.44	14.43	28.71
Domestic Natural Gas at Wellhead (dollars per thousand cubic feet)	1.61	2.24	2.54	1.91	2.97	2.45	2.58
Domestic Coal at Minemouth (dollars per short ton)	19.25	18.50	13.27	13.14	13.50	13.16	13.28
Average Electricity Price (cents per kilowatthour).	7.0	6.9	5.5	5.0	5.8	5.4	5.5
Economic Indicators							
Real Gross Domestic Product (billion 1992 dollars)	6,742	6,928	10,900	9,533	12,191	10,953	10,873
(annual change, 1996--2020)	--	--	1.9%	1.3%	2.4%	1.9%	1.9%
GDP Implicit Price Deflator (index, 1992=1.00)	1.08	1.10	2.26	3.20	1.69	2.27	2.25
(annual change, 1996--2020)	--	--	3.0%	4.5%	1.8%	3.1%	3.0%
Real Disposable Personal Income (billion 1992 dollars)	4,964	5,077	8,217	7,336	9,006	8,289	8,171
(annual change, 1996--2020)	--	--	2.0%	1.5%	2.4%	2.1%	2.0%
Index of Manufacturing Gross Output (index, 1987=1.00).	1.264	1.299	2.125	1.761	2.444	2.124	2.121
(annual change, 1996--2020)	--	--	2.1%	1.3%	2.7%	2.1%	2.1%
Energy Intensity (thousand Btu per 1992 dollar of GDP) . . .	13.52	13.57	10.89	11.31	10.60	10.96	10.84
(annual change, 1996--2020).	--	--	-0.9%	-0.8%	-1.0%	-0.9%	-0.9%
Carbon Emissions (million metric tons). .	**1,411**	**1,463**	**1,956**	**1,770**	**2,134**	**1,990**	**1,940**

Notes: Assumptions underlying the alternative cases are defined in the Economic Activity and International Oil Markets sections, beginning on page 34. Quantities are derived from historical volumes and assumed thermal conversion factors. Other production includes liquid hydrogen, methanol, supplemental natural gas, and some inputs to refineries. Net imports of petroleum include crude oil, petroleum products, unfinished oils, alcohols, ethers, and blending components. Other net imports include coal coke and electricity. Some refinery inputs appear as petroleum product consumption. Other consumption includes net electricity imports, liquid hydrogen, and methanol.

Source: *Annual Energy Outlook 1998*, Energy Information Administration, Washington, DC, 1997

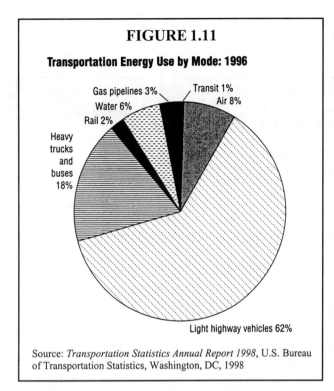

FIGURE 1.11

Transportation Energy Use by Mode: 1996

- Gas pipelines 3%
- Transit 1%
- Water 6%
- Air 8%
- Rail 2%
- Heavy trucks and buses 18%
- Light highway vehicles 62%

Source: *Transportation Statistics Annual Report 1998*, U.S. Bureau of Transportation Statistics, Washington, DC, 1998

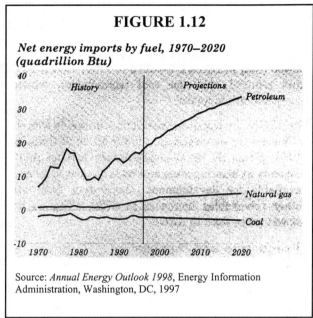

FIGURE 1.12

Net energy imports by fuel, 1970–2020 (quadrillion Btu)

History — Projections

Petroleum

Natural gas

Coal

Source: *Annual Energy Outlook 1998*, Energy Information Administration, Washington, DC, 1997

Energy production from nuclear power will decline significantly through 2020, with no new plants being built, while petroleum and renewables are expected to remain steady. Coal and natural gas energy will rise greatly to meet the increased demand for electricity and the decline in nuclear power. The total production is expected to reach approximately 83 quadrillion Btu. (See Table 1.7.) Declining production and rising consumption will lead to increasing petroleum imports through 2020 (Figure 1.12).

World oil production per person has been declining since 1979. Estimates of when total global oil production will peak range from 2011 to 2025. Although people born in 1950 saw per capita oil production double in a few decades, those born in 2000 are likely to see it cut in half, dropping below 1950 levels. Meeting increasing demand will also require more storage and transportation infrastructure.

While, historically, the production, consumption, and price of energy has largely been driven by supply and demand of petroleum, environmental concerns will now play a greater role.

However, it will not be fuel scarcity that may constrain future growth in energy consumption, but rather concerns about climate change and air and water quality.... A shift to renewable energy sources, such as solar energy and wind power, in addition to continued efficiency gains for power plants, cars, and appliances, holds great promise for meeting future energy demands without adverse ecological consequences. — Worldwatch Institute, *Beyond Malthus: Sixteen Dimensions of the Population Problem*, 1998

Whether the American public will adjust their energy use out of concern for their environment remains unclear.

CHAPTER II

PETROLEUM — SHORTAGE, GLUT, OR ENOUGH?

There is one single, dominant point to keep in mind about energy policy. Oil determines pretty much how the rest of the energy menu goes. — Chemical and Engineering News (July 1991)

THE QUEST FOR OIL

On August 27, 1859, near Titusville, Pennsylvania, Edwin Drake "struck oil" 69 feet below the surface, the first successful modern well drilled in the search for crude oil, and ushered in the "Age of Petroleum." Companies were seeking to meet the growing demand for new and better fuels for heat and illumination. Just as the invention of the steam engine and the creation of better processes for smelting and reforming iron ore led to a huge demand for coal, the development of the internal combustion engine opened a huge market for oil products.

SOURCES OF OIL

Oil is a limited resource. Almost all oil comes from underground reservoirs. Most scientists believe that petroleum (oil and natural gas) is the product of intense heat and pressure applied over millions of years to organic (formerly alive) sediments buried in geological formations. A few scientists, however, believe that at least some of the deposits are accumulations of methane gas seeping out from the molten core of the earth.

At one time, it was believed that crude oil flowed in underground streams and accumulated in lakes or caverns in the earth. Today, scientists know that a petroleum reservoir is usually a solid sandstone or limestone formation overlaid with a layer of impermeable rock or shale that creates a shield. The petroleum accumulates within the pores and fractures of the rock and is trapped beneath the seal. Anticlines, faults, and salt domes are common trapping formations (Figure 2.1). The oil (and natural gas) deposits are at varying depths. Wells are drilled to reach the reservoirs and extract the oil (Figure 2.2). Deep wells are more expensive to

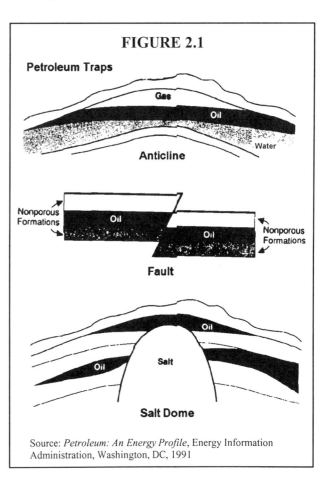

FIGURE 2.1

Petroleum Traps

Source: *Petroleum: An Energy Profile*, Energy Information Administration, Washington, DC, 1991

19

FIGURE 2.2

Oil pumping unit and drilling rig, Texas.

Source: *Annual Energy Review 1997*, Energy Information Administration, Washington, DC, 1998

drill and, therefore, are attempted only to reach large reservoirs or when the price of oil is high.

The Effects of Changing Oil Prices on Oil Exploration

Oil is crucial to the economies of developed nations, and oil production is strongly influenced by market prices. Exploring for new deposits and drilling exploratory wells is expensive. It is also costly to drill, maintain, and operate production wells. Figure 2.3 shows a diagram of a rotary drilling system. If the price of a barrel of oil falls too low, operators will shut off expensive wells because they cannot recover their higher operating costs.

Oil deposits are not distributed evenly over the world, and some that have been exploited for de-

cades are being exhausted. As an oil reservoir is depleted, various techniques can be used to recover additional petroleum. These include the injection of water, chemicals, or steam to force more oil from the rock. Because these recovery techniques can be expensive, they are used only when the price of oil is relatively high.

When oil prices are high, oil companies drill; when prices are low, drilling drops off. In 1996, after a decade of low oil prices, the demand for rigs collapsed, and new rig construction stopped altogether. Thousands of rigs were mothballed, sold for scrap metal, or shipped overseas, and their crews were put out of work. Idle rigs became a source of spare parts for those still operating. In 1997, following a rise in oil prices, the demand for rigs soared, but, by 1998, the market for rigs had once again dwindled as oil prices sank.

TYPES OF OIL

While crude oil is usually dark when it comes from the ground, it may also be almost colorless or green, red, or yellow, depending on its chemical composition and the amount of sulfur, oxygen, nitrogen, and trace minerals present. Its viscosity (resistance to flow or how thick it appears) can range from water-thin to tar-like. Of limited use in its natural form, crude oil has to be refined in order to be made into thousands of useful products.

Crude oils vary in quality. "Sweet" crudes have little sulfur, refine easily, and are worth more than "sour" crudes, which contain more impurities. "Light" crudes have more short molecules, which yield more gasoline and are more profitable than "heavy" crudes, which bring a lower price in the market.

In addition to crude oil, there are two other sources of primary petroleum: lease condensate and natural gas plant liquids. Lease condensate is the liquid condensed from natural gas at or near the wellhead during production operations. It consists primarily of penthanes and heavier hydrocarbons and is generally blended with crude oil for refining. Natural gas plant liquids are collected when natural gas is refined. (See Chapter III.)

HOW OIL IS REFINED

Before oil can be used by consumers, the crude oil, lease condensate, and natural gas plant liquids must be processed into finished products. In distillation, the first step in refining, crude oil molecules are separated according to size and weight. After the crude oil is heated and vaporized, it enters the bottom of a distillation tower where the vaporized crude rises and condenses on trays — gasoline on the top, distillates in the middle, and the heavy residual fuels at the bottom. Each separate portion can then be further refined through the processes of cracking and reforming to transform the condensed molecules into other forms of petroleum. Cracking converts the heaviest fractions of separated petroleum into lighter fractions to produce jet fuel, motor gasolines, home heating oils, and less-residual fuel oil (heavier oils left after distillation of other petroleum products and used for naval ships, commercial and industrial heating, and some power generation). Reforming is used to increase the octane rating of gasolines. (See Figure 2.4.)

Refining is a continuous process, with crude oil entering the refinery while finished products leave by pipeline, truck, and train. Although refineries are surrounded by storage tanks, they have limited capacity. If there is a malfunction and intermediate products cannot be processed, they may be burned (flared) off if no storage facility is available. While a small flare is normal at a refinery or a chemical plant, a large flare, or many flares, likely indicates a processing problem.

FIGURE 2.3
A Rotary Drilling System

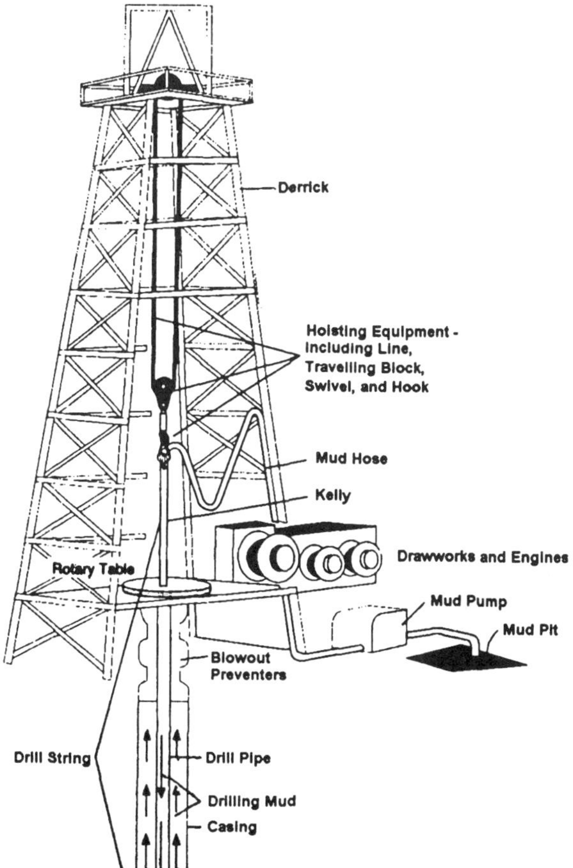

Derrick

Hoisting Equipment - Including Line, Travelling Block, Swivel, and Hook

Mud Hose

Kelly

Drawworks and Engines

Mud Pump

Mud Pit

Rotary Table

Blowout Preventers

Drill String

Drill Pipe

Drilling Mud

Casing

Bit

Source: *Petroleum: An Energy Profile*, Energy Information Administration, Washington, DC, 1991

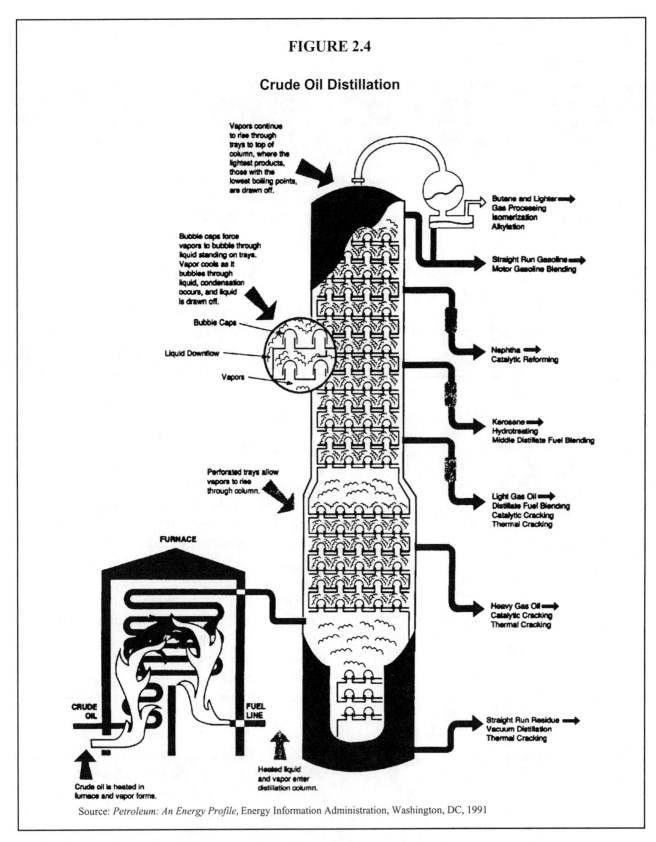

FIGURE 2.4

Crude Oil Distillation

Vapors continue to rise through trays to top of column, where the lightest products, those with the lowest boiling points, are drawn off.

Bubble caps force vapors to bubble through liquid standing on trays. Vapor cools as it bubbles through liquid, condensation occurs, and liquid is drawn off.

Bubble Caps

Liquid Downflow

Vapors

Perforated trays allow vapors to rise through column.

FURNACE

CRUDE OIL

FUEL LINE

Crude oil is heated in furnace and vapor forms.

Heated liquid and vapor enter distillation column.

Butane and Lighter ➡
Gas Processing
Isomerization
Alkylation

Straight Run Gasoline ➡
Motor Gasoline Blending

Naphtha ➡
Catalytic Reforming

Kerosene ➡
Hydrotreating
Middle Distillate Fuel Blending

Light Gas Oil ➡
Distillate Fuel Blending
Catalytic Cracking
Thermal Cracking

Heavy Gas Oil ➡
Catalytic Cracking
Thermal Cracking

Straight Run Residue ➡
Vacuum Distillation
Thermal Cracking

Source: *Petroleum: An Energy Profile*, Energy Information Administration, Washington, DC, 1991

USES FOR OIL

Many of the uses of petroleum are well known: gasoline, diesel fuel, jet fuel, and lubricants for transportation; heating oil, residual oil, and kerosene for heat; and heavy residuals for paving and roofing. Petroleum byproducts are also vital to the chemical industry, ending up in foams used for

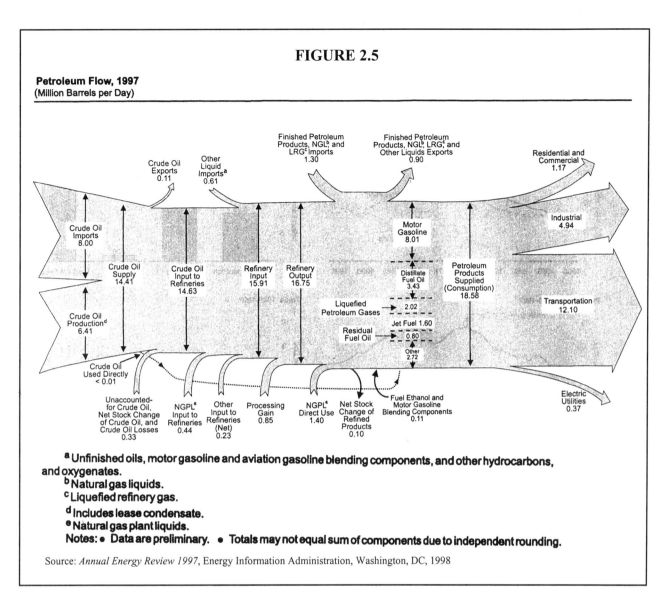

FIGURE 2.5

Petroleum Flow, 1997
(Million Barrels per Day)

Crude Oil Exports 0.11

Other Liquid Imports[a] 0.61

Finished Petroleum Products, NGL[b] and LRG[c] Imports 1.30

Finished Petroleum Products, NGL[b], LRG[c] and Other Liquids Exports 0.90

Residential and Commercial 1.17

Crude Oil Imports 8.00

Crude Oil Supply 14.41

Crude Oil Input to Refineries 14.63

Refinery Input 15.91

Refinery Output 16.75

Motor Gasoline 8.01

Industrial 4.94

Distillate Fuel Oil 3.43

Petroleum Products Supplied (Consumption) 18.58

Crude Oil Production[d] 6.41

Liquefied Petroleum Gases 2.02

Jet Fuel 1.60

Transportation 12.10

Residual Fuel Oil 0.80

Other 2.72

Crude Oil Used Directly < 0.01

Unaccounted-for Crude Oil, Net Stock Change of Crude Oil, and Crude Oil Losses 0.33

NGPL[e] Input to Refineries 0.44

Other Input to Refineries (Net) 0.23

Processing Gain 0.85

NGPL[e] Direct Use 1.40

Net Stock Change of Refined Products 0.10

Fuel Ethanol and Motor Gasoline Blending Components 0.11

Electric Utilities 0.37

[a] Unfinished oils, motor gasoline and aviation gasoline blending components, and other hydrocarbons, and oxygenates.
[b] Natural gas liquids.
[c] Liquefied refinery gas.
[d] Includes lease condensate.
[e] Natural gas plant liquids.
Notes: • Data are preliminary. • Totals may not equal sum of components due to independent rounding.

Source: *Annual Energy Review 1997*, Energy Information Administration, Washington, DC, 1998

packaging, furniture, and padding; many different plastics; synthetic fabrics; paints, dyes, and inks; and drugs. Most chemical plants, because of their dependence on petroleum, are directly connected by pipelines to nearby refineries.

The demand for petroleum products can vary. Heating oil demand (as well as price) rises during the winter. A cold spell, which leads to a sharp rise in demand, may result in a corresponding price rise. A warm winter may be reflected in lower charges as suppliers try to clear out their supplies. Gasoline demand rises during the summer when people drive more on vacations and for recreation.

Petroleum demand also reflects the general condition of the economy. During a recession, when demand for and production of many items incorporating petroleum products drops, demand for oil products also falls and may be reflected in lower prices. (Figure 2.5 shows the flow of oil in the United States.)

DOMESTIC PRODUCTION

U.S. production of petroleum reached its highest level in 1970 at 11.3 million barrels per day and then turned downward. By 1997, U.S. domestic production of crude oil averaged about 6.4 million barrels per day (Table 2.1 and Figure 2.6). Texas, Alaska, Louisiana, California, and the offshore areas around these and other states produce about 75 percent of the nation's oil. Supplies from Alaska, which increased with the construction of

TABLE 2.1

Petroleum Overview, 1949-1997
(Million Barrels per Day)

| Year | Production | | | Other Domestic Supply[2] | Crude Oil Imports[3] | Petroleum Product Imports[4] | Trade | | | Crude Oil Losses | Stock Change[6] | Petroleum Products Supplied |
	Crude Oil[1]	Natural Gas Plant Liquids	Total Petroleum				Total Imports	Total Exports	Net Imports[5]			
1949	5.05	0.43	5.48	(s)	0.42	0.22	0.65	0.33	0.32	0.04	-0.01	5.76
1950	5.41	0.50	5.91	(s)	0.49	0.36	0.85	0.30	0.55	0.05	-0.06	6.46
1951	6.16	0.56	6.72	0.01	0.57	0.35	0.84	0.42	0.42	0.03	0.10	7.02
1952	6.26	0.61	6.87	0.01	0.65	0.38	0.95	0.43	0.52	0.02	0.11	7.27
1953	6.46	0.65	7.11	0.02	0.65	0.39	1.03	0.40	0.63	0.02	0.14	7.60
1954	6.34	0.69	7.03	0.02	0.66	0.40	1.05	0.36	0.70	0.03	-0.03	7.76
1955	6.81	0.77	7.58	0.04	0.78	0.47	1.25	0.37	0.88	0.04	(s)	8.46
1956	7.15	0.80	7.95	0.04	0.93	0.50	1.44	0.43	1.01	0.05	0.18	8.78
1957	7.17	0.81	7.98	0.04	1.02	0.55	1.57	0.57	1.01	0.05	0.17	8.81
1958	6.71	0.81	7.52	0.06	0.95	0.75	1.70	0.28	1.42	0.03	-0.14	9.12
1959	7.05	0.88	7.93	0.09	0.97	0.81	1.78	0.21	1.57	0.01	0.05	9.53
1960	7.04	0.93	7.96	0.15	1.02	0.80	1.81	0.20	1.61	0.01	-0.08	9.80
1961	7.18	0.99	8.17	0.18	1.05	0.87	1.92	0.17	1.74	0.01	0.11	9.98
1962	7.33	1.02	8.35	0.18	1.13	0.96	2.08	0.17	1.91	0.01	0.03	10.40
1963	7.54	1.10	8.64	0.20	1.13	0.99	2.12	0.21	1.91	0.01	(s)	10.74
1964	7.61	1.15	8.77	0.22	1.20	1.06	2.26	0.20	2.06	0.01	0.01	11.02
1965	7.80	1.21	9.01	0.22	1.24	1.23	2.47	0.19	2.28	0.01	-0.01	11.51
1966	8.30	1.28	9.58	0.25	1.22	1.35	2.57	0.20	2.37	0.01	0.10	12.08
1967	8.81	1.41	10.22	0.29	1.13	1.41	2.54	0.31	2.23	0.01	0.17	12.56
1968	9.10	1.50	10.60	0.35	1.29	1.55	2.84	0.23	2.61	0.01	0.15	13.39
1969	9.24	1.59	10.83	0.34	1.41	1.76	3.17	0.23	2.93	0.01	-0.05	14.14
1970	9.64	1.66	11.30	0.35	1.32	2.10	3.42	0.26	3.16	0.01	0.10	14.70
1971	9.46	1.69	11.16	0.44	1.68	2.25	3.93	0.22	3.70	0.01	0.07	15.21
1972	9.44	1.74	11.18	0.44	2.22	2.53	4.74	0.22	4.52	0.01	-0.23	16.37
1973	9.21	1.74	10.95	0.49	3.24	3.01	6.26	0.23	6.02	0.01	0.14	17.31
1974	8.77	1.69	10.46	0.49	3.48	2.64	6.11	0.22	5.89	0.01	0.18	16.65
1975	8.37	1.63	10.01	0.51	4.10	1.95	6.06	0.21	5.85	0.01	0.03	16.32
1976	8.13	1.60	9.74	0.59	5.29	2.03	7.31	0.22	7.09	0.01	-0.06	17.46
1977	8.24	1.62	9.86	0.57	6.61	2.19	8.81	0.24	8.56	0.02	0.55	18.43
1978	8.71	1.57	10.27	0.49	6.36	2.01	8.36	0.36	8.00	0.02	-0.09	18.85
1979	8.55	1.58	10.14	0.58	6.52	1.94	8.46	0.47	7.99	0.02	0.17	18.51
1980	8.60	1.57	10.17	0.68	5.26	1.65	6.91	0.54	6.36	0.01	0.14	17.06
1981	8.57	1.61	10.18	0.64	4.40	1.60	6.00	0.59	5.40	(s)	0.16	16.00
1982	8.65	1.55	10.20	0.65	3.49	1.63	5.11	0.82	4.30	(s)	-0.15	15.30
1983	8.69	1.56	10.25	0.65	3.33	1.72	5.05	0.74	4.31	(s)	-0.02	15.23
1984	8.88	1.63	10.51	0.78	3.43	2.01	5.44	0.72	4.72	(s)	0.28	15.73
1985	8.97	1.61	10.58	0.76	3.20	1.87	5.07	0.78	4.29	(s)	-0.10	15.73
1986	8.68	1.55	10.23	0.81	4.18	2.05	6.22	0.78	5.44	(s)	0.20	16.28
1987	8.35	1.60	9.94	0.85	4.67	2.00	6.68	0.76	5.91	(s)	0.04	16.67
1988	8.14	1.62	9.76	0.90	5.11	2.30	7.40	0.82	6.59	(s)	-0.03	17.28
1989	7.61	1.55	9.16	0.92	5.84	2.22	8.06	0.86	7.20	(s)	-0.04	17.33
1990	7.36	1.56	8.91	1.02	5.89	2.12	8.02	0.86	7.16	(s)	0.11	16.99
1991	7.42	1.66	9.08	1.00	5.78	1.84	7.63	1.00	6.63	(s)	-0.01	16.71
1992	7.17	1.70	8.87	1.16	6.08	1.80	7.89	0.95	6.94	(s)	-0.07	17.03
1993	6.85	1.74	8.58	1.19	6.79	1.83	8.62	1.00	7.62	(s)	0.15	17.24
1994	6.66	1.73	8.39	1.29	7.06	1.93	9.00	0.94	8.05	(s)	0.02	17.72
1995	6.56	1.76	8.32	1.27	7.23	1.61	8.83	0.95	7.89	(s)	-0.25	17.72
1996	R6.46	R1.83	R8.29	R1.36	R7.51	R1.97	R9.48	0.98	R8.50	(s)	R-0.15	R18.31
1997P	6.41	1.84	8.25	1.57	8.00	1.91	9.91	1.00	8.90	0.00	0.14	18.58

[1] Includes lease condensate.
[2] Includes benzol, other hydrocarbons, oxygenates, gasoline blending components, finished petroleum products, hydrogen, alcohol, processing gains, and unaccounted-for crude oil.
[3] Includes imports for the Strategic Petroleum Reserve, which began in 1977.
[4] For 1981 forward, includes motor gasoline blending components and aviation gasoline blending components.
[5] Net imports = imports minus exports.
[6] A negative value indicates a decrease in stocks; a positive value indicates an increase in stocks.
R=Revised. P=Preliminary. (s)=Less than 0.005 million barrels per day and greater than -0.005 million barrels per day.

Notes:
• Totals may not equal sum of components due to independent rounding.

Sources: • 1949-1975—Bureau of Mines, Mineral Industry Surveys, *Petroleum Statement, Annual*. • 1976-1980—Energy Information Administration (EIA), Energy Data Reports, *Petroleum Statement, Annual*. • 1981-1996—EIA, *Petroleum Supply Annual*. • 1997—EIA, *Petroleum Supply Monthly* (February 1998).

Source: *Annual Energy Review 1997*, Energy Information Administration, Washington, DC, 1998

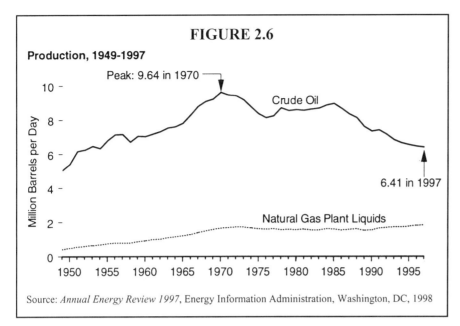

FIGURE 2.6

Production, 1949-1997

Peak: 9.64 in 1970

Crude Oil

6.41 in 1997

Natural Gas Plant Liquids

Source: *Annual Energy Review 1997*, Energy Information Administration, Washington, DC, 1998

a direct pipeline in the late 1970s, have begun to decline as supplies are used up (Figure 2.7).

Any new discoveries are unlikely to lead to a significant increase in domestic production in the near future because of the long lead-time needed to prepare for production. Most oil (75 percent) comes from onshore drilling (Figure 2.8). The 574 thousand producing wells in the United States produced an average of 11.2 barrels per day per well, significantly below peak levels of over 18 barrels per day in the early 1970s. (For a discussion of offshore drilling, see Chapter IV.)

less than half the rate of the early 1970s. Of the country's 13 largest oil fields, seven are at least 80 percent depleted (used up). Geological studies estimate that 34 percent of the U.S. undiscovered recoverable resources are in Alaska, but it is uncertain whether they will ever be recovered.

Middle Eastern producers can drill and bring out crude oil from enormous, easily accessible reservoirs for around $2 a barrel. In contrast, the U.S. Department of Energy estimates it costs an American oil producer about $14 to produce a barrel of oil (not counting royalty payments and taxes, which add to the cost).

Of all the successful domestic oil wells drilled, only approximately 1 percent have been "wildcat" wells that have led to the discovery of new fields, and these discoveries have provided only minor amounts to the total proved reserve additions. The new discoveries have mostly been small — finding new oil in the United States is getting much harder. (See Chapter IV for a more complete discussion of reserves.) The leading oil producing

In a Mature Phase

Even with oil prices expected to increase somewhat, future U.S. oil production will likely continue to drop. The Alaskan oil boom appears to be at an end, and oil production is expected to fall. The United States is considered to be in a "mature" oil development phase, meaning that most of the oil has been found and the nation is producing what it can. The amount of oil discovered per foot of exploratory well in the United States has fallen to

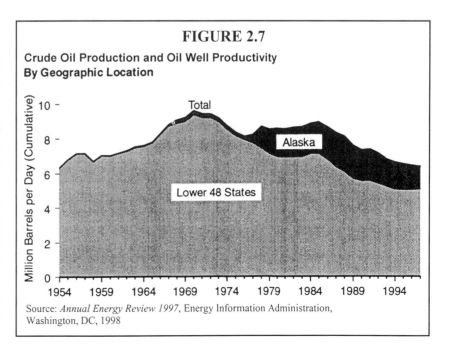

FIGURE 2.7

Crude Oil Production and Oil Well Productivity By Geographic Location

Total

Alaska

Lower 48 States

Source: *Annual Energy Review 1997*, Energy Information Administration, Washington, DC, 1998

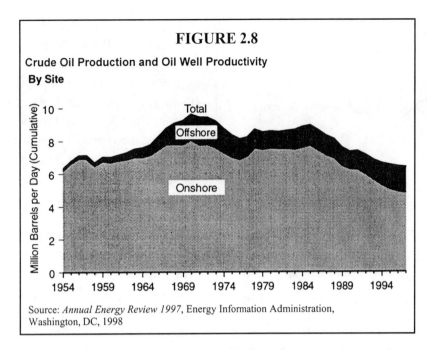

FIGURE 2.8

Crude Oil Production and Oil Well Productivity By Site

Source: *Annual Energy Review 1997*, Energy Information Administration, Washington, DC, 1998

to economic recession, to a very busy utilization rate of 97 percent in 1997 (Table 2.2). The National Petroleum Refiners Association notes that no major refiner has plans to begin construction of any refineries, a process that takes three to five years to complete.

CONSUMPTION BY TYPE

In 1997, most petroleum, by far, was used for transportation (65 percent), followed by industrial use (27 percent), residential and commercial use (6 percent), and electric utilities (2 percent) (Figure 2.10).

companies in the United States are Exxon, Standard Oil (part of British Petroleum), and ARCO.

REFINERIES

Once oil is discovered and drilled, it must be processed or "refined." In 1997, 164 refineries were operating in the United States, a continued drop from 336 in 1949 and 324 in 1981. In 1997, refinery capacity was about 15.5 million barrels per day, well below the 1981 peak of 18.6 million barrels (Table 2.2). The petroleum industry has been going through "rationalization," shutting down older, inefficient refineries and concentrating production in more efficient plants, usually newer and larger. Consolidation within the industry has also played a role. For example, the merger of Gulf Oil Corporation into Chevron Corporation led to the closing of two large refineries, one in Bakersfield, California, and the other in Cincinnati, Ohio. (Figure 2.9 shows a picture of a refinery.) In 1998, Exxon initiated a buyout of Mobile Oil.

In addition, the decision of many OPEC countries (see below), particularly Saudi Arabia, to refine their own oil has led to a drop in demand for U.S. refineries. Currently, the smaller number of refineries is operating near or at full capacity. Utilization rates have steadily increased from the low of 69 percent in 1981, a period of low demand due

Most petroleum used for transportation is for motor gasoline. In the residential and commercial sectors, distillate fuel oil (refined fuels used for space heaters, diesel engines, and electric power generation) accounts for most petroleum use. LPG (Liquid Petroleum Gas) is the primary use for oil in the industrial sector. In electric utilities, residual fuel oils are used most.

A modest decline in residual fuel oil consumption has been caused by the conversion of electric utilities and plants from heavy oil to coal or natural gas energy. An initial decline in the amount of motor gasoline used beginning in 1978 was attributed to the federal CAFE (Corporate Average Fuel Economy) regulations, which required increased miles-per-gallon efficiency in new automobiles. However, that amount has increased steadily since, partly from an increase in users and partly from a leveling off in vehicle efficiency as consumers once again have shown a growing preference for less efficient vehicles, such as larger automobiles and sport-utility vehicles (SUVs).

SELLING AND BUYING — IMPORTS AND EXPORTS

Few countries are able to produce exactly the amount of petroleum they require. Those with a surplus (Saudi Arabia, for example) sells its ex-

TABLE 2.2

Refinery Capacity and Utilization, 1949-1997

Year	Operable Refineries		Gross Input to Distillation Units[3] (million barrels per day)	Utilization[3] (percent)
	Number[4]	Capacity[1] (million barrels per day)		
1949	336	6.23	5.56	89.2
1950	320	6.22	5.98	92.5
1951	325	6.70	6.76	97.5
1952	327	7.16	6.93	93.8
1953	315	7.62	7.26	93.1
1954	308	7.98	7.27	88.8
1955	296	8.39	7.82	92.2
1956	317	8.58	8.25	93.5
1957	317	9.07	8.22	89.2
1958	315	9.36	8.02	83.9
1959	313	9.76	8.36	85.2
1960	309	9.84	8.44	85.1
1961	309	10.00	8.57	85.7
1962	309	10.01	8.83	88.2
1963	304	10.01	9.14	90.0
1964	298	10.31	9.28	89.6
1965	293	10.42	9.56	91.8
1966	280	10.39	9.99	94.9
1967	276	10.66	10.39	94.4
1968	282	11.35	10.89	94.5
1969	279	11.70	11.25	94.8
1970	276	12.02	11.52	92.6
1971	272	12.86	11.88	90.9
1972	274	13.29	12.43	92.3
1973	268	13.64	13.15	93.9
1974	273	14.36	12.69	86.6
1975	279	14.96	12.90	85.5
1976	276	15.24	13.88	87.8
1977	282	16.40	14.98	89.6
1978	296	17.05	15.07	87.4
1979	308	17.44	14.96	84.4
1980	319	17.99	13.80	75.4
1981	324	18.62	12.75	68.6
1982	301	17.89	12.17	69.9
1983	258	16.86	11.95	71.7
1984	247	16.14	12.22	76.2
1985	223	15.66	12.17	77.6
1986	216	15.46	12.83	82.9
1987	219	15.57	13.00	83.1
1988	213	15.92	13.45	84.7
1989	204	15.65	13.55	86.6
1990	205	15.57	13.61	87.1
1991	202	15.68	13.51	86.0
1992	199	15.70	13.60	87.9
1993	187	15.12	13.85	91.5
1994	179	15.03	14.03	92.6
1995	175	15.43	14.12	92.0
1996	R170	15.33	14.34	R94.1
1997P	164	15.45	14.82	97.2

[1] Capacity in million barrels per calendar day on January 1.

[3] For 1949-1980, utilization is derived by dividing gross input to distillation units by one-half of the current year January 1 capacity and the following year January 1 capacity. Percentages were derived from unrounded numbers. For 1981 forward, utilization is derived by averaging reported monthly utilization.

[4] Prior to 1956, the number of refineries included only those in operation on January 1. For 1957 forward, the number of refineries has included all operable refineries on January 1. See Glossary. R=Revised. P=Preliminary.

Sources: **Operable Refineries:** • 1949-1961—Bureau of Mines Information Circular, "Petroleum Refineries, Including Cracking Plants in the United States." • 1962-1977—Bureau of Mines, Mineral Industry Surveys, *Petroleum Refineries, Annual*. • 1978-1981—Energy Information Administration (EIA), Energy Data Reports, *Petroleum Refineries in the United States*. • 1982-1997—EIA, *Petroleum Supply Annual*. • **Gross Input to Distillation Units:** • 1949-1966—Bureau of Mines, *Minerals Yearbook*, "Natural Gas Liquids" and "Crude Petroleum and Petroleum Products" chapters. • 1967-1977—Bureau of Mines, Mineral Industry Surveys, *Petroleum Refineries, Annual*. • 1978-1980—EIA, Energy Data Reports, *Petroleum Refineries in the United States and U.S. Territories*. • 1981-1997—EIA, *Petroleum Supply Annual*. • **Utilization:** • 1949-1980—Calculated. • 1981-1997—EIA, *Petroleum Supply Annual*.

Source: *Annual Energy Review 1997*, Energy Information Administration, Washington, DC, 1998

FIGURE 2.9

Modern refineries employ many different processes to convert crude oil into useful products.

Source: *Petroleum: An Energy Profile*, Energy Information Administration, Washington, DC, 1991

cess to others (the United States, Japan, and European countries) that need more than they can produce. Petroleum is sold as crude oil or as refined products. World trade has been moving towards refined products as the petroleum exporting countries realize that they can make more profit from refined oil products than from crude oil and have, therefore, begun refining some of their own crude oil.

American Imports

While the United States produces a significant amount of petroleum, it has been importing oil since World War II. This reflects the gradual exhaustion of reserves in the United States and the growing energy demand caused by population growth and economic expansion. The relatively low price of foreign oil has encouraged dependence on imported oil as American industry and economic life have been built on oil's easy and cheap availability.

Relatively low crude oil prices and the resulting reduced domestic oil production are the major cause of an increase in imports since 1985. From a low total net import (imports minus exports) of 4.3 million barrels per day in 1985, oil net imports in 1997 were an all-time high of 8.9 million barrels per day. (See Table 2.1.) In 1985, imported oil supplied only 27 percent of American oil consumption. Just five years later, in 1990, the proportion had risen to 42 percent and, by 1997, to 47.9 percent as demand continued to grow (Figure 2.11). Venezuela, Saudi Arabia, Canada, Mexico, and Nigeria were the leading suppliers of petroleum to the United States.

PETROLEUM PRICES

The law of supply and demand, which means that the price of goods reflects a relationship between the supply (availability) and the demand (need), usually explains oil price changes. Changes in the price of oil affect both supply and demand:

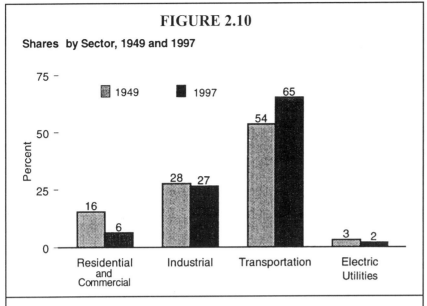

FIGURE 2.10

Shares by Sector, 1949 and 1997

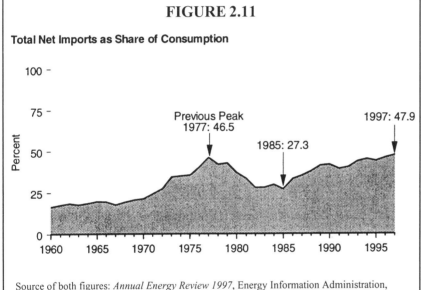

FIGURE 2.11

Total Net Imports as Share of Consumption

Source of both figures: *Annual Energy Review 1997*, Energy Information Administration, Washington, DC, 1998

(marketing group) called the Organization of Petroleum Exporting Countries (OPEC*) to try to manipulate the market. Over the past decade, OPEC has tried to control the supply in order to achieve higher prices. Over this period, each individual producer has been tempted to sell more oil, although an increased supply causes the price to drop. OPEC has also faced long-term problems because earlier higher prices encouraged conservation, reducing demand for oil, which led to a sharp decline in oil prices and reduced their income. As a result of the decreased demand for oil and lower prices, OPEC has lost the ability to control its members and virtually all the power it once had over prices. In 1997, 50 percent of the oil that the United States imported came from OPEC nations. In 1998, gas is cheaper than it has ever been.

Factors That Influence the Price of Oil

Not only senior citizens can reminisce about the "good old days" of cheap gas. A middle-aged person can remember when gas cost $.50 a gallon in the early 1970s. From 1973 to 1981, the price of a gallon of gas (in current dollars that do not consider inflation) more than tripled, although the price in real dollars (that account for inflation) rose only 77 percent. However, since 1981, as a result of the international oil glut, real prices have tumbled. In real dollars, the price of a gallon of regular unleaded gasoline was $2.09 in 1981; by 1997, the price was only $1.10 (Table 2.3). In 1998, prices fell below $1 a gallon, an economic disaster for oil producing nations.

a higher price will increase production as it becomes profitable to operate more expensive wells and reduce demand as consumers reduce activity and increase conservation. The factors also work the other way: reduced demand or increased supply will generally cause the price of oil to drop.

While consumers prefer low prices that allow them to save money or get more of the commodity for the same price, producers naturally prefer to keep prices high. Oil producers formed a cartel

---

* OPEC member countries are Algeria, Indonesia, Iran, Iraq, Kuwait, Libya, Qatar, Saudi Arabia, United Arab Emirates, and Venezuela.

TABLE 2.3

Retail Motor Gasoline and On-Highway Diesel Fuel Prices, 1949-1997
(Cents per Gallon)

Year	Motor Gasoline by Grade — Leaded Regular[1] Nominal	Real[2]	Unleaded Regular Nominal	Real[2]	Unleaded Premium Nominal	Real[2]	All Types Nominal	Real[2]	Regular Motor Gasoline by Area Type[3,4] Conventional	Oxygenated	Oxygenated and Reformulated	Reformulated	All Area Types	On-Highway Diesel Fuel
1949	26.8	R148.1	NA	NA	NA	NA	NA	NA	NA	NA	NA	NA	NA	NA
1950	26.8	R146.4	NA	NA	NA	NA	NA	NA	NA	NA	NA	NA	NA	NA
1951	27.2	R138.8	NA	NA	NA	NA	NA	NA	NA	NA	NA	NA	NA	NA
1952	27.4	R137.7	NA	NA	NA	NA	NA	NA	NA	NA	NA	NA	NA	NA
1953	28.7	R142.1	NA	NA	NA	NA	NA	NA	NA	NA	NA	NA	NA	NA
1954	29.0	R142.2	NA	NA	NA	NA	NA	NA	NA	NA	NA	NA	NA	NA
1955	29.1	R140.6	NA	NA	NA	NA	NA	NA	NA	NA	NA	NA	NA	NA
1956	29.9	R139.1	NA	NA	NA	NA	NA	NA	NA	NA	NA	NA	NA	NA
1957	31.0	R139.8	NA	NA	NA	NA	NA	NA	NA	NA	NA	NA	NA	NA
1958	30.4	R133.9	NA	NA	NA	NA	NA	NA	NA	NA	NA	NA	NA	NA
1959	30.5	R132.6	NA	NA	NA	NA	NA	NA	NA	NA	NA	NA	NA	NA
1960	31.1	R133.5	NA	NA	NA	NA	NA	NA	NA	NA	NA	NA	NA	NA
1961	30.8	R131.1	NA	NA	NA	NA	NA	NA	NA	NA	NA	NA	NA	NA
1962	30.6	R128.6	NA	NA	NA	NA	NA	NA	NA	NA	NA	NA	NA	NA
1963	30.4	R126.1	NA	NA	NA	NA	NA	NA	NA	NA	NA	NA	NA	NA
1964	30.4	124.1	NA	NA	NA	NA	NA	NA	NA	NA	NA	NA	NA	NA
1965	31.2	124.8	NA	NA	NA	NA	NA	NA	NA	NA	NA	NA	NA	NA
1966	32.1	124.9	NA	NA	NA	NA	NA	NA	NA	NA	NA	NA	NA	NA
1967	33.2	125.3	NA	NA	NA	NA	NA	NA	NA	NA	NA	NA	NA	NA
1968	33.7	122.1	NA	NA	NA	NA	NA	NA	NA	NA	NA	NA	NA	NA
1969	34.8	R120.4	NA	NA	NA	NA	NA	NA	NA	NA	NA	NA	NA	NA
1970	35.7	R117.0	NA	NA	NA	NA	NA	NA	NA	NA	NA	NA	NA	NA
1971	36.4	R113.4	NA	NA	NA	NA	NA	NA	NA	NA	NA	NA	NA	NA
1972	36.1	R108.1	NA	NA	NA	NA	NA	NA	NA	NA	NA	NA	NA	NA
1973	38.8	R109.9	NA	NA	NA	NA	NA	NA	NA	NA	NA	NA	NA	NA
1974	53.2	138.2	NA	NA	NA	NA	NA	NA	NA	NA	NA	NA	NA	NA
1975	56.7	R134.7	NA	NA	NA	NA	NA	NA	NA	NA	NA	NA	NA	NA
1976	59.0	132.3	61.4	137.7	NA	NA	65.2	R128.1	NA	NA	NA	NA	NA	NA
1977	62.2	131.2	65.6	138.4	NA	NA	NA	NA	NA	NA	NA	NA	NA	NA
1978	62.6	R123.0	67.0	R131.6	NA	NA	88.2	R159.8	NA	NA	NA	NA	NA	NA
1979	85.7	R155.3	90.3	R163.6	NA	NA	122.1	R202.5	NA	NA	NA	NA	NA	NA
1980	119.1	R197.5	124.5	R206.5	NA	NA	135.3	R205.0	NA	NA	NA	NA	NA	NA
1981	131.1	R198.6	137.8	R208.8	147.0	R222.7	128.1	NA	NA	NA	NA	NA	NA	NA
1982	122.2	R174.1	129.6	R184.6	141.5	R201.6	122.5	R182.5	NA	NA	NA	NA	NA	NA
1983	115.7	R158.1	124.1	R169.5	138.3	R188.9	119.8	R167.3	NA	NA	NA	NA	NA	NA
1984	112.9	R148.7	121.2	R159.7	136.6	R180.0	119.6	R157.8	NA	NA	NA	NA	NA	NA
1985	111.5	R142.0	120.2	R153.1	134.0	R170.7	119.6	R152.4	NA	NA	NA	NA	NA	NA
1986	85.7	106.3	92.7	115.0	108.5	134.6	93.1	115.5	NA	NA	NA	NA	NA	NA
1987	89.7	R107.9	94.8	114.1	109.3	131.5	95.7	115.2	NA	NA	NA	NA	NA	NA
1988	89.9	R104.4	94.6	109.9	110.7	128.6	96.3	111.8	NA	NA	NA	NA	NA	NA
1989	99.8	R111.3	102.1	113.8	119.7	133.4	106.0	118.2	NA	NA	NA	NA	NA	NA
1990	114.9	R122.8	116.4	124.4	134.9	144.1	121.7	130.0	110.0	NA	NA	NA	110.0	NA
1991	NA	NA	114.0	117.2	132.1	135.8	119.6	122.9	110.0	NA	NA	NA	110.0	NA
1992	NA	NA	112.7	112.7	131.6	131.6	119.0	119.0	108.7	NA	NA	NA	108.7	NA
1993	NA	NA	110.8	108.0	130.2	126.9	117.3	114.3	104.8	NA	NA	NA	106.7	NA
1994	NA	NA	111.2	R105.8	130.5	R124.2	117.4	R111.7	105.5	113.8	NA	NA	107.5	NA
1995	NA	NA	114.7	R106.4	133.6	R123.9	120.5	R111.8	109.0	113.5	118.2	115.9	111.1	110.9
1996	NA	NA	123.1	R111.7	141.3	R128.2	128.8	R116.9	117.8	116.0	126.5	123.9	119.9	123.5
1997	NA	NA	123.4	109.8	141.6	126.0	129.1	114.9	117.9	126.2	127.5	125.0	119.8	119.8

[1] Average motor gasoline prices are calculated from a sample of service stations providing all types of service (i.e., full-, mini-, and self-serve). Geographic coverage - 1949-1973, 55 representative cities; 1974-1977, 56 urban areas; 1978 forward, 85 urban areas.

[2] In chained (1992) cents, calculated by using gross domestic product implicit price deflators.

[3] Area refers to the areas of the country in which specific types of motor gasoline are sold as designated by the Environmental Protection Agency. Only self-service prices are included.

[4] Nominal cents.

R=Revised. NA=Not available.

Sources: **Motor Gasoline by Grade:** • 1949-1973—*Platt's Oil Price Handbook and Oilmanac, 1974,* 51st Edition. • 1974 forward—Energy Information Administration (EIA), simple annual averages of monthly data from Bureau of Labor Statistics, *Consumer Prices: Energy.* **Motor Gasoline by Area Type:** EIA, Form EIA-878, "Motor Gasoline Price Survey." **On-Highway Diesel:** EIA, Form EIA-888, "On-Highway Diesel Fuel Price Survey."

Source: *Annual Energy Review 1997,* Energy Information Administration, Washington, DC, 1998

This led many oil-producing nations to cut oil production. Saudi Arabia, Mexico, and Venezuela agreed to cut production by 1.6 to 2 million barrels a day in an attempt to halt the downward slide of prices. Many other oil-producing nations also limited their production.

The Persian Gulf crisis in 1990-1991 caused a sharp, momentary spike in prices as Iraqi and Kuwaiti oil was withdrawn from the market while demand increased as consumers built stockpiles. The price then dropped as other oil producers, particularly Saudi Arabia, increased production, and economic recession dampened demand. The price paid by refiners for crude oil in 1997 averaged $19.08 per barrel, $16.98 adjusted for inflation, compared to $53.39 (inflation adjusted) per barrel in 1981.

LESS CONCERN ABOUT OIL DEPENDENCY

Two decades ago, the United States and its leaders were very concerned that so much of the U.S. productive ability, based so heavily on oil, was in the hands of the OPEC countries. Oil resources became an issue of national security, and OPEC countries, especially the Arab members, were often portrayed as potentially strangling the United States. Now, while over two-fifths of the nation's oil comes from outside the country, with half coming from OPEC nations, there seems to be little public concern.

For Americans, yesterday's issues often fade quickly. The Reagan and Bush Administrations' decisions to permit the energy issue to be handled by the marketplace, while consistent with their economic philosophy, indicated that they saw oil supply as an economic, not a political issue. This downplayed the international political side of the energy problem.

Why There Is Little Concern

The decline in concern is due to several factors. First, the United States and European nations have developed substantial oil reserves to ride out an oil stoppage. This includes the Strategic Petroleum Reserve (SPR) in the United States (see below) and the government stocks and government-required private company reserves in Europe. Demand for oil has dropped, mainly through the conservation efforts of many industrialized nations. This has contributed to an abundant supply of oil in the world. Furthermore, in an emergency, non-OPEC oil producers, such as the United Kingdom and Norway, could increase their supplies.

The falling prices of oil have made the oil-producing nations more dependent on the oil they sell. In fact, for the first time, many Middle Eastern OPEC producers have run into financial problems, and without their oil income, these problems could become very serious. In response, in order to guarantee their market, many OPEC members have developed "downstream" marketing — the country refines its oil products in the country where the oil products are sold.

The increased use of pipelines across Saudi Arabia and through Iraq (until the Gulf War) and Turkey has resulted in a growing number of tankers picking up their oil in either the Red Sea or the Mediterranean Sea and then delivering it to Europe or the United States. These ships do not have to go through the potentially dangerous Persian Gulf. In addition, since many American strategists like to focus on the "choke-point" of the Straits of Hormuz, where a future enemy could supposedly stop the flow of oil to the West, shipment through pipeline lessens the importance of the waterway. On the other hand, such pipelines can be relatively easily destroyed. (See Figure 2.12 for a map of the Middle East.)

The Unpredictability of World Response

Based on these factors, if the oil shortages that developed in 1973 or 1979 occurred again, the result would not likely be the same. Despite the United States' role as protector of Kuwaiti oil in the Persian Gulf, there seems to be little real concern that America's dependence on foreign oil,

FIGURE 2.12

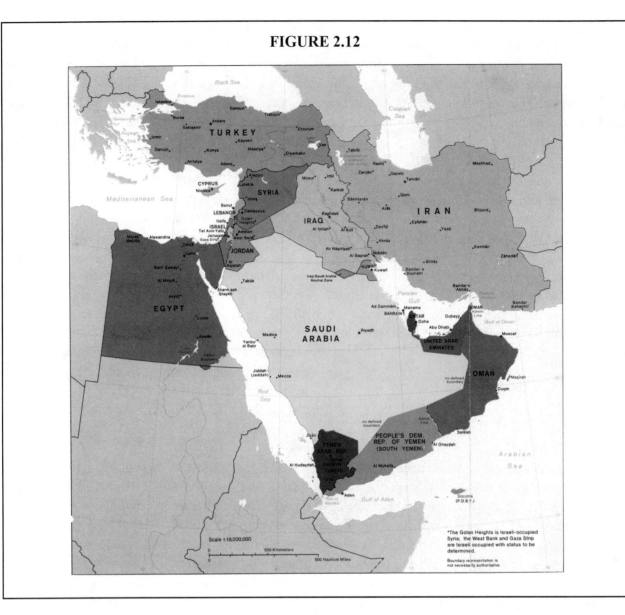

especially OPEC oil, represents a threat to national security or national stability.

The 1990-1991 Persian Gulf War illustrated the effectiveness of both the reserves and market mechanisms. Prices rose in reaction to the loss of Iraqi and Kuwaiti oil supplies and in expectation of hostilities that could restrict other Gulf suppliers from the market. The price rises were somewhat moderated by the availability of reserve supplies. The United States and other western nations agreed on a policy for release of supplies from the reserves, and the United States did actually sell some of its oil. Demand dropped sharply in reaction to the higher prices, one factor in the recession that followed.

Nonetheless, the war also highlighted the dependence on oil of the United States and its Western allies. In order to guarantee its oil, the United States and its allies committed 500,000 troops to war. While world leaders spoke of stopping aggression, most observers wondered if the reaction would have been the same if Kuwait were known for mangos and not oil.

In 1991, the World Bank predicted that prices could go as high as $65 a barrel. Instead, prices have plummeted. Saudi Arabia and other producers, taking advantage of the war-reduced supply and higher prices, increased production. Production continued to rise even as demand fell, resulting in record-high world petroleum stockpiles. As the imbalance persisted, oil prices fell to below the pre-crisis level. Gulf oil production remained high after the war.

CONSERVATION AND OIL DEMAND

Among the principal reasons for the relatively slow growth in total demand are the conservation measures adopted in response to the oil price shocks in the 1970s. Oil companies have reworked existing refineries and built more efficient new ones. These measures will become increasingly effective as oil-powered equipment continues to be replaced and energy users switch to other forms of fuel, perhaps renewable sources (see Chapter IX).

Many quick and relatively inexpensive conservation measures have also been introduced, including more efficient burners, insulation of the heaters and the buildings heated, and reducing use by, for example, lowering thermostat settings. Moderate investments in insulation and burner efficiency in existing buildings can cut fuel needs for these buildings by 25 percent. Most of the increase in oil demand has been for transportation. For information on automobile fuel efficiency measures, see Chapter XI.

When oil prices remain low, companies are less likely to promote conservation and fuel substitution measures because they may not provide an adequate financial return. Car manufacturers have responded by producing fewer smaller, fuel-efficient cars and making a growing number of larger cars and sport-utility vehicles (SUVs). On the other hand, it is important to note that today's large car is much smaller and lighter than a large car of the 1960s

and 1970s. Electric utilities are less likely to substitute natural gas or coal. Building owners are less likely to invest in more insulation.

Since the United States is a "mature" oil-producing nation, an increased national commitment to conservation could be an important way to resolve the problem of an ever-greater dependence on foreign oil, since it will become more costly to get ever smaller amounts of domestic oil out of the ground. Some observers believe it is better to develop programs promoting conservation now because the cost would be less, at this time, than if steps were taken in a hurried manner at some time in the future.

Others feel, however, that should the situation arise, the marketplace will resolve the problem. Today, most observers do not consider continued heavy dependence on foreign oil as a problem or as one likely to develop in such a way that it would threaten the economic well-being of the United States. As a result, the once important issue of "energy independence" is no longer generally considered a national concern.

FIGURE 2.13

Much of the petroleum imported each year arrives via tankers at Gulf Coast facilities.

Source: *Petroleum: An Energy Profile*, Energy Information Administration, Washington, DC, 1991

THE INCREASING IMPORTANCE OF ENVIRONMENTAL CONCERNS

Fossil fuels have been responsible for much contamination of the environment. Because of public sentiment and legislation passed to slow the environmental damage, efforts are being made to shift to the use of other means of energy production, to conserve existing oil supplies, and to find cleaner ways to produce and burn oil. According to the U.S. Department of the Interior, the cause of most spills is oil tanker accidents, like the grounding of the *Exxon Valdez* in 1989. (For further discussion of environmental issues, see *The Environment — A Revolution in Attitudes*, Information Plus, Wylie, Texas, 1998.)

The *Exxon Valdez* Oil Spill

A number of events of the past decade have influenced American attitudes towards oil production and use. In March 1989, the *Exxon Valdez* oil tanker hit a reef in Alaska, spilling 11 million gallons of crude oil into the waters of Prince William Sound — the largest oil spill ever. The cleanup cost Exxon $1.28 billion, which does not include the legal costs or the cost of the value of the lost wildlife. Ironically, the measures used to clean up the spill (washing the beaches with hot water) often proved to be additionally damaging.

The *Exxon Valdez* spill also led to debate about added safety measures in the design of tankers. Tankers are bigger than ever before. In 1945, the largest tanker held 16,500 tons of oil; today, the supertankers carry more than 550,000 tons. These supertankers are harder to maneuver because of their size and are likely to spill more oil if damaged. Al-

though there have been fewer spills since 1973, the amount of oil lost is roughly the same. Figures 2.13 and 2.14 show tankers and marine terminals on the Gulf Coast.

The Oil Pollution Act of 1990

The *Exxon Valdez* oil spill led Congress to pass the Oil Pollution Act of 1990 (PL 101-380) after having debated the issue for 16 years. The bill increases, but still limits, oil spillers' federal liability (financial responsibility) as long as a spill is not the result of "gross negligence" and compensates those economically injured by oil-spill accidents. Damages that can be charged to the oil company are limited to $60 million for tanker accidents and $75 million for accidents at offshore facilities. The rest of the cleanup costs are paid from a $500 million oil-spill fund generated by a 1.3 cents-per-barrel tax on oil. The individual states still maintain the right to impose unlimited liability on spillers. Furthermore, oil companies are required to phase in double hulls on oil vessels over a 25-year period.

FIGURE 2.14

Domestic and foreign crude oil is unloaded from tankers at marine terminals such as this one on the Gulf Coast.

Source: *Petroleum: An Energy Profile*, Energy Information Administration, Washington, DC, 1991

THE SHRINKING U.S. OIL INDUSTRY

During the past decade, the U.S. petroleum industry has experienced a severe loss of jobs. Oil availability and some shift to alternative energy sources have lessened the interest among the general public in reducing U.S. dependency on foreign oil. The American Petroleum Institute (API) claims the downturn in the petroleum industry is due to its lack of access to promising new territories for exploration. The number of seismic land crews and marine vessels searching for oil in the United States and its waters has decreased sharply since 1981. From 1982 to 1992 alone, oil-extraction companies lost 51 percent of their work force, and petroleum refiners experienced a decline of 28 percent. In Texas alone, once the seat of the U.S. oil industry, jobs in the industry plummeted from 80,000 in 1981 to only 25,000 in 1996. In 1998, the Texas Comptroller of Public Accounts estimated that for every dollar drop in the price of oil, 10,000 jobs are lost in the Texas economy. That translated into 100,000 jobs lost in the Texas oil industry from October 1997 to December 1998.

Unlike many other industries, the API predicts today's robust economy will not reverse the situation. Major U.S. oil companies are reporting lower earnings and profits. Industry leaders claim the strong economy will not reverse the con-

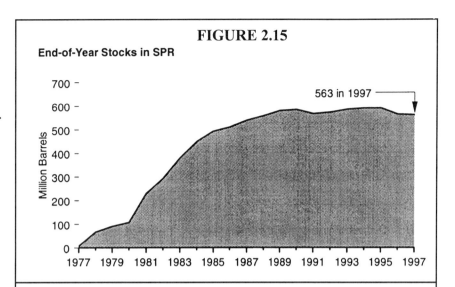

FIGURE 2.15

End-of-Year Stocks in SPR

563 in 1997

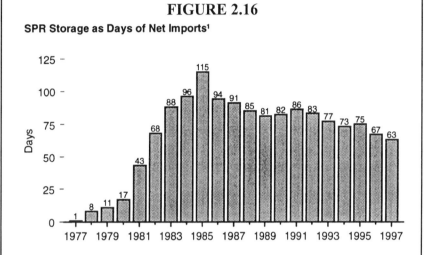

FIGURE 2.16

SPR Storage as Days of Net Imports[1]

[1] Derived by dividing end-of-year Strategic Petroleum Reserve stocks by average daily net imports of all petroleum.
Notes: • SPR=Strategic Petroleum Reserve.

Source of both figures above: *Annual Energy Review 1997*, Energy Information Administration, Washington, DC, 1998

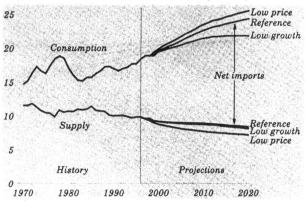

FIGURE 2.17

Petroleum supply, consumption, and imports, 1970-2020 (million barrels per day)

Source: *Annual Energy Outlook 1998*, Energy Information Administration, Washington, DC, 1997

TABLE 2.4

World Crude Oil Production, 1960-1997
(Million Barrels per Day)

Year	Persian Gulf Nations[2]	Selected OPEC[1] Producers								Selected Non-OPEC Producers									World
		Iran	Iraq[3]	Kuwait[3]	Nigeria	Saudi Arabia[3]	United Arab Emirates	Venezuela	Total OPEC	Canada	China	Mexico	Norway	Former U.S.S.R.	Russia	United Kingdom	United States	Total Non-OPEC[4]	
1960	5.27	1.07	0.97	1.69	0.02	1.31	0.00	2.85	8.70	0.52	0.10	0.27	0.00	2.91	—	(s)	7.04	12.29	20.99
1961	5.65	1.20	1.01	1.74	0.05	1.48	0.00	2.92	9.36	0.61	0.11	0.29	0.00	3.28	—	(s)	7.18	13.09	22.45
1962	6.19	1.33	1.01	1.96	0.07	1.64	0.01	3.20	10.51	0.67	0.12	0.31	0.00	3.67	—	(s)	7.33	13.84	24.35
1963	6.82	1.49	1.16	2.10	0.08	1.79	0.05	3.25	11.51	0.71	0.13	0.31	0.00	4.07	—	(s)	7.54	14.62	26.13
1964	7.61	1.71	1.26	2.30	0.12	1.90	0.19	3.39	12.98	0.75	0.18	0.32	0.00	4.60	—	(s)	7.61	15.20	28.18
1965	8.37	1.91	1.32	2.36	0.27	2.21	0.28	3.47	14.35	0.81	0.23	0.32	0.00	4.79	—	(s)	7.80	15.98	30.33
1966	9.32	2.13	1.39	2.48	0.42	2.60	0.36	3.37	15.77	0.88	0.29	0.33	0.00	5.23	—	(s)	8.30	17.19	32.96
1967	9.91	2.60	1.23	2.50	0.32	2.81	0.38	3.54	16.85	0.96	0.28	0.36	0.00	5.68	—	(s)	8.81	18.54	35.39
1968	10.91	2.84	1.50	2.61	0.14	3.04	0.50	3.60	18.79	1.19	0.30	0.39	0.00	6.08	—	(s)	9.10	19.84	38.63
1969	11.95	3.38	1.52	2.77	0.54	3.22	0.63	3.59	20.91	1.13	0.48	0.46	0.00	6.48	—	(s)	9.24	20.79	41.70
1970	13.39	3.83	1.55	2.99	1.08	3.80	0.78	3.71	23.30	1.26	0.60	0.49	0.00	6.99	—	(s)	9.64	22.59	45.89
1971	15.77	4.54	1.69	3.20	1.53	4.77	1.06	3.55	25.21	1.35	0.78	0.49	0.01	7.48	—	(s)	9.46	23.31	48.52
1972	17.54	5.02	1.47	3.28	1.82	6.02	1.20	3.22	26.89	1.53	0.90	0.51	0.03	7.89	—	(s)	9.44	24.25	51.14
1973	20.67	5.86	2.02	3.02	2.05	7.60	1.53	3.37	30.63	1.80	1.09	0.47	0.03	8.32	—	(s)	9.21	25.05	55.68
1974	21.28	6.02	1.97	2.55	2.26	8.48	1.68	2.98	30.35	1.55	1.32	0.57	0.04	8.91	—	(s)	8.77	25.37	55.72
1975	18.93	5.35	2.26	2.08	1.78	7.08	1.66	2.35	26.77	1.43	1.49	0.71	0.19	9.52	—	0.01	8.37	26.06	52.83
1976	21.51	5.88	2.42	2.15	2.07	8.58	1.94	2.29	30.33	1.31	1.67	0.83	0.28	10.06	—	0.25	8.13	27.01	57.34
1977	21.73	5.66	2.35	1.97	2.09	9.25	2.00	2.24	30.89	1.32	1.87	0.98	0.28	10.60	—	0.77	8.24	28.82	59.71
1978	20.61	5.24	2.56	2.13	1.90	8.30	1.83	2.17	29.46	1.32	2.08	1.21	0.36	11.11	—	1.08	8.71	30.70	60.16
1979	21.07	3.17	3.48	2.50	2.30	9.53	1.83	2.36	30.58	1.50	2.12	1.46	0.40	11.38	—	1.57	8.55	32.09	62.67
1980	17.96	1.66	2.51	1.66	2.06	9.90	1.71	2.17	26.61	1.44	2.11	1.94	0.53	11.71	—	1.62	8.60	32.99	59.60
1981	15.25	1.38	1.00	1.13	1.43	9.82	1.47	2.10	22.48	1.29	2.01	2.31	0.50	11.85	—	1.81	8.57	33.60	56.08
1982	12.16	2.21	1.01	0.82	1.30	6.48	1.25	1.90	18.78	1.27	2.05	2.75	0.52	11.91	—	2.07	8.65	34.70	53.48
1983	11.08	2.44	1.01	1.06	1.24	5.09	1.15	1.80	17.50	1.36	2.12	2.69	0.61	11.97	—	2.29	8.69	35.76	53.26
1984	10.78	2.17	1.21	1.16	1.39	4.66	1.19	1.68	17.44	1.44	2.30	2.78	0.70	11.86	—	2.48	8.88	37.05	54.49
1985	9.63	2.25	1.43	1.02	1.50	3.39	1.33	1.79	16.18	1.47	2.51	2.75	0.79	11.59	—	2.53	8.97	37.80	53.98
1986	11.70	2.04	1.69	1.42	1.47	4.87	1.54	1.75	18.28	1.47	2.62	2.44	0.87	11.90	—	2.54	8.68	37.95	56.23
1987	12.10	2.30	2.08	1.59	1.34	4.27	1.54	1.75	18.52	1.54	2.69	2.55	1.02	12.05	—	2.41	8.35	38.15	56.67
1988	13.46	2.24	2.69	1.49	1.45	5.09	1.57	1.90	20.32	1.62	2.73	2.51	1.16	12.05	—	2.23	8.14	38.42	58.74
1989	14.84	2.81	2.90	1.78	1.72	5.06	1.86	1.91	22.07	1.56	2.76	2.52	1.55	11.72	—	1.80	7.61	37.79	59.86
1990	15.28	3.09	2.04	1.18	1.81	6.41	2.12	2.14	23.20	1.55	2.77	2.55	1.70	10.98	—	1.82	7.36	37.37	60.57
1991	14.74	3.31	0.31	0.19	1.89	8.12	2.39	2.38	23.27	1.55	2.84	2.68	1.89	9.99	—	1.80	7.42	36.94	60.21
1992	15.97	3.43	0.43	1.06	1.94	8.33	2.27	2.37	24.40	1.61	2.85	2.67	2.23	—	7.63	1.83	7.17	35.82	60.22
1993	16.71	3.54	0.51	1.85	1.96	8.20	2.16	2.45	25.12	1.68	2.89	2.67	2.35	—	6.73	1.92	6.85	35.13	60.25
1994	16.96	3.62	0.55	2.03	1.93	8.12	2.19	2.59	25.51	1.75	2.94	2.69	2.52	—	6.14	2.37	6.66	35.49	61.00
1995	17.30	3.64	0.56	2.06	1.99	8.23	2.28	2.75	26.09	1.81	2.99	2.62	2.77	—	6.00	2.49	6.56	36.36	62.45
1996	17.37	3.69	0.58	2.06	2.19	8.22	2.28	3.05	26.77	1.82	3.13	R2.86	3.10	—	R5.77	2.57	R6.46	R37.20	R63.97
1997P	18.50	3.66	1.19	2.08	2.32	8.56	2.32	3.31	28.36	1.89	3.20	3.03	3.15	—	5.88	2.52	6.41	37.91	66.27

[1] Organization of Petroleum Exporting Countries. See Glossary for membership.
[2] Persian Gulf Nations are Bahrain, Iran, Iraq, Kuwait, Qatar, Saudi Arabia, and United Arab Emirates.
[3] Includes about one-half of the production in the Neutral Zone between Kuwait and Saudi Arabia.
[4] Ecuador, which withdrew from OPEC on December 31, 1992, and Gabon, which withdrew on December 31, 1994, are included in "Non-OPEC" for all years.
R=Revised. P=Preliminary. — = Not applicable. (s)=Less than 5,000 barrels per day.
Notes: • Includes lease condensate, excludes natural gas plant liquids. • Totals may not equal sum of components due to independent rounding.

Sources: China: • 1960-1972—Central Intelligence Agency, unpublished data. • 1973-1979—Energy Information Administration (EIA), International Energy Annual 1983, Table 8. • 1980-1996—EIA, International Energy Database, March 1998. • 1997—EIA, Monthly Energy Review (March 1998), Table 10.1. United States: • 1960-1975—Bureau of Mines, Mineral Industry Surveys, Petroleum Statement, Annual. • 1976-1980—EIA, Energy Data Reports, Petroleum Statement, Annual. • 1981-1996—EIA, Petroleum Supply Annual. • 1997—EIA, Monthly Energy Review (March 1998), Table 10.1. Former U.S.S.R.: • 1960-1969—U.S.S.R. Central Statistical Office, Narodnoye Khozyaystvo SSSR (National Economy USSR). • 1970-1991—EIA, International Petroleum Statistics Report, February 1996, Table 4.1c. Russia: • 1992 forward—EIA, Office of Energy Markets and End Use, International Energy Database, March 1998. OPEC Nations: • 1960-1972—Organization of Petroleum Exporting Countries, Annual Statistical Bulletin 1979. • 1973-1979—EIA, International Energy Annual 1983, Table 8. • 1980-1996—EIA, Office of Energy Markets and End Use, International Energy Database, March 1998. • 1997—EIA, Monthly Energy Review (March 1998), Table 10.1. All Other Countries: • 1960-1969—Bureau of Mines, International Petroleum Annual, 1969. • 1970-1972—EIA, International Petroleum Annual, 1978. • 1973-1979—EIA, International Energy Annual 1983, Table 8. • 1980-1996—EIA, International Energy Annual 1996 (February 1998), Table 2.2, and the International Energy Database, March 1998. • 1997—EIA, Monthly Energy Review (March 1998), Table 10.1.

Source: Annual Energy Review 1997, Energy Information Administration, Washington, DC, 1998

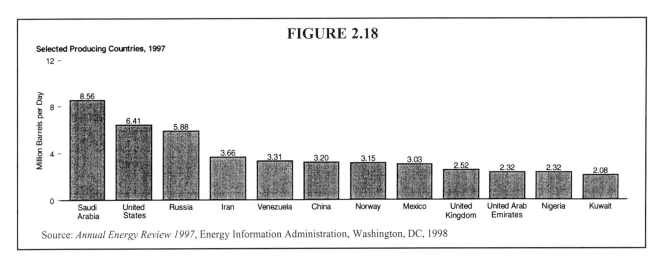

FIGURE 2.18

Selected Producing Countries, 1997

Million Barrels per Day

| Saudi Arabia | United States | Russia | Iran | Venezuela | China | Norway | Mexico | United Kingdom | United Arab Emirates | Nigeria | Kuwait |
| 8.56 | 6.41 | 5.88 | 3.66 | 3.31 | 3.20 | 3.15 | 3.03 | 2.52 | 2.32 | 2.32 | 2.08 |

Source: *Annual Energy Review 1997*, Energy Information Administration, Washington, DC, 1998

traction in the industry because restrictive laws and environmental constrictions have hobbled the industry.

STRATEGIC PETROLEUM RESERVES

In 1923, the Harding Administration set up the Petroleum Reserve to ensure the U.S. Navy would have adequate fuel in the event of war. In 1975, in response to the then-growing concern over America's energy dependence on other nations, Congress, under the Energy Policy and Conservation Act (PL 94-163), turned the Strategic Petroleum Reserve (SPR) over to the Interior Department. This was extended by PL 101-383, which reauthorized and expanded the SPR and created a second reserve for refined products. A small amount of oil was drawn from the reserves at the start of the Persian Gulf War, but it quickly became clear that this was unnecessary.

The oil is stored in deep salt caverns located at four storage sites in Louisiana and two in Texas (oil does not dissolve salt the way water does). The caverns vary in capacity, but most can hold approximately 10 million barrels of oil. The SPR system currently has 41 such caverns. If the United States suddenly found its supplies cut off, the reserve system would be connected to existing commercial lines and start pumping the oil.

A large strategic stockpile is difficult to create in a short period because of the time involved in finding storage capacity and filling sites. Market events, such as the worldwide shortage of oil in

early 1979 or the Persian Gulf War in 1991, also affect SPR filling rates. Also, additional demand for the SPR in a tight economic situation would cause oil prices to rise, affecting the United States and its allies.

At the end of 1997, the SPR contained about 563 million barrels (Figure 2.15), about enough to equal 63 days of imports should the supply be cut off (Figure 2.16). This is over one-third of the total stocks available should an emergency develop. The remaining two-thirds is in the hands of private oil companies. The decline in the days of net petroleum imports did not fall from a high of 115 days in 1985 to the current 63 days because of a drop in quantity. Rather, it reflects the increase in imports over the past several years. As the nation has imported a greater amount of oil, the days of import replacement represented by the amount of oil in the SPR have dropped.

In 1999, the Clinton Administration announced that, in order to shore up the nation's shrinking oil reserves, it would add oil to the reserves for the first time since 1994. The government will replace the 28 million barrels sold over the past few years at a rate of about 150,000 barrels a day.

SYNTHETIC FUELS

Oil is not the only source of fuel — fuel can be produced from other energy sources, including coal, natural gas, grain, garbage, and oil shale. Some common examples of synthetic fuels are alcohol, methane gas, methanol, and gasohol. Many

37

TABLE 2.5

World Petroleum Consumption, 1960-1996
(Million Barrels per Day)

Year	Selected OECD [1] Consumers											Selected Non-OECD Consumers						World
	Canada	France	Germany [2]	Italy	Japan	Mexico [3]	South Korea [3]	Spain	United Kingdom	United States	Total OECD [4]	Brazil	China	India	Former U.S.S.R.	Russia	Total Non-OECD	World
1960	0.84	0.56	0.63	0.44	0.66	0.30	0.01	0.10	0.94	9.80	R15.78	0.27	0.17	0.16	2.38	—	R5.56	21.34
1961	0.87	0.63	0.79	0.54	0.82	0.29	0.02	0.12	1.04	9.98	R16.77	0.28	0.17	0.17	2.57	—	R6.23	23.00
1962	0.92	0.73	1.00	0.67	0.93	0.30	0.02	0.12	1.12	10.40	R18.06	0.31	0.14	0.18	2.87	—	R6.83	24.89
1963	0.99	0.86	1.17	0.77	1.21	0.31	0.03	0.12	1.27	10.74	R19.60	0.34	0.17	0.21	3.15	—	R7.32	26.92
1964	1.05	0.98	1.36	0.90	1.48	0.33	0.02	0.20	1.36	11.02	R21.05	0.35	0.20	0.22	3.58	—	R8.03	29.08
1965	1.14	1.09	1.61	0.96	1.74	0.34	0.03	0.23	1.49	11.51	R22.81	0.33	0.23	0.25	3.61	—	R8.33	31.14
1966	1.21	1.19	1.80	1.08	1.98	0.36	0.04	0.31	1.58	12.08	R24.60	0.38	0.30	0.28	3.87	—	R8.96	33.56
1967	1.25	1.34	1.86	1.19	2.14	0.39	0.07	0.36	1.64	12.56	R25.94	0.38	0.28	0.26	4.22	—	R9.65	35.59
1968	1.34	1.46	1.99	1.40	2.66	0.41	0.10	0.46	1.82	13.39	R28.56	0.46	0.31	0.31	4.48	—	R10.40	38.96
1969	1.42	1.66	2.33	1.69	3.25	0.45	0.15	0.49	1.98	14.14	R31.54	0.48	0.44	0.34	4.87	—	R11.35	42.89
1970	1.52	1.94	2.83	1.71	3.82	0.50	0.20	0.58	2.10	14.70	R34.49	0.53	0.62	0.40	5.31	—	R12.32	46.81
1971	1.56	2.12	2.94	1.84	4.14	0.52	0.23	0.64	2.14	15.21	R36.07	0.58	0.79	0.42	5.66	—	R13.35	49.42
1972	1.66	2.32	3.13	1.95	4.36	0.59	0.23	0.68	2.28	16.37	R38.74	0.66	0.91	0.46	6.12	—	R14.35	53.09
1973	1.73	2.60	3.34	2.07	4.95	0.67	0.28	0.78	2.34	17.31	R41.53	0.78	1.12	0.49	6.60	—	R15.71	57.24
1974	1.78	2.45	3.06	2.00	4.86	0.71	0.29	0.86	2.21	16.65	R40.12	0.86	1.19	0.47	7.28	—	R16.56	56.68
1975	1.78	2.25	2.96	1.86	4.62	0.75	0.31	0.87	1.91	16.32	R38.82	0.92	1.36	0.50	7.52	—	R17.38	56.20
1976	1.82	2.42	3.21	1.97	4.84	0.83	0.36	0.97	1.89	17.46	R41.39	1.00	1.53	0.51	7.78	—	R18.28	59.67
1977	1.85	2.29	3.21	1.90	4.88	0.88	0.42	0.94	1.91	18.43	R42.43	1.02	1.64	0.55	8.18	—	R19.40	61.83
1978	1.90	2.41	3.29	1.95	4.95	0.99	0.48	0.98	1.94	18.85	R43.62	1.11	1.79	0.62	8.48	—	R20.54	64.16
1979	1.97	2.46	3.37	2.04	5.05	1.10	0.53	1.02	1.97	18.51	R44.01	1.18	1.84	0.66	8.64	—	R21.21	65.22
1980	1.87	2.26	3.08	1.93	4.96	1.27	0.54	0.99	1.73	17.06	R41.41	1.15	1.77	0.64	9.00	—	R21.66	63.07
1981	1.77	2.02	2.80	1.87	4.85	1.40	0.54	0.94	1.59	16.06	R39.14	1.09	1.71	0.73	8.94	—	R21.76	60.90
1982	1.58	1.88	2.74	1.78	4.58	1.48	0.53	1.00	1.59	15.30	R37.45	1.06	1.66	0.74	9.08	—	R22.05	59.50
1983	1.45	1.84	2.66	1.75	4.40	1.35	0.56	1.01	1.53	15.23	R36.59	0.98	1.73	0.77	8.95	—	R22.15	58.74
1984	1.47	1.75	2.66	1.65	4.58	1.45	0.59	0.91	1.85	15.73	R37.43	1.03	1.74	0.82	8.91	—	R22.41	59.84
1985	1.50	1.78	2.70	1.72	4.38	1.47	0.57	0.85	1.63	15.73	R37.23	1.08	1.89	0.90	8.95	—	R22.87	60.10
1986	1.51	1.77	2.86	1.74	4.44	1.49	0.61	0.88	1.65	16.28	R38.28	1.24	2.00	0.95	8.98	—	R23.48	61.76
1987	1.55	1.79	2.77	1.86	4.48	1.52	0.64	0.90	1.60	16.67	R38.96	1.26	2.12	0.99	9.00	—	R24.04	63.00
1988	1.69	1.80	2.74	1.84	4.75	1.55	0.73	0.98	1.70	17.28	R40.24	1.30	2.28	1.08	8.89	—	R24.58	64.82
1989	1.73	1.86	2.58	1.93	4.98	1.64	0.84	1.03	1.74	17.33	R40.88	1.32	2.38	1.15	8.74	—	R25.04	65.92
1990	1.69	1.82	2.66	1.87	5.14	1.68	1.03	1.01	1.75	16.99	R40.92	1.34	2.30	1.17	8.39	—	R25.07	65.99
1991	1.62	1.94	2.83	1.86	5.28	1.70	1.20	1.07	1.80	16.71	R41.40	1.35	2.50	1.19	8.35	—	R25.18	66.58
1992	1.64	1.93	2.84	1.94	5.45	1.72	1.46	1.11	1.80	17.03	R42.41	1.37	2.66	1.28	—	4.42	R24.33	66.74
1993	1.69	1.88	2.90	1.85	5.40	1.78	1.69	1.06	1.82	17.24	R43.05	1.40	2.96	1.31	—	3.75	R23.99	67.04
1994	1.73	1.83	2.88	1.84	5.67	1.82	1.86	1.13	1.84	17.72	R44.20	1.45	3.14	1.41	—	3.18	R24.11	68.31
1995	1.76	1.90	2.88	2.05	5.71	R1.86	R2.03	1.26	R1.84	17.72	R45.07	R1.49	R3.33	R1.57	—	P2.98	R24.86	R69.93
1996P	1.80	1.93	2.91	2.06	5.87	1.90	2.16	1.18	1.85	18.31	46.15	1.53	3.55	1.66	—	2.73	25.37	71.52

[1] Organization for Economic Cooperation and Development. See Glossary for membership.
[2] Through 1969, the data for Germany are for the former West Germany only. For 1970 through 1990, this is East and West Germany. Beginning in 1991, this is unified Germany.
[3] Mexico, which joined the OECD on May 18, 1994, and South Korea, which joined the OECD on December 12, 1996, are included in the OECD for all years shown in this table.
[4] Hungary and Poland, which joined the OECD on May 7, 1996, and November 22, 1996, respectively, are included in Total OECD beginning in 1970, the first year that data for these countries were available.

The Czech Republic, which joined the OECD on December 21, 1995, is included in Total OECD beginning in 1993, the year that it came into existence.
R=Revised. P=Preliminary. — = Not applicable.
Note: Totals may not equal sum of components due to independent rounding.

Source: Energy Information Administration, *International Energy Annual 1996* (February 1998), Tables 1.1 and 1.2, and the International Energy Database, March 1998.

Source: *Annual Energy Review 1997*, Energy Information Administration, Washington, DC, 1998

years ago, kerosene was made from coal oil, so it was an early synthetic fuel.

In 1980, President Jimmy Carter signed legislation creating the Synthetic Fuels Corporation Act of 1985 (PL 96-294) in an attempt to make the United States less dependent on foreign oil in the future. The legislation was intended to provide funding for plants that would turn coal, shale oil, and tar sands into oil and natural gas. Congress originally financed the program with $15 billion because people feared the price of oil had no upper limit (experts spoke of oil reaching $90 a barrel). The synthetic fuels industry quickly lost support when, in the 1980s, the United States experienced a recession and world oil prices began to drop, making synthetic fuels uneconomical. It cost much less to import oil than to manufacture synthetic fuels, and the whole idea of "energy independence" quickly faded away. In its five-year existence, the Synthetic Fuels Corporation planned six plants (one each in California, Louisiana, North Dakota, and Texas and two in Colorado). After gradual reductions in financing, the entire program was discontinued in 1985.

The United States government has continued a program to study and subsidize the use of ethanol (grain alcohol usually produced from corn) as a gasoline extender or substitute. The subsidy, in the form of fuel tax exemptions, helps compensate for the higher cost of the ethanol. The ethanol-gasoline mixture is usually 10 percent ethanol and 90 percent gasoline. Gasoline with higher percentages of ethanol tends to corrode parts of automobile fuel systems, makes cold engines hard to start, and produces less energy per gallon, thus reducing fuel efficiency. Brazil currently pursues an aggressive program to substitute fuels from grain (often called biomass) for gasoline, with mixed results.

THE FUTURE OF PETROLEUM USE IN THE UNITED STATES

The Energy Information Administration (EIA) of the U.S. Department of Energy, in its *Annual Energy Outlook 1998* (1997), forecasts the nation's energy supply, demand, and prices through the year 2020. The projections are based on federal, state, and local laws in effect in July 1997 and are used by governments, trade associations, and decisionmakers. The EIA has projected that domestic crude oil will continue to decline by 1.1 percent per year, from 6.5 million barrels per day in 1996 to 4.9 million barrels per day in 2020.

The EIA also predicts that, as domestic oil production falls off and demand increases, additional petroleum imports will be needed to fill the widening gap. The EIA estimates that, in 2020, the United States will need to import between 13.7 and 18.4 million barrels per day (Figure 2.17). Dependence on petroleum imports is predicted to reach 66 percent of total U.S. consumption in 2020.

INTERNATIONAL PETROLEUM USAGE

World Production

Total world petroleum production has generally increased over the past decade and a half, reaching 66 million barrels per day in 1997 (Table 2.4). The major producers have been Saudi Arabia, the United States, and Russia. Together, these three countries account for 31.5 percent of the world's crude oil production. Other leading oil producers include Iran, Venezuela, China, Norway, Mexico, the United Kingdom, United Arab Emirates, Nigeria, and Kuwait. (See Figure 2.18.)

World Consumption

World petroleum consumption in 1996 was estimated at more than 71.5 million barrels per day. The United States was, by far, the leading consumer (18.3 million barrels per day), followed by Japan (5.9 million barrels per day), China (3.55 million barrels a day), Germany (2.91 million barrels a day), and Russia (2.73 million barrels per day). (See Table 2.5.)

CHAPTER III

NATURAL GAS

Natural gas is an important source of energy in the United States. The natural gas industry first developed out of the growing petroleum industry. Wells drilled for oil often produced considerable amounts of natural gas, but the early oilmen had no idea what to do with it.

Natural gas is mostly a mixture of methane, ethane, and propane, with methane making up 73 to 95 percent. Originally considered a waste by-product of oil production, no market existed for gas, nor were transmission lines available to deliver it even if a use could have been found. As a result, the gas was burned off (flared). Pictures of southeast Texas at the turn of the century showed thousands of wooden drilling rigs topped like burn-

ing candles with flaming plumes of gas. (See Figure 3.1.) Even today, flaring sites are sometimes the brightest areas visible in nighttime satellite images, outshining even the brightest urban areas.

Nonetheless, researchers soon found ways to use natural gas. In 1925, the first welded pipeline over 200 miles in length was built from Louisiana to Texas. U.S demand grew rapidly, especially after World War II. By the 1950s, natural gas was providing one-quarter of the nation's energy needs. Today, a vast pipeline transmission system connects the production facilities in the United States, Canada, and Mexico with the natural gas distributors. (Figure 3.2 shows a natural gas pipeline.) Natural gas is second only to petroleum in the share

FIGURE 3.1

Source: *Natural Gas Annual 1989*, Energy Information Administration, Washington, DC, 1990

FIGURE 3.2

Natural gas pipeline, El Paso County, Texas. Source: U.S. Department of Energy.

Source: *Annual Energy Review 1997*, Energy Information Administration, Washington, DC, 1998

of U.S. energy produced. (Figures 3.3 and 3.4 show the flow of natural gas.)

THE PRODUCTION OF NATURAL GAS

Natural gas is produced from gas wells and oil wells. Except for the gas placed in storage, there is little delay between production and consumption. Changes in demand are almost immediately reflected by changes in wellhead flows.

Total gas production reached 19 trillion cubic feet in 1997, well below the levels during the early 1970s (Figure 3.5). Although production levels are being driven up by increasing demand and rising prices, production continues to be outpaced by consumption. Imported gas makes up the difference between supply and demand. Texas, Louisiana, and Oklahoma accounted for over half the natural gas produced in the United States in 1997.

Natural gas from the North Slope fields of Alaska is projected to begin flowing to the lower 48 states in about 2005 with the construction of the Alaskan Natural Gas Transportation System. This system is expected to deliver more than 800 billion cubic feet of gas per year to the lower 48 states.

Natural Gas Wells

An all-time high of 304,000 gas wells were in operation in 1997 (Figure 3.6), although average productivity of these wells has remained relatively low since the 1980s (Figure 3.7). The annual changes in the number of producing wells are due partly to drilling activity for new sources of gas, the rate of abandoning old wells, weather conditions, and the economic vigor of the nation. Wells are abandoned when they can no longer produce economically.

Offshore Production

Offshore drilling for natural gas accounted for one-fourth of the total U.S. production in 1997

FIGURE 3.3

Natural Gas Flow, 1997
(Trillion Cubic Feet)

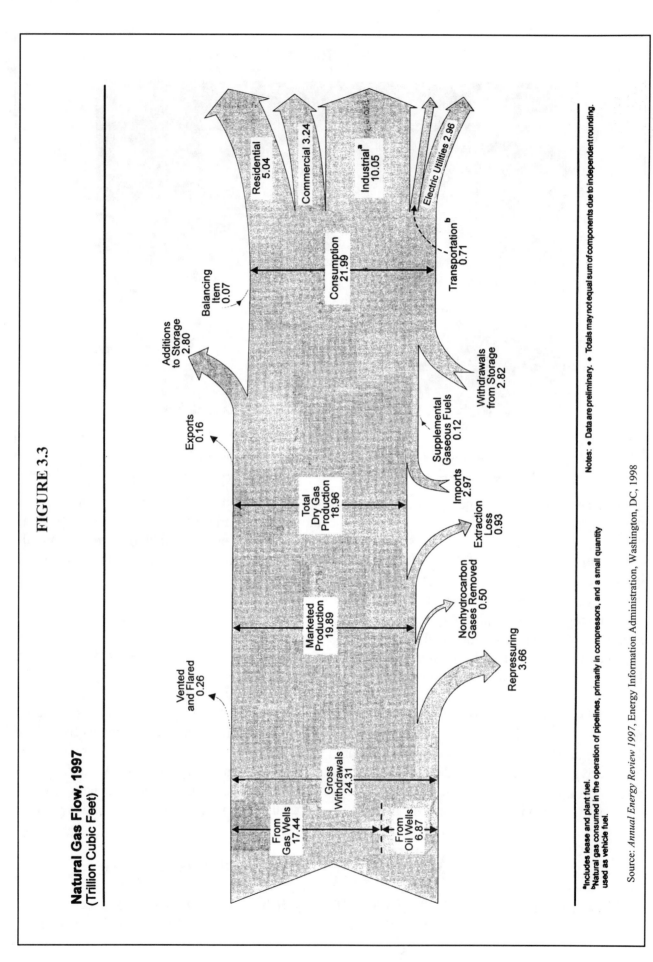

Source: *Annual Energy Review 1997*, Energy Information Administration, Washington, DC, 1998

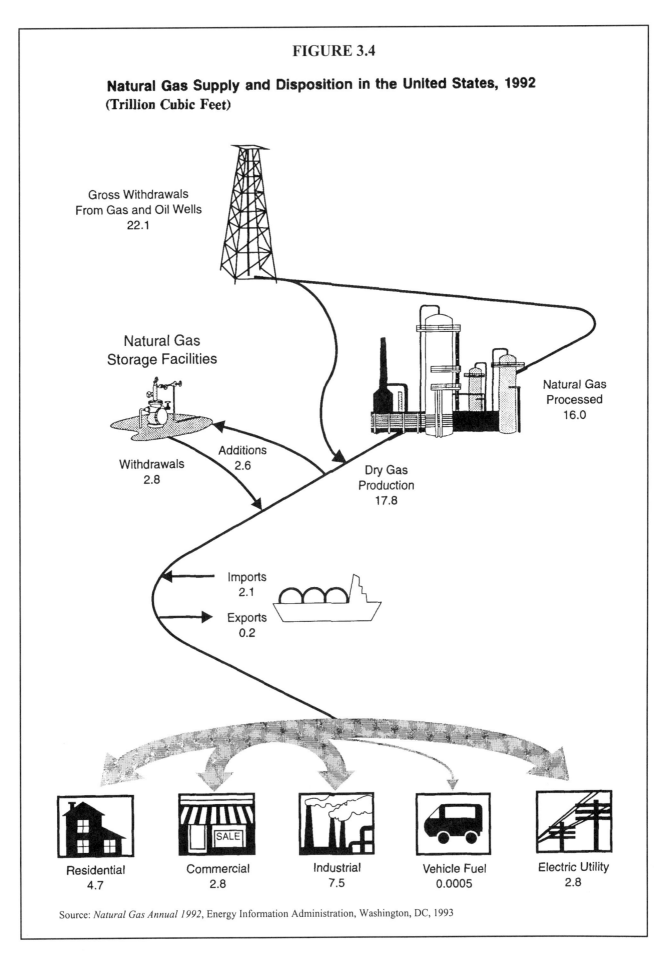

FIGURE 3.4

Natural Gas Supply and Disposition in the United States, 1992
(Trillion Cubic Feet)

Gross Withdrawals
From Gas and Oil Wells
22.1

Natural Gas
Storage Facilities

Natural Gas
Processed
16.0

Additions
2.6

Withdrawals
2.8

Dry Gas
Production
17.8

Imports
2.1

Exports
0.2

Residential
4.7

Commercial
2.8

Industrial
7.5

Vehicle Fuel
0.0005

Electric Utility
2.8

Source: *Natural Gas Annual 1992*, Energy Information Administration, Washington, DC, 1993

43

(Figure 3.8). Almost all natural gas produced offshore comes from the Gulf of Mexico and offshore California. U.S. offshore production is expected to increase to meet the nation's growing need for energy, although this type of production could be slowed by environmental restrictions and public concerns.

Offshore drilling generally occurs on the outer "continental shelf," the submerged area off shore to a depth of 200 meters (656 feet). Figure 3.9 shows a diagram of a continental margin. The continental shelf varies from one coastal area to another. The shelf is relatively narrow along the Pacific coast, wide along much of the Atlantic coast and the Gulf of Alaska, and widest in the Gulf of Mexico. Offshore waters contain state and federal leases involving more than 1.5 billion acres.

The development of offshore oil and gas resources began with the drilling of the Summerland oil field in California in 1896 (Figure 3.10), where about 400 wells were drilled. In the search for oil and gas in offshore areas, the industry has continually extended and improved drilling technology. Today, deep-water petroleum exploration occurs from platforms and drill ships and, in shallow water, from gravel islands and mobile units (Figures 3.11 - 3.13).

Even though natural gas is transported mostly by pipelines, not tankers, the 1989 Exxon oil spill in Prince William Sound, Alaska, and other oil spills have

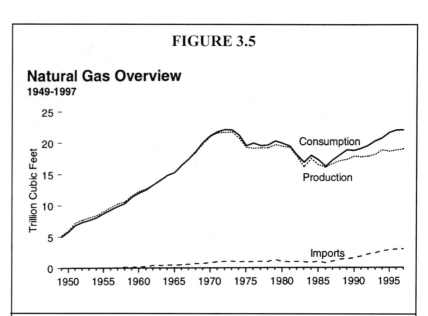

FIGURE 3.5

Natural Gas Overview
1949-1997

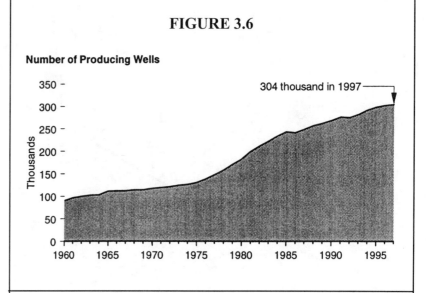

FIGURE 3.6

Number of Producing Wells

304 thousand in 1997

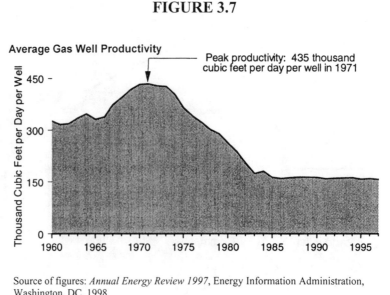

FIGURE 3.7

Average Gas Well Productivity

Peak productivity: 435 thousand cubic feet per day per well in 1971

Source of figures: *Annual Energy Review 1997*, Energy Information Administration, Washington, DC, 1998

44

focused national attention on all types of offshore drilling. Even before the *Exxon Valdez* oil spill, environmentalists were calling for curtailment of offshore drilling of both oil and gas.

Natural Gas Reserves

Reserves are volumes of gas estimated to exist in known deposits and believed to be recoverable in the future. Proved reserves are those gas volumes that geological and engineering data show with reasonable certainty to be recoverable. Proved reserves of natural gas remained steady at about 175.1 trillion cubic feet in 1996 (Table 3.1). Texas, the Gulf of Mexico, Oklahoma, and Louisiana are the leading gas-producing areas. The reserves in these regions make up approximately half the total.

(See Chapter IV for a discussion of offshore reserves.)

Underground Storage

Because of seasonal, daily, and even hourly changes in gas demand, substantial natural gas storage facilities have been created to meet peak supply needs. Many of these storage centers are depleted gas reservoirs located near transmission lines and marketing areas. Gas is injected into storage when market needs are lower than the available gas flow, and gas is withdrawn from storage when supplies from producing fields and/or the capacity of transmission lines are not adequate to meet peak demands. At the end of 1997, gas in underground storage totaled 6.5 trillion cubic feet (Figure 3.14).

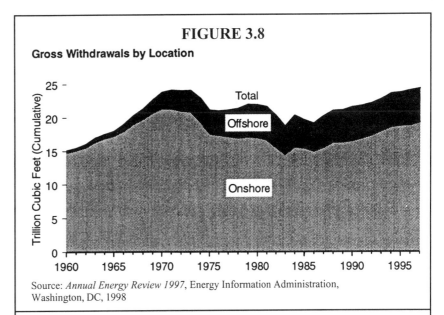

FIGURE 3.8

Gross Withdrawals by Location

Source: *Annual Energy Review 1997*, Energy Information Administration, Washington, DC, 1998

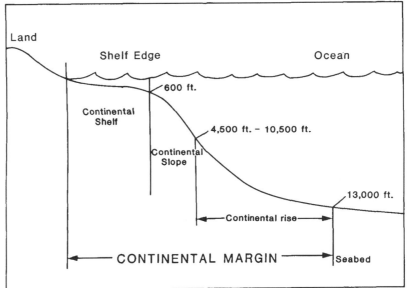

FIGURE 3.9

Generalized Profile of the Continental Margin

NOTE: Depths and gradients are approximate.

Source: *Managing Oil and Gas Operations on the Outer Continental Shelf*, U.S. Department of Interior, Washington, DC, 1986

Natural gas reserves in North America are generally more abundant than crude oil reserves. At one time, the U.S. Department of Energy had estimated that proven supplies of recoverable gas in the United States would last fewer than eight years, the same time as recoverable oil. New discoveries and technological improvements in efficiency, however, have increased the estimated recoverable supply to 50 years or more.

FIGURE 3.10
Summerland Oil Field, California, in the Late 1880s

FIGURE 3.11
Gravel Island

Source of both figures: *Managing Oil and Gas Operations on the Outer Continental Shelf*, U.S. Department of Interior, Washington, DC, 1986

TRANSMISSION OF NATURAL GAS

A vast network of natural gas pipelines criss-crosses the United States, connecting every state except Alaska, Hawaii, and Vermont. (Vermont receives its gas from Canada.) The natural gas in this quarter-million mile system generally flows northeastward, primarily from Texas and Louisiana, the two major gas-producing states, and to a lesser extent, from Oklahoma and New Mexico. It also flows west to California. (See Figure 3.15.)

In 1997, Texas and Louisiana provided approximately 53 percent of the nation's total gas use. The remainder of gas shipments came mainly from Oklahoma and New Mexico, with much smaller amounts coming from Idaho, Kansas, Minnesota, and Montana. The largest users were California,

FIGURE 3.12
Ice-strengthened Drillship

FIGURE 3.13
Concrete Island Drilling System

Source of both figures: *Managing Oil and Gas Operations on the Outer Continental Shelf*, U.S. Department of Interior, Washington, DC, 1986

Illinois, Michigan, New York, Ohio, and Pennsylvania.

NATURAL GAS CONSUMPTION

Nationally, natural gas consumption has been rising since 1986, when the demand was the lowest in 21 years. Since the 1986 low point, natural gas consumption has risen, reaching almost 22 trillion cubic feet in 1997. (See Table 3.2.)

Natural gas fills an important part of the country's energy needs. It is an attractive fuel, not only because the current prices are relatively low,

(continued on page 51)

47

TABLE 3.1

Crude Oil and Natural Gas Field Counts, Cumulative Production, Proved Reserves, and Ultimate Recovery, End of Year 1977-1996

Year	Cumulative Number of Fields with Crude Oil and/or Natural Gas	Cumulative Number of Fields with Crude Oil	Crude Oil [1] (billion barrels)			Cumulative Number of Fields with Natural Gas	Natural Gas [2] (trillion cubic feet)		
			Cumulative Production	Proved Reserves	Ultimate Recovery		Cumulative Production	Proved Reserves	Ultimate Recovery
1977	31,725	28,057	121.4	33.6	155.0	24,266	558.3	209.5	767.8
1978	32,755	28,877	124.6	33.1	157.6	25,126	578.4	210.1	788.5
1979	33,898	29,810	127.7	31.2	158.9	26,094	599.1	208.3	807.4
1980	35,196	30,860	130.8	31.3	162.2	27,129	619.4	206.3	825.6
1981	36,727	32,124	133.9	31.0	165.0	28,331	639.4	209.4	848.9
1982	38,110	33,289	137.1	29.5	166.6	29,374	658.1	209.3	867.4
1983	39,403	34,345	140.3	29.3	169.6	30,349	675.1	209.0	884.1
1984	40,865	35,558	143.5	30.0	173.5	31,449	693.5	206.0	899.5
1985	42,114	36,590	146.8	29.9	176.7	32,419	710.9	202.2	913.1
1986	42,869	37,195	150.0	28.3	178.3	32,963	727.8	201.1	928.9
1987	43,535	37,703	153.0	28.7	181.7	33,469	745.4	196.4	941.8
1988	44,197	38,215	156.0	28.2	184.2	33,996	763.4	177.0	940.4
1989	44,655	38,555	158.8	27.9	186.7	34,367	781.7	175.4	957.1
1990	45,157	38,933	161.5	27.6	189.0	34,757	800.4	177.6	978.0
1991	45,539	39,233	164.2	25.9	190.1	35,022	819.1	175.3	994.4
1992	45,898	39,508	166.8	25.0	191.8	35,283	838.0	173.3	1,011.3
1993	46,220	39,737	169.3	24.1	193.4	35,490	857.2	170.5	1,027.7
1994	46,597	40,001	172.5	23.6	196.2	35,724	877.1	171.9	1,049.1
1995	46,872	40,165	R175.0	23.5	198.5	35,836	896.9	173.5	1,070.4
1996	47,322	40,483	177.3	23.3	200.6	36,052	917.0	175.1	1,092.1

[1] Includes lease condensate.
[2] Wet, after lease separation.
R=Revised.

Sources: **1992:** Energy Information Administration (EIA), Office of Oil and Gas, Oil and Gas Integrated Field File (OGIFF), (July 1995). **1977-1991 and 1993-1996:** • Crude Oil Cumulative Production—EIA, *Petroleum Supply Annual 1996, Volume 1* (June 1997). • Natural Gas Cumulative Production—EIA, *Natural Gas Annual 1996* (September 1997). • Proved Reserves—EIA, *U.S. Crude Oil, Natural Gas, and Natural Gas Liquids Reserves Annual Report 1996* (December 1997). • Field Counts—EIA, *Oil and Gas Field Code Master List 1997* (February 1998) and OGIFF.

Source: *Annual Energy Review 1997*, Energy Information Administration, Washington, DC, 1998

FIGURE 3.14

Natural Gas in Underground Storage, End of Year 1954-1997

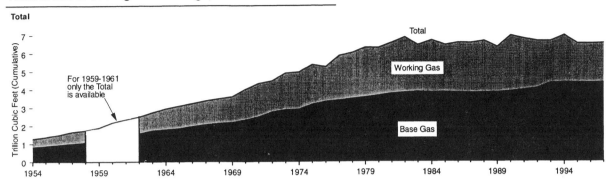

Source: *Annual Energy Review 1997*, Energy Information Administration, Washington, DC, 1998

FIGURE 3.15

Principal Interstate Natural Gas Flow Summary, 1994

Source: *Natural Gas Annual 1994*, Energy Information Administration, Washington, DC, 1995

TABLE 3.2

Natural Gas Consumption by Sector, 1949-1997
(Trillion Cubic Feet)

Year	Residential	Commercial[1]	Industrial			Transportation			Electric Utilities	Total
			Lease and Plant Fuel	Other	Total	Pipeline Fuel[2]	Vehicle Fuel	Total		
1949	0.99	0.35	0.84	2.25	3.08	NA	NA	NA	0.55	4.97
1950	1.20	0.39	0.93	2.50	3.43	0.13	NA	0.13	0.63	5.77
1951	1.47	0.48	1.15	2.77	3.91	0.19	NA	0.19	0.76	6.81
1952	1.62	0.52	1.16	2.87	4.04	0.21	NA	0.21	0.91	7.29
1953	1.69	0.53	1.13	3.03	4.16	0.23	NA	0.23	1.03	7.64
1954	1.89	0.58	1.10	3.07	4.17	0.23	NA	0.23	1.17	8.05
1955	2.12	0.63	1.13	3.41	4.54	0.25	NA	0.25	1.15	8.69
1956	2.33	0.72	1.00	3.71	4.71	0.30	NA	0.30	1.24	9.29
1957	2.50	0.78	1.05	3.89	4.93	0.30	NA	0.30	1.34	9.85
1958	2.71	0.87	1.15	3.89	5.03	0.31	NA	0.31	1.37	10.30
1959	2.91	0.98	1.24	4.22	5.46	0.35	NA	0.35	1.63	11.32
1960	3.10	1.02	1.24	4.53	5.77	0.35	NA	0.35	1.72	11.97
1961	3.25	1.08	1.29	4.67	5.96	0.38	NA	0.38	1.83	12.49
1962	3.48	1.21	1.37	4.86	6.23	0.38	NA	0.38	1.97	13.27
1963	3.59	1.27	1.41	5.13	6.55	0.42	NA	0.42	2.14	13.97
1964	3.79	1.37	1.37	5.52	6.89	0.44	NA	0.44	2.32	14.81
1965	3.90	1.44	1.16	5.96	7.11	0.50	NA	0.50	2.32	15.28
1966	4.14	1.62	1.03	6.51	7.55	0.54	NA	0.54	2.61	16.45
1967	4.31	1.96	1.14	6.65	7.79	0.58	NA	0.58	2.75	17.39
1968	4.45	2.08	1.24	7.13	8.37	0.59	NA	0.59	3.15	18.63
1969	4.73	2.25	1.35	7.61	8.96	0.63	NA	0.63	3.49	20.06
1970	4.84	2.40	1.40	7.85	9.25	0.72	NA	0.72	3.93	21.14
1971	4.97	2.51	1.41	8.18	9.59	0.74	NA	0.74	3.98	21.79
1972	5.13	2.61	1.46	8.17	9.62	0.77	NA	0.77	3.98	22.10
1973	4.88	2.60	1.50	8.69	10.18	0.73	NA	0.73	3.66	22.05
1974	4.79	2.56	1.48	8.29	9.77	0.67	NA	0.67	3.44	21.22
1975	4.92	2.51	1.40	6.97	8.36	0.58	NA	0.58	3.16	19.54
1976	5.05	2.67	1.63	6.96	8.60	0.55	NA	0.55	3.08	19.95
1977	4.82	2.50	1.66	6.82	8.47	0.53	NA	0.53	3.19	19.52
1978	4.90	2.60	1.65	6.76	8.40	0.53	NA	0.53	3.19	19.63
1979	4.97	2.79	1.50	6.90	8.40	0.60	NA	0.60	3.49	20.24
1980	4.75	2.61	1.03	7.17	8.20	0.63	NA	0.63	3.68	19.88
1981	4.55	2.52	0.93	7.13	8.06	0.64	NA	0.64	3.64	19.40
1982	4.63	2.61	1.11	5.83	6.94	0.60	NA	0.60	3.23	18.00
1983	4.38	2.43	0.98	5.64	6.62	0.49	NA	0.49	2.91	16.83
1984	4.56	2.52	1.08	6.15	7.23	0.63	NA	0.63	3.11	17.95
1985	4.43	2.43	0.97	5.90	6.87	0.50	NA	0.50	3.04	17.28
1986	4.31	2.32	0.92	5.58	6.50	0.49	NA	0.49	2.60	16.22
1987	4.31	2.43	1.15	5.95	7.10	0.52	NA	0.52	2.84	17.21
1988	4.63	2.67	1.10	6.38	7.48	0.61	NA	0.61	2.64	18.03
1989	4.78	2.72	1.07	6.82	7.89	0.63	NA	0.63	2.79	18.80
1990	4.39	2.62	1.24	7.02	8.25	0.66	NA	0.66	2.79	18.72
1991	4.56	2.73	1.13	7.23	8.36	0.60	(s)	0.60	2.79	19.04
1992	4.69	2.80	1.17	7.53	8.70	0.59	(s)	0.59	2.77	19.54
1993	4.96	2.86	1.17	7.98	9.15	0.62	(s)	0.63	2.68	20.28
1994	4.85	2.90	1.12	8.17	9.29	0.69	(s)	0.69	2.99	20.71
1995	4.85	3.03	1.22	8.58	9.80	0.70	(s)	0.70	3.20	21.58
1996	R5.24	R3.16	1.25	R8.87	R10.12	0.71	(s)	0.71	R2.73	R21.97
1997P	5.04	3.24	1.25	8.80	10.05	0.71	NA	0.71	2.96	21.99

[1] Includes deliveries to municipalities and public authorities for institutional heating and other purposes.
[2] Natural gas consumed in the operation of pipelines, primarily in compressors.
R=Revised. P=Preliminary. NA=Not available. (s)=Less than 5 billion cubic feet.
Notes: • Beginning with 1965, all volumes are shown on a pressure base of 14.73 p.s.i.a. at 60° F. For prior years, the pressure base was 14.65 p.s.i.a. at 60° F.
• Totals may not equal sum of components due to independent rounding.

Source: *Annual Energy Review 1997*, Energy Information Administration, Washington, DC, 1998

FIGURE 3.16

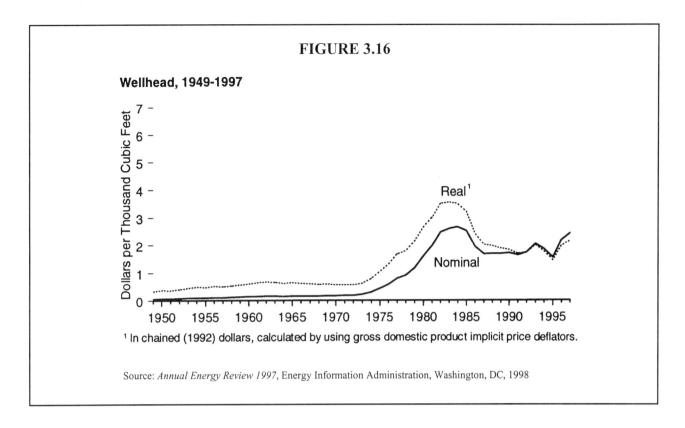

Wellhead, 1949-1997

[1] In chained (1992) dollars, calculated by using gross domestic product implicit price deflators.

Source: *Annual Energy Review 1997*, Energy Information Administration, Washington, DC, 1998

but also because it is efficient and can help the country meet both its environmental goals and its energy needs.

Of the total amount of natural gas used in 1997, 46 percent was delivered to industry, 23 percent to residences, 13 percent to electric utilities, 15 percent to commercial customers, and 3 percent to transportation consumers.

Residential Consumption

The residential sector used 5.04 trillion cubic feet in 1997 (Table 3.2). Energy consumption in this area depends heavily on weather-related home heating demands. The colder it gets, the more gas is used. Weather, however, is not the only factor in demand for gas in the home. Residential consumption patterns also depend on the number of consumers and the amount of conservation consumers practice. According to the U.S. Department of Commerce, approximately one-half of all residential energy consumers in the United States use gas to heat their homes.

Commercial Consumption

The use of natural gas continues to grow in the commercial sector, reaching a record high of 3.24 trillion cubic feet in 1997 (Table 3.2). Like residential consumers, use in the commercial area depends heavily on seasonal requirements, as well as the number of users and conservation measures taken by commercial establishments. Commercial customers are also particularly sensitive to changes in gas prices and to changes in the economy.

Industrial Consumption

Historically, the industrial sector has been the largest consumer of natural gas. Consumption in this sector rose in 1997 to 10.05 trillion cubic feet, approaching the highs reached in the early 1970s, when natural gas consumption peaked at 10.18 trillion cubic feet used in 1973. The increases in natural gas consumption in the industrial sector were due partly to fuel switching from petroleum.

Consumption by electric utilities rose and then fell in the last half of the 1980s. In 1997, electric

51

TABLE 3.3

Natural Gas Prices by Sector, 1967-1997

(Price: Dollars¹ per Thousand Cubic Feet; Share of Total Volume Delivered: Percentage)

Year	Residential Price [4]	Commercial [2] Price	Commercial [2] Share of Total Volume Delivered	Industrial Price	Industrial Share of Total Volume Delivered	Vehicle Fuel [3] Price	Vehicle Fuel [3] Share of Total Volume Delivered	Electric Utilities Price [5]
1967	1.04	0.74	NA	0.34	NA	NA	NA	0.28
1968	1.04	0.73	NA	0.34	NA	NA	NA	0.22
1969	1.05	0.74	NA	0.35	NA	NA	NA	0.27
1970	1.09	0.77	NA	0.37	NA	NA	NA	0.29
1971	1.15	0.82	NA	0.41	NA	NA	NA	0.32
1972	1.21	0.88	NA	0.45	NA	NA	NA	0.34
1973	1.29	0.94	NA	0.50	NA	NA	NA	0.38
1974	1.43	1.07	NA	0.67	NA	NA	NA	0.51
1975	1.71	1.35	NA	0.96	NA	NA	NA	0.77
1976	1.98	1.64	NA	1.24	NA	NA	NA	1.06
1977	2.35	2.04	NA	1.50	NA	NA	NA	1.32
1978	2.56	2.23	NA	1.70	NA	NA	NA	1.48
1979	2.98	2.73	NA	1.99	NA	NA	NA	1.81
1980	3.68	3.39	NA	2.56	NA	NA	NA	2.27
1981	4.29	4.00	NA	3.14	NA	NA	NA	2.89
1982	5.17	4.82	NA	3.87	85.1	NA	NA	3.48
1983	6.06	5.59	NA	4.18	80.7	NA	NA	3.58
1984	6.12	5.55	NA	4.22	74.7	NA	NA	3.70
1985	6.12	5.50	NA	3.95	68.8	NA	NA	3.55
1986	5.83	5.08	NA	3.23	59.8	NA	NA	2.43
1987	5.54	4.77	93.1	2.94	47.4	NA	NA	2.32
1988	5.47	4.63	90.7	2.95	42.6	NA	NA	2.33
1989	5.64	4.74	89.1	2.96	36.9	NA	NA	2.43
1990	5.80	4.83	86.6	2.93	35.2	NA	NA	2.38
1991	5.82	4.81	85.1	2.69	32.7	3.39	NA	2.18
1992	5.89	4.88	83.2	2.84	30.3	3.96	NA	2.36
1993	6.16	5.22	83.9	3.07	29.7	4.05	87.8	2.61
1994	6.41	5.44	79.3	3.05	25.5	R4.11	86.9	2.28
1995	6.06	5.05	76.7	2.71	24.5	3.98	86.6	2.02
1996	R6.34	R5.40	R77.6	R3.42	R20.2	R4.34	R94.0	R2.69
1997ᴾ	6.89	5.75	65.0	3.53	15.3	NA	NA	NA

¹ Nominal dollars.
² Includes deliveries to municipalities and public authorities for institutional heating and other purposes.
³ Much of the natural gas delivered for vehicle fuel represents deliveries to fueling stations that are used primarily or exclusively by respondents' fleet vehicles. Thus, the prices are often those associated with the operation of fleet vehicles.
⁴ Based on 100 percent of volume delivered.
⁵ Based on all steam-electric utility plants with a combined capacity of 50 megawatts or greater.
R=Revised. P=Preliminary. NA=Not available.
Notes: • Natural gas includes supplemental gaseous fuels. • Residential, commercial, and industrial

price data represent prices of natural gas sold and delivered by local distribution companies to residential, commercial, and industrial consumers, respectively. The data do not reflect prices of natural gas transported for the account of others. • The average for each end-use sector is calculated by dividing the total value of the gas consumed by each sector by the total quantity consumed.

Vehicle Fuel: 1990-1996—EIA, *Natural Gas Annual 1996 (September 1997), Table 102.* All
Other Data: • 1967-1990—EIA, *Natural Gas Annual 1996* (September 1997), Table 102. • 1991 forward—EIA, *Natural Gas Monthly* (March 1998), Table 4.

Source: *Annual Energy Review 1997*, Energy Information Administration, Washington, DC, 1998

utilities accounted for 2.96 trillion cubic feet of natural gas use.

NATURAL GAS PRICES

Due to different federal and state rate structures, there are many price categories for natural gas. In addition, prices to consumers vary by region. For example, prices are lower in major producing areas where transmission costs are lower.

Through the early 1970s, natural gas prices were relatively stable. Thereafter, deregulation and industry restructuring brought about a period of price fluctuations, with the average price of all categories of natural gas at the wellhead at $2.15 per 1,000 cubic feet in 1997 (Figure 3.16).

Nonetheless, at a retail price level, residential customers paid the highest price ever for natural gas in 1997 — $6.89 per thousand cubic feet. Commercial consumers paid $5.75 per thousand cubic feet, while industrial consumers paid only $3.53 per thousand cubic feet. (See Table 3.3.)

Much of the variation in natural gas prices through the years can be attributed to changes that have occurred in the natural gas industry. The passage of the Natural Gas Policy Act of 1978 (NGPA; PL 95-621) triggered a dramatic transformation in the natural gas industry. The NGPA allowed gas prices at the wellhead to rise gradually. On January 1, 1985, new gas prices were decontrolled, and additional volumes of onshore production were decontrolled on July 1, 1987. In 1989, former President Ronald Reagan signed legislation removing all remaining natural gas wellhead price controls by 1993.

The NGPA allowed prices to go up, but it also opened the market to the forces of supply and demand. Now that prices are decontrolled and the industry is no longer constrained by federal regu-

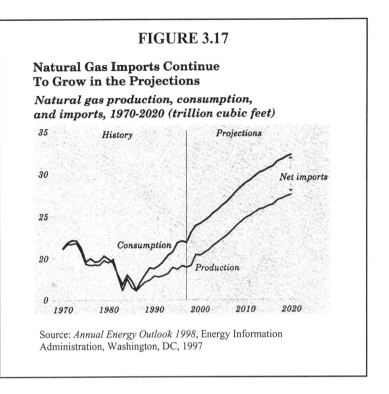

FIGURE 3.17

Natural Gas Imports Continue To Grow in the Projections

Natural gas production, consumption, and imports, 1970-2020 (trillion cubic feet)

Source: *Annual Energy Outlook 1998*, Energy Information Administration, Washington, DC, 1997

lations, the natural gas industry has become more sensitive to market signals and able to respond more quickly to changes in economic conditions.

IMPORTS AND EXPORTS

U.S. natural gas trade was limited to the border countries of Mexico and Canada until shipping natural gas in liquefied form became a feasible alternative to pipelines. In 1969, the first shipments of liquefied natural gas (LNG) were sent from the United States to Japan, and U.S. imports of LNG from Algeria began the following year.

In 1997, U.S. net imports of natural gas by all routes totaled 2.9 trillion cubic feet, approximately 12.8 percent of domestic consumption. Historically, Canada has been, by far, the major supplier of U.S. natural gas imports, accounting for about 2.9 trillion cubic feet in 1997.

The United States exported 157 billion cubic feet of natural gas in 1997. Of the gas exported by the United States, Japan bought the largest amount (62 billion cubic feet). Canada purchased 51 billion cubic feet and Mexico, 44 billion cubic feet.

TABLE 3.4

World Dry Natural Gas Production, 1987-1996
(Trillion Cubic Feet)

Region and Country	1987	1988	1989	1990	1991	1992	1993	1994	1995	1996 P
North, Central, and South America	**22.33**	**23.47**	**24.16**	**24.62**	**24.84**	**25.42**	**26.20**	**27.44**	**R27.76**	**28.52**
Argentina	0.53	0.63	0.72	0.63	0.70	0.71	0.76	0.79	R0.88	1.02
Canada	3.10	3.57	3.80	3.85	4.06	4.52	4.91	5.26	R5.64	5.85
Mexico	0.86	0.92	0.93	0.94	0.94	0.92	0.90	0.91	0.94	0.99
United States	16.62	17.10	17.31	17.81	17.70	17.84	18.10	18.82	18.60	18.79
Venezuela	0.66	0.66	0.77	0.76	0.79	0.76	0.82	0.88	R0.89	0.96
Other	0.56	0.58	0.64	0.62	0.65	0.66	0.73	0.78	R0.81	0.91
Western Europe	**7.44**	**7.07**	**7.32**	**7.24**	**7.83**	**7.89**	**8.32**	**8.40**	**R8.75**	**10.08**
Germany [1]	0.92	0.90	0.86	0.72	0.67	0.68	0.68	0.67	R0.71	0.78
Italy	0.58	0.59	0.60	0.61	0.61	0.64	0.69	0.73	R0.72	0.71
Netherlands	2.77	2.45	2.67	2.69	3.04	3.06	3.11	2.95	R2.97	3.37
Norway	1.06	1.05	1.09	0.98	0.97	1.04	0.97	1.04	R1.08	1.45
United Kingdom	1.68	1.62	1.58	1.75	2.01	1.93	2.31	2.47	R2.67	3.17
Other	0.44	0.47	0.51	0.50	0.53	0.54	0.56	0.54	R0.60	0.60
Eastern Europe and Former U.S.S.R.	**27.14**	**28.95**	**29.70**	**30.13**	**29.85**	**28.58**	**27.99**	**26.47**	**R25.93**	**26.27**
Romania	1.32	1.28	1.13	1.00	0.88	0.78	0.75	0.69	0.68	0.63
Former U.S.S.R.	25.36	27.19	28.11	28.78	28.62	—	—	—	—	—
Russia	—	—	—	—	—	22.62	21.81	21.45	21.01	21.23
Turkmenistan	—	—	—	—	—	2.02	2.29	1.26	1.14	1.31
Ukraine	—	—	—	—	—	0.74	0.68	0.64	0.62	0.64
Uzbekistan	—	—	—	—	—	1.51	1.59	1.67	1.70	1.70
Other	0.47	0.48	0.46	0.35	0.35	0.91	0.87	0.76	0.78	0.76
Middle East and Africa	**5.13**	**5.55**	**6.08**	**6.17**	**6.52**	**6.91**	**7.24**	**7.41**	**R8.00**	**8.64**
Algeria	1.52	1.63	1.71	1.79	1.93	1.97	1.90	1.81	2.05	2.19
Egypt	0.22	0.24	0.27	0.29	0.32	0.35	0.40	0.42	0.44	0.47
Iran	0.57	0.71	0.78	0.84	0.92	0.88	0.96	1.12	R1.25	1.38
Qatar	0.20	0.21	0.22	0.28	0.33	0.40	0.48	0.48	0.48	0.48
Saudi Arabia	0.95	1.03	1.05	1.08	1.13	1.20	1.27	1.33	R1.34	1.46
United Arab Emirates	0.68	0.66	0.81	0.78	0.92	1.02	0.94	0.91	R1.11	1.28
Other	1.00	1.07	1.24	1.13	0.98	1.08	1.30	1.34	R1.33	1.38
Far East and Oceania	**4.50**	**4.78**	**4.98**	**5.44**	**5.76**	**6.07**	**6.55**	**7.09**	**R7.49**	**8.22**
Australia	0.53	0.56	0.57	0.72	0.75	0.82	0.86	0.92	R1.03	1.06
China	0.49	0.49	0.51	0.51	0.53	0.53	0.56	0.59	0.60	0.67
India	0.23	0.31	0.32	0.40	0.45	0.48	0.53	0.59	R0.63	0.70
Indonesia	1.29	1.34	1.42	1.53	1.72	1.79	1.97	2.21	R2.24	2.38
Malaysia	0.55	0.58	0.61	0.65	0.75	0.80	0.88	0.92	R1.02	1.30
Pakistan	0.42	0.44	0.47	0.48	0.53	0.55	0.58	0.63	R0.65	0.70
Other	0.98	1.06	1.09	1.15	1.03	1.10	1.16	1.23	R1.32	1.41
World	**66.54**	**69.81**	**72.25**	**73.61**	**74.81**	**74.87**	**76.30**	**76.80**	**R77.92**	**81.73**

[1] Through 1990, this is East and West Germany. Beginning in 1991, this is unified Germany.
R=Revised. P=Preliminary. — = Not applicable.
Note: Totals may not equal sum of components due to independent rounding and the inclusion of more recent U.S. data from an alternative source.

Source: *Annual Energy Review 1997*, Energy Information Administration, Washington, DC, 1998

54

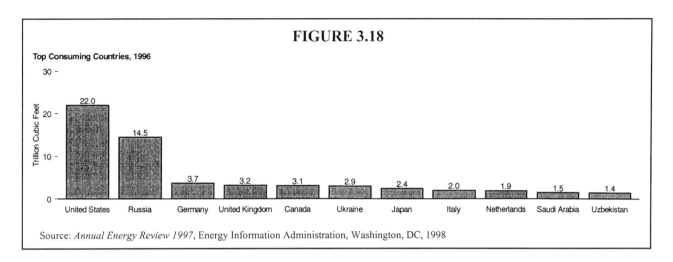

FIGURE 3.18

Top Consuming Countries, 1996

Source: *Annual Energy Review 1997*, Energy Information Administration, Washington, DC, 1998

FUTURE TRENDS IN THE GAS INDUSTRY

Projected Gas Use

The Energy Information Administration (EIA) of the U.S. Department of Energy, in its *Annual Energy Outlook 1998* (1997), projects energy supply, demand, and prices through the year 2020. The EIA predicts that natural gas demand will increase steadily, as will consumption, pipeline expansion, and imports.

By 2020, annual consumption will reach between 29.4 and 34.5 trillion cubic feet. Demand will outstrip existing pipeline capacity, resulting in expansion at a rate of 1.5 percent per year, especially along the corridors that move Canadian and Gulf Coast supplies to the eastern United States. Imports will increase from 12.4 percent of total gas consumption in 1996 to 15.2 percent in 2020. (See Figure 3.17.) Most of the increase will come from Canada. Natural gas exports to Mexico will continue, with exports increasing due to mandated conversions of power plants from heavy fuel oil to natural gas, in compliance with new environmental regulations.

The EIA predicts that although natural gas prices to the industrial, electricity, and transportation sectors will generally increase, prices to the residential and commercial sectors will decline.

Liquid Natural Gas

Imports of liquefied natural gas (LNG) are not expected to serve as a major source of gas imports, growing from 79 billion cubic feet in 1990 to 0.04 trillion cubic feet in 1996 to roughly 0.36 trillion cubic feet in 2020. Liquefied gas is the only economically feasible non-pipeline method of transporting natural gas in large amounts.

INTERNATIONAL NATURAL GAS SUPPLY AND CONSUMPTION

Worldwide Natural Gas Production (Supply)

The world's gross production of natural gas totaled 81.73 trillion cubic feet in 1996, approximately 22 percent of world energy production. Russia was the major producer (21.23 trillion cubic feet), with the United States second (18.79 trillion cubic feet). (See Table 3.4.)

Worldwide Natural Gas Consumption (Demand)

The world's consumption of natural gas has continued to increase since 1980, from 53 trillion cubic feet to 82.2 trillion cubic feet in 1996. The United States, followed by Russia, consumed the largest amount of natural gas. (Figure 3.18). Combined, they accounted for 44 percent of world consumption.

CHAPTER IV

ENERGY RESERVES — OIL, GAS, COAL, AND URANIUM

Fossil fuels are nonrenewable resources. Nonrenewable resources are defined as concentrations of naturally occurring solid, liquid, or gaseous hydrocarbons in or near the earth's surface in such a form that economic recovery is currently or potentially feasible. Once used, these substances cannot be replaced. It is important, therefore, to know the recoverable quantities of crude oil, natural gas, coal, and uranium resources in the United States and on Earth. Such estimates are essential to the development, implementation, and evaluation of national energy policy and legislation, and Congress requires the U.S. Department of Energy to prepare these estimates.

Proved reserves are reserves that geological and engineering data demonstrate, with reasonable certainty, can be recovered in the future under today's economic and operating conditions from known locations. *Undiscovered recoverable resources* are those quantities of fuel, as yet undiscovered, which are thought to exist in favorable geologic settings and would be feasible to retrieve under existing technological conditions (although they may not be feasible to recover under current economic conditions).

CRUDE OIL

Over the past decade, U.S. crude oil proved reserves have been declining (Figure 4.1). The U.S. had 22,017 million barrels of crude oil proved reserves as of December 31, 1996. This is about 2 percent less than in 1995 and the ninth consecu-

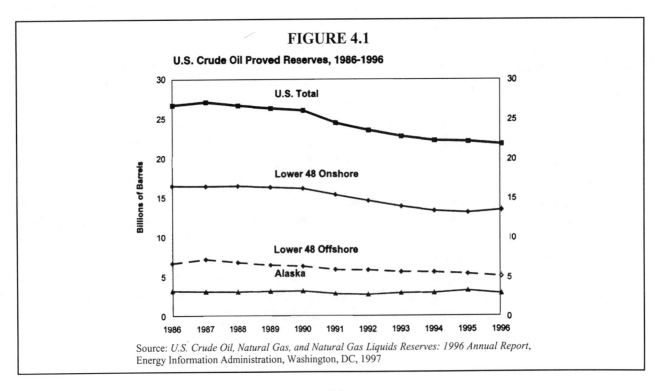

FIGURE 4.1

U.S. Crude Oil Proved Reserves, 1986-1996

Source: *U.S. Crude Oil, Natural Gas, and Natural Gas Liquids Reserves: 1996 Annual Report,* Energy Information Administration, Washington, DC, 1997

TABLE 4.1

Proved Reserves

U.S. proved reserves of crude oil as of December 31, 1996, by selected States and State subdivisions.

Area	% of U.S. Oil Reserves
Texas	26
Alaska	24
California	16
Gulf of Mexico Federal Offshore	12
Total	**78**

Source: *U.S. Crude Oil, Natural Gas, and Natural Gas Liquids Reserves: 1996 Annual Report*, Energy Information Administration, Washington, DC, 1997

tive year that crude oil proved reserves have declined. Alaska, the state with the second largest crude oil reserves in the United States (Table 4.1 shows the four areas that account for most of U.S. crude oil reserves), reported the largest decline in 1996 — a decrease of 5.5 percent from 1995. In 1996, the largest addition to new crude oil proved reserves came from the Gulf of Mexico Federal Offshore, which added 2 percent (49 million bar-

rels) in reserves. Figure 4.2 shows crude oil reserves by area in 1996.

Alaska

Proved reserves of crude oil and natural gas rose with the 1970 inclusion of Alaska's North Slope. Since then they have steadily declined. In 1987, Alaska was estimated to have 13.2 billion barrels of crude oil; by 1996, it had only 5.6 million barrels. However, the discovery of a new field in 1996 — the Alpine field on Alaska's North Slope, owned by Arco — is expected to raise recovery to 40,000 barrels per day in 2000 and 70,000 by 2001. The Northstar field on Seal Island, where an estimated 130 million barrels of recoverable oil have been discovered, is being considered for development.

The Gulf of Mexico

Projects in the Gulf of Mexico Federal Offshore provided the largest increase of crude oil re-

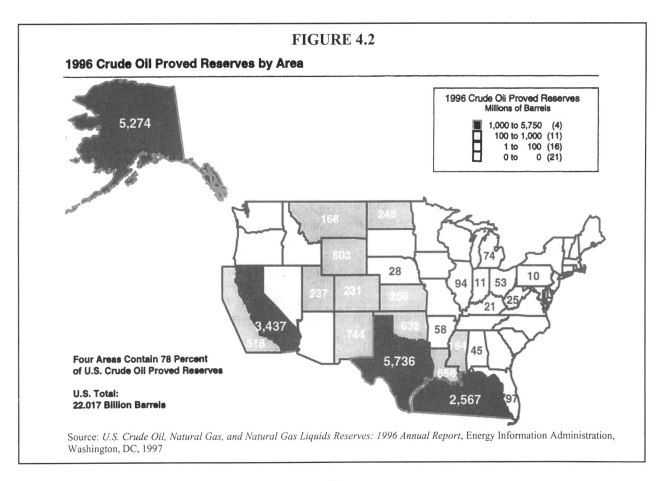

FIGURE 4.2

1996 Crude Oil Proved Reserves by Area

1996 Crude Oil Proved Reserves
Millions of Barrels

1,000 to 5,750 (4)
100 to 1,000 (11)
1 to 100 (16)
0 to 0 (21)

Four Areas Contain 78 Percent of U.S. Crude Oil Proved Reserves

U.S. Total: 22.017 Billion Barrels

Source: *U.S. Crude Oil, Natural Gas, and Natural Gas Liquids Reserves: 1996 Annual Report*, Energy Information Administration, Washington, DC, 1997

FIGURE 4.3

Semisubmersible drilling rig in the Gulf of Mexico. U.S. Department of Energy.

Source: *Annual Energy Review 1997*, Energy Information Administration, Washington, DC, 1998

serves in 1996, the fourth consecutive year that crude oil reserves have increased in that area. The improvement in deepwater drilling systems — floating platforms and subsea wells — has allowed the industry to expand into deeper Gulf waters (Figure 4.3). The Gulf of Mexico produced about 303 million barrels of crude oil in 1996, up from 292 million barrels in 1995.

The Permian Basin

In 1996, scientists turned their attention to the Permian Basin of West Texas and southeastern New Mexico, where plenty of dry-land potential for crude oil was found, making it one of the most active onshore areas.

NATURAL GAS

The United States had 166.5 trillion cubic feet of dry natural gas and 7.8 billion barrels of natural gas liquid proved reserves in 1996. This represented a three-year increase in natural gas resources. (See Figures 4.4 and 4.5.)

UNDISCOVERED RESOURCES

In addition to those proved resources, other resources, based on past geological experience, are believed to exist, although they are not yet proven. In 1996, the Energy Information Administration (EIA) reported there were an estimated 77.9 billion barrels of crude oil, 884.7 quadrillion cubic feet of natural gas, and 11.1 billion barrels of natural gas liquids of undiscovered resources in the United States (Table 4.2).

LOOKING FOR OIL AND GAS

Finding oil and gas is usually a two-step process. First, geological and geophysical (primarily

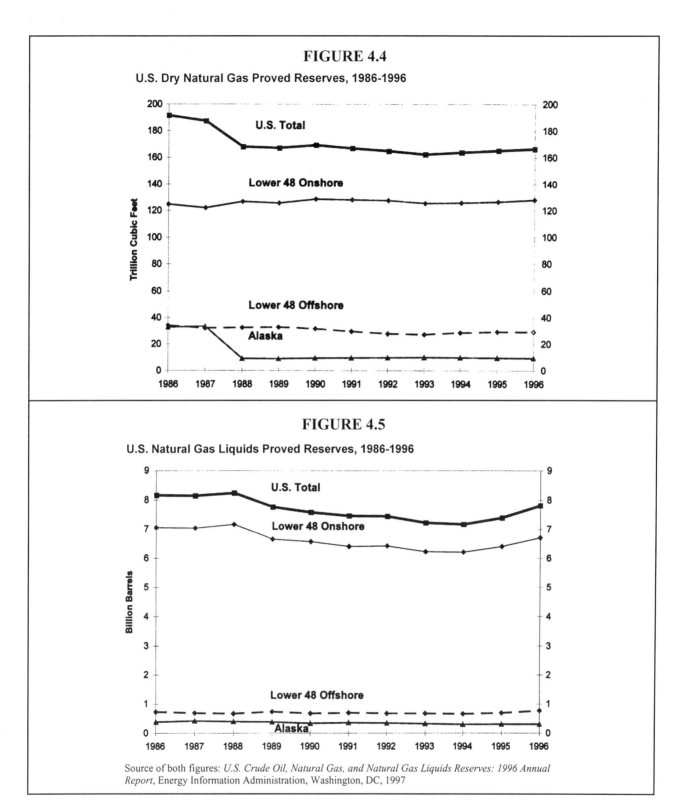

FIGURE 4.4

U.S. Dry Natural Gas Proved Reserves, 1986-1996

U.S. Total

Lower 48 Onshore

Lower 48 Offshore

Alaska

Trillion Cubic Feet

1986 1987 1988 1989 1990 1991 1992 1993 1994 1995 1996

FIGURE 4.5

U.S. Natural Gas Liquids Proved Reserves, 1986-1996

U.S. Total

Lower 48 Onshore

Lower 48 Offshore

Alaska

Billion Barrels

1986 1987 1988 1989 1990 1991 1992 1993 1994 1995 1996

Source of both figures: *U.S. Crude Oil, Natural Gas, and Natural Gas Liquids Reserves: 1996 Annual Report*, Energy Information Administration, Washington, DC, 1997

seismic, which measures the movement of the earth) exploration identifies the areas where oil and gas may most likely be found. Then exploratory wells are drilled to determine if oil or gas is present.

Market conditions and technological developments shape exploration for oil and gas. The eco-nomic problems of the oil industry can be seen in the drop in the number of exploratory oil and gas wells completed. Drilling activity has declined dra-matically since the early 1980s. Table 4.3 shows the number of wells that were explored and drilled. In 1981, a peak of 91,470 exploratory wells was drilled, with 70 percent of those successful. In

59

TABLE 4.2

Estimated Oil and Gas Reserves and Mean Estimates of Technically Recoverable Oil and Gas Resources

Categories	Crude Oil[a] (million barrels)	Natural Gas (Wet) (billion cubic feet)	Natural Gas Liquids (million barrels)
Lower 48 States			
Discovered			
Proved Reserves (EIA, 1996)...............................	16,743	[b]165,851	7,486
Reserve Growth - conventional, onshore[c] (USGS, 1991)	[d]47,000	290,000	12,900
Reserve Growth - conventional, Federal Offshore (MMS, 1994)....	[e]2,200	[e]32,700	NE
Unproved Reserves, Federal Offshore (MMS, 1994)	1,500	5,500	NE
Undiscovered, Technically Recoverable			
Conventional, onshore[c] (USGS, 1993).......................	21,810	190,280	6,080
Continuous-type - sandstone, shale, chalk; onshore[c] (USGS, 1993).	2,066	308,080	2,119
Continuous-type - coalbeds, onshore[c] (USGS, 1993)	NA	49,910	NA
Federal Offshore - conventional (MMS, 1994).................	21,300	142,100	[f]<1,800
Subtotal	**112,619**	**1,184,421**	**NA**
Alaska			
Discovered			
Proved Reserves (EIA, 1996)...............................	5,274	9,296	337
Reserve Growth - conventional, onshore[c] (USGS, 1991)	[g]13,000	32,000	500
Reserve Growth conventional, Federal Offshore (MMS, 1994).....	0	0	NE
Unproved Reserves, Federal Offshore (MMS, 1994)	400	700	NE
Undiscovered, Technically Recoverable			
Conventional onshore[c] (USGS, 1993)	8,440	68,410	1,120
Continuous-type - sandstone, shale, chalk; onshore[c] (USGS, 1993).	NE	NE	NE
Continuous-type - coalbeds, onshore[c] (USGS, 1993)	NA	NE	NA
Federal Offshore - conventional (MMS, 1994)	24,300	125,900	[f]<1,800
Subtotal	**51,414**	**236,306**	**NA**
Total Lower 48 States and Alaska...........................	**164,033**	**1,420,727**	**32,342**
Deductions for Production and Proved Reserves Changes,			
1991-1996	**-7,632**	**-79,898**	**-4,008**
U.S. Total, 1996..	**156,401**	**1,340,829**	**28,334**

[a] Condensate is included with crude oil for MMS estimates in Federal Offshore regions.

[b] Includes 10,566 billion cubic feet of coalbed methane (EIA, 1996).

[c] Includes USGS estimates for all onshore plus State Offshore (near-shore and shallow-water areas under State jurisdiction).

[d] Using USGS definition, 1,924 million barrels of indicated additional oil reserves in the lower 48 States were included (EIA, 1996).

[e] Reserve growth in the Pacific Federal offshore is not included and was not estimated by the MMS.

[f] Total undiscovered natural gas liquids for Federal offshore are 1,800 million barrels; MMS source did not separate lower 48 and Alaska estimates of undiscovered natural gas liquids (1986).

[g] Using USGS definition, 952 million barrels of indicated additional oil reserves in Alaska were included (EIA, 1996).

NE = not estimated.

NA = not applicable.

Notes: Federal Onshore indicates MMS estimates for Federal Offshore jurisdictions (Outer Continental Shelf and deeper water areas seaward of State Offshore). Energy Information Administration (EIA), onshore and offshore estimated reserves. U.S. Geological Survey (USGS): 1995 National Assessment mean estimates as of the end of 1993 (onshore and State Offshore). Minerals Management Service (MMS): 1996 National Assessment mean estimates as of the end of 1994. The MMS also has end-1994 estimates for economically recoverable resources. Probable and Possible reserves are considered by USGS definition to be part of USGS Reserve Growth, but are separately considered by the MMS as its Unproved Reserves term. The USGS did not set a time limit for the duration of Reserve Growth; the MMS set the year 2020 as the time limit in its estimates of Reserve Growth in existing fields of the Gulf of Mexico. Excluded from the estimates are undiscovered oil resources in tar deposits and oil shales, and undiscovered gas resources in geopressured brines and gas hydrates.

Energy Information Administration, Office of Oil and Gas; USGS and MMS - _Estimates of Undiscovered Conventional Oil and Gas Resources in the United States—A Part of the Nation's Energy Endowment_ (1989), U.S. Department of the Interior; _1995 National Assessment of United States Oil and Gas Resources_, USGS Circular 1118, U.S. Department of the Interior; and _An Assessment of the Undiscovered Hydrocarbon Potential of the Nation's Outer Continental Shelf_ (1996), U.S. Department of the Interior.

Source: _U.S. Crude Oil, Natural Gas, and Natural Gas Liquids Reserves: 1996 Annual Report_, Energy Information Administration, Washington, DC, 1997

TABLE 4.3

Oil and Gas Exploratory and Development Wells, 1949-1997

Year	Wells Drilled (thousands)				Successful Wells (percent)	Footage Drilled (million feet)				Average Depth (feet per well)			
	Oil	Gas	Dry Holes	Total		Oil	Gas	Dry Holes	Total	Oil	Gas	Dry Holes	Total
1949	21.35	3.36	12.60	37.31	66.2	79.4	12.4	43.8	135.6	3,720	3,698	3,473	3,635
1950	23.81	3.44	14.80	42.05	64.8	92.7	13.7	51.0	157.4	3,893	3,979	3,445	3,742
1951	23.18	3.44	17.03	43.64	61.0	95.1	13.9	63.1	172.1	4,103	4,056	3,706	3,944
1952	23.29	3.51	17.76	44.56	60.1	98.1	15.3	70.7	184.1	4,214	4,342	3,983	4,132
1953	25.32	3.97	18.45	47.74	61.4	102.1	18.2	73.9	194.2	4,033	4,599	4,004	4,069
1954	28.14	4.04	18.93	51.11	63.0	113.4	18.9	75.8	208.0	4,028	4,670	4,004	4,070
1955	30.43	4.27	20.45	55.15	62.9	121.1	19.9	85.1	226.2	3,981	4,672	4,161	4,101
1956	30.53	4.53	22.11	57.17	61.3	120.4	22.7	90.2	233.3	3,942	5,018	4,079	4,080
1957	27.36	4.48	20.16	52.00	61.2	110.0	23.8	83.2	217.0	4,021	5,326	4,126	4,174
1958	23.77	5.01	18.16	46.94	61.3	93.1	25.6	74.6	193.3	3,916	5,106	4,110	4,118
1959	24.04	4.93	18.59	47.56	60.9	94.6	26.6	79.5	200.7	3,935	5,396	4,275	4,220
1960	22.26	5.15	18.21	45.62	60.1	86.6	28.2	77.4	192.2	3,889	5,486	4,248	4,213
1961	21.44	5.49	17.33	44.25	60.8	85.6	29.3	74.7	189.6	3,994	5,339	4,311	4,285
1962	21.73	5.35	17.08	44.16	61.3	88.4	28.9	77.3	194.6	4,070	5,408	4,524	4,408
1963	20.14	4.57	16.76	41.47	59.6	81.8	24.5	76.3	182.6	4,063	5,368	4,552	4,405
1964	19.91	4.69	17.69	42.29	58.2	80.5	25.6	81.4	187.4	4,042	5,453	4,598	4,431
1965	18.07	4.48	16.23	38.77	58.2	73.3	24.9	76.6	174.9	4,059	5,562	4,723	4,510
1966	16.78	4.38	15.23	36.38	58.1	67.3	25.9	69.6	162.9	4,013	5,928	4,573	4,478
1967	15.33	3.66	13.25	32.23	58.9	58.6	21.6	61.1	141.4	3,825	5,898	4,616	4,385
1968	14.33	3.46	12.81	30.60	58.1	59.5	20.7	64.7	145.0	4,153	5,994	5,053	4,738
1969	14.37	4.08	13.74	32.19	57.3	61.6	24.2	71.4	157.1	4,286	5,918	5,195	4,881
1970	R12.97	4.03	R11.03	R28.03	R60.6	R56.9	23.6	58.1	138.6	R4,385	R5,860	R5,265	R4,943
1971	11.90	3.98	R10.31	R26.20	R60.6	49.1	23.5	54.7	127.3	R4,126	R5,890	R5,305	R4,858
1972	R11.38	R5.44	R10.89	R27.71	R60.7	R49.3	R30.0	R58.6	R137.8	R4,330	R5,516	R5,377	R4,974
1973	R10.17	R6.93	R10.32	R27.42	R62.4	R44.4	38.0	55.8	R138.2	R4,367	R5,487	R5,406	R5,041
1974	13.66	7.17	R12.12	R32.95	R63.2	R52.0	38.5	63.0	R153.5	R3,807	R5,365	R5,198	R4,657
1975	R16.98	R8.13	R13.65	R38.75	R64.8	R67.0	44.5	R69.5	181.0	R3,948	R5,477	R5,091	R4,671
1976	17.70	9.44	13.81	40.94	66.3	R68.9	49.2	R69.1	R187.2	R3,894	R5,212	R5,007	R4,573
1977	18.70	12.12	15.04	45.86	67.2	R75.4	R63.6	R76.8	R215.8	R4,034	R5,250	R5,105	R4,707
1978	R19.18	14.41	16.59	R50.18	66.9	R77.0	R75.8	R85.8	R238.6	R4,014	R5,259	R5,173	R4,754
1979	R20.85	R15.25	16.04	52.14	R69.2	R82.5	R80.4	R81.6	R244.5	R3,959	R5,270	R5,089	R4,690
1980	R32.59	R17.28	R20.61	R70.49	R70.7	R124.1	R91.3	R98.8	R314.2	R3,809	R5,283	R4,792	R4,457
1981	R43.57	R20.13	R27.78	R91.47	R69.6	R171.1	R107.8	R134.1	R413.1	R3,927	R5,358	R4,830	R4,516
1982	R39.13	R18.95	R26.22	R84.30	R68.9	R148.9	R106.8	R123.0	R378.7	R3,806	R5,638	R4,689	R4,492
1983	R37.10	14.56	R24.16	R75.82	R68.1	R136.2	77.6	R104.4	R318.2	R3,670	R5,333	R4,323	R4,197
1984	R42.54	R17.04	R25.66	R85.23	R69.9	R161.9	R90.7	R119.2	R371.9	R3,807	R5,324	R4,647	R4,363
1985	R34.93	R14.19	R21.03	R70.15	R70.0	R137.2	75.9	R99.9	R313.1	R3,929	R5,349	R4,751	R4,463
1986	R18.98	R8.50	R12.65	R40.13	R68.5	R76.3	44.7	R60.4	R181.5	R4,023	R5,261	R4,778	R4,523
1987	R16.09	R8.05	R11.09	R35.23	R68.5	R66.3	R42.5	R53.4	R162.1	R4,117	R5,279	R4,815	R4,602
1988	R13.56	R8.55	R10.03	R32.14	R68.8	R58.6	R45.4	R52.3	R156.3	R4,322	R5,305	R5,216	R4,862
1989	R10.18	R9.53	R8.17	R27.88	R70.7	R43.2	49.2	R52.3	R134.3	R4,245	R5,168	R5,124	R4,818
1990	R12.18	R11.04	R8.30	R31.52	R73.7	R54.2	R56.3	R43.1	R153.6	R4,453	R5,097	R5,193	R4,874
1991	R11.72	R9.48	R7.60	R28.81	R73.6	R54.0	50.0	R39.0	R143.0	R4,610	R5,279	R5,119	R4,964
1992	R8.76	R8.16	R6.11	R23.03	R73.5	R43.8	46.1	R31.2	R121.1	R4,992	R5,655	R5,109	R5,258
1993E	R8.25	R9.94	R6.22	R24.42	R74.5	R41.9	R59.6	R32.3	R133.8	R5,080	R6,000	R5,185	R5,481
1994E	R6.59	R9.55	R5.24	R21.38	R75.5	R35.9	59.5	R29.2	R124.5	R5,443	R6,229	R5,568	R5,824
1995E	R7.50	R8.25	R5.04	R20.79	R75.8	R37.6	50.6	27.5	R115.8	R5,018	R6,135	R5,463	R5,569
1996E	R8.00	R9.05	R5.16	R22.21	R76.8	R38.7	R55.4	R28.8	R123.0	R4,839	R6,125	R5,585	R5,535
1997E	8.93	10.73	5.23	24.88	79.0	46.6	65.6	28.5	140.7	5,219	6,114	5,457	5,655

R=Revised. E=Estimated.

Notes: • Service wells, stratigraphic tests, and core tests are excluded. • For 1949-1959, data represent wells completed in a given year. For 1960-1969, data are for well completion reports received by the American Petroleum Institute during the reporting year. For 1970 forward, the data represent wells completed in a given year. • Totals may not equal sum of components due to independent rounding. Average depth may not equal average of components due to independent rounding. • 1949-1965—Gulf Publishing Company, *World Oil*, "Forecast-Review" issue. • 1966-1969—American Petroleum Institute, *Quarterly Review of Drilling Statistics for the United States*, annual summaries and monthly reports. • 1970 forward—Energy Information Administration computations based on well reports submitted to the American Petroleum Institute (1970-1994) and to the Petroleum Information Corporation (1995 forward).

Source: *Annual Energy Review 1997*, Energy Information Administration, Washington, DC, 1998

1997, only 24,880 were attempted, 79 percent successfully. In 1981, 3,970 rotary rigs were in operation; by 1997, only 943 were operating. In 1997, 564 rigs drilled for gas; 376, for oil. (See Figure 4.6.) Most (821) rigs were onshore; 122 were offshore. The average depth of wells has steadily increased from 3,842 feet in 1949 to 6,554 feet in 1997. Gas wells (6,051 feet) are typically somewhat deeper than oil wells (5,013 feet).

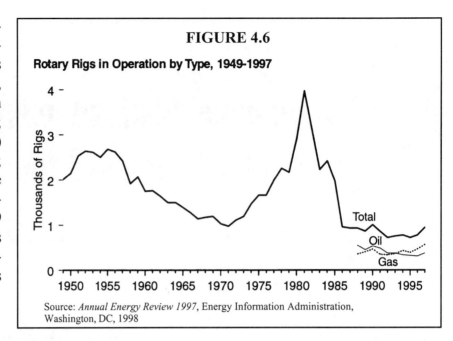

FIGURE 4.6

Rotary Rigs in Operation by Type, 1949-1997

Source: *Annual Energy Review 1997*, Energy Information Administration, Washington, DC, 1998

The Cost to Drill

In 1996, an average well cost $496,100 to drill, or $88.92 per foot. A gas well ($616,000) cost more than an oil well ($341,000) to drill because it is deeper. That is why the average cost per foot of a gas well ($98.67) is more than an oil well ($70.60). Although drilling costs have fluctuated in recent years, it costs considerably more to drill a well today than it did in the 1960s and early 1970s, not only because of inflation but also because wells must now be drilled deeper in order to reach either gas or oil. (Note the fluctuations in Table 4.4.)

SPENDING ON EXPLORATION AND DEVELOPMENT

The estimated expenditures by United States major energy-producing companies on exploration and development of oil and gas peaked at $48 billion in 1984. The $14.6 billion spent in 1996 was barely one-fourth that amount, about 46 percent of the total worldwide expenditure ($31.7 billion). (See Table 4.5.) The drop in oil prices and the declining probability of finding new fields have contributed to this huge decline in exploration funding.

In fact, the chance of finding a major oil or gas field has become increasingly small. Oil explorers are spending more of their time looking for less and less oil. This does not necessarily imply that the nation will soon be facing a shortage of gas or oil. The reserves are still considerable, especially of gas. It does show, however, that this is a "mature" oil and gas industry that is fully developed. The discovered reserves are likely to be most of what will be available. Finding new reserves will become increasingly difficult and more expensive, and unless the prices of oil and gas rise sharply, fewer and fewer companies will go looking for it.

DRILLING IN THE ARCTIC NATIONAL WILDLIFE REFUGE?

Considerable controversy developed over opening the Arctic National Wildlife Refuge (ANWR) in Alaska to oil drilling. Prudhoe Bay, directly to the west of the refuge, supplies about 20 percent of the country's domestic oil. Its potential is estimated at 8 billion barrels, and production is dropping as the oil is used up. In 1980, Congress passed the Alaska National Interest Lands Conservation Act (PL 96-487), which set aside more than 104 million acres for parks, refuges, and wilderness areas, including the Arctic Refuge (18 million acres), but it did not include the coastal plain.

The Department of the Interior, in a 1987 report to Congress, recommended that the 1.5 mil-

TABLE 4.4

Costs of Oil and Gas Wells Drilled, 1960-1996

Year	Costs per Well (thousand dollars)					Costs per Foot (dollars)				
	Oil (nominal)	Gas (nominal)	Dry Holes (nominal)	All (nominal)	All (real)¹	Oil (nominal)	Gas (nominal)	Dry Holes (nominal)	All (nominal)	All (real)¹
1960	52.2	102.7	44.0	54.9	235.8	13.22	18.57	10.56	13.01	55.84
1961	51.3	94.7	45.2	54.5	R232.0	13.11	17.65	10.56	12.85	R54.68
1962	54.2	97.1	50.8	55.6	246.4	13.41	18.10	11.20	13.31	R55.92
1963	51.8	92.4	48.2	55.0	R228.3	13.20	17.19	10.58	12.69	R52.66
1964	50.6	104.8	48.5	55.8	227.8	13.12	18.57	10.64	12.86	52.49
1965	56.6	101.9	53.1	60.6	242.6	13.94	18.35	11.21	13.44	53.76
1966	62.2	133.8	56.9	68.4	266.1	15.04	21.75	12.34	14.95	58.17
1967	66.6	141.0	61.5	72.9	275.1	16.61	23.05	12.87	15.97	60.26
1968	79.1	148.5	66.2	81.5	R295.2	18.63	24.05	12.88	16.83	R60.98
1969	86.5	154.3	70.2	88.6	R306.4	19.28	25.58	13.23	17.56	R60.76
1970	86.7	160.7	80.9	94.9	R311.1	19.29	26.75	15.21	18.84	R61.77
1971	78.4	166.6	86.8	94.7	R295.0	18.41	27.70	16.02	19.03	R59.28
1972	93.5	157.8	94.9	106.4	R318.6	20.77	27.78	17.28	20.76	R62.16
1973	103.8	155.3	105.8	117.2	R331.9	22.54	27.46	19.22	22.50	R63.74
1974	110.2	189.2	141.7	138.7	360.3	27.82	34.11	26.76	28.93	75.14
1975	138.6	262.0	177.2	177.8	R422.3	34.17	46.23	33.86	36.99	R87.86
1976	151.1	270.4	190.3	191.6	429.6	37.35	49.78	36.94	40.46	90.72
1977	170.0	313.5	230.2	227.2	479.3	41.16	57.57	43.49	46.81	98.76
1978	208.0	374.2	281.7	280.0	R550.0	49.72	68.37	52.55	56.63	R111.26
1979	243.1	443.1	339.6	331.4	R600.3	58.29	80.66	64.60	67.70	R122.64
1980	272.1	536.4	376.5	367.7	R609.8	86.36	95.16	73.70	77.02	R127.73
1981	336.3	698.6	464.0	453.7	R687.4	80.40	122.17	90.03	94.30	R142.88
1982	347.4	864.3	515.4	514.4	R732.7	86.34	146.20	104.09	108.73	R154.89
1983	283.8	608.1	366.5	371.7	R507.8	72.65	108.37	79.10	83.34	R113.85
1984	262.1	489.8	329.2	326.5	430.1	66.32	88.80	67.18	71.90	94.73
1985	270.4	508.7	372.3	349.4	445.1	66.78	93.09	73.69	75.35	P95.99
1986	284.9	522.9	389.2	364.6	452.3	68.35	93.02	76.53	76.86	95.38
1987	246.0	380.4	259.1	279.6	336.5	58.35	69.55	51.05	58.71	70.65
1988	279.4	460.3	366.4	354.7	412.0	62.28	84.65	66.96	70.23	81.57
1989	282.3	457.8	355.4	362.2	403.8	64.92	88.86	67.61	73.55	82.00
1990	321.8	471.3	367.5	383.6	409.8	69.17	90.73	67.49	76.07	81.27
1991	346.9	506.6	441.2	421.5	433.1	73.75	93.10	83.05	82.64	84.93
1992	362.3	426.1	357.6	382.6	382.6	69.50	72.83	67.82	70.27	70.27
1993	356.6	521.2	387.7	426.8	416.0	67.52	83.15	72.56	75.30	73.39
1994	409.5	535.1	491.5	483.2	R459.8	70.57	81.90	86.60	79.49	R75.63
1995	415.8	629.7	481.2	513.4	R476.3	78.09	95.97	84.60	87.22	P90.91
1996	341.0	616.0	541.0	496.1	450.2	70.60	98.67	95.74	88.92	80.69

¹ In chained (1992) dollars, calculated by using gross domestic product implicit price deflators.

R=Revised.

Notes: • The information reported for 1965 and prior years is not strictly comparable to that in the more recent surveys. • Average cost is the arithmetic mean and includes all costs for drilling and equipping wells and for surface-producing facilities. Wells drilled include exploratory and development wells; excludes service wells, stratigraphic tests, and core tests.

American Petroleum Institute, Independent Petroleum Association of America, Mid-Continent Oil and Gas Association, *1996 Joint Association Survey on Drilling Costs*.

Source: *Annual Energy Review 1997*, Energy Information Administration, Washington, DC, 1998

TABLE 4.5

Major Energy Producers' Expenditures for Oil and Gas Exploration and Development by Region, 1974-1996
(Billion Dollars[1])

| Year | United States | | | Foreign | | | | | | | Total |
	Onshore	Offshore	Total	Canada	Europe	Africa	Middle East	Other Eastern Hemisphere [2]	Other Western Hemisphere [3]	Total	
1974	NA	NA	8.7	NA	NA	NA	NA	NA	NA	3.8	12.5
1975	NA	NA	7.8	NA	NA	NA	NA	NA	NA	5.3	13.1
1976	NA	NA	9.5	NA	NA	NA	NA	NA	NA	5.2	14.7
1977	6.7	4.0	10.7	1.5	2.5	0.7	0.2	0.3	0.4	5.6	16.3
1978	7.5	4.3	11.8	1.6	2.6	0.8	0.3	0.4	0.6	6.4	18.2
1979	13.0	8.3	21.3	2.3	3.0	0.8	0.2	0.5	0.8	7.8	29.1
1980	16.8	9.4	26.2	3.1	4.3	1.4	0.2	0.8	1.0	11.0	37.2
1981	19.9	13.0	33.0	1.8	5.0	2.1	0.3	1.9	1.3	12.4	45.4
1982	27.2	11.9	39.1	1.9	6.3	2.1	0.4	2.4	1.1	14.2	53.3
1983	16.0	11.1	27.1	1.6	4.3	1.7	0.5	2.0	0.6	10.7	37.7
1984	32.1	16.0	48.1	5.4	5.5	3.4	0.5	2.0	0.5	17.3	65.3
1985	20.0	8.5	28.5	1.9	3.7	1.6	0.9	1.3	0.7	10.1	38.6
1986	12.5	4.9	17.4	1.1	3.2	1.1	0.3	1.2	0.6	7.5	24.9
1987	9.7	4.5	14.3	1.9	3.0	0.8	0.4	2.8	0.5	9.2	23.5
1988	12.9	8.1	21.0	5.4	4.3	0.8	0.4	1.4	0.7	13.0	34.1
1989	9.0	6.0	15.0	6.3	3.5	1.0	0.4	2.3	0.6	14.1	29.1
1990	10.2	4.9	15.1	1.8	6.6	1.4	0.6	2.4	0.7	13.6	28.7
1991	9.6	4.6	14.2	1.7	6.8	1.5	0.5	2.4	0.7	13.7	27.9
1992	7.3	3.0	10.3	1.1	6.8	1.4	0.6	2.4	0.6	12.9	23.2
1993	7.2	3.7	10.9	1.6	5.7	1.5	0.7	2.5	0.6	12.5	23.5
1994	7.8	4.8	12.6	1.8	4.7	1.4	0.4	2.8	0.7	11.9	24.5
1995	7.7	4.7	12.4	1.9	5.6	2.0	0.4	2.4	0.9	13.2	25.6
1996	7.9	6.7	14.6	1.6	6.0	2.8	0.5	4.6	1.6	17.1	31.7

[1] Nominal dollars.
[2] This region includes areas that are eastward of the Greenwich prime meridian to 180 longitude and that are not included in other specified domestic or foreign classifications.
[3] This region includes areas that are westward of the Greenwich prime meridian to 180 longitude and that are not included in other domestic or foreign classifications.
NA=Not available.
Note: • Major Energy Producers are the top publicly-owned crude oil producers that form the Financial Reporting System (FRS). • Totals may not equal sum of components due to independent rounding. • 1974–1976—Energy Information Administration (EIA), Office of Energy Markets and End Use, Financial Reporting System Database, November 1997. • 1977–1995—EIA, *Performance Profiles of Major Energy Producers*, annual report. • 1996—EIA, *Performance Profiles of Major Energy Producers, 1996* (January 1998), Tables B32 and B34.

Source: *Annual Energy Review 1997*, Energy Information Administration, Washington, DC, 1998

TABLE 4.6

Coal Demonstrated Reserve Base, January 1, 1997
(Billion Short Tons)

Region and State	Anthracite Underground and Surface [2]	Bituminous Coal [1] Underground	Bituminous Coal [1] Surface	Lignite Surface [3]	Total Underground	Total Surface	Total
Appalachian	**7.3**	**75.3**	**24.4**	**1.1**	**79.2**	**28.9**	**108.1**
Alabama	0.0	1.3	2.2	1.1	1.3	3.3	4.5
Kentucky, Eastern	0.0	2.2	9.8	0.0	2.2	9.8	12.1
Ohio	0.0	17.8	5.9	0.0	17.8	5.9	23.7
Pennsylvania	7.2	20.4	1.0	0.0	24.2	4.4	28.6
Virginia	0.1	1.4	0.7	0.0	1.5	0.7	2.2
West Virginia	0.0	31.0	4.4	0.0	31.0	4.4	35.4
Other [4]	0.0	1.2	0.4	0.0	1.2	0.4	1.5
Interior	**0.1**	**118.3**	**27.8**	**13.4**	**118.4**	**41.2**	**159.6**
Illinois	0.0	88.5	16.6	0.0	88.5	16.6	105.1
Indiana	0.0	8.9	1.1	0.0	8.9	1.1	9.9
Iowa	0.0	1.7	0.5	0.0	1.7	0.5	2.2
Kentucky, Western	0.0	16.3	3.7	0.0	16.3	3.7	20.0
Missouri	0.0	1.5	4.5	0.0	1.5	4.5	6.0
Oklahoma	0.0	1.2	0.3	0.0	1.2	0.3	1.6
Texas	0.0	0.0	0.0	12.9	0.0	12.9	12.9
Other [5]	0.1	0.3	1.1	0.5	0.4	1.6	2.0
Western	**0.0**	**144.1**	**66.2**	**29.7**	**144.1**	**95.9**	**240.0**
Alaska	0.0	5.4	0.7	0.0	5.4	0.7	6.1
Colorado	0.0	12.0	0.6	4.2	12.0	4.8	16.8
Montana	0.0	71.0	33.0	15.8	71.0	48.7	119.7
New Mexico	0.0	6.2	6.3	0.0	6.2	6.3	12.5
North Dakota	0.0	0.0	0.0	9.4	0.0	9.4	9.4
Utah	0.0	5.6	0.3	0.0	5.6	0.3	5.9
Washington	0.0	1.3	0.0	0.0	1.3	0.1	1.4
Wyoming	0.0	42.5	25.3	0.0	42.5	25.3	67.8
Other [6]	0.0	0.1	0.1	0.4	0.1	0.4	0.5
U.S. Total	**7.5**	**337.7**	**118.3**	**44.2**	**341.8**	**166.0**	**507.7**
States East of the Mississippi River	7.3	189.0	45.8	1.1	192.9	50.2	243.2
States West of the Mississippi River	0.1	148.7	72.6	43.2	148.8	115.7	264.6

[1] Includes subbituminous coal.
[2] Includes 3,385.4 million short tons of surface-minable resources, of which 3,370.0 million tons are in Pennsylvania and 15.5 million tons are in Arkansas.
[3] Lignite resources are not mined underground in the United States.
[4] Georgia, Maryland, North Carolina, and Tennessee.
[5] Arkansas, Kansas, Louisiana, and Michigan.
[6] Arizona, Idaho, Oregon, and South Dakota.

Notes: • Data represent known measured and indicated coal resources meeting minimum seam and depth criteria, in the ground as of January 1, 1997. These coal resources are not totally recoverable. Net recoverability ranges from less than 0 percent to more than 90 percent. Fifty-four percent of the demonstrated reserve base of coal in the United States is estimated to be recoverable. • Totals may not equal sum of components due to independent rounding.

Energy Information Administration, U.S. Coal Reserves 1997 update (April 1998).

Source: *Annual Energy Review 1997*, Energy Information Administration, Washington, DC, 1998

lion-acre coastal plain be opened for exploration and extraction. Alaskan corporations supported the proposal in hopes of sharing in the proceeds. Environmentalists strongly opposed the plan because of the destruction digging could do to the native wildlife, such as caribou, polar and grizzly bears, musk oxen, wolves, Arctic foxes, and millions of nesting birds.

The Department of Interior's Fish and Wildlife Service estimated that 3.2 billion barrels of recoverable oil exists in the contested area. The Department of Interior estimated that there was a 46 percent chance of recovering the oil, a high figure by industry standards. Considering the generally declining American production, this could account for as much as one-third of American production in the next century.

The report further stated, however, that there could be a major effect on the migratory caribou herds, which number about 180,000 animals. While environmentalists felt 20 to 40 percent of the animals would be endangered, Interior Department officials thought the caribou would change their migratory habits. However, while the report spoke of a short-term occupation by man, the energy developers could be there for a long time. If major oil reserves were found, oil companies might operate on the coastal plain for several decades. Also, the potential cannot be ignored for producing vast quantities of natural gas likely to be found. This, and possible development of offshore oil fields with onshore support in ANWR, could mean significant human activity in the area for the next century.

To date, the ANWR remains withheld from oil exploration, due both to environmental concerns and all-time low oil prices, which make exploration unlikely.

COAL RESERVES

The Energy Information Administration estimates the reserves of coal at 507.7 billion short tons as of 1997. Most (337.7 billion short tons) of

that reserve is underground bituminous coal. (See Table 4.6.) Montana, Illinois, and Wyoming have the largest amounts of coal reserves.

In addition to untapped coal reserves, coal producers and distributors, as well as major consumers such as electric utility companies and coke plants, maintain large stockpiles to compensate for possible interruptions in supply. Although there is little seasonal change in demand for coal, production of coal can vary due to factors such as coal miners' strikes and bad weather. In 1995, coal stockpiles totaled 169 million short tons. Electric utilities held over 70 percent of this coal, and coal producers and distributors stocked most of the remainder.

URANIUM RESOURCES

The United States possesses enough uranium to fuel existing reactors and any that will be built over the next 40 years. (At this time no more are expected to be built.) In 1997, uranium reserves totaled 1,466 million pounds of uranium oxide, most of which are in Wyoming and New Mexico (Table 4.7). Exploration for uranium has reflected changes in energy markets. The number of exploratory and development holes drilled peaked in 1978 at 104,000 and declined to just 7,800 in 1997 (Figure 4.6).

WORLD RESERVES

Crude Oil

Most of the estimated world crude oil reserves of approximately 1,100 billion barrels (as of January 1997) are located in the Middle East (Table 4.8). Saudi Arabia, Iraq, Iran, Kuwait, and the United Arab Emirates have the largest reserves. With an estimated 22 billion barrels of reserves, or only about 2 percent of the world's oil reserves total, the United States can no longer be able to depend on its own oil reserves. If current consumption rates continue, the world's oil reserves could be used up in 50 to 90 years.

TABLE 4.7

Uranium Reserves and Resources, End of Year 1997
(Million Pounds U₃O₈)

Resource Category and State	Forward Cost Category (dollars per pound)[1]		
	$30 or Less	$50 or Less	$100 or Less
Reserves[2]	**281**	**931**	**1,466**
New Mexico	84	350	578
Wyoming	116	381	602
Texas	8	26	42
Arizona, Colorado, Utah	42	119	164
Others[3]	32	56	79
Potential Resources[4]			
Estimated Additional Resources	2,180	3,310	4,850
Speculative Resources	1,310	2,230	3,480

[1] Forward costs are all operating and capital costs (in current dollars) yet to be incurred in the production of uranium from estimated resources. Excluded are previous expenditures (such as exploration and land acquisitions), taxes, profit, and the cost of money. Generally, forward costs are lower than market prices. Resource values in forward-cost categories are cumulative; that is, the quantity at each level of forward-cost includes all reserves/resources at the lower cost in that category.
[2] The Energy Information Administration category of uranium reserves is equivalent to the internationally reported category of Reasonably Assured Resources (RAR).
[3] California, Idaho, Nebraska, Nevada, North Dakota, Oregon, South Dakota, and Washington.
[4] Shown are the mean values for the distribution of estimates for each forward-cost category, rounded to the nearest million pounds U₃O₈.

• Forward Costs $30 or Less or $50 or Less—Energy Information Administration (EIA), *Uranium Industry Annual 1997* (April 1998), Tables B1 and B4. • Forward Costs $100 or Less—EIA, Office of Coal, Nuclear, Electric and Alternate Fuels database as of December 31, 1997.

FIGURE 4.7

Uranium Exploration and Development Drilling, 1949-1997

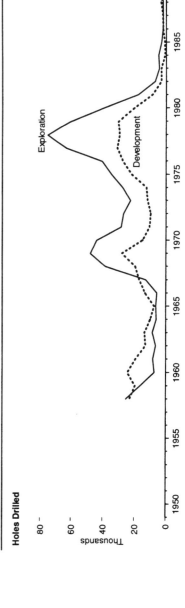

Source of table and figure: *Annual Energy Review 1997*, Energy Information Administration, Washington, DC, 1998

TABLE 4.8

World Crude Oil and Natural Gas Reserves, January 1, 1997

Region and Country	Crude Oil (billion barrels)		Natural Gas (trillion cubic feet)	
	Oil and Gas Journal	World Oil	Oil and Gas Journal	World Oil
North America	**75.7**	**76.0**	**302.3**	**298.5**
Canada	4.9	5.5	68.1	68.1
Mexico	48.8	48.5	67.7	63.9
United States	22.0	22.0	166.5	166.5
Central and South America	**79.1**	**91.2**	**208.5**	**213.9**
Argentina	2.4	2.6	21.9	24.3
Bolivia	0.1	0.1	4.5	4.4
Brazil	4.8	7.0	5.4	8.3
Colombia	2.8	3.4	8.3	8.0
Ecuador	2.1	3.3	3.7	3.4
Peru	0.8	0.7	7.0	7.0
Trinidad and Tobago	0.6	0.6	12.4	12.1
Venezuela	64.9	72.6	141.6	143.0
Other	0.7	1.1	3.7	3.5
Western Europe	**18.5**	**34.9**	**167.9**	**242.3**
Denmark	1.0	0.9	3.9	3.7
Germany	0.4	0.4	11.6	12.1
Italy	0.7	0.7	10.5	9.8
Netherlands	0.1	0.1	64.1	62.3
Norway	11.2	26.9	47.7	123.3
United Kingdom	4.5	5.0	24.7	26.8
Other	0.6	0.9	5.4	4.2
Eastern Europe and Former U.S.S.R.	**59.0**	**185.1**	**2,000.4**	**1,953.6**
Hungary	0.1	0.1	3.3	3.1
Romania	1.6	1.0	14.0	4.5
Former U.S.S.R.	57.0	183.8	1,977.0	1,939.3
Other ¹	0.2	0.2	6.1	6.7
Middle East	**676.4**	**635.7**	**1,617.1**	**1,675.0**
Bahrain	0.2	0.1	5.2	5.0
Iran	93.0	90.5	741.6	812.2
Iraq	112.0	112.0	118.0	118.5
Kuwait	96.5	94.7	52.9	52.7
Oman	5.1	3.6	30.0	21.1
Qatar	3.7	3.9	250.0	244.8
Saudi Arabia	261.5	261.8	189.1	191.5
Syria	2.5	2.4	8.3	8.2
United Arab Emirates	97.8	63.5	204.9	203.6
Yemen	4.0	3.1	16.9	17.0
Other	0.0	0.0	0.2	0.2
Africa	**67.6**	**76.2**	**328.6**	**344.6**
Algeria	9.2	13.0	130.3	138.9
Angola	5.4	3.6	1.7	1.7
Cameroon	0.4	0.1	3.9	3.9
Congo	1.5	1.6	3.2	4.3
Egypt	3.7	3.7	20.4	20.4
Libya	29.5	29.5	46.3	46.3
Nigeria	15.5	20.8	104.7	109.7
Tunisia	0.3	0.3	2.4	2.7
Other	2.0	3.6	15.7	16.7
Far East and Oceania	**42.3**	**60.8**	**321.8**	**448.7**
Australia	1.8	3.7	19.4	83.5
Brunei	1.4	1.1	14.1	13.5
China	24.0	34.1	41.4	39.6
India	4.3	5.0	24.2	19.5
Indonesia	5.0	9.2	72.3	135.9
Malaysia	4.0	5.2	80.2	79.1
New Zealand	0.1	0.1	2.4	2.2
Pakistan	0.2	0.2	22.0	18.3
Papua New Guinea	0.3	0.2	1.5	8.6
Thailand	0.3	0.3	7.1	7.1
Other	0.9	1.6	37.3	41.3
World	**1,018.5**	**1,160.1**	**4,946.7**	**5,176.6**

¹ Albania, Bulgaria, former Czech Republic, Poland, and Slovakia.

Notes: • Data for Kuwait and Saudi Arabia include one-half of the reserves in the Neutral Zone between Kuwait and Saudi Arabia. • All reserve figures except those for the former U.S.S.R. and natural gas reserves in Canada are proved reserves recoverable with present technology and prices. Former U.S.S.R. figures are "explored reserves," which include proved, probable, and some partially possible. The Canadian natural gas figure includes proved and some probable. The latest Energy Information Administration data for the United States are for December 31, 1996. • Totals may not equal sum of components due to independent rounding.

United States: Energy Information Administration (EIA), U.S. Crude Oil, Natural Gas, and Natural Gas Liquids Reserves, Annual Report 1996 (December 1997). All Other Data: PennWell Publishing Company, Oil and Gas Journal, December 30, 1996. Gulf Publishing Company, World Oil, August 1997.

Source: Annual Energy Review 1997, Energy Information Administration, Washington, DC, 1998

TABLE 4.9

World Recoverable Reserves of Coal
(Million Short Tons)

Region and Country	Anthracite and Bituminous Coal	Subbituminous Coal and Lignite	Total
North America	R 128,110	R 153,832	R 281,942
Canada	4,970	4,535	9,505
Greenland	0	202	202
Mexico	948	387	1,335
United States [1]	R 122,192	R 148,708	R 270,901
Central and South America	6,227	5,013	11,240
Brazil	0	3,136	3,136
Chile	34	1,268	1,302
Colombia	4,674	330	5,003
Peru	1,058	110	1,168
Other	461	170	631
Western Europe	30,544	78,281	108,825
Germany	26,455	47,730	74,186
Greece	0	3,307	3,307
Spain	937	661	1,598
Turkey	179	7,701	7,879
United Kingdom	2,205	551	2,756
Former Yugoslavia	70	18,152	18,222
Other	698	179	877
Eastern Europe and Former U.S.S.R.	149,200	179,232	328,431
Albania	0	(s)	(s)
Bulgaria	14	2,974	2,988
Czech Republic	1,810	3,858	5,668
Hungary	657	4,260	4,917
Poland	32,077	14,330	46,407
Romania	1	3,436	3,437
Slovakia	0	251	251
Former U.S.S.R.	114,640	150,122	264,762
Africa	66,585	1,397	67,982
Botswana	3,858	0	3,858
South Africa	60,994	0	60,994
Swaziland	128	1,101	1,229
Zimbabwe	809	0	809
Other	796	295	1,091
Middle East, Far East, and Oceania	196,630	146,941	343,571
Australia	49,979	50,265	100,244
China	68,564	57,651	126,215
India	75,009	2,094	77,103
Indonesia	1,060	34,283	35,343
Japan	886	19	905
Pakistan	0	809	809
Thailand	(s)	1,101	1,101
Other	1,132	719	1,850
World	R 577,296	R 564,696	R 1,141,992

[1] U.S. data are more current than other data on this table. They represent recoverable reserves as of January 1, 1997; data for the other countries are as of December 31, 1993, the most recent period for which they are available. U.S. reserves represent both measured and indicated tonnage. The U.S. term "measured" approximates the term "proved," which is used by the World Energy Council. The U.S. "measured and indicated" data have been combined prior to depletion adjustments and cannot be recaptured as "measured alone."
R=Revised. (s)=Less than 500 thousand short tons.
Notes: • World Energy Council definition of "Proved Recoverable Reserves" is the tonnage of Proved

Amount in Place that can be recovered (extracted from the earth in raw form) under present and expected local economic conditions with existing technology. • The EIA does not certify the international reserves data but reproduces the information as a matter of convenience for the reader. • Totals may not equal sum of components due to independent rounding.

United States: Energy Information Administration, Unpublished File Data of the Coal Reserves Database, (December 1997). **All Other Data:** World Energy Council, *1995 Survey of Energy Resources.* World Energy Conference (1995).

Source: *Annual Energy Review 1997,* Energy Information Administration, Washington, DC, 1998

Oil industry experts say that even though the world, at the moment, is sufficiently supplied with oil, the need will rise in the future as economies such as China and India expand. This knowledge drives oil companies to seek new sources for oil. Companies from many nations have, in recent months, turned their attention to the Caspian Sea, Azerbaijan, and Kazakstan (formerly in the Soviet Union) for oil exploration. Geologists believe that many billions of barrels of oil will be found there.

Many energy experts predict increased exploration in deep water. Roger Anderson, Director of Petroleum Research, Columbia University, reported in 1998, "We've pretty much put drill pipe into every basin in the world, with a couple exceptions in China north of Tibet, and so there aren't many frontiers left on land that haven't been explored." Areas they expect drilling to occur include the Gulf of Mexico (see above) and the coast of Brazil. Under-sea exploration is extremely expensive, but if oil prices rise, as they surely must, the oil industry will increasingly launch deep-water explorations.

Natural Gas

The former U.S.S.R. and the Middle East have most of the world's estimated 5,000 trillion cubic feet (as of January 1997) of natural gas reserves (Table 4.8). Russia has more than twice as much natural gas reserves as any other country, while Iran possesses, by far, the largest natural gas reserves in the Middle East. Large reserves are also located in the United Arab Emirates, Saudi Arabia, Qatar, the United States, Indonesia, Nigeria, Algeria, and Venezuela.

Coal

Recoverable reserves of coal were estimated to be 1.1 trillion short tons (Table 4.9; note that the data for the United States are for 1997; other countries, 1993, the latest available). The three countries with the most plentiful coal reserves are the United States (271 billion short tons), the former U.S.S.R. (265 billion short tons), China (126 billion short tons), and Australia (100 billion short tons).

CHAPTER V

COAL — CHANGING PATTERNS OF USE

A BRIEF HISTORY OF COAL

The first large-scale use of coal occurred during the Industrial Revolution in England. The sky was filled with huge billowing columns of black smoke, soot covered the towns, and workers breathed the thick coal dust swirling around them. At that time, most people were not concerned with environmental issues, since the Industrial Revolution meant jobs to the workers, and factory owners had little desire to control the pollution their factories were making. It was not generally understood that the environment was being harmed.

In America, colonists used wood to heat their homes because it was so plentiful; coal was less common. Prior to the Civil War (1861-1865), some industries used coal as a source of energy, but its greatest use as an energy source was tied to the building of the railroads prior to and during the Civil War. After the Civil War ended, America began to expand its railroad system westward and increase its manufacturing capacity. Coal became such a fundamental part of American industrialization that some have called this era "The Coal Age." As in England, Americans considered the development of industry a source of national pride. Photographs and postcards of the era proudly featured railroad trains and steel mills with smokestacks belching dark pollutants into gray skies.

By the 1900s, coal had become the nation's major fuel source, accounting for nearly 90 percent of the nation's energy requirements. By the end of World War II, however, coal accounted for only 38 percent of the energy supply as oil began to heat homes and offices and the growing number

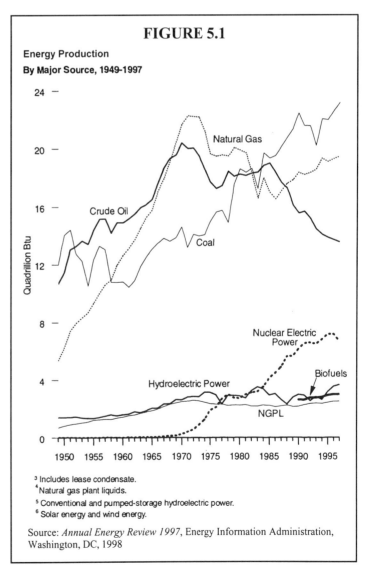

FIGURE 5.1

Energy Production
By Major Source, 1949-1997

[3] Includes lease condensate.
[4] Natural gas plant liquids.
[5] Conventional and pumped-storage hydroelectric power.
[6] Solar energy and wind energy.

Source: *Annual Energy Review 1997*, Energy Information Administration, Washington, DC, 1998

71

TABLE 5.1

Coal Production, 1949-1997
(Million Short Tons)

Year	Rank — Bituminous Coal	Rank — Subbituminous Coal	Rank — Lignite	Rank — Anthracite	Mining Method — Underground	Mining Method — Surface	Location — West of the Mississippi	Location — East of the Mississippi	Total
1949	437.9	(¹)	(¹)	42.7	358.9	121.7	36.4	444.2	480.6
1950	516.3	(¹)	(¹)	44.1	421.0	139.4	36.0	524.4	560.4
1951	533.7	(¹)	(¹)	42.7	442.2	134.2	34.6	541.7	576.3
1952	466.8	(¹)	(¹)	40.6	381.2	126.3	32.7	474.8	507.4
1953	457.3	(¹)	(¹)	30.9	367.4	120.8	30.6	457.7	488.2
1954	391.7	(¹)	(¹)	29.1	306.0	114.8	25.4	395.4	420.8
1955	464.6	(¹)	(¹)	26.2	358.0	132.9	26.6	464.2	490.8
1956	500.9	(¹)	(¹)	28.9	380.8	148.9	25.8	504.0	529.8
1957	492.7	(¹)	(¹)	25.3	373.6	144.5	24.7	493.4	518.0
1958	410.4	(¹)	(¹)	21.2	297.6	134.0	20.3	411.3	431.6
1959	412.0	(¹)	(¹)	20.6	292.8	139.8	20.3	412.4	432.7
1960	415.5	(¹)	(¹)	18.8	292.6	141.7	21.3	413.0	434.3
1961	403.0	(¹)	(¹)	17.4	279.6	140.9	21.8	398.6	420.4
1962	422.1	(¹)	(¹)	16.9	287.9	151.1	21.4	417.6	439.0
1963	458.9	(¹)	(¹)	18.3	309.0	168.2	23.7	453.5	472.2
1964	487.0	(¹)	(¹)	17.2	327.7	176.5	25.7	478.5	504.2
1965	512.1	(¹)	(¹)	14.9	338.0	189.0	27.4	499.5	527.0
1966	533.9	(¹)	(¹)	12.9	342.6	204.2	28.0	518.8	546.8
1967	552.6	(¹)	(¹)	12.3	352.4	212.5	28.9	536.0	564.9
1968	545.2	(¹)	(¹)	11.5	346.6	210.1	29.7	527.0	556.7
1969	547.2	8.3	5.0	10.5	349.2	221.7	33.3	537.7	571.0
1970	578.5	16.4	8.0	9.7	340.5	272.1	44.9	567.8	612.7
1971	521.3	22.2	8.7	8.7	277.2	283.7	51.0	509.9	560.9
1972	556.8	27.5	11.0	7.1	305.0	297.4	64.3	538.2	602.5
1973	543.5	33.9	14.3	6.8	300.1	298.5	76.4	522.1	598.6
1974	545.7	42.2	15.5	6.6	278.0	332.1	91.9	518.1	610.0
1975	577.5	51.1	19.8	6.2	293.5	361.2	110.9	543.7	654.6
1976	588.4	64.8	25.5	6.2	295.5	389.4	136.1	548.8	684.9
1977	581.0	82.1	28.2	5.9	266.6	430.6	163.9	533.3	697.2
1978	534.0	96.8	34.4	5.0	242.8	427.4	183.0	487.2	670.2
1979	612.3	121.5	42.5	4.8	320.9	460.2	221.4	559.7	781.1
1980	628.8	147.7	47.2	6.1	337.5	492.2	251.0	578.7	829.7
1981	608.0	159.7	50.7	5.4	316.5	507.3	269.9	553.9	823.8
1982	620.2	160.9	52.4	4.6	339.2	499.0	273.9	564.3	838.1
1983	568.6	151.0	58.3	4.1	300.4	481.7	274.7	507.4	782.1
1984	649.5	179.2	63.1	4.2	352.1	543.9	308.3	587.6	895.9
1985	613.9	192.7	72.4	4.7	350.8	532.8	324.9	558.7	883.6
1986	620.1	189.6	76.4	4.3	360.4	529.9	325.9	564.4	890.3
1987	636.6	200.2	78.4	3.6	372.9	545.9	336.8	581.9	918.8
1988	638.1	223.5	85.1	3.6	382.2	568.1	370.7	579.6	950.3
1989	659.8	231.2	86.4	3.3	393.8	586.9	381.7	599.0	980.7
1990	693.2	244.3	88.1	3.5	424.5	604.5	398.9	630.2	1,029.1
1991	650.7	255.3	86.5	3.4	407.2	588.8	404.7	591.3	996.0
1992	R651.8	R252.2	90.1	3.5	407.2	590.3	409.0	588.6	997.5
1993	576.7	274.9	89.5	4.3	351.1	594.4	429.2	516.2	945.4
1994	640.3	300.5	88.1	4.6	399.1	634.4	467.2	566.3	1,033.5
1995	613.8	328.0	86.5	4.7	396.2	636.7	488.7	544.2	1,033.0
1996	R630.8	R340.3	R88.1	R4.8	R409.8	R654.0	R500.2	R563.7	R1,063.9
1997	E629.3	E366.9	E87.6	P4.9	E419.1	E669.5	P511.3	P577.3	P1,088.6

¹ Included in bituminous coal.
R=Revised. E=Estimated.
Note: Totals may not equal sum of components due to independent rounding.

Sources: • 1949-1975—Bureau of Mines, *Minerals Yearbook*, "Coal-Bituminous and Lignite" and "Coal-Pennsylvania Anthracite" chapters. • 1976—Energy Information Administration (EIA), Energy Data Report, *Coal-Bituminous and Lignite in 1976* and *Coal-Pennsylvania Anthracite 1976.* • 1977 and 1978—EIA, Energy Data Report, *Bituminous Coal and Lignite Production and Mine Operations-1977; 1978, Coal-Pennsylvania Anthracite 1977; 1978,* and *Coal Production* (annual). • 1979 and 1980—EIA, Energy Data Report, *Weekly Coal Report* and *Coal Production* (annual). • 1981-1992—EIA, *Weekly Coal Production* and *Coal Production* (annual). • 1993-1996—EIA, *Coal Industry Annual 1996* (November 1997), Tables 1, 3, and 9. • 1997—EIA estimates.

Source: *Annual Energy Review 1997,* Energy Information Administration, Washington, DC, 1998

72

of cars used more gasoline. Coal fell further out of favor as an energy source in the 1950s and 1960s as oil became more attractive. This decline continued, with coal producing as little as 18 percent of the energy used during the early 1970s due to concerns about environmental pollution and the emergence of nuclear power as a primary energy source.

By 1973, Americans recognized they could no longer rely on imported oil for their energy — the Arab oil embargo clearly demonstrated the nation's heavy reliance on foreign sources of energy and its potentially crippling effect on the American economy. Consequently, the nation revived its interest in domestic coal as a plentiful and economical energy source.

After the 1973 Arab oil embargo, coal and nuclear fuel received more attention, especially in the electric utility sector. In 1977, President Jimmy Carter called for a two-thirds annual increase in national coal production by 1985. He also asked utility companies and other large industries to convert their operations to coal and proposed a 10-year, $10 billion program to encourage domestic coal production. In 1997, coal contributed more to America's energy (23 quadrillion Btu [British thermal units], or 31 percent) than any other source (Figure 5.1).

WHAT IS COAL?

Coal is a black, combustible, mineral solid that develops from the partial decomposition of plant matter in an airless space, under increased temperature and pressure over a period of millions of years. Coal is used as a fuel and in the production of coke, coal gas, water gas, and many coal-tar compounds.

Coal beds, sometimes called seams, are found between beds of sandstone, shale, and limestone and range in thickness from less than an inch to more than a hundred feet. About five to 10 feet of composted plant material have been compressed to create each foot of coal.

When coal is burned, its fossil energy is released. Coal produces an average of 22 million Btu

per ton, about the same heating value as 22,000 cubic feet of natural gas, 159 gallons of distillate fuel oil, or one cord of seasoned firewood.

CLASSIFICATIONS OF COAL

There are four basic types of coal. Their classification, or "coal rank," is based on how much carbon, volatile matter, and heating value are contained in each type of coal.

- Anthracite, or hard coal, is the highest ranked coal. It is hard and jet black, with a moisture content of less than 15 percent. Anthracite is used mainly for generating electricity and space heating. It contains approximately 22 to 28 million Btu per ton, with an ignition temperature of approximately 925 to 970 degrees Fahrenheit. Anthracite is mined in northeastern Pennsylvania.

- Bituminous, or soft coal, is the most common coal. It is dense and black, with a moisture content of less than 20 percent. Soft coal has an ignition range from 700 to 900 degrees Fahrenheit. Bituminous coal is used to generate electricity, produce coke (the substance left after coal gas and coal tar have been extracted from coal, used as fuel), and provide space heating in homes. It contains a heating value range of 19 to 30 million Btu per ton. Bituminous coal is mined chiefly in the Appalachian and Interior regions (see below).

- Subbituminous coal, or black lignite, is dull black and generally contains 20 to 30 percent moisture. Black lignite is used for generating electricity and for space heating. It contains 16 to 24 million Btu per ton. Black lignite is primarily mined in the western United States.

- Lignite, the lowest rank of coal, is brownish-black in color and has high moisture content. It tends to disintegrate when exposed to weather. Lignite is used mainly to generate electricity and contains about 9 to 17 million Btu per ton. Lignite has an ignition temperature of approximately 600 degrees Fahrenheit

FIGURE 5.2

Coal Areas of the United States

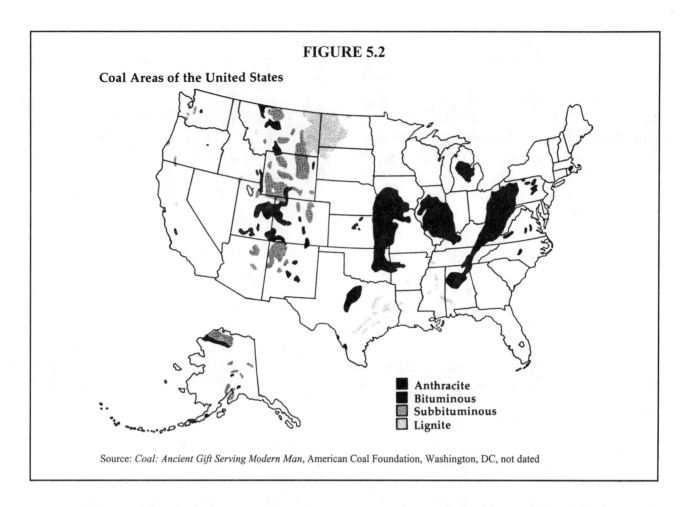

Anthracite
Bituminous
Subbituminous
Lignite

Source: *Coal: Ancient Gift Serving Modern Man*, American Coal Foundation, Washington, DC, not dated

and is mined in North Dakota, Montana, Texas, California, and Louisiana.

Bituminous coal accounts for, by far, the largest share of all coal production. In 1997, production of all types of coal totaled 1,089 million short tons (a short ton of coal is a unit of weight equal to 2,000 pounds), of which 996 million were bituminous and subbituminous coal. (See Table 5.1.) Lignite and anthracite accounted for the remainder.

LOCATION OF COAL DEPOSITS

The source of coal supply is determined primarily by the type of coal in demand, the level of demand, long-term contracts, the location of the consumer, and the delivered price of the coal per Btu. Coal is found in about 13 percent of the nation's total land area — less than 458,600 square miles of the United States.

Geologists have geographically divided U.S. coal fields into three regions — Appalachian, In-

terior, and Western. The Appalachian Region is subdivided into three areas: Northern (Ohio, Pennsylvania, Maryland and northern West Virginia); Central (Virginia, southern West Virginia, eastern Kentucky and Tennessee); and Southern Appalachia (Alabama). Coal production in the Interior Region occurs in Illinois, Indiana, western Kentucky, Iowa, Missouri, Kansas, Arkansas, Oklahoma, Louisiana and Texas. The Western Region includes the Northern Great Plains (Montana, Wyoming, northern Colorado, North and South Dakota), the Rocky Mountains, the Southwest area (southern Colorado, Utah, Arizona, and New Mexico), and the Northwest (Washington and Alaska). (See Figure 5.2.)

More coal is mined east of the Mississippi than in the West, but the West's proportion of total production has increased almost every year since 1965. In 1965, the production of coal in the West was 27 million short tons, only 5 percent of total production. By 1997, western production had increased

FIGURE 5.3

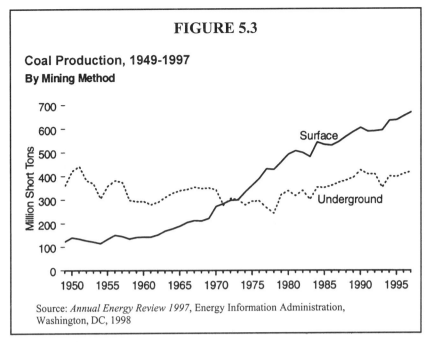

Coal Production, 1949-1997
By Mining Method

Source: *Annual Energy Review 1997*, Energy Information Administration, Washington, DC, 1998

demand for low-sulfur coal, which is concentrated in the West. In addition, surface mining, which has a higher average production, is more prevalent in the West. Finally, improved rail service has made it easier to deliver this low-sulfur coal to utility plants located east of the Mississippi River.

COAL MINING METHODS

Historically, most coal has been taken from underground mines. Since the early 1970s, however, coal production shifted from underground mines to surface mines (Figure 5.3 and Table 5.1). Because surface mines are easier to work, their yield averages two to three times that of underground mines.

almost 15-fold, to 511 million short tons — 47 percent of the total. The amount of coal mined east of the Mississippi was 577 million short tons in 1997. (See Table 5.1.) The growth in production of coal in the western regions has been partly due to environmental concerns that have led to an increased

The method used to mine coal depends on the terrain and the depth of the coal. Underground

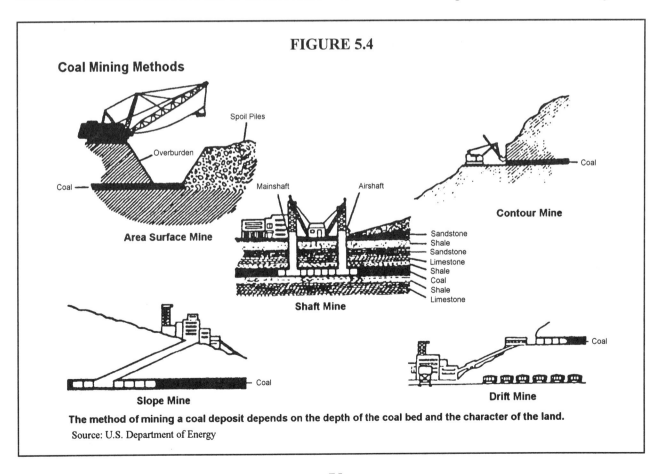

FIGURE 5.4

Coal Mining Methods

The method of mining a coal deposit depends on the depth of the coal bed and the character of the land.

Source: U.S. Department of Energy

75

FIGURE 5.5

Coal Yard, Curtis Bay, Maryland

Source: *Annual Energy Review 1997*, Energy Information Administration, Washington, DC, 1998

mining is required when the coal lies deeper than about 200 feet below ground level. The depth of most underground mines is less than 1,000 feet, but a few go down as far as 1,500 to 2,000 feet. In underground mines, some coal must be left untouched to form pillars needed to prevent the mine from caving in. In both underground mines and surface mines, natural features such as folded, faulted, and interlaid rock strata reduce the amount of coal that can actually be recovered. (See Figure 5.4.)

The first use of a steam-powered excavator in a surface coal mine occurred in Illinois in 1866. Surface mines are usually less than 200 feet deep and can be developed in either flat or hilly terrain. Area surface mining is practiced on rela-

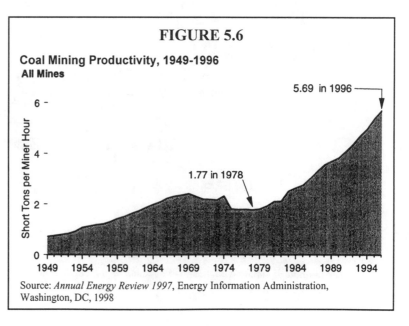

FIGURE 5.6

Coal Mining Productivity, 1949-1996
All Mines

5.69 in 1996

1.77 in 1978

Short Tons per Miner Hour

Source: *Annual Energy Review 1997*, Energy Information Administration, Washington, DC, 1998

76

tively flat ground, while contour surface mining follows a coal bed along hillsides. Open pit mining is used to mine thick, steeply inclined coal beds and uses a combination of contour and area mining methods. Figure 5.5 shows a coal yard.

The growing importance of surface coal mining and the closing of nonproductive mines led to increases in coal mining productivity in the 1980s and 1990s. In 1996, average productivity reached an all-time high of 5.69 short tons per miner hour (Figure 5.6). That year, productivity of underground mines (except for anthracite coal production) was 3.6 short tons per miner hour, while productivity of surface mines (excluding anthracite) was 9.3 short tons per miner hour.

Some coal deposits lie under towns and cities and, consequently, cannot be mined. Nonetheless, the coal reserves in the United States are believed to be the largest in the world (see Chapter IV).

COAL'S ROLE IN THE U.S. ENERGY PICTURE

Production and Consumption

From 1949 through 1951, coal was the leading source of energy produced in the United States. From 1952 to 1984, crude oil and natural gas vied for first place, but in 1984, coal regained the top position and has remained the leader since. In 1997, the United States produced 23 quadrillion Btu of energy — 1,089 million short tons — from coal (Table 5.1).

Sparked by the 1973-74 oil embargo and the resulting energy price increases, U.S. coal consumption has increased rapidly and steadily. In 1975, the nation consumed 563 million short tons of coal; by 1997, this number had grown to 1,027 million short tons. (Figure 5.7 shows the flow of coal in 1997.) The share of coal in total national energy consumption grew from 18 percent in 1975

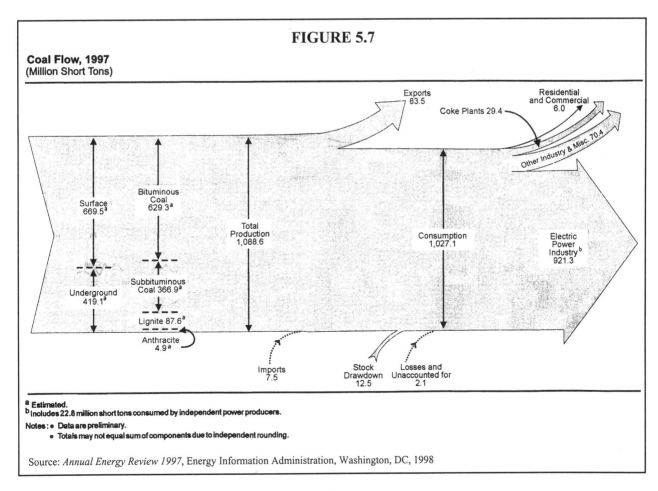

FIGURE 5.7

Coal Flow, 1997
(Million Short Tons)

Exports 83.5
Coke Plants 29.4
Residential and Commercial 6.0
Other Industry & Misc. 70.4

Surface 669.5[a]
Bituminous Coal 629.3[a]
Total Production 1,088.6
Consumption 1,027.1
Electric Power Industry[b] 921.3
Underground 419.1[a]
Subbituminous Coal 366.9[a]
Lignite 87.6[a]
Anthracite 4.9[a]
Imports 7.5
Stock Drawdown 12.5
Losses and Unaccounted for 2.1

[a] Estimated.
[b] Includes 22.8 million short tons consumed by independent power producers.

Notes: • Data are preliminary.
• Totals may not equal sum of components due to independent rounding.

Source: *Annual Energy Review 1997*, Energy Information Administration, Washington, DC, 1998

77

to 31 percent in 1997. The increases in coal consumption were greatest in the electric utility sector, as many existing electric power plants were switched to coal from the more expensive oil and gas, and many new coal-fired power plants were constructed during the 1970s (see below).

Electric Utilities — The Largest Coal Consumers

Electric utility companies are, by far, the primary users of coal. The coal is pulverized and burned to produce steam, which then drives electric generators. Each ton of coal used by the electric generator produces about 2,000 kilowatt hours of electricity. In household terms, each pound of coal produces enough electricity to light ten 100-watt light bulbs for one hour. As the main coal consumer, electric utility companies accounted for 90 percent of domestic coal consumption — 921 million short tons — in 1997 (Figure 5.8).

Demand for Coal by the Industrial Sector

Industrial steam coal is the second-largest component of coal demand, accounting for 10 percent of coal use in 1997 (Figure 5.8). Coal is used in the chemical, cement, paper, synthetic fuels, metals, and food-processing industries. Industrial use of coal in 1997 accounted for 106 million tons.

Residential and Commercial Uses of Coal

Coal was once the major fuel in the residential and commercial sector. However, since the late 1940s, cleaner, more convenient oil, natural gas, and electricity have rapidly replaced it. By 1970, only 16 million tons of coal were used for residential and commercial buildings. Since then, residential and commercial coal use has continued to de-

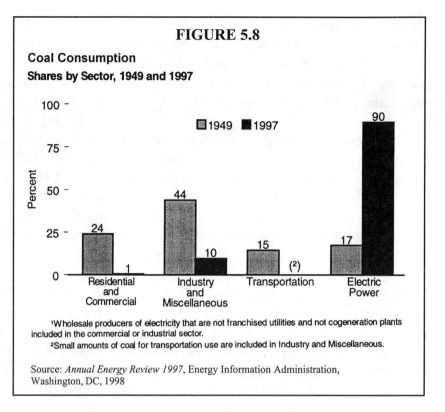

FIGURE 5.8

Coal Consumption Shares by Sector, 1949 and 1997

[1] Wholesale producers of electricity that are not franchised utilities and not cogeneration plants included in the commercial or industrial sector.
[2] Small amounts of coal for transportation use are included in Industry and Miscellaneous.

Source: *Annual Energy Review 1997*, Energy Information Administration, Washington, DC, 1998

cline, falling to 6 million short tons (1 percent of total coal use) in 1997 (Figure 5.8).

The Price of Coal

In 1997, the average price of coal fell to $23.27 per short ton, down for the fifteenth year in a row and less than half the 1982 price (Table 5.2). On a Btu basis, coal remains the least expensive fossil fuel; in 1997 dollars, the cost for bituminous coal, subbituminous coal, and lignite was 85 cents per million Btu, compared to $2.18 per million Btu for natural gas and $2.97 per million for crude oil.

ENVIRONMENTAL CONCERNS ABOUT COAL

All energy use has unwanted effects of one kind or another. Even a campfire produces, in addition to warmth, smoke that stings the eyes and pollutes the air. This is not only a recent problem. King Edward I of England so objected to the noxious smoke and fumes from London's many coal-burning fires that, in 1306, he banned its use by every-

TABLE 5.2

Coal Prices, 1949-1997
(Dollars per Short Ton)

Year	Bituminous Coal[1] and Lignite, F.O.B.[2] Mines		Anthracite, At Plants and Mines[3]		All Coal, CIF[4] Electric Utility Power Plants	
	Nominal	Real[5]	Nominal	Real[5]	Nominal	Real[5]
1949	4.88	R26.96	8.90	R49.17	NA	NA
1950	4.84	R26.45	9.34	R51.04	NA	NA
1951	4.92	R25.10	9.84	R50.71	NA	NA
1952	4.90	R24.62	9.58	R48.14	6.61	R33.22
1953	4.92	R24.36	9.87	R48.86	6.61	R32.72
1954	4.52	R22.16	8.76	R42.94	6.31	R30.93
1955	4.50	R21.74	8.00	R38.65	6.07	R29.32
1956	4.82	R22.42	8.33	R38.74	6.32	R29.40
1957	5.08	R22.88	9.11	R41.04	6.64	R29.91
1958	4.86	R21.41	9.14	R40.26	6.58	R28.99
1959	4.77	R20.74	8.55	R37.17	6.37	R27.70
1960	4.69	20.13	8.01	34.38	6.26	26.87
1961	4.58	R19.49	8.26	R35.15	6.20	R26.38
1962	4.48	R18.82	7.99	R33.57	6.02	R25.29
1963	4.39	R18.22	8.64	R35.85	5.66	R24.32
1964	4.45	18.16	8.93	36.45	5.74	23.43
1965	4.44	17.76	8.51	34.04	5.71	22.84
1966	4.54	17.67	8.08	31.44	5.76	22.41
1967	4.62	17.43	8.15	30.75	5.85	22.08
1968	4.67	16.92	8.78	31.81	5.93	21.49
1969	4.99	R17.27	9.91	R34.29	6.13	R21.21
1970	6.26	R20.52	11.03	R36.16	7.13	R23.38
1971	7.07	22.02	12.08	37.63	8.00	24.92
1972	7.66	R22.93	12.40	R37.13	8.44	R25.27
1973	8.53	24.16	13.65	38.67	9.01	25.52
1974	15.75	40.91	22.19	57.64	15.46	40.16
1975	19.23	R45.68	32.28	R76.63	17.63	R41.88
1976	19.43	43.57	33.92	76.05	18.38	41.21
1977	19.82	41.81	34.86	73.54	20.37	42.97
1978	21.78	R42.79	35.25	R69.25	23.75	R46.66
1979	23.65	R42.84	41.06	R74.38	26.15	R47.37
1980	24.52	R40.66	42.51	R70.50	28.76	R47.69
1981	26.23	R39.83	44.28	R67.09	32.32	R48.97
1982	27.14	38.66	49.85	71.01	34.91	R49.73
1983	25.85	R35.31	52.29	R71.43	34.99	R47.80
1984	25.51	33.61	48.22	63.53	35.12	46.27
1985	25.10	R31.97	45.80	R58.34	34.53	R43.99
1986	23.70	29.40	44.12	54.74	33.30	41.32
1987	23.00	27.68	43.65	52.53	31.83	38.30
1988	22.00	25.55	44.16	51.29	30.64	35.59
1989	21.76	24.26	42.93	47.86	30.15	33.61
1990	21.71	23.19	39.40	42.09	30.45	32.53
1991	21.45	22.05	36.34	37.35	30.02	30.85
1992	R20.99	20.99	34.24	34.24	29.36	29.36
1993	19.79	R18.40	32.94	32.11	28.58	27.86
1994	19.34	R17.38	36.07	R34.32	28.03	R26.67
1995	18.74	R16.93	39.78	R36.90	27.01	R25.06
1996	R18.42	R16.72	R36.78	R33.38	R26.45	R24.00
1997	E18.11	E16.11	E34.01	E30.26	26.16	23.27

[1] Includes subbituminous coal.
[2] Free on board. See Glossary.
[3] For 1949-1978, prices are f.o.b. preparation plants. For 1979 forward, prices are f.o.b. mines.
[4] Cost, Insurance, and Freight. See Glossary.
[5] In chained (1992) dollars, calculated by using gross domestic product implicit price deflators.

R=Revised. E=Estimated. NA=Not available.
Web Page: http://www.eia.doe.gov/fuelcoal.html.
Sources: **Bituminous Coal and Lignite, F.O.B. Mines:** • 1949-1975—Bureau of Mines, *Minerals Yearbook*, "Coal-Bituminous and Lignite" chapter. • 1976—Energy Information Administration (EIA), "Coal-Bituminous and Lignite" chapter. • 1977 and 1978—EIA, *Energy Data Report, Coal-Bituminous and Lignite in 1976.* • 1977 and 1978—EIA, *Energy Data Report,* *Bituminous Coal and Lignite Production and Mine Operations-1977; 1978.* • 1979-1992—EIA, *Coal Production,* (annual). • 1993-1996—EIA, Form EIA-7A, "Coal Production Report." • 1997—EIA estimates. **Anthracite:** • 1949-1976—Bureau of Mines, *Minerals Yearbook,* "Coal-Pennsylvania Anthracite" chapter. • 1977 and 1978—EIA, *Energy Data Report, Coal-Pennsylvania Anthracite 1977; 1978.* • 1979—EIA, Form EIA-7A, "Coal Production Report." • 1980-1992—EIA, *Coal Production,* (annual). • 1993-1996—EIA, Form EIA-7A, "Coal Production Report." • 1997—EIA estimates. **All Coal, CIF Electric Utility Power Plants:** • 1949-1972—National Coal Association, *Steam Electric Plant Factors.* • 1973-1982—Federal Power Commission, Form FPC-423, "Monthly Report of Cost and Quality of Fuels for Electric Plants." • 1983-1990—Federal Energy Regulatory Commission, Form FERC-423, "Monthly Report of Cost and Quality of Fuel for Electric Utilities." • 1991 forward—EIA, *Quarterly Coal Report October-December 1997,* Table 21.

Source: *Annual Energy Review 1997,* Energy Information Administration, Washington, DC, 1998

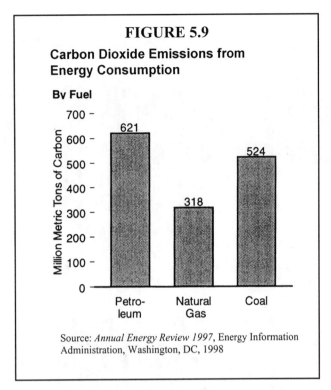

FIGURE 5.9

Carbon Dioxide Emissions from Energy Consumption

By Fuel

Source: *Annual Energy Review 1997*, Energy Information Administration, Washington, DC, 1998

one except blacksmiths. But the enormous scale of today's energy use has increased concerns.

Coal-fired electric power plants emit gases that are harmful to the environment. Many scientists believe they cause the "greenhouse effect," warming the climate and threatening Earth's environment. Coal-burning also contributes to the formation of acid rain (see below). (For more information on environmental pollution, see *The Environment — A Revolution in Attitudes*, Information Plus, Wylie, Texas, 1998.)

Carbon dioxide accounts for the largest share of these greenhouse gas emissions. In 1996, the combustion of coal in the United States produced more than half a billion metric tons of carbon, 36 percent of total carbon dioxide emissions from all sources (Figure 5.9).

What Is Acid Rain?

Acid rain can be described as any form of precipitation that contains a greater than normal amount of acid. Chemicals, such as oxides of sulfur and nitrogen, are emitted from coal-fired power

plants. These emissions chemically change as they travel through the atmosphere and eventually fall to Earth as acidic rain, snow, fog, or dust, creating air pollution. In nature, the combination of rain and oxides is part of a natural balance that nourishes plants and aquatic life. When oxides in the atmosphere increase because of industrial and power plant pollution, automobile exhaust, or other fossil fuel combustion processes, the balance of nature is upset.

The Clean Coal Technology Law

In 1984, Congress established the Department of Energy's (DOE) Clean Coal Technology (CCT) program (PL 98-473). Congress directed the DOE to direct cost-shared (industry and government-financed) projects to demonstrate clean coal technologies. Clean coal technologies include a variety of processes by which potentially harmful emissions are reduced when coal or coal products are burned for energy production. The demonstration projects were to use coal in a more environmentally responsive, economic, and efficient manner than the existing coal-fueled technologies.

Clean Coal Technology and the Clean Air Act

The stated goal of both Congress and the DOE has been to develop cost-effective ways to burn coal more cleanly, both to control acid rain and to improve the nation's energy security by reducing dependence on imported oil and gas. One suggested strategy is a slow, phased-in approach whereby utility companies and states would reduce their emissions in stages.

Under the Clean Air Act of 1990 (PL 101-549), restrictions on sulfur dioxide and nitrogen oxide emissions, which contribute heavily to air pollution, took effect in 1995 and will tighten in 2000. Each round of regulation will require more coal-burning utilities to find lower-sulfur coal or to install scrubbers or other cleanup technology. When the first Clean Air Act was passed in 1970, it was aimed at changing the air quality standards at new generating stations, but older coal-using plants were exempt. Under the new act, older plants are also covered by the regulations.

An Environmental Protection Agency (EPA) analysis prepared by ICF Resources, Inc., predicted that the 1990 Clean Air Act would cut coal production from the high-sulfur areas of the Middle West and northern Appalachia by 2005. The low-sulfur replacement coal will come mostly from central Appalachia and the West. Coal from these two regions is very low in sulfur. The only major barrier for western coal is the cost of transportation, but recent improvements in rail service have relieved this problem.

How Coal Can Be Cleaned

When the sulfur in coal is burned, it forms sulfur dioxide gas. The EPA considers this pollutant a respiratory threat, and the gas can also mix with the moisture in the atmosphere and become acid rain. Coal may be cleaned by physical or chemical methods. Scrubbers, which are the most commonly used physical method used to reduce sulfur dioxide emissions, filter the polluted gas after the coal has been burned by spraying lime or a calcium compound and water across the emission stream before it escapes out of the smokestack. (Figure 5.10 shows a scrubber.) The sulfur dioxide bonds to the spray and settles as a mud-like substance that can be pumped out for disposal. The process is expensive. Chemical cleaning, a relatively new technology, involves the use of biological or chemical agents.

Coal-burning electricity plants built to meet current emission standards while using eastern high-sulfur coal now spend 30 percent of the construction costs on pollution control equipment and use 3 to 5 percent of the plant's power output to operate this equipment. Under the new environmental regulations, plants with coal-generated boilers must be built to reduce sulfur emissions by 70 to 90 percent. Research to lower these costs is important because most of the electricity produced in the United States is generated with coal. In addition, 30 percent of all power plants use the high-sulfur coal mined east of the Mississippi.

The Department of Energy reports that coal-fired plants account for 300 gigawatts of electrical capacity, or 44 percent of the total generating capacity. Of this total coal-fired capacity, 70 gigawatts are already treated with scrubbers. Additional plants with a total of 42 gigawatts of capacity will probably switch to low-sulfur coal, and larger

FIGURE 5.10

Example of a Scrubber

Photo used by permission of Air Products and Chemicals, Inc.

Source: *Air Pollution Allowance Trading Offers an Opportunity to Reduce Emissions at Less Cost*, U.S. General Accounting Office, Washington, DC, 1994

TABLE 5.3

Coal Exports by Country of Destination, 1960-1997
(Million Short Tons)

Year	Canada	Brazil	Europe										Japan	Other	Total
			Belgium/ Luxembourg	Denmark	France	Germany[1]	Italy	Netherlands	Spain	United Kingdom	Other	Total			
1960	12.8	1.1	1.1	0.1	0.8	4.6	4.9	2.8	0.3	0.0	2.4	17.1	5.6	1.3	38.0
1961	12.1	1.0	1.0	0.1	0.7	4.3	4.8	2.6	0.2	0.0	2.0	15.7	6.6	1.0	36.4
1962	12.3	1.3	1.3	(s)	0.9	5.1	6.0	3.3	0.8	(s)	1.8	19.1	6.5	1.0	40.2
1963	14.6	1.2	2.7	(s)	2.7	5.6	7.9	5.0	1.5	0.0	2.4	27.7	6.1	0.9	50.4
1964	14.8	1.1	2.3	(s)	2.2	5.2	8.1	4.2	1.4	0.0	2.6	26.0	6.5	1.1	49.5
1965	16.3	1.2	2.2	(s)	2.1	4.7	9.0	3.4	1.4	(s)	2.3	25.1	7.5	0.9	51.0
1966	16.5	1.7	1.8	(s)	1.6	4.9	7.8	3.2	1.2	0.0	2.5	23.1	7.8	1.0	50.1
1967	15.8	1.7	1.4	0.0	2.1	4.7	5.9	2.2	1.0	0.0	2.1	19.4	12.2	1.0	50.1
1968	17.1	1.8	1.1	0.0	1.5	3.8	4.3	1.5	1.5	0.0	1.9	15.5	15.8	0.9	51.2
1969	17.3	1.8	0.9	0.0	2.3	3.5	3.7	1.6	1.8	0.0	1.3	15.2	21.4	1.2	56.9
1970	19.1	2.0	1.9	0.0	3.6	5.0	4.3	2.1	3.2	(s)	1.8	21.8	27.6	1.2	71.7
1971	18.0	1.9	0.8	0.0	3.2	2.9	2.7	1.6	2.6	1.7	1.1	16.6	19.7	1.1	57.3
1972	18.7	1.9	1.1	0.0	1.7	2.4	3.7	2.3	2.1	2.4	1.1	16.9	18.0	1.2	56.7
1973	16.7	1.6	1.2	0.0	2.0	1.6	3.3	1.8	2.2	0.9	1.3	14.4	19.2	1.6	53.6
1974	14.2	1.3	1.1	0.0	2.7	1.5	3.9	2.6	2.0	1.4	0.9	16.1	27.3	1.8	60.7
1975	17.3	2.0	0.6	0.0	3.6	2.0	4.5	2.1	2.7	1.9	1.6	19.0	25.4	2.6	66.3
1976	16.9	2.2	2.2	(s)	3.5	1.0	4.2	3.5	2.5	0.8	2.1	19.9	18.8	2.1	60.0
1977	17.7	2.3	1.5	0.1	2.1	0.9	4.1	2.0	1.6	0.6	2.1	15.0	15.9	3.5	54.3
1978	15.7	1.5	1.1	0.0	1.7	0.6	3.2	1.1	0.8	0.4	2.2	11.0	10.1	2.5	40.7
1979	19.5	2.8	3.2	0.2	3.9	2.6	5.0	2.0	1.4	1.4	4.4	23.9	15.7	4.1	66.0
1980	17.5	3.3	4.6	1.7	7.8	2.5	7.1	4.7	3.4	4.1	6.0	41.9	23.1	6.0	91.7
1981	18.2	2.7	4.3	3.9	9.7	4.3	10.5	6.8	6.4	2.3	8.8	57.0	25.9	8.7	112.5
1982	18.6	3.1	4.8	2.8	9.0	2.3	11.3	5.9	5.6	2.0	7.6	51.3	25.8	7.5	106.3
1983	17.2	3.6	2.5	1.7	4.2	1.5	8.1	4.2	3.3	1.2	6.4	33.1	17.9	8.1	77.8
1984	20.4	4.7	3.9	0.6	3.8	0.9	7.6	5.5	2.3	2.9	5.3	32.8	16.3	7.2	81.5
1985	16.4	5.9	4.4	2.2	4.5	1.1	10.3	6.3	3.5	2.7	10.3	45.1	15.4	9.9	92.7
1986	14.5	5.7	4.4	2.1	5.4	0.8	10.4	5.6	2.6	2.9	8.4	42.6	11.4	11.4	85.5
1987	16.2	5.8	4.6	0.9	2.9	0.5	9.5	4.1	2.5	2.6	6.6	34.2	11.1	12.3	79.6
1988	19.2	5.3	6.5	2.8	4.3	0.7	11.1	5.1	2.5	3.7	8.5	45.1	14.1	11.3	95.0
1989	16.8	5.7	7.1	3.2	6.5	0.7	11.2	6.1	3.3	4.5	8.9	51.6	13.8	12.9	100.8
1990	15.5	5.8	8.5	3.2	6.9	1.1	11.9	8.4	3.8	5.2	9.5	58.4	13.3	12.7	105.8
1991	11.2	7.1	7.5	4.7	9.5	1.7	11.3	9.6	4.7	6.2	10.4	65.5	12.3	13.0	109.0
1992	15.1	6.4	7.2	3.8	8.1	1.0	9.3	9.1	4.5	5.6	8.5	57.3	12.3	11.4	102.5
1993	8.9	5.2	5.2	0.3	4.0	0.5	6.9	5.6	4.1	4.1	6.9	37.6	11.9	11.0	74.5
1994	9.2	5.5	4.9	0.5	2.9	0.3	7.5	4.9	4.1	3.4	7.3	35.8	10.2	10.7	71.4
1995	9.4	6.4	4.5	2.1	3.7	2.0	9.1	7.3	4.7	4.7	R9.8	48.6	11.8	12.4	88.5
1996	12.0	6.5	4.6	1.3	3.9	1.1	9.2	7.1	4.1	6.2	9.8	47.2	10.5	14.2	90.5
1997	15.0	7.5	4.3	0.4	3.4	0.9	7.0	4.8	4.1	7.2	9.2	41.3	8.0	11.8	83.5

[1] Through 1990, the data for Germany are for the former West Germany only. Beginning with 1991, the data for Germany are for the unified Germany, i.e., the former East Germany and West Germany.
(s)=Less than 50,000 tons.
Note: Totals may not equal sum of components due to independent rounding.

Sources: • 1960-1988—U.S. Department of Commerce, Bureau of the Census. *U.S. Exports by Schedule B Commodities, EM 522.* • 1989 forward—U.S. Department of Commerce, Bureau of the Census, Monthly Reports, EM-545.

Source: *Annual Energy Review 1997,* Energy Information Administration, Washington, DC, 1998

FIGURE 5.11

Coal is shipped by rail or barge where it is loaded aboard large ocean-going bulk carriers for shipment to Europe, Asia, and other major markets.

Source: *Coal Industry Annual 1996*, Energy Information Administration., Washington, DC, 1997

---

plants with 92 gigawatts or more of capacity will install scrubbers.

U.S. COAL EXPORTS

Since 1950, the United States has produced more coal that it has consumed. The excess production allowed the United States to become a significant exporter of coal to other nations. In 1997, the United States exported 83.5 million short tons, down from 109 million short tons in 1991, account-ing for 48 percent of all U.S. energy exports. Almost half of U.S. coal exports went to Europe. The individual countries buying the most U.S. coal were Canada, Japan, Brazil, United Kingdom, and Italy. (See Table 5.3.) While the amount of coal leaving the nation is considerable, it still represents only about 10 percent of the Btu content of the petroleum coming into the United States each year. (Figure 5.11 shows rail cars transporting coal to ocean barges for export.)

FIGURE 5.12

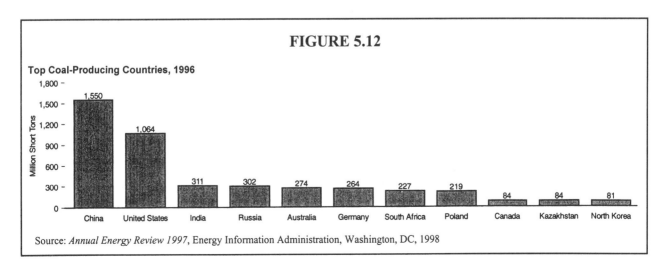

Top Coal-Producing Countries, 1996

Source: *Annual Energy Review 1997*, Energy Information Administration, Washington, DC, 1998

INTERNATIONAL COAL — SUPPLY AND DEMAND

World coal production exceeded 5.0 billion short tons in 1996 and accounted for 25 percent of world energy production. China led the world in coal production, mining 1,550 million short tons, followed by the United States at 1,064 million short tons. Other major producers were India, Russia, Australia, Germany, South Africa, and Poland. (See Figure 5.12.)

World consumption of coal in 1996 totaled 5.2 billion short tons. China was also the largest consumer of coal in 1996, using 1.5 billion short tons, followed by the United States, which consumed 1.01 billion short tons. Other major consumers included India, Russia, and Germany. (See Figure 5.13.)

COAL USE INTO THE TWENTY-FIRST CENTURY

The Energy Information Administration (EIA) of the U.S. Department of Energy, in its *Annual Energy Outlook 1998* (December 1997), forecasts that domestic coal production will increase annually, reaching a level of 1,326 million short tons by 2015 and 1,376 million short tons by 2020 (Table 5.4). Almost all of this increase will be due to a growth of electric utility demand, although industrial steam coal use is also expected to grow.

As older buildings convert from coal furnaces to natural gas, the use of coal as a means of energy in the residential and commercial sectors will likely disappear over the next 20 years.

The EIA expects the Western Region will surpass the Eastern Region in coal production. Eastern mines will likely lose market share to less expensive, low-sulfur coal from western mines. Coal transportation and labor costs are expected to decline, resulting in lower costs overall.

Due to the U.S. economy's increasing dependence on fossil fuels, especially coal, it can be expected that today's environmental concerns with acid rain and global warming will grow. The outlook for the U.S. coal industry could be affected significantly by acid rain legislation, the development of clean coal technologies, and, over the longer term, the problem of global warming.

The EIA predicts a major expansion of world coal trade in the future. This large projected growth is based upon a rapid expansion in the world market for steam coal in both Western Europe and Asia, especially China. China, with nearly five times the population of the United States and an apparently rapidly growing economy, will likely surpass the United States in carbon emissions by 2020.

Annual coal imports by the countries in Western Europe are predicted to rise by 227 million tons

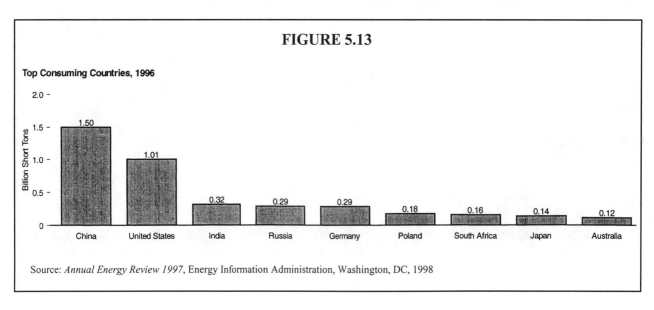

FIGURE 5.13

Top Consuming Countries, 1996

Source: *Annual Energy Review 1997*, Energy Information Administration, Washington, DC, 1998

TABLE 5.4

Comparison of coal forecasts (million short tons, except where noted)

Projection	AEO98			Other forecasts		
	Reference	Low economic growth	High economic growth	WEFA	GRI	DRI
2015						
Production	*1,326*	*1,223*	*1,415*	*1,263*	*1,427*	*1,365*
Consumption by sector						
Electricity generation[a]	*1,103*	*1,012*	*1,183*	*1,050*	*1,262*	*1,188*
Coking plants	*24*	*24*	*24*	*37*	*25*	*22*
Industrial/other	*88*	*77*	*97*	*66*	*70*	*75*
Total	*1,215*	*1,113*	*1,305*	*1,153*	*1,357*	*1,284*
Net coal exports	*112*	*112*	*112*	*108*	*71*	*79*
Minemouth price						
(1996 dollars per short ton)	*13.99*	*13.87*	*14.05*	*15.20*	*13.42*	*NA*
(1996 dollars per million Btu)	*0.67*	*0.66*	*0.67*	*0.70*	*0.64*	*NA*
Average delivered price, electricity						
(1996 dollars per short ton)	*20.72*	*20.26*	*20.99*	*NA*	*23.93*	*21.58*
(1996 dollars per million Btu)	*1.03*	*1.00*	*1.04*	*1.12*	*1.15*	*1.05*
2020						
Production	*1,376*	*1,258*	*1,501*	*1,368*	*NA*	*1,424*
Consumption by sector						
Electricity generation[a]	*1,147*	*1,042*	*1,258*	*1,138*	*NA*	*1,246*
Coking plants	*23*	*23*	*23*	*37*	*NA*	*20*
Industrial/other	*87*	*73*	*101*	*67*	*NA*	*76*
Total	*1,257*	*1,138*	*1,382*	*1,242*	*NA*	*1,342*
Net coal exports	*120*	*120*	*120*	*122*	*NA*	*80*
Minemouth price						
(1996 dollars per short ton)	*13.27*	*13.14*	*13.50*	*15.10*	*NA*	*NA*
(1996 dollars per million Btu)	*0.64*	*0.63*	*0.65*	*0.70*	*NA*	*NA*
Average delivered price, electricity						
(1996 dollars per short ton)	*19.52*	*18.91*	*20.01*	*NA*	*NA*	*20.86*
(1996 dollars per million Btu)	*0.97*	*0.95*	*0.99*	*1.11*	*NA*	*1.01*

[a]The DRI and *AEO98* forecasts for electricity generation include nonutility generators. Consumption by industrial cogenerators is included in industrial consumption. The WEFA values for electricity consumption have been adjusted by including consumption by nonutility generators (11.2 million tons in 2015 and 2020).
NA = Not available.
Btu = British thermal unit.
Sources: **AEO98:** AEO98 National Energy Modeling System, runs AEO98B.D100197A (reference case), LMAC98.D100197A (low economic growth case), and HMAC98.D100197A (high economic growth case). **WEFA:** The WEFA Group, *U.S. Energy Outlook* (Spring/Summer 1997). **GRI:** Gas Research Institute, *GRI Baseline Projection of U.S. Energy Supply and Demand*, 1998 Edition, and *Coal Demand and Price Projections*, Vol. I, GRI-95/0493.1 (February 1996), Table 4-3. **DRI:** DRI/McGraw-Hill, *World Energy Service: U.S. Outlook, Spring 1997* (April 1997).

Source: *Annual Energy Outlook 1998*, Energy Information Administration, Washington, DC, 1997

over the next 20 years — over 71 percent of the total growth in projected international coal trade. The annual coal imports by countries in Asia will account for almost all of the remaining expected growth in international coal trade. All of the growth in U.S. coal exports is expected to be in steam coal. (Steam coal is all coal other than the coal used for metallurgical purposes and is suitable for use for heat and power.)

CHAPTER VI

NUCLEAR ENERGY

CONQUERING OIL DEPENDENCY, OR THREATENING THE FUTURE OF THE ENVIRONMENT?

Much environmental contamination is directly related to the use of fossil fuels. To prevent further damage, many energy experts have turned their attention to other means of energy production. Some observers consider nuclear energy an attractive alternative because it does not pollute the atmosphere as burning coal does. On the other hand, nuclear energy depends on a non-renewable source (uranium) for its production. In addition, safe disposal of the radioactivity and radioactive wastes, which are the by-products of nuclear energy, has proven difficult. (See Chapter VII.)

Many citizens do not want nuclear power plants in their neighborhoods, while others oppose nuclear power for broader environmental reasons. In the four decades since the first commercial nuclear reactor went into operation, the nuclear power industry has not been able to persuade many Americans of the safety of its enterprise. The 1979 near-disaster at Three Mile Island (Pennsylvania) and the catastrophe at Chernobyl (USSR) in 1986 (see below), as well as reports of design flaws, cracks, and leaks in other reactors, greatly increased public concerns about the safety of nuclear power. In the early 1970s, most Americans favored the use of nuclear power; nearly three decades later, most Americans, indeed, most people around the world, oppose building additional nuclear power plants.

Supporters of nuclear power believe that nuclear power, if carefully monitored, is safer than any other form of energy production. They point to the growing concern over global warming. This condition may well be accelerated by coal use, other environmental problems tied to coal such as acid rain, the damage to the environment caused by strip mining, and the hazards associated with extracting and transporting coal and oil. In fact, this growing concern over fossil fuels has led a small number of environmentalists who had previously opposed nuclear power to reconsider their position. Nonetheless, environmental, safety, and economic concerns have restrained growth in the nuclear industry since the mid-1970s. Unwillingness to commission new nuclear plants became especially evident in 1992, when the number of operating units began to decline (see below).

Other alternative fuels include renewable sources, such as sunshine (solar), wind, and water (hydropower). In 1997, nuclear energy provided 20 percent (629 billion kilowatt-hours) of U.S. electrical energy and 9 percent of total U.S. energy. (See Figure 6.1.)

THE SOURCE OF NUCLEAR ENERGY

Nuclear energy is currently used for steam generation at electric utilities, for ship propulsion, and for nuclear weapons. In a nuclear power plant, fuel (uranium in the United States) in the reactor generates a nuclear reaction (fission) that produces heat. The heat from the reaction is carried away by water under high pressure, which heats a second water stream to produce steam. The steam runs through a turbine (similar to a jet engine) making it and the attached electrical generator spin, which produces electricity. The steam is cooled and re-circulated (Figure 6.2). The large, hourglass-shaped cooling towers associated with nuclear plants are used to cool the steam after it has run through the turbines.

The key problems in operating a nuclear power reactor include finding material (uranium 235) that will sustain a chain reaction, maintaining the reaction at a level which yields heat but does not escalate out of control and become an explosion, and coping with the radiation produced by the chain reaction.

What Is Radioactivity?

Radioactivity is a state of instability that occurs when there is an imbalance of protons (particles of matter with positive electric charge) and neutrons (particles with no electric charge) in the nucleus of an atom. The production and explosion of nuclear weapons involve splitting the atoms by bombarding them with neutrons or fusing atoms together. (Figure 6.3 shows this chain reaction.) The transformation to stability is called radioactive decay, a process during which radiation is emitted. All radioactive elements eventually decay into lead, a stable element.

Some radioactivity occurs in nature. This natural radiation makes up the majority of the radiation to which people are exposed. It occurs from elements within the earth and from cosmic rays that filter into Earth's atmosphere from outer space. Certain areas experience higher levels of radiation than others; residents of higher elevations, such as Denver, Colorado, receive roughly twice as much radiation as people who live in Amsterdam, the Netherlands, which is below sea level.

Other radiation is created by humans. The largest doses of radiation from non-natural sources come from radiation used for medical diagnosis and treatment. Color television and video games also account for a considerable amount of man-made radiation. Figure 6.4 shows radiation sources.

Mining of Nuclear Fuel

There are no natural deposits of material that are immediately suitable for use in a reactor. Such nuclear deposits would have immediately started reacting in the ground (exploding) when they were first formed millions or billions of years ago and would have long since been scattered by the resulting explosions. Therefore, a material must be found that will sustain a chain reaction resulting in the production of energy. In the United States, uranium 235, found in the form of ore, is used. In a nuclear reactor, the chain reaction produces heat, which powers generators to make electricity.

Ore that contains uranium is first located by geological methods such as drilling. Uranium-bearing ores are mined by methods similar to those used

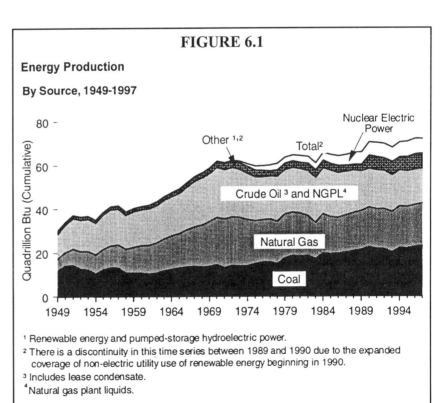

FIGURE 6.1

Energy Production

By Source, 1949-1997

[1] Renewable energy and pumped-storage hydroelectric power.
[2] There is a discontinuity in this time series between 1989 and 1990 due to the expanded coverage of non-electric utility use of renewable energy beginning in 1990.
[3] Includes lease condensate.
[4] Natural gas plant liquids.

Source: *Annual Energy Review 1997*, Energy Information Administration, Washington, DC, 1998

FIGURE 6.2

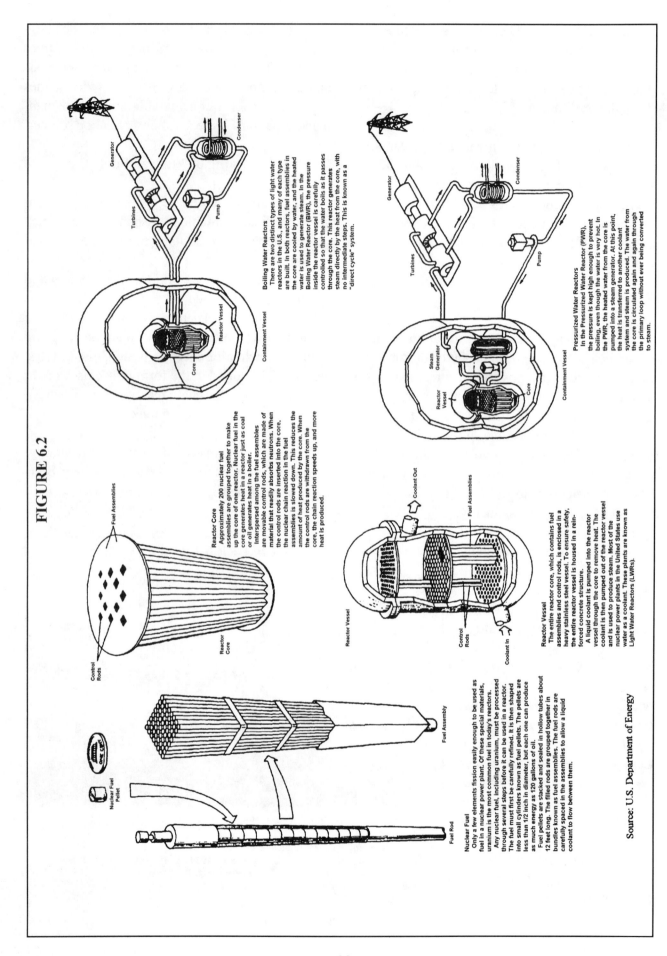

Boiling Water Reactors

There are two distinct types of light water reactors in the U.S., and many of each type are built. In both reactors, fuel assemblies in the core are cooled by water, and the heated water is used to generate steam. In the Boiling Water Reactor (BWR), the pressure inside the reactor vessel is carefully controlled so that the water boils as it passes through the core. This reactor generates steam directly by the heat from the core, with no intermediate steps. This is known as a "direct cycle" system.

Pressurized Water Reactors

In the Pressurized Water Reactor (PWR), the pressure is kept high enough to prevent boiling, even though the water is very hot. In the PWR, the heated water from the core is pumped into a steam generator. At this point, the heat is transferred to another coolant system and steam is produced. The water from the core is circulated again and again through the primary loop without ever being converted to steam.

Reactor Core

Approximately 200 nuclear fuel assemblies are grouped together to make up the core of one reactor. Nuclear fuel in the core generates heat in a reactor just as coal or oil generates heat in a boiler.

Interspersed among the fuel assemblies are movable control rods, which are made of material that readily absorbs neutrons. When the control rods are inserted into the core, the nuclear chain reaction in the fuel assemblies is slowed down. This reduces the amount of heat produced by the core. When the control rods are withdrawn from the core, the chain reaction speeds up, and more heat is produced.

Reactor Vessel

The entire reactor core, which contains fuel assemblies and control rods, is enclosed in a heavy stainless steel vessel. To ensure safety, the entire reactor vessel is housed in a reinforced concrete structure.

A liquid coolant is pumped into the reactor vessel. The coolant is then pumped out of the reactor vessel and is used to produce steam. Most of the nuclear power plants in the United States use water as a coolant. These plants are known as Light Water Reactors (LWRs).

Nuclear Fuel

Only a few elements fission easily enough to be used as fuel in a nuclear power plant. Of these special materials, uranium is the most common fuel in today's reactors. Any nuclear fuel, including uranium, must be processed through several steps before it can be used in a reactor. The fuel must first be carefully refined. It is then shaped into small cylinders known as fuel pellets. The pellets are less than 1/2 inch in diameter, but each one can produce as much energy as 120 gallons of oil.

Fuel pellets are stacked and sealed in hollow tubes about 12 feet long. The filled rods are grouped together in bundles known as fuel assemblies. The fuel rods are carefully spaced in the assemblies to allow a liquid coolant to flow between them.

Source: U.S. Department of Energy

88

for other metal ores. The mining of uranium is dangerous because uranium atoms split by themselves at a slow rate, causing radioactive substances such as radon to slowly accumulate in the deposits.

PROPORTION OF TOTAL ENERGY PRODUCTION

When it was introduced in the 1950s, nuclear power was presented as the energy of the future, a source so cheap it would eliminate the need for electric meters. The dreams never came true. Construction costs skyrocketed as expenditures far exceeded early estimates. The technology was considerably more complicated than originally thought, and it turned out to be increasingly expensive to develop reactors that would meet Nuclear Regulatory Commission (NRC) standards.

The percentage of U.S. electricity supplied by nuclear power grew considerably during the 1970s and 1980s before leveling off in the 1990s. In 1973, nuclear power supplied only 4.5 percent of the total U.S. electricity generated; by 1997, nuclear power accounted for 20.1 percent, down somewhat from the 1995 all-time high of 22.5 percent. (See Table 6.1.)

NUCLEAR POWER PRODUCTION IN THE UNITED STATES

In December 1997, 107 nuclear reactors were operating in 32 states, with a total net capacity of 100.8 million kilowatts (Figures 6.5 and 6.6). Most of these reactors are located east of the Mississippi River, where the demand for electrical energy is high. Six other units have received construction permits, although construction has been deferred indefinitely on those units. The numbers are far below the 226 reactors in planning, construction, and operation in 1974. Since 1978, no new

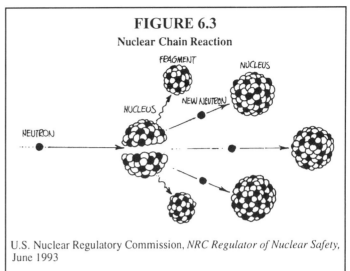

FIGURE 6.3
Nuclear Chain Reaction

U.S. Nuclear Regulatory Commission, *NRC Regulator of Nuclear Safety,* June 1993

Source: Katherine A. Mahoney and Linda K. Murakami, *Farewell to Arms: Cleaning Up Nuclear Weapons Facilities*, National Conference of State Legislatures, Denver, CO, 1993

nuclear power plants have been ordered. (See Table 6.2.)

Nuclear plants produced a record 675 net billion kilowatthours of electricity in 1996. That year, U.S. nuclear units achieved an overall average capacity factor of 76 percent, up from the 58 percent in 1979 (the year of the Three Mile Island accident). Better training for operators, longer operating cycles between refueling, and control system improvements contributed to improved plant performance.

INTERNATIONAL PRODUCTION

Nuclear power now provides about 12 percent of the world's electricity and 5 percent of total en-

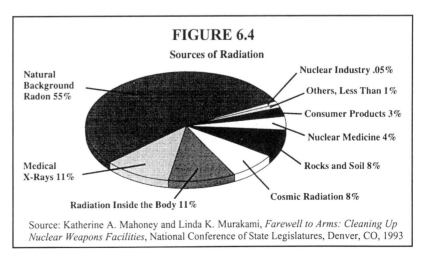

FIGURE 6.4
Sources of Radiation

Natural Background Radon 55%

Nuclear Industry .05%

Others, Less Than 1%

Consumer Products 3%

Nuclear Medicine 4%

Medical X-Rays 11%

Rocks and Soil 8%

Radiation Inside the Body 11%

Cosmic Radiation 8%

Source: Katherine A. Mahoney and Linda K. Murakami, *Farewell to Arms: Cleaning Up Nuclear Weapons Facilities*, National Conference of State Legislatures, Denver, CO, 1993

TABLE 6.1

Nuclear Power Plant Operations, 1957-1997

Year	Nuclear Electricity Net Generation	Nuclear Share of Electric Utility Net Generation	Net Summer Capability of Operable Units [1,2]	Capacity Factor [2]
	Billion Kilowatthours	Percent	Million Kilowatts	Percent
1957	(s)	(s)	0.1	NA
1958	0.2	(s)	0.1	NA
1959	0.2	(s)	0.1	NA
1960	0.5	0.1	0.4	NA
1961	1.7	0.2	0.4	NA
1962	2.3	0.3	0.7	NA
1963	3.2	0.4	0.8	NA
1964	3.3	0.3	0.8	NA
1965	3.7	0.3	0.8	NA
1966	5.5	0.5	1.7	NA
1967	7.7	0.6	2.7	NA
1968	12.5	0.9	2.7	NA
1969	13.9	1.0	4.4	NA
1970	21.8	1.4	7.0	NA
1971	38.1	2.4	9.0	NA
1972	54.1	3.1	14.5	NA
1973	83.5	4.5	22.7	53.5
1974	114.0	6.1	31.9	47.8
1975	172.5	9.0	37.3	55.9
1976	191.1	9.4	43.8	54.7
1977	250.9	11.8	46.3	63.3
1978	276.4	12.5	50.8	64.5
1979	255.2	11.4	49.7	58.4
1980	251.1	11.0	51.8	56.3
1981	272.7	11.9	56.0	58.2
1982	282.8	12.6	60.0	56.6
1983	293.7	12.7	63.0	54.4
1984	327.6	13.6	69.7	56.3
1985	383.7	15.5	79.4	58.0
1986	414.0	16.6	85.2	56.9
1987	455.3	17.7	93.6	57.4
1988	527.0	19.5	94.7	63.5
1989	529.4	19.0	98.2	62.2
1990	576.9	20.5	99.6	66.0
1991	612.6	21.7	99.6	70.2
1992	618.8	22.1	99.0	70.9
1993	610.3	21.2	99.0	70.5
1994	640.4	22.0	99.1	73.8
1995	673.4	22.5	99.5	77.4
1996	R674.7	21.9	100.8	R76.3
1997P	629.4	20.1	100.8	70.8

[1] At end of year.
[2] See Note 2 at end of section.
R=Revised. P=Preliminary. NA=Not available. (s)=Less than 0.05 billion kilowatthours or less than 0.05 percent.

Note: The performance data shown in this table are based on a universe of reactor units that differ in some respects from the reactor universe used to profile the nuclear power industry in Table 9.1, especially in the years prior to 1973.

Sources: **Operable Units:** • 1957-1972—Federal Power Commission (FPC), Form FPC-4, "Monthly Power Plant Report." • 1973 forward—Nuclear Regulatory Commission, *Licensed Operating Reactors*, (NUREG-0020), monthly. **Electricity Generation:** • 1957-September 1977—FPC, Form FPC-4, "Monthly Power Plant Report." • October 1977-1981—Federal Energy Regulatory Commission, Form FPC-4, "Monthly Power Plant Report." • 1982 forward—Energy Information Administration (EIA), Form EIA-759, "Monthly Power Plant Report." **Net Summer Capability of Operable Units:** • 1957-1983—See Note 2 at end of section. • 1984 forward—EIA, Form EIA-860, "Annual Electric Generator Report."

Source: *Annual Energy Review 1997*, Energy Information Administration, Washington, DC, 1998

ergy, levels unlikely to increase much in the future. Although the United States is the largest producer of nuclear power, it trails other Western countries in the proportion of a nation's electrical production generated by nuclear power. That is primarily because oil, natural gas, and coal have been more accessible in the United States than in other countries.

In 1996, the United States led the world in nuclear power generation (675 billion kilowatthours), followed by France (376 billion kilowatthours) and Japan (283 billion kilowatthours) (Table 6.3). These three countries generated almost 60 percent of the world's nuclear electric power. France had, by far, the highest proportion (78 percent) of its electrical power produced by nuclear energy, followed by Belgium (55 percent), Sweden (48 percent), and Switzerland (38 percent).

In 1996, 436 reactors operated worldwide. Construction started on nine more reactors —four in South Korea, two each in Taiwan and China, and one in Japan. In Western Europe, France is the only country still building

FIGURE 6.5

Nuclear Generating Units

Operable Units by Site, End of Year 1997

Source: *Annual Energy Review 1997*, Energy Information Administration, Washington, DC, 1998

nuclear plants, with three units under construction. Asia, excluding Japan, is the only region where nuclear power is expected to expand significantly. In Japan, political support for nuclear power has declined since 1996, following a major accident at the fast-breeder reactor at Monju.

South Korea currently leads the world in construction, with 9 reactors being built and 11 in operation. Local opposition there, however, has stalled construction on two reactors, and the government is still unable to find radioactive waste facilities due to public protest. Russian officials have announced their intention to fire up 26 new nuclear reactors by 2010 in an effort to overcome a growing energy shortage. This plan, if implemented, would more than double the number of reactors operating in Russia, although the Russian government often fails to reach its goals. China may pass South Korea as the world's leading builder; official plans call for an increase from the current 2,100 megawatts of capacity to 20,000 megawatts by 2010.

Worldwide, 81 reactors have already been taken out of service. On average, they were in use less than 17 years, far fewer years than had been estimated. Dozens of larger plants will likely be shut down over the next few years with an anticipated drop in the overall amount of generating capacity.

International Agreement on Safety

In September 1994, 40 nations signed the International Convention on Nuclear Safety, an agreement that requires them to shut down nuclear power plants if necessary safety measures cannot be guaranteed. The agreement applies to land-based civil nuclear power plants and seeks to avert accidents like the 1986 explosion at Chernobyl, the world's worst civil nuclear disaster (see below). Ukraine, which inherited the Chernobyl plant after the collapse of the Soviet Union, signed the agreement. Signers must immediately submit reports on atomic installations and, if necessary, make improvements to upgrade safety of the sites. Neighboring countries may call for an urgent study if they are concerned about a reactor's safety and the potential fallout that could affect their own population or crops.

THE INTERNATIONAL RESPONSE TO GLOBAL WARMING

For some, concern about the greenhouse effect has been a consideration in the future construction of nuclear power plants. The increases in greenhouse gases in the atmosphere are mainly caused by burning fossil fuels and worldwide deforestation. Nuclear fuel emits no greenhouse gases and can substitute for fossil-fueled electricity.

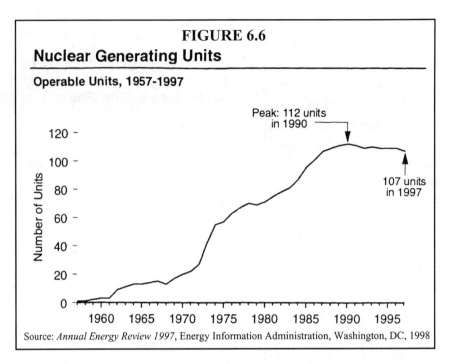

FIGURE 6.6

Nuclear Generating Units

Operable Units, 1957-1997

Peak: 112 units in 1990

107 units in 1997

Source: *Annual Energy Review 1997*, Energy Information Administration, Washington, DC, 1998

Nonetheless, despite concerns about greenhouse gases, no nation has yet considered nuclear power as the complete solution to its energy needs. Sweden legislated a nuclear phase-out by 2010 (although it is not clear that this is an obtainable goal since about half of Sweden's electricity comes from nuclear power), while the Netherlands and Germany have strong conservation policies and well-organized anti-nuclear movements. Although other countries are concerned about global warming, their governments claim that, at this time, the evidence of global warming is not yet strong enough to offset the cost and safety concerns of nuclear power. France's huge dependency on nuclear energy is based on a scarcity of other energy resources and has nothing to do with concerns about global warming.

THE AGING OF NUCLEAR POWER PLANTS

Problems with Nuclear Reactor Construction

Several factors have contributed to the slowdown in U.S. nuclear reactor construction. The demand for electricity has grown at a slower rate than expected. Overall costs have increased as a result of more expensive financing, partly influenced by longer lead time for licensing and construction and overruns in construction costs caused by regulations that were instituted as a result of the Three Mile Island incident (see below). Backfits (modifications to existing plants to conform to new requirements) have been estimated to cost $90 million at each of the nation's 35 oldest plants.

A critical problem is the premature aging of nuclear power plants. The plants were originally expected to last 40 years, but many showed serious levels of deterioration after as few as 15 years. Pipes cracked or suffered "wasting," a situation in which pipe walls become thinner with use. Steam generators cause one of the main aging problems. The old steam generators will be radioactive for centuries and will have to be disposed of in huge mausoleums with thick walls. Originally, nuclear fuel operators projected that, with brief pauses for refueling, the plants could run almost 90 percent of the time, but this has not been the case. Indian Point 3 (New York), for example, has been operational only about 50 percent of the time.

Dismantling a Nuclear Power Plant

Eventually, the more than 400 nuclear plants now operating worldwide will need to be retired. The oldest commercial nuclear generating plant,

TABLE 6.2

Nuclear Generating Units, End of Year 1953-1997

Year	Orders [1]	Construction Permits [2]	LPOL [3]	New Operable Units [4]	Shutdowns [5]	Total Operable Units [6]	Cancellations	Cumulative Cancellations
1953	1	0	0	0	0	0	0	0
1954	0	0	0	0	0	0	0	0
1955	3	1	0	0	0	0	0	0
1956	1	3	0	0	0	0	0	0
1957	2	1	1	1	0	1	0	0
1958	4	0	0	0	0	1	0	0
1959	4	3	1	1	0	2	0	0
1960	1	7	1	1	0	3	0	0
1961	0	0	0	0	0	3	0	0
1962	2	1	7	6	0	9	0	0
1963	4	1	3	2	0	11	0	0
1964	0	3	2	3	1	13	0	0
1965	7	1	0	0	0	13	0	0
1966	20	5	1	2	1	14	0	0
1967	29	14	3	3	2	15	0	0
1968	16	23	0	0	2	13	0	0
1969	9	7	4	4	0	17	0	0
1970	14	10	4	3	0	20	0	0
1971	21	4	5	2	0	22	0	0
1972	38	8	6	6	1	27	7	7
1973	42	14	12	15	0	42	0	7
1974	28	23	14	15	2	55	9	16
1975	4	9	3	2	0	57	13	29
1976	3	9	7	7	1	63	1	30
1977	4	15	4	4	0	67	10	40
1978	2	13	3	4	1	70	13	53
1979	0	2	0	0	1	69	6	59
1980	0	0	5	2	0	71	15	74
1981	0	0	3	4	0	75	9	83
1982	0	0	6	4	1	78	18	101
1983	0	0	3	3	0	81	6	107
1984	0	0	7	6	0	87	6	113
1985	0	0	7	9	0	96	2	115
1986	0	0	7	5	0	101	2	117
1987	0	0	6	8	2	107	0	117
1988	0	0	1	2	0	109	3	120
1989	0	0	3	4	2	111	0	120
1990	0	0	1	2	1	112	1	121
1991	0	0	0	0	1	111	0	121
1992	0	0	0	0	2	109	0	121
1993	0	0	1	1	0	110	0	121
1994	0	0	0	0	1	109	1	122
1995	0	0	1	0	0	109	2	124
1996	0	0	0	1	1	109	0	124
1997	0	0	0	0	2	107	0	124

[1] Placement of an order by a utility or government agency for a nuclear steam supply system.

[2] Issuance by regulatory authority of a permit, or equivalent permission, to begin construction. Numbers reflect permits issued in a given year, not extant permits.

[3] Low-power operating license: Issuance by regulatory authority of license, or equivalent permission, to conduct testing but not to operate at full power.

[4] Issuance by regulatory authority of full-power operating license, or equivalent permission. Units generally did not begin immediate operation.

[5] Ceased operation permanently, irrespective of intent.

[6] Total of units holding full-power licenses, or equivalent permission to operate, at the end of the year. See Note 1 at end of section.

[7] Cancellation by utilities of ordered units. Does not include three units (Bellefonte 1 and 2 and Watts Bar 2) where construction has been stopped indefinitely.

Sources: **Orders:** Energy Information Administration, *Commercial Nuclear Power 1991,* Appendix E, September 1991, and Nuclear Energy Institute, *Historical Profile of U.S. Nuclear Power Development,* 1988 edition; U.S. Atomic Energy Commission, *1973 Annual Report to Congress, Volume 2, Regulatory Activities;* various utilities. **Construction Permits:** Nuclear Regulatory Commission, *Information Digest,* 1997 edition, Appendix A; and Nuclear Energy Institute, *Historical Profile of U.S. Nuclear Power Development,* 1988 edition; various utility, Federal, and contractor officials. **Low-Power Operating Licenses:** Nuclear Energy Institute, *Historical Profile of U.S. Nuclear Power Development,* 1988 edition; U.S. Department of Energy, *Nuclear Reactors Built, Being Built, and Planned: 1995;* and various utility, Federal, and contractor officials. **New Operable Units:** Nuclear Regulatory Commission, *Information Digest,* 1997 edition, Table 11 and Appendices A and B; various utility, Federal, and contractor officials. **Shutdowns:** Energy Information Administration, *Commercial Nuclear Power 1991,* Appendix E, Nuclear Regulatory Commission, *Information Digest,* 1997 edition, Appendix B; U.S. Department of Energy, *Nuclear Reactors Built, Being Built, and Planned: 1995;* Tennessee Valley Authority officials. **Total Operable Units:** Running sum of licenses minus permanent shutdowns. **Cancellations:** Energy Information Administration, *Commercial Nuclear Power 1991,* Appendix E, September 1991; Nuclear Regulatory Commission, *Information Digest,* 1997 editon, Appendix C; and Nuclear Energy Institute, *Historical Profile of U.S. Nuclear Power Development,* 1988 edition.

Source: *Annual Energy Review 1997,* Energy Information Administration, Washington, DC, 1998

located in Shippingsport, Pennsylvania, started generating electricity in 1957. In 1986, dismantling procedures began at that plant, costing an estimated $100 million. The dismantling was expected to take about five years to complete but is still not finished.

There are three methods of retiring ("decommissioning") a reactor — mothballing, entombment, and dismantling. Mothballing involves removing the fuel, monitoring the radiation, and guarding the structure (which will be contaminated for centuries) to prevent anyone from entering it.

TABLE 6.3

World Net Nuclear Electric Power Generation, 1987 - 1996
(Billion Kilowatthours)

Region Country	1987	1988	1989	1990	1991	1992	1993	1994	1995	1996[1]
North America										
Canada	72.9	78.2	75.4	69.2	80.7	76.6	90.1	102.4	93.0	88.1
Mexico	0.0	0.0	0.0	2.8	4.0	3.7	4.7	4.0	8.0	7.5
United States	455.3	527.0	529.4	577.0	612.6	618.8	610.4	640.5	673.4	674.7
Total	**528.2**	**605.1**	**604.8**	**649.0**	**697.4**	**699.1**	**705.1**	**747.0**	**774.4**	**770.3**
Central & South America										
Argentina	6.1	4.8	4.8	7.0	7.7	6.7	7.3	7.8	7.1	6.9
Brazil	0.9	0.3	1.5	1.9	1.4	1.7	0.4	0.1	2.4	2.3
Total	**7.1**	**5.2**	**6.3**	**9.0**	**9.1**	**8.4**	**7.7**	**7.9**	**9.5**	**9.2**
Western Europe										
Belgium	39.8	40.9	39.1	40.6	40.7	41.3	39.8	38.6	39.3	41.2
Finland	18.5	18.4	18.0	18.3	18.5	18.3	18.9	18.5	18.3	18.8
France	249.3	260.3	288.7	298.4	314.8	321.5	349.8	342.0	358.4	376.2
Germany	--	--	--	--	140.1	150.9	145.8	143.6	146.4	153.5
Germany, East	10.7	11.1	11.1	5.3	--	--	--	--	--	--
Germany, West	130.5	145.1	140.4	139.8	--	--	--	--	--	--
Italy	(s)	0.0	0.0	0.0	0.0	0.0	0.0	0.0	0.0	0.0
Netherlands	3.4	3.5	3.8	3.3	3.2	3.6	3.8	3.8	3.8	4.0
Spain	41.3	48.3	53.7	51.6	52.8	53.0	53.3	52.5	52.7	53.5
Sweden	64.3	65.6	62.8	64.8	72.9	60.4	58.3	69.5	66.4	71.1
Switzerland	20.5	21.5	21.5	22.4	21.7	22.3	22.2	23.1	23.7	23.7
United Kingdom	48.2	55.6	63.6	58.7	62.8	69.1	76.9	76.0	76.6	81.5
Former Yugoslavia	4.2	3.9	4.5	4.4	4.2	--	--	--	--	--
Slovenia	--	--	--	--	--	3.8	3.8	4.3	4.5	4.4
Total	**630.6**	**674.2**	**707.3**	**707.5**	**731.6**	**744.1**	**772.6**	**771.9**	**789.9**	**828.0**
Eastern Europe & Former U.S.S.R.										
Bulgaria	11.7	15.1	14.6	13.5	12.4	11.0	13.3	14.6	16.4	17.8
Former Czechoslovakia	20.9	21.9	23.2	23.4	22.5	23.3	--	--	--	--
Czech Republic	--	--	--	--	--	--	12.0	12.3	11.6	12.2
Slovakia	--	--	--	--	--	--	11.6	11.5	10.9	11.3
Hungary	10.4	12.7	13.1	13.0	13.0	13.3	13.1	13.3	13.3	13.5
Romania	0.0	0.0	0.0	0.0	0.0	0.0	0.0	0.0	0.0	0.9
Former U.S.S.R.	176.3	203.7	212.7	201.3	201.5	--	--	--	--	--
Armenia	--	--	--	--	--	0.0	0.0	0.0	0.0	2.1
Kazakhstan	--	--	--	--	--	0.5	0.4	0.4	0.1	0.1
Lithuania	--	--	--	--	--	13.9	12.3	7.3	10.6	12.7
Russia	--	--	--	--	--	113.6	113.2	92.9	94.3	103.3
Ukraine	--	--	--	--	--	70.1	71.4	65.4	67.0	76.0
Total	**219.3**	**253.4**	**263.5**	**251.3**	**249.5**	**245.6**	**247.3**	**217.7**	**224.3**	**249.8**
Africa										
South Africa	6.2	10.5	11.1	8.4	9.1	9.3	7.3	9.7	11.3	11.8
Total	**6.2**	**10.5**	**11.1**	**8.4**	**9.1**	**9.3**	**7.3**	**9.7**	**11.3**	**11.8**
Far East & Oceania										
China	0.0	0.0	0.0	0.0	0.0	0.5	2.5	13.5	12.4	13.6
India	4.7	5.2	3.8	5.6	5.2	6.0	5.9	4.7	6.5	7.4
Japan	188.6	173.9	174.5	192.2	202.8	212.1	236.8	255.7	276.7	283.0
Korea, South	37.1	37.8	45.0	50.2	53.5	53.7	55.2	55.7	63.7	70.2
Pakistan	0.5	0.2	0.1	0.4	0.4	0.5	0.4	0.6	0.5	0.3
Taiwan	31.8	29.4	27.1	31.6	33.5	32.5	33.0	33.5	33.9	36.3
Total	**262.7**	**246.5**	**250.5**	**279.9**	**295.4**	**305.3**	**333.8**	**363.6**	**393.6**	**410.9**
World Total	**1,654.0**	**1,794.8**	**1,843.4**	**1,905.1**	**1,992.0**	**2,011.8**	**2,073.7**	**2,117.8**	**2,203.0**	**2,280.0**

[1] Preliminary.

-- = Not applicable.

(s) = Value less than 50 million kilowatthours.

Notes: Sum of components may not equal total due to independent rounding.
Generation data consist of both utility and nonutility sources. Data are reported as net generation as opposed to gross. Net generation excludes
the energy consumed by the generating unit.
No generation is reported for Middle East.

Source: *International Energy Annual 1996*, Energy Information Administration, Washington, DC, 1998

Entombment, which was used at Chernobyl, involves removing the fuel and permanently encasing the structure in thick concrete. This process exposes more workers to radiation than the mothballing method. Dismantling, the method used at Shippingsport, is initially more costly but removes the long-term costs of monitoring both the structure and the radiation levels. It also frees the site for other uses, possibly even another nuclear

94

power plant. Of the three methods, dismantling involves the highest worker exposure to radiation.

The decommissioning process can take 60 years or longer at a price of $124 million to $205 million. An additional cost of decommissioning is the storage of spent nuclear fuel. The U.S. Department of Energy does not have an interim facility to store the fuel, and such storage may not be available for another decade. Storing spent fuel on site beyond the expiration of a plant's operating license and after revenues are no longer generated is costly.

A Bold Investment?

Paying for closing, decontaminating, and dismantling nuclear plants has become an issue of intense public policy debate. Early closing of several plants due to poor economic performance and safety concerns has raised the question of how to pay for decommissioning when the utility industry cannot. Reports issued by the investment firm of Shearson Lehman and by Moody's Investors Services contend that the cost of decommissioning retired plants and handling radioactive wastes will continue to escalate, causing serious financial problems for electric utilities. Most electric utilities have concluded that nuclear power is no longer competitive with other power sources. Not only coal plants, but also new technologies, such as wind turbines and geothermal energy, are, overall, less expensive than nuclear energy plants.

Retrofitting for Alternative Uses

As nuclear plants are dismantled, officials are seeking alternative uses for the nuclear shells, including the conversion of old nuclear plants to gas-fired plants. When the Shoreham Nuclear Power Station was decommissioned in 1991, research began on ways to adapt turbines, power lines, and the control room into a gas-fired plant. In 1993, in a controversial action, nuclear fuel from the defunct Shoreham plant began being shipped to France for reprocessing, at a cost of $74 million to utility customers.

PROBLEMS PLAGUING THE INDUSTRY*

Grave problems have plagued the nuclear industry almost from its beginnings. Plant site selections have been considered questionable, especially those built near earthquake fault lines. Internal quality control has often been lax. The Nuclear Regulatory Commission (NRC) has come under fire for failure to adequately follow up on the observations of so-called "whistle-blowers" who report inadequacies in plant construction or operation.

Peach Bottom

In 1987, the Nuclear Regulatory Commission shut down the Peach Bottom nuclear plant in Delta, Pennsylvania, because control room operators were found sleeping on duty. This was the first plant to shut down solely because of operator violations and misconduct. Many industry observers note that attempts to improve nuclear plant safety focus mainly on technical design improvements and do not recognize the "people problems," which are just as serious as the mechanical problems.

A nuclear analyst and spokesman for Public Citizen, the Ralph Nader consumer-advocacy group, observed that, while the function of the NRC is primarily technological, people, or "human error," has been responsible for almost all nuclear accidents. Even supporters of nuclear power recognize that many of the jobs in question are quite boring, although they take a great deal of training to master. One expert compared it to training a racehorse and then making it stay in its stall.

Three Mile Island

Three Mile Island (TMI), near Harrisburg, Pennsylvania, was the worst nuclear accident in American history (March 28, 1979). Information released several years after the accident revealed that the plant came much closer to meltdown than either the NRC or the industry had previously indicated. Temperatures inside the reactor were first

---

* For a discussion of nuclear waste disposal and nuclear weapons, see Chapter VII.

said to have been 3,500 degrees Fahrenheit, but are now known to have reached at least 4,800 degrees. (The temperature needed to melt uranium dioxide fuel is 5,080 degrees Fahrenheit.)

The emergency core cooling system at TMI was designed to dump water on the hot core and spray water into the reactor building to stop the production of steam, but during the accident, the valves leading to the emergency water pumps closed. Another valve was stuck in the open position, drawing water away from the core, which then became partially uncovered and began to melt. (When meltdown occurs, an uncontrolled explosion may result, unlike the controlled nuclear reaction of normal operation; see Chernobyl, below.) The emergency core cooling system then began drawing water out of the basement supply and reusing it, contaminating the reactor pump, although limiting the radiation contamination of the interior of the building.

The Worst Nuclear Power Plant Disaster Ever — Chernobyl — Ten Years Later

On April 26, 1986, the most serious nuclear accident ever occurred at Chernobyl, a four-reactor nuclear plant complex located in the former Soviet Union near Kiev (now Ukraine). At least 31 people died, and hundreds were injured in the explosion. About 500 people were hospitalized, and medical experts expect from 6,000 to 24,000 cancer-related deaths over the years as a result of the released radiation.

The cleanup was one of the biggest projects of its kind ever undertaken. Helicopters dropped 5,000 tons of limestone, sand, clay, lead, and boron on the smoldering reactor to stop the radiation leakage and reduce the heat. Workers built a giant steel and cement sarcophagus to enshrine the remains of the reactor and contain the radioactive waste. Approximately 135,000 people were evacuated from a 300-square-mile area around the power station. Topsoil had to be removed in the 19-mile evacuation area and buried as nuclear waste. Buildings were washed down, and the newly contaminated water and soil carted away and buried. Agri-

cultural products from areas nearby were declared unmarketable throughout Europe. Many of the 600,000 people involved in the immediate cleanup have suffered long-term effects of radiation exposure.

Some people at Chernobyl received 400 rems of radiation immediately following the explosion. (A rem is a standard measure of the whole-body dose of radiation. Under normal conditions, a person receives about one-tenth of a rem annually.) With a dose of 25 rems, a person's blood begins to change. The DNA is damaged, preventing the red and white cells from reproducing. Sickness starts at 100 rems and severe sickness at 200 rems. Death of half the population occurs at 400 rems, and death to everyone within a week can be expected at 600 rems. One estimate is that 17.5 million people (including 2.5 million children under 7 years old) have had some significant exposure to radiation from Chernobyl, but other estimates are half that high.

In 1995, the United Nations reported that illnesses of all kinds were up 30 percent above normal in Ukraine; the incidence of depression, alcoholism, and divorce were on the rise. Thyroid cancers were 285 times pre-Chernobyl levels in Belarus, a nation bordering Ukraine, especially among children. (Although the Chernobyl reactor is in Ukraine, Belarus, a nation of 10 million people, suffered more human and ecological damage from fallout because of prevailing winds.) Belarus' cabinet minister claimed that a quarter of his country's national income was being spent on alleviating the effects of the disaster. About 375,000 people in Belarus, Ukraine, and Russia remain displaced and often homeless. Contaminated forests spread radioactivity through fires, and seepage from the reactor is polluting waterways as far away as the Black Sea.

In April 1996, a fire in the woods near the Chernobyl reactor once more alarmed observers who feared further danger to the entombed reactor and the release of radioactivity from soils and vegetation in the area. In addition, the sarcophagus built to contain the damaged reactor is reported to be crumbling. However, Ukraine, which suffers from 40 percent unemployment and other enormous economic woes, claims it needs the power from the remaining reactor and that completely shutting down Chernobyl would cost too much.

Some high technology companies have offered robots to clean up hazardous sites, such as Chernobyl. Such efforts would, however, produce yet another problem — what to do with the nuclear waste once the Chernobyl sarcophagus is entered and cleaned up.

Other Problems with Soviet-Built Reactors

A 1995 U.S. Energy Department report underscored previous concerns about the danger of Soviet-built reactors and declared 10 reactors in Ukraine, Slovakia, Lithuania, Russia, and Bulgaria at high risk of failure. The 10 reactors, at five power plant facilities including Chernobyl, "pose significant safety risks," the report said. Although Russian officials claimed the reactors were "comparable or superior to American designs," they admitted that, due to economic difficulty throughout the region, funds were not available to repair and staff some facilities. Among the findings, the report stated, "Today, conditions at the Chernobyl plant are in many ways worse than those that existed prior to the 1986 accident." Many of the plants are old and scheduled for retirement, but economic pressures have kept them open. Figure 10.7 shows the location of Soviet-designed nuclear plants.

A nuclear plant in Metzamor, Armenia, which sits near two major and several minor geologic faults, was closed following an earthquake in 1988. In 1995, despite Western protests, the energy-starved nation restarted the reactor. In turning to the Metzamor reactor for power, Armenia is relying on a Soviet design that American scientists consider among the world's most dangerous. American scientists cite the lack of a dome-shaped containment vessel that is standard on Western reactors.

The United States has pledged to send more than $150 million in nuclear safety assistance to Russia, Ukraine, Bulgaria, Hungary, Lithuania, the Czech Republic, and Slovakia. (Figure 6.8 shows the planned distribution of those funds.) The bulk of the funding is targeted for Russia and Ukraine to help reduce the risk of operating older, least-safe reactors until economic conditions allow them to be shut down or until alternate sources of power can be provided.

The Minami Plant in Japan

On February 9, 1991, the Minami nuclear power plant in Mihama, Japan (220 miles west of Tokyo) almost suffered a meltdown when a pipe carrying super-heated radioactive water broke in the 19-year-old plant. (See above for the aging of nuclear power plants.) The water leaked, contaminating the water in the steam generator. A reported 20 tons of water were released before the plant shut down. After initially denying any radiation leak, the electric company said that an amount equal to about 8 percent of the plant's annual emissions had been released into the atmosphere. A sister plant was closed the next month because it had the same design flaw that existed at Minami. A storm of protest gave new life to the Japanese anti-nuclear movement.

The Japanese are in a difficult position concerning nuclear power. Japan has very few natural energy resources and is heavily dependent on Middle Eastern oil. The Japanese government wanted nuclear power to provide increasing proportions of its electric energy, but there has been growing opposition from many Japanese people, including survivors of the nuclear bombings of Hiroshima and Nagasaki in World War II. With several of its biggest plants out of operation due to concern about safety issues, Japan's demand for electricity is likely to come close to its generating capacity. In order to avoid that, Japan spends three times more than American industry on nuclear energy research of alternative designs or on nuclear fusion (see below).

A Retreat from Nuclear Power?

In December 1997, the U.S. Nuclear Regulatory Commission (NRC) fined Northeast Utilities $2.1 million for a host of violations of federal regu-

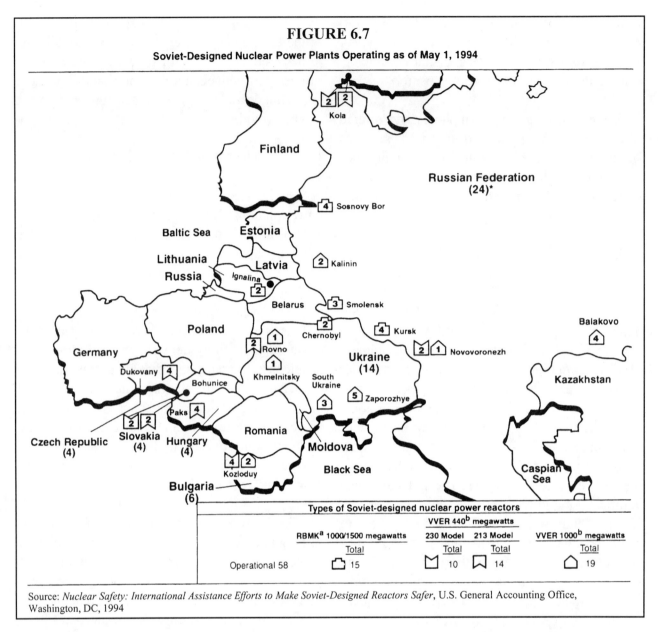

FIGURE 6.7

Soviet-Designed Nuclear Power Plants Operating as of May 1, 1994

		Types of Soviet-designed nuclear power reactors			
	RBMK[a] 1000/1500 megawatts	VVER 440[b] megawatts		VVER 1000[b] megawatts	
		230 Model	213 Model		
	Total	Total	Total	Total	
Operational 58	15	10	14	19	

Source: *Nuclear Safety: International Assistance Efforts to Make Soviet-Designed Reactors Safer*, U.S. General Accounting Office, Washington, DC, 1994

lations at three nuclear reactors at the Millstone Nuclear Power Station in Waterford, Connecticut. The fine was nearly double the next-largest fine ever imposed by the NRC, and agency officials stated they might seek criminal prosecution as well. (The previous largest fine — $1.25 million — was assessed in 1988 against Philadelphia Electric Company's Peach Bottom plant.)

The commission had previously shut down the three Millstone reactors out of safety concerns, citing more than 50 violations from October 1995 to December 1996. Northeast Utilities will not be allowed to restart the reactors without approval from an independent consultant and the NRC. Other plants have undergone reviews, but Mill-

stone was the first in which the commission required the company to hire an independent consulting firm to examine it.

Critics of the industry claimed the fine was not severe enough and that revocation of license would have been a more appropriate penalty and a message to the rest of the industry. The fine was another blow to the already troubled nuclear industry. While nuclear energy was once viewed as the energy of the future, deregulation of the electric industry has raised questions about whether expensive nuclear power plants, which must comply with extensive government oversight, can compete. Since nuclear energy faces increased competition from cheaper energy sources, regulators worry that nuclear utilities may try to lower expenses by cutting corners on safety measures. The aging of the nation's reactors compounds the need for vigilance. Each year, maintenance problems grow more complex and expensive, increasing the need to ensure that plant operations are thoroughly supervised.

In January 1998, Commonwealth Edison announced that it would close two of its 12 nuclear reactors (in Zion, Illinois) because they were too expensive to operate under industry deregulation. The closing will cost $515 million. Spent fuel will be stored on site until 2014, when final decommissioning will begin. In addition to Zion, four other Commonwealth Edison plants are on the NRC's watch list. Industry experts predict Commonwealth Edison will be forced to close two of the other sites in order to focus on the remaining reactors.

NEW TECHNOLOGY?

Without new orders for nuclear plants, the U.S. nuclear industry will likely go out of business in a generation. The industry has had no new orders since 1977. Since the last order, suppliers have re-thought plant design and reactor safety. In what government and industry officials optimistically hope will be a new era in nuclear power, they are now proposing smaller, standardized, and more simplified reactors that they claim will be 300 times safer than current regulations require. The modular plants would take half as long to build at barely a quarter of the cost. Designers claim that the plants will be serviced, in part, by robots, and rely on natural convection for emergency cooling, thus requiring fewer engineered safety features. The smaller plants will use standardized parts that can be produced in commercial factories rather than custom, on-site assembly.

THE PRICE-ANDERSON ACT — PAYING FOR A NUCLEAR ACCIDENT

Immediately following the Chernobyl incident in 1987, the Price-Anderson Act (PL95-256, amended), a law which limited how much a nuclear utility owner would have to pay to cover the costs of a nuclear accident, came up for renewal. At the time, the Price-Anderson Act required nuclear reactor owners to carry $650 million of off-site liability insurance, the amount to which the law limited their liability in the event of a nuclear accident. If damages from an accident exceeded $650 million, all nuclear plants could be charged up to $5 million per reactor to help cover the costs. Following the Chernobyl accident, legislation was enacted to increase the liability cap to $7.4 billion.

A ROLE FOR NUCLEAR POWER?

Expressing the thoughts of those who advocate the use of nuclear power, Ratib Karan, director of the Neely Nuclear Research Center at Georgia Tech University contends, "Nuclear energy is now the only major source of power that does not produce carbon dioxide. In terms of global society, nuclear power plants are essential." Some critics suggest that the threat to climate change could lead to a truce between the nuclear power industry and some environmentalists, long-time bitter enemies. Nonetheless, many Americans remain ambivalent about nuclear power.

NUCLEAR FUSION

On November 1, 1952, a thermonuclear bomb equivalent to 10 million tons of TNT was detonated at Eniwetok atoll in the Pacific. That moment was both a nightmare — the potential of even more destruction — and a great dream — the possibility of generating cheap and abundant electricity by fusing hydrogen nuclei together. That dream survives today, but just barely.

In an effort to develop energy sources free of the dangers of nuclear fission, scientists have been experimenting with nuclear fusion as a potential major source of power for the twenty-first century. Fusion is the process by which two atomic particles are joined together under certain conditions to release vast amounts of heat energy. In a fusion reaction, deuterium and tritium atoms fuse, or come together, creating helium and energetic neutrons. The neutrons escape through a chamber wall into

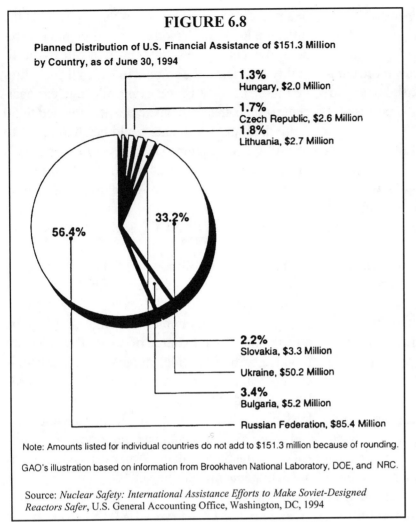

FIGURE 6.8

Planned Distribution of U.S. Financial Assistance of $151.3 Million by Country, as of June 30, 1994

1.3%
Hungary, $2.0 Million

1.7%
Czech Republic, $2.6 Million

1.8%
Lithuania, $2.7 Million

33.2%

56.4%

2.2%
Slovakia, $3.3 Million

Ukraine, $50.2 Million

3.4%
Bulgaria, $5.2 Million

Russian Federation, $85.4 Million

Note: Amounts listed for individual countries do not add to $151.3 million because of rounding.

GAO's illustration based on information from Brookhaven National Laboratory, DOE, and NRC.

Source: *Nuclear Safety: International Assistance Efforts to Make Soviet-Designed Reactors Safer*, U.S. General Accounting Office, Washington, DC, 1994

a surrounding "basket," which absorbs heat that is used to create steam for generating electricity.

The closest natural example of fusion is the sun, where the temperature at the core is 14 million degrees centigrade, and gravitational pressure is crushing. There, atomic nuclei are driven so close together that they fuse and release vast energy. In a fusion reactor, the temperature must be even higher, around 200 million degrees centigrade, since there is less compression than at the center of the sun.

Fusion has several advantages over fossil fuels and nuclear fission power. Fusion does not create air pollutants that contribute to acid rain or global warming. Deuterium is available in essentially unlimited supply from seawater, and tritium can

be generated on site as part of the fusion process. In theory, fusion could produce far more energy from the top two inches of Lake Erie than exists in all of Earth's known oil reserves.

Fusion experts believe the prospects for building fusion power plants that actually produce electricity in useful amounts are bleak. Dr. Martha Krebs, who heads the Office of Energy Research at the Department of Energy, observes that, "The department's [DOE] fusion program is now at a turning point because there will be dramatically fewer dollars [for research] in the foreseeable future." In 1996, Congress slashed federal support for fusion research by one-third, to $244 million a year. The reductions cut into the work at the Princeton Plasma Physics Laboratory, which operates the most powerful "magnetic confinement" fusion machine in the world: the Tokamak Fusion Test Reactor. Tokamaks are donut-shaped vessels in which an element is compressed and heated to millions of degrees.

No fusion reactor has, so far, produced more energy than it has used. The highest power ever reached, 10.6 million watts, was maintained for only a fraction of a second by the Princeton Tokamak in 1995. The Fusion Energy Advisory Committee, a panel of scientists that advise the DOE, recently concluded that the United States would have to join with the European Community, Japan, and Russia to jointly design an international experimental reactor to further test the concept. "The pursuit of fusion energy is of such cost and complexity that it can only be achieved through international collaboration," the committee concluded. Budget constraints will likely force the DOE to shut down the Tokamak Fusion Test reactor.

CHAPTER VII

NUCLEAR WASTE

Nuclear waste has sometimes been called the Achilles' heel of the nuclear power industry; much of the controversy over nuclear power centers on the lack of a disposal system for the highly radioactive spent fuel that must be regularly removed from operating reactors. As a result, progress on nuclear waste disposal is widely considered a prerequisite for any future growth of nuclear power. — Congressional Research Service, August 1998

In 1942, humanity's relationship with nature changed forever. Working in a laboratory in Chicago, Illinois, Italian physicist Enrico Fermi assembled enough uranium to cause a nuclear fission reaction. His discovery transformed both warfare and energy production. But his experiment also produced a small packet of radioactive waste materials that will remain dangerous for hundreds of thousands of years. That original waste lies buried under a foot of concrete and two feet of dirt on a hillside in Illinois. Scientists and governments have yet to find a way to dispose of this deadly residue or the many hundreds of thousands of tons that have since been generated.

Radioactive waste material is produced at all stages of the nuclear energy process (used in nuclear power plants, nuclear weapons plants, hospitals, and scientific research), from the initial mining of the uranium to the final disposal of the spent fuel from the reactor. (Figure 7.1 shows the nuclear fuel cycle.) Disposing of this waste is unquestionably one of the major problems associated with the development of nuclear power. Although federal policy is based on the assumption that nuclear waste can be disposed of safely, new storage and disposal facilities for all types of radioactive waste have frequently been delayed or blocked by concerns about safety, health, and the environment.

The highly toxic wastes must be isolated from the environment until the radioactivity decays to a safe level. In the case of plutonium, one of the most deadly substances known to man, the half-life (the time it takes for half the atoms to disintegrate) is 26,000 years. At this rate, it will take at least 100,000 years before it is no longer dangerous. Any facilities to store such materials must last virtually forever.

The failure to handle such deadly wastes properly has led to the pollution of the surrounding water supplies and plant life. A massive cleanup operation will be required that may well test the capabilities of modern technology as well as the nation's financial resources.

From the 1940s, when the nation began to develop nuclear weapons, until the late 1980s, the predecessors of the U.S. Department of Energy (DOE) and the Nuclear Regulatory Commission (NRC) paid little attention to the environmental consequences of their activities. As a result, many DOE sites are now contaminated with radioactive and hazardous wastes, and the DOE faces the most complex clean-up task in the country, estimated to cost anywhere between $300 billion and $41 trillion. Congress is especially divided over this issue; nonetheless, when it comes to storing nuclear

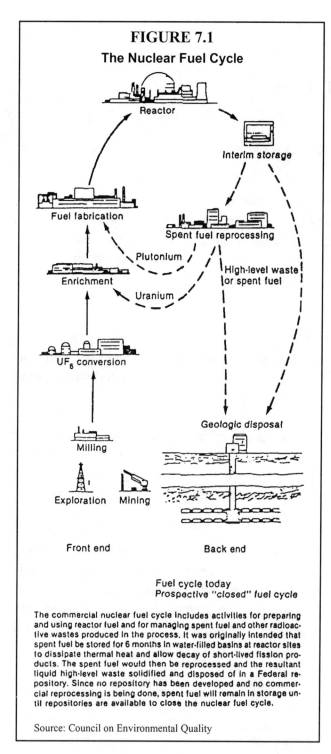

FIGURE 7.1

The Nuclear Fuel Cycle

Reactor

Interim storage

Fuel fabrication

Spent fuel reprocessing

Plutonium

High-level waste or spent fuel

Enrichment

Uranium

UF$_6$ conversion

Milling

Geologic disposal

Exploration   Mining

Front end   Back end

Fuel cycle today
Prospective "closed" fuel cycle

The commercial nuclear fuel cycle includes activities for preparing and using reactor fuel and for managing spent fuel and other radioactive wastes produced in the process. It was originally intended that spent fuel be stored for 6 months in water-filled basins at reactor sites to dissipate thermal heat and allow decay of short-lived fission products. The spent fuel would then be reprocessed and the resultant liquid high-level waste solidified and disposed of in a Federal repository. Since no repository has been developed and no commercial reprocessing is being done, spent fuel will remain in storage until repositories are available to close the nuclear fuel cycle.

Source: Council on Environmental Quality

handle, while other types are intensely hot in both temperature and radioactivity. Some waste decays to safe levels of radioactivity in a matter of days or weeks, while other types will remain dangerous for thousands of years. The DOE and the NRC define the major types of radioactive waste as (Figure 7.2):

- *Uranium mill tailings* are sand-like wastes produced in uranium refining operations. Although they emit low levels of radiation, their large volumes pose a hazard, particularly from radon emissions or groundwater contamination.

- *Low-level waste* contains varying lesser levels of radioactivity, including trash, contaminated clothing, and hardware. In general, low-level waste decays relatively quickly.

- *Spent fuel* is "used" reactor fuel that will be classified as waste if not reprocessed to recover the usable uranium and plutonium. In reprocessing, the used uranium and plutonium in spent reactor fuel can be removed for use again as nuclear reactor fuel. It is the most radioactive type of civilian nuclear waste.

- *High-level waste* is the by-product of a reprocessing plant, containing highly toxic and extremely dangerous fission products. Although most of the uranium and plutonium has usually been removed for reuse, enough long-lived radioactive elements remain to require isolation for 10,000 years or more.

- *Transuranic (TRU) wastes* are 11 man-made radioactive elements with an atomic number greater than that of uranium (92) and half-lives of thousands of years. They are found in refuse produced mainly by nuclear weapons plants and, therefore, are part of the nuclear waste problem but not directly the concern of nuclear power utilities.

- *Mixed waste* is high-level, low-level, or TRU waste that contains hazardous non-radioactive

waste, NIMBY (not in my back yard) has been the position of most congressional representatives.

NUCLEAR ENERGY WASTE DISPOSAL

Radioactive waste is a term that encompasses a broad range of material with widely varying characteristics. Some is barely radioactive and safe to

FIGURE 7.2

Radioactive Waste in the United States

Radioactive wastes, which are generated at each stage of the processing of nuclear materials, are divided into five categories by the U.S. federal government. The total accumulations of radioactive waste in the United States, including wastes from defense uses, are shown below.

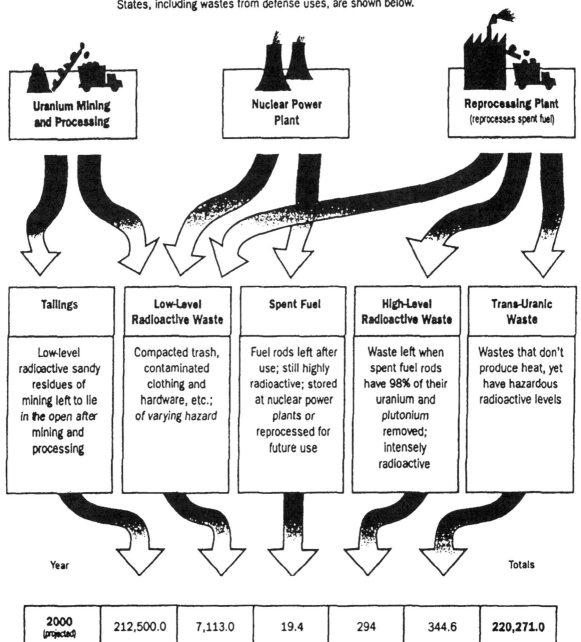

| Uranium Mining and Processing | Nuclear Power Plant | Reprocessing Plant (reprocesses spent fuel) |

Tailings	Low-Level Radioactive Waste	Spent Fuel	High-Level Radioactive Waste	Trans-Uranic Waste
Low-level radioactive sandy residues of mining left to lie in the open after mining and processing	Compacted trash, contaminated clothing and hardware, etc.; of varying hazard	Fuel rods left after use; still highly radioactive; stored at nuclear power plants or reprocessed for future use	Waste left when spent fuel rods have 98% of their uranium and plutonium removed; intensely radioactive	Wastes that don't produce heat, yet have hazardous radioactive levels

Year						Totals
2000 (projected)	212,500.0	7,113.0	19.4	294	344.6	**220,271.0**

Accumulated Radioactive Waste in the United States, from Commercial and Defense Use, in Thousands of Cubic Meters*

* Cubic Meter = 1.308 Cubic Yards
Sources: Natural Resources Defense Council; Worldwatch Paper 75: "Reassessing Nuclear Power: The Fallout from Chernobyl," by Christopher Revin, Worldwatch Institute, March 1987.

waste. Such waste poses serious institutional problems, because the radioactive portion is regulated by the DOE or NRC under the Atomic Energy Act, while the Environmental Protection Agency (EPA) regulates the non-radioactive elements under the Resource Conservation and Recovery Act (RCRA; PL 95-510).

Uranium Mill Tailings

These sand-like wastes emit low levels of radiation that can contaminate water and air. Most of these tailing sites are west of the Mississippi River, primarily in Utah, Colorado, New Mexico, and Arizona.

Prior to the early 1970s, the tailings were believed to have such low levels of radiation that they were not harmful to humans. Miners, many of whom were Native Americans, received little protection from the radiation. Now, many of these workers are reporting very high rates of cancer. Tailings were also left in scattered piles without warnings or safeguards, exposing anyone who came near. Some tailings were even used as landfill, and homes were built on top of them. Although too late for many, authorities now recognize that the handling and disposal of mill tailings must be properly managed to control radiation exposure.

Proper management of uranium mill tailings is particularly important as they are generated in relatively large volumes — about 10 to 15 million tons annually. About 15 percent of the radioactivity is removed during the milling process, while the remainder (85 percent) stays in the tailings. Radium-226, the major radioactive waste product, retains its radioactivity for thousands of years and produces two potentially hazardous radiation components — gamma radiation and gaseous radon. There is a proven causal relationship between these radioactive elements and leukemia and lung cancer.

In response to growing concern, Congress passed the Uranium Mill Tailing Radiation Control Act of 1978 (PL 95-604) to regulate mill tailing operations. The law called for the cleanup of abandoned mill sites, primarily at federal expense, although owners of still-active mines were financially responsible for their own cleanup. The legislation also required the EPA to prepare standards for the cleanup of both inactive and active sites, although it took the EPA until 1983 to issue such standards.

Low-Level Radioactive Waste

Low-level radioactive waste decays in 10 to 100 years. Until the 1960s, the United States dumped low-level wastes into the ocean. The first commercial site to house such waste was opened in 1962, and by 1971, six sites were licensed for disposal.

By 1979, only three commercial low-level waste sites were still operating — Hanford, Washington; Beatty, Nevada; and Barnwell, South Carolina. In response to the threatened closing of the South Carolina site, Congress passed the Low-Level Radioactive Waste Policy Act of 1980 (PL 96-573), calling for the establishment of a national system of such facilities. Every state would be responsible for finding a low-level disposal site for wastes generated within its borders by 1986. It also gave states the right to bar low-level wastes if they were engaged in regional compacts for waste disposal. The disposal of high-level wastes, however, remains a federal responsibility.

The volume of low-level waste increased during the initial years (1963-1980) of commercially generated waste disposal, until the Low-Level Radioactive Waste Policy Act of 1980. Since then, volume has decreased (Figure 7.3).

Compacts

The 1980 law encouraged states to organize themselves into compacts to develop new dumps. As of 1998, nine such compacts have been approved by Congress, and a compact among Texas, Maine, and Vermont is pending. But only two commercial low-level waste sites currently operate, one in the state of Washington and the other in South Carolina. The Washington facility accepts waste

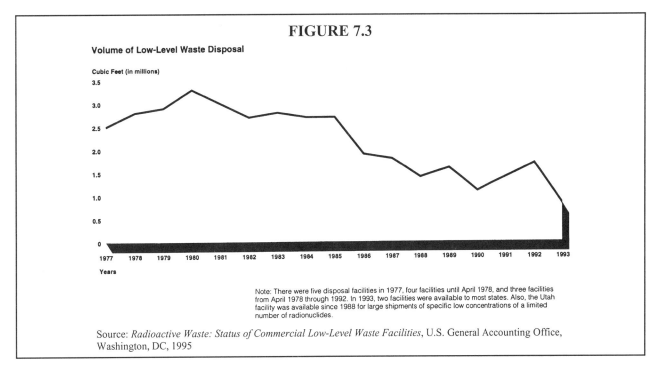

FIGURE 7.3

Volume of Low-Level Waste Disposal

Cubic Feet (in millions)

Years

Note: There were five disposal facilities in 1977, four facilities until April 1978, and three facilities from April 1978 through 1992. In 1993, two facilities were available to most states. Also, the Utah facility was available since 1988 for large shipments of specific low concentrations of a limited number of radionuclides.

Source: *Radioactive Waste: Status of Commercial Low-Level Waste Facilities*, U.S. General Accounting Office, Washington, DC, 1995

just from within the Northwest and Rocky Mountain regional compacts.

A Short-Term Solution

In 1994, the Barnwell, South Carolina, facility, as part of a planned phase-out, was closed to waste generators outside the Southeast Compact, leaving no repository for states outside the compact. States with no plans for their own disposal sites had no place to send their wastes. (The dump in Beatty, Nevada, was closed in 1992.) Their low-level wastes were to have been "managed and stored" (held on site) until new facilities established by the compacts were operational.

However, in 1995, after the compacts failed to arrange new disposal sites, Barnwell reopened for a 10-year period, taking waste from every state willing to pay sharply increased rates. The facility charged $315 per cubic foot, up from $200 per cubic foot before the 1994 closing. Because of the failure of the states to manage these low-level wastes, many observers believe the federal government may be forced to re-enter the picture. In fact, some observers think the reopening of Barnwell lessens the pressure on the states, leading them to put their planning processes on hold.

Storage Problems

Developing storage areas for hazardous waste is difficult because regulatory requirements mandate a buffer zone of land surrounding each site. This acreage will require monitoring and limited land-use applications for at least a century. Although larger sites would collectively reduce the total number of acres required, some state officials believe that having more numerous local facilities would be safer by reducing the number of transportation accidents.

In addition, officials are concerned about degradation of the packages that contain stored waste. Depending on the environment, degradation can occur from temperature fluctuations, corrosion, and containers becoming brittle. Some state officials worry that, as the amounts of waste accumulate, with fewer sites for disposal, illegal dumping will increase. Finally, waste accumulation may lead to the reduction of nuclear health care and medical research to avoid adding to the waste problems.

Spent Fuel and High-Level Radioactive Waste

Approximately once a year, one-third of the nuclear fuel (uranium) inside a reactor is removed and replaced with fresh fuel. The used or "spent fuel" is the primary form of high-level nuclear waste. Spent fuel is not completely "spent." It contains highly penetrating and toxic radioactivity and requires isolation from living things for thousands of years. It still contains significant amounts of uranium, as well as plutonium created during the nuclear fission process. Spent fuel is a problem for nuclear power plants that will be decommissioned before the projected availability of a long-term, high-level waste disposal repository. (See Figure 7.4 for the locations of high-level and spent nuclear fuel accumulations.) Unless a temporary site becomes available, utilities have the following options:

- Leave the fuel on site.

- Use on-site casks. This is not an option for hot fuel (fuel that is less than five years out of the core).

- Ship the spent fuel to France or Britain for reprocessing. Nuclear watch groups, including the Friends of the Earth and the Union of Concerned Scientists, oppose reprocessing abroad because they fear the possibility of theft or accidental spread of nuclear materials.

- Ship the fuel to a monitored retrievable storage facility, if there is one available.

- Continue to operate the unit.

Only the natural decaying process, which can take hundreds of thousands of years, diminishes the radioactivity of nuclear waste. The original "solution" was to bury the waste deep in the earth, but many scientists now believe that the deadly debris cannot be guaranteed to remain sealed off from the biosphere for hundreds of centuries. None of the options guarantee protection of Earth from radiation. Due to the scientific and political diffi-

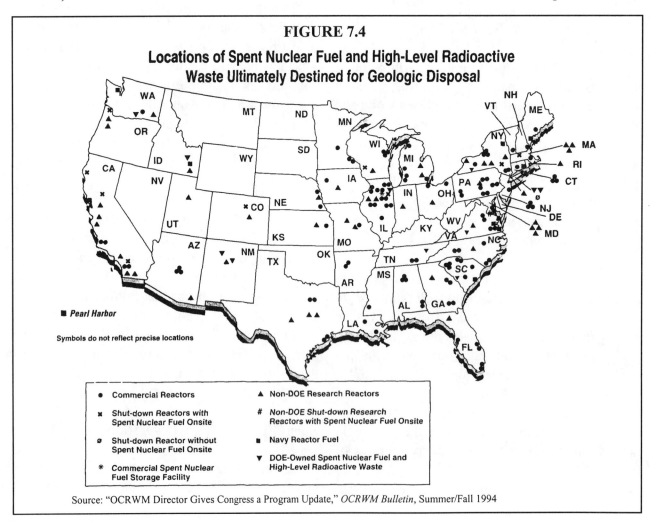

FIGURE 7.4

Locations of Spent Nuclear Fuel and High-Level Radioactive Waste Ultimately Destined for Geologic Disposal

■ *Pearl Harbor*

Symbols do not reflect precise locations

- Commercial Reactors
✕ Shut-down Reactors with Spent Nuclear Fuel Onsite
ø Shut-down Reactor without Spent Nuclear Fuel Onsite
✳ Commercial Spent Nuclear Fuel Storage Facility
▲ Non-DOE Research Reactors
Non-DOE Shut-down Research Reactors with Spent Nuclear Fuel Onsite
■ Navy Reactor Fuel
▼ DOE-Owned Spent Nuclear Fuel and High-Level Radioactive Waste

Source: "OCRWM Director Gives Congress a Program Update," *OCRWM Bulletin*, Summer/Fall 1994

culties with geologic burial and other methods, above-ground "temporary" storage, despite the dangers, may remain the preferred option well into the twenty-first century.

Pantex

Pantex employs an estimated 3,500 workers at its 16,000-acre site 17 miles northeast of Amarillo in the Texas Panhandle. The Pantex plant assembled nuclear weapons for the U.S. military until 1989. When the Cold War ended, the plant's major mission shifted to dismantling those same weapons. The federal government plans to take apart as many as 15,000 warheads and store them at Pantex. More than 46,000 pounds of weapons-grade plutonium (a man-made radioactive element produced by irradiating uranium in nuclear reactors) will be stored in above-ground bunkers at Pantex by the time weapons disassembly is completed in 2003 (most experts believe the DOE is unlikely to meet this target). The government must then decontaminate buildings used at those facilities, dispose of millions of gallons of boiling radioactive water, and decontaminate hundreds of square miles of land at test sites.

The plutonium held by the DOE is in several forms — metals, oxides (fine powders), residues, and solutions (materials with lower plutonium content) and "pits." A pit is the spherical central core of a nuclear weapon. It is compressed with high explosives to create a nuclear explosion. The DOE currently stores pits in containers known as AL-R8s, which were originally designed only to transport pits (Figure 7.5).

The perpetual storage of radioactive materials at Pantex and the "temporary" storage at other sites raise the possibility that an accident involving plutonium could ruin agriculture and cost jobs in those areas. Hanford (Washington; see below), Savannah River (South Carolina), Los Alamos National Laboratory (New Mexico), Rocky Flats Environ-

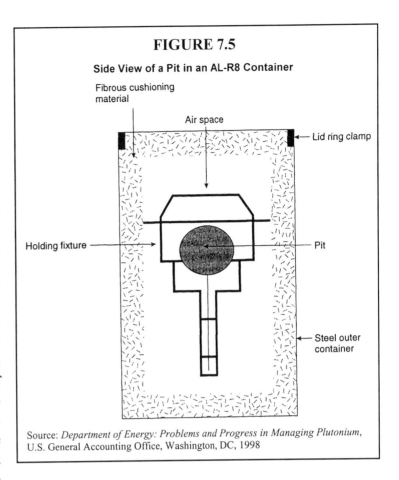

FIGURE 7.5

Side View of a Pit in an AL-R8 Container

Source: *Department of Energy: Problems and Progress in Managing Plutonium*, U.S. General Accounting Office, Washington, DC, 1998

mental Technology Site (Colorado), and Lawrence Livermore National Laboratory (California) store the majority of the plutonium (Figure 7.6). Table 7.1 shows the amount of plutonium still being held at the five former weapons plants (Pantex stores only plutonium in pits).

Theoretically, the plutonium also poses a dilemma because it could be stolen by terrorists or end up in the hands of unfriendly nations seeking nuclear weapons capability. To date, government officials claim they can account for every ounce of plutonium that has been removed from nuclear weapons. Options for dealing with the plutonium include:

• Mix the plutonium with other radioactive waste, encase it in glass logs ("vitrification"), seal the logs in metal cylinders, and store them in remote geological formations.

• Mix the plutonium into an unusable form, inject it into a borehole one or two miles deep, and seal it with concrete.

107

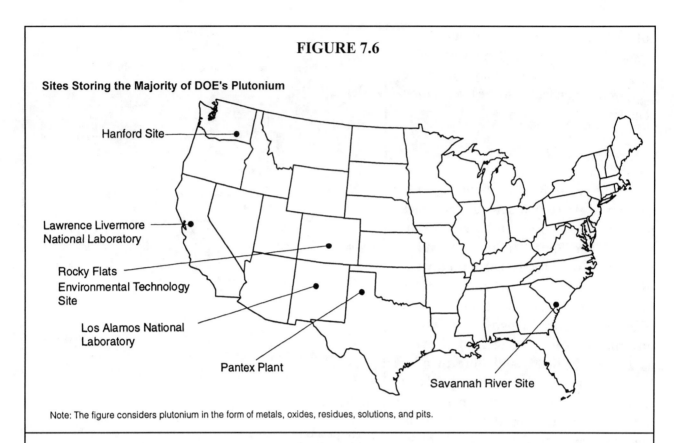

FIGURE 7.6

Sites Storing the Majority of DOE's Plutonium

Hanford Site

Lawrence Livermore
National Laboratory

Rocky Flats
Environmental Technology
Site

Los Alamos National
Laboratory

Pantex Plant

Savannah River Site

Note: The figure considers plutonium in the form of metals, oxides, residues, solutions, and pits.

TABLE 7.1

Plutonium Inventory, by Form, at Five DOE Sites With Plutonium Stabilization Activities

Metric tons

Site	Total plutonium inventory[a]	Plutonium metals	Plutonium oxides	Plutonium residues	Plutonium solutions
Rocky Flats Environmental Technology Site	12.7	6.5	1.6	4.5	0.1
Hanford Site	3.5	0.8	2.0	0.4	0.3
Savannah River Site	1.8	0.7	0.7	0.1	0.3
Los Alamos National Laboratory	2.5	1.2	0.0	1.3	0.0
Lawrence Livermore National Laboratory	0.3	0.1	0.1	0.1	0.0
Total	**20.8**	**9.3**	**4.4**	**6.4**	**0.7**

[a]Inventory amounts are as of 1994; any updated amounts would be classified information.
Amounts exclude spent nuclear fuel, reactor fuel, and special isotopes of plutonium.

Source of figure and table: *Department of Energy: Problems and Progress in Managing Plutonium*, U.S. General Accounting Office, Washington, DC, 1998

- Reformulate the plutonium into a substance called mixed-oxide fuel, or MOX, and use the fuel to power nuclear reactors to produce electricity.

- Take no action. A small portion of plutonium pits will be retained as strategic reserves for use in weapons in the future, if necessary.

NUCLEAR WASTE LEGISLATION

Nuclear Waste Policy Act — 1982

A major step toward shifting the responsibility for disposal of high-level nuclear wastes from the nuclear power industry to the federal government was taken in 1982. Congress passed the Nuclear Waste Policy Act (PL 97-425), which provided the first national, comprehensive policy and detailed timetable for the management and disposal of high-level nuclear waste. The major provisions of the act were to:

- Authorize construction of the first waste repository.

- Provide a schedule for the site selection and operation.

- Define the means of achieving cooperation with the host state.

- Assure funding for the program by charging 1 mill (0.1 cent) per kilowatt-hour of electricity generated by nuclear energy (this measure has been in effect since 1983, adding between 2 and 6 percent to the consumer's cost of electricity).

- Provide for the president to decide if civilian repositories may accept nuclear waste from military activities.

- Establish an interim storage program to ease the backlog of spent nuclear fuel at power plants.

- Direct the DOE to design a monitored retrievable storage program for long-term storage of spent fuel.

1987 Congressional Amendments

In 1987, Congress amended the Nuclear Waste Policy Act as part of the Omnibus Budget Reconciliation Act (PL 100-203). Because costs continued to escalate (from $23 to $30 billion), Congress directed the DOE to investigate only the Yucca Mountain site in Nevada (see below) as a potential site for the first repository. Congress limited the amount of waste that could be disposed of in the repository until a second repository was made ready.

The DOE was also authorized to develop a facility to receive and temporarily store waste until the second repository was built. In 1987, the DOE proposed developing a facility in Tennessee for temporary waste storage to begin accepting waste in 1998. Congress authorized the plan, but it cannot go into effect until the Nuclear Regulatory Commission (NRC) has authorized the construction of the Yucca Mountain repository, which is still pending (see below).

NUCLEAR WASTE REPOSITORIES — WASTE ISOLATION PILOT PLANT AND YUCCA MOUNTAIN

In the United States, the government is focusing on two locations as eventual geologic repositories: the Waste Isolation Pilot Plant (WIPP) in southeastern New Mexico for defense (transuranic) waste and Nevada's Yucca Mountain for civilian waste.

The Waste Isolation Pilot Plant (WIPP)

In May 1998, federal regulators gave final approval to the WIPP, the world's first deep depository for nuclear waste. The large facility near Carlsbad, New Mexico, which will be restricted to defense (transuranic) waste, was authorized to accept defense-related waste in late 1998. However, waste is not expected to be shipped to the WIPP until the summer of 1999 because a number of regulations of the state of New Mexico remain unmet. The WIPP is 655 meters below the surface, in the salt beds of the Salado Formation, and is intended to house up to 6.25 million cubic feet of transuranic waste for more than 10,000 years.

Currently, more than 99 percent of transuranic waste is temporarily stored in drums at nuclear defense sites in California, Colorado, Idaho, Illinois, Nevada, New Mexico, Ohio, Tennessee, South Carolina, and Washington. Under Congressional mandate, the WIPP facility will not receive commercial or high-level waste; only transuranic waste will be accepted. Some environmentalists oppose the Carlsbad site and threaten to block shipments of the waste or stage peaceful protests at the site.

TABLE 7.2

Existing and Projected Volumes of Contact-Handled Transuranic Waste

In cubic meters

Storage site	Existing	Projected	Total
Hanford, Washington	11,028	34,909	45,937
Idaho	64,158[a]	0	64,158
Los Alamos, New Mexico	10,953	7,351	18,304
Oak Ridge, Tennessee	1,326	256	1,582
Rocky Flats, Colorado	1,869	3,205	5,074
Savannah River, South Carolina	6,551	8,946	15,497
Subtotal	**95,885**	**54,667**	**150,552**
All others	1,160	1,241	2,401
Total	**97,045**	**55,908**	**152,953**

[a]Includes 24,903 cubic meters of low-level radioactive waste that is contaminated with transuranic elements and is commingled with contact-handled transuranic waste stored at the site. DOE intends to treat both the low-level and transuranic waste in a treatment facility and then dispose of the residual waste in WIPP.

GAO's presentation of data from the Transuranic Waste Baseline Inventory Report, Revision 2 (DOE/CAO-95-1121, Dec. 1995).

Source: *Nuclear Waste: Uncertainties About Opening Waste Isolation Pilot Project*, U.S. General Accounting Office, Washington, DC, 1996

Waste will be transported to the WIPP via interstate highways in 30 states using the TRUPACT-II, a container designed specifically to be carried on trucks and that has passed drop, puncture, and burn safety tests. Initially, one truckload of waste will arrive from Los Alamos. As more sites receive EPA certification, shipments will increase. Under full operation, the site will receive as many as two shipments a day from various locations.

For the first several years of the WIPP's operation, the DOE expects to dispose of contact-handled waste* (Table 7.2) at less than one-quarter of the designed disposal rate of the repository, primarily because few transportation containers are available. The DOE does not expect to begin disposing of remote-handled waste until 2002. Most of the remote-handled waste is at Oak Ridge, although the DOE expects to generate much more of this waste at the Hanford site. (See Table 7.3.)

Originally, the DOE planned to ship waste from Idaho Falls, Rocky Flats, and Los Alamos in 1998 and from Savannah River in 1999. Thereafter, DOE

will make almost 1,300 shipments to the WIPP at an accelerating rate over the approximately five-year period ending December 2002 (Table 7.4). The repository was to have opened in 1998, although, as indicated earlier, laws of the state of New Mexico will likely prevent that until summer 1999.

A Sierra Blanca Dump?

A second waste disposal site is planned near Sierra Blanca, Texas, 90 miles from El Paso, Texas, to handle radioactive waste generated from hospitals, utilities, and universities in Texas. In September 1998, Congress passed the Texas Low-Level Radioactive Waste Disposal Compact (PL 105-236) that will allow Maine and Vermont to ship their low-level waste to the site as well. Vermont and Maine have agreed to pay Texas $55 million to bury their low-level waste.

Mexican officials protested the plant, contending that it would violate a 1983 agreement between the United States and Mexico to curb pollution along the border. Mexico claimed it would protest the action as far as the United Nations or will even boycott Texas merchants, if necessary. In October 1998, however, the Texas Natural Resource Conservation Commission denied a permit for the proposed dump based on concerns about its safety.

Yucca Mountain

The centerpiece of the geologic disposal of highly radioactive civilian (nuclear electric power) waste is the Yucca Mountain site. The Nuclear Waste Policy Act of 1982 (see above) requires the

---

* Contact-handled waste can be handled with limited precaution, as opposed to "remote-handled waste" that emits higher levels of radiation and requires special handling and disposal.

Secretary of Energy to investigate the site and, if it is suitable, recommend to the president that the site be established.

Yucca Mountain is a flat-topped ridge, running six miles from north to south, which has changed little over the past million years. The site has a desert climate, important because water movement is the primary means by which radioactive waste could be transported from a repository into the environment. The repository would be built about 1,000 feet below the surface and 1,000 feet above the water table.

It is not clear, however, that Yucca Mountain (Figures 7.7 and 7.8) is suitable. It is located near volcanic and earthquake activity, and local Native American tribes are contesting rights to the land.

TABLE 7.3

Existing and Projected Volumes of Remote-Handled Transuranic Waste
In cubic meters

Storage site	Existing	Projected	Total
Hanford	201	21,521	21,722
Idaho	200	0	200
Los Alamos	93	34	127
Oak Ridge	1,832	344	2,176
Rocky Flats	0	0	0
Savannah River	0	0	0
Subtotal	**2,326**	**21,899**	**24,225**
All other sites	608	34	642
Total	**2,934**	**21,933**	**24,867**

GAO's presentation of data from the Transuranic Waste Baseline Inventory Report, Revision 2.

TABLE 7.4

Planned Shipments to and Operational Capabilities of WIPP Through 2002
Number of shipments

Year	Planned shipments	Operational capability	Unused capability
1998	64	64	0
1999	198	200	2
2000	197	350	153
2001	425	566	141
2002	412	740	328
Total	**1,296**	**1,920**	**624**

GAO's presentation of data from DOE's Carlsbad Area Office.

Source of both tables: *Nuclear Waste: Uncertainties About Opening Waste Isolation Pilot Project*, U.S. General Accounting Office, Washington, DC, 1996

Scientists have discovered areas of "perched water" (water that has seeped in between layers of the earth's crust) above the water table. Although these areas may not ultimately prove to be a problem, researchers must determine their size and number in order to determine the seriousness of the situation. Scientists are also concerned by recent studies that found the area more geologically unstable than previously thought.

The Nuclear Waste Policy Act set forth a multistep process for deciding whether to proceed with the development of a repository at Yucca Mountain. A negative decision at any step would stop the process and require the Secretary of Energy and the Congress to develop a different approach to solving the nation's nuclear waste problem. Before deciding whether to recommend the Yucca Mountain site, the Secretary of Energy will con-

duct a formal evaluation of the site and hold public hearings in the vicinity of Yucca Mountain to inform local residents and receive comments. The current schedule calls for the Secretary of Energy to decide in 2001 whether to recommend the site. If approval is granted at each step and there are no delays in the process, waste placement could begin in 2010.

In December 1998, Secretary of Energy Bill Richardson submitted a Viability Assessment to the President and Congress. Secretary Richardson found no "show stoppers" at Yucca Mountain. The report concluded that scientific and technical work should proceed to support a decision by the secretary of energy in 2001 on whether to recommend the site to the president. The cost to license, construct, operate, monitor, and close the repository is estimated at $18.7 billion in 1998 dollars. This

FIGURE 7.7

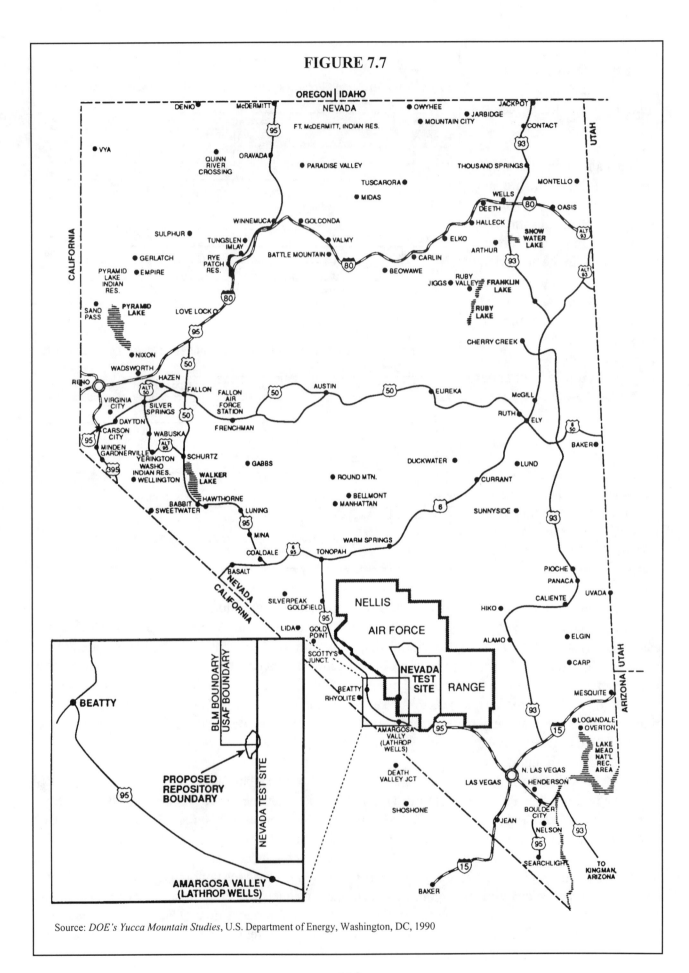

Source: *DOE's Yucca Mountain Studies*, U.S. Department of Energy, Washington, DC, 1990

FIGURE 7.8

Yucca Mountain, Nevada: Candidate site for the first U.S. geologic repository

Source: *Managing the Nation's Nuclear Waste*, U.S. Department of Energy, Washington, DC, 1990

cost includes monitoring the repository for 100 years and disposing of 70,000 metric tons of spent nuclear fuel and high-level waste, currently the legal limit of what can be disposed.

Some western states feel they have long been targeted for hazardous facilities. If Yucca Mountain is found to be acceptable, the president approves it, and a recommendation goes to the Congress, the state of Nevada is expected to file a notice of disapproval. For more detailed discussion of nuclear waste, see *Garbage and Other Pollution*, Information Plus, Wylie, Texas, 1998.

Shipping Waste to Yucca Mountain

From a cooling pool at a power plant, spent fuel would be packaged for shipment either to a temporary, central storage facility or to a repository. Spent fuel would be hoisted by remote control into strong, heavily shielded shipping casks designed to withstand severe accidents. (Figure 7.9 shows a transport cask.) Transportation casks for radioactive waste must pass rigorous crash and fire

tests to be certified by the Nuclear Regulatory Commission (NRC).

The U.S. Department of Transportation (DOT) and the NRC regulate the shipment of nuclear materials. Studies are being done to determine which method of shipping to a repository — road, rail, or a combination of the two — is best and which possible routes are safest. The approximate number of shipments to a repository each year is estimated to be 250 by rail and 1,000 by truck. When nuclear shipments to Yucca Mountain begin, extensive safety checks will be required by drivers and state inspectors before a shipment leaves, en route, and when the shipment arrives at Yucca Mountain. Before a repository opens, highway patrol officers, firefighters, emergency medical personnel, and other public safety workers will have to be trained and provided with emergency response equipment.

On arrival at the repository, the cask would be unloaded by remote control and inspected for damage. The fuel would be removed from the cask and put into a canister, which would be welded shut. The waste canisters would then be taken by special vehicles down a ramp to rooms deep underground. There, by remote control, the waste would be placed inside holes in the tunnel floors and plugged with a heavy shield.

What Would a Repository Look Like?

The proposed repository would look like a large mining complex. It would have two types of facilities — a facility on the surface for handling and packaging nuclear waste and a large mine about 1,000 feet underground. Plans call for the waste to be placed in sealed metal canisters placed vertically in the floor of underground tunnels.

Many kinds of different facilities would be built on the surface, including roads, utilities, fire and medical areas, administrative offices, repair shops, water and sewage treatment plants, warehouses, and machine shops. These facilities would cover approximately 400 acres and be surrounded by a three-mile buffer zone. Underground, about 1,400 acres would be mined, consisting of tunnels lead-

FIGURE 7.9

How Some Waste Is Transported

Source: *Radioactive Waste: Status of Commercial Low-Level Waste Facilities*, U.S. General Accounting Office, Washington, DC, 1995

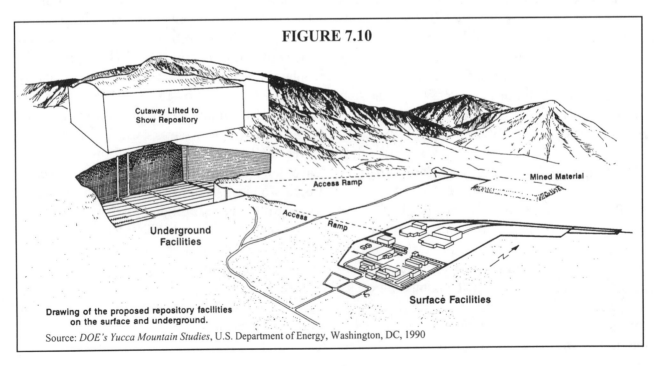

FIGURE 7.10

Cutaway Lifted to Show Repository

Access Ramp

Mined Material

Underground Facilities

Access Ramp

Surface Facilities

Drawing of the proposed repository facilities on the surface and underground.

Source: *DOE's Yucca Mountain Studies*, U.S. Department of Energy, Washington, DC, 1990

ing to the areas where waste containers would be placed and service areas near the shafts and ramps that provide access from the surface. (See Figure 7.10.)

What Happens When the Yucca Mountain Repository Is Full?

The repository would be designed to contain the radioactive material by using layers of shielding, by sealing the containers, and eventually by filling the holes — using layers of man-made and natural barriers. Regulations require that a repository isolate waste until the radiation levels decrease naturally ("decay") to a level that is about the same as that from a natural, underground uranium deposit. This decay time is estimated at about 10,000 years.

After the repository has been filled to capacity, regulations require the DOE to keep the facility open and to monitor it for at least 50 years from the fill date. This will allow experts to monitor conditions inside the repository and retrieve spent fuel if necessary. Eventually, the repository shafts will be filled with rock and earth and sealed. At the ground level, facilities will be removed, and to the extent possible, DOE will take steps to return the site to its original condition.

Scientists assume that over thousands of years, some of the man-made barriers in a repository will break down. Once that happens, natural barriers will be counted on to stop or slow the movement of radiation particles. The most likely way for particles to reach humans and the environment would be through water, which is why water tables are of such concern to scientists. In 1995, scientists studying Yucca Mountain announced they had found water table intrusion into areas of deep rock that were previously thought to be dry. Studies to determine the condition of water tables at Yucca Mountain continue (see above). However, Yucca Mountain has certain chemical properties that act as another barrier to the movement of radiative particles. Minerals in the rock called "zeolites" would stick to the particles and slow their movement throughout the environment.

Who Pays for Nuclear Waste Management?

Customers who use nuclear power pay for the deposit of spent fuel. The federal government collects a fee of one-tenth of a cent per kilowatt-hour of nuclear-generated electricity from utilities, which goes into the Nuclear Waste Fund. In addition, the federal government will pay for disposal of military defense high-level waste.

CAN CONTAINMENT STANDARDS BE MET?

In order for a repository to be built, the DOE must satisfactorily demonstrate to the NRC that the combination of the site and repository design complies with the standards set forth by the EPA. The EPA standards use numerical probabilities to establish requirements for containing radioactivity within the repository:

- Cumulative releases of radioactivity from a repository must have a likelihood of less than one chance in 10 of exceeding limits established in the standard and a likelihood of less than one chance in 1,000 of exceeding 10 times the limits for a period of 10,000 years.

- Exposures of radiation to individual members of the public for 1,000 years must not exceed specified limits.

- Limits are placed on the concentration of radioactivity for 1,000 years (after disposal) from the repository to a nearby source of groundwater that 1) currently supplies drinking water for thousands of persons, and 2) is irreplaceable.

- Prescribed technical or institutional procedures or steps must provide confidence that the containment requirements are likely to be met.

Serious Leaks of Radioactive Waste

Hanford

In 1997, scientists discovered that about 900,000 gallons of radioactive waste had leaked into the soil from 68 of the 149 tanks at the nuclear weapons plant in Hanford, Washington (Figure 7.11). The Hanford site has one of the greatest concentrations of radioactive waste in the world. Eventually all the Hanford tanks are expected to leak. The leaks have contaminated underground water moving toward the Columbia River.

Managers at the plant had maintained that the leaks were insignificant because the radioactive materials would be trapped by the area above the water table, the "vadose zone." Furthermore, officials had been claiming for decades that no waste from the tanks would reach the groundwater in the next 10,000 years. Nonetheless, the groundwater under more than 85 square miles of the site is already contaminated. Figure 7.12 shows the migration of nuclear waste through the vadose zone at Hanford. Washington's governor Gary Locke calls Hanford a "Chernobyl waiting to happen." State and federal officials have agreed to a timetable to clean up two indoor pools that are 400 yards from the Columbia River and hold 2,300 tons of spent nuclear fuel by 2007.

Brookhaven National Laboratory

Brookhaven National Laboratory (BNL) is a federally funded research facility, owned by the U.S. Department of Energy, on Long Island, New York. In January 1997, groundwater samples taken at BNL revealed concentrations of tritium that were twice the allowable federal drinking water standards. Some later samples found levels 32 times the standard. BNL employs about 3,200 people, including 900 scientists and engineers.

Tritium was found to be leaking from the spent fuel pool of the laboratory's High Flux Beam Re-

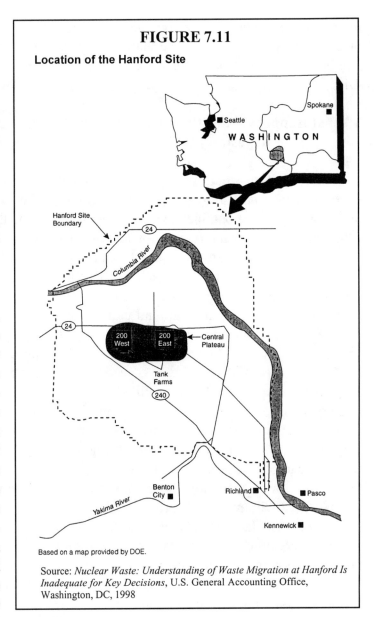

FIGURE 7.11

Location of the Hanford Site

Based on a map provided by DOE.

Source: *Nuclear Waste: Understanding of Waste Migration at Hanford Is Inadequate for Key Decisions*, U.S. General Accounting Office, Washington, DC, 1998

actor into the aquifer that provides drinking water for local residents. An investigation revealed that the tritium had been leaking for as long as 12 years. Because Brookhaven did not monitor its reactor's spent-fuel pool for leaks, years passed before the tritium contamination was discovered.

The High Flux Beam Reactor is the larger of the two research reactors. Its main purpose is to produce neutrons for scientific experiments. The reactor's cooling water became contaminated with the radioactive element tritium during operations. Built in the early 1960s, the spent-fuel pool is made of concrete but does not have a secondary container, such as a stainless steel liner, to protect

FIGURE 7.12

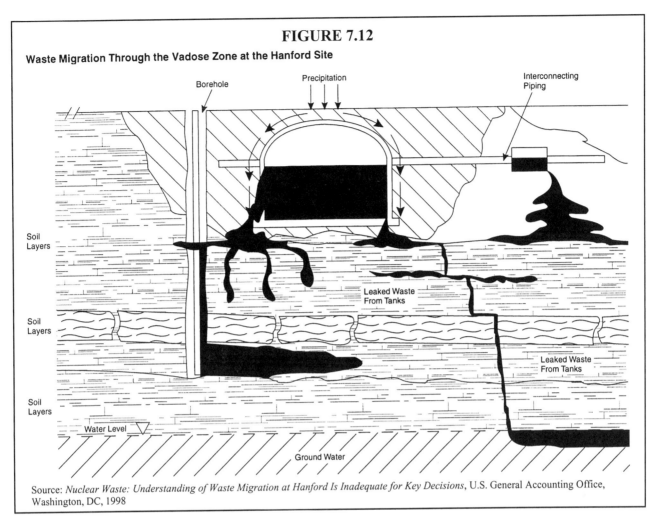

Waste Migration Through the Vadose Zone at the Hanford Site

Source: *Nuclear Waste: Understanding of Waste Migration at Hanford Is Inadequate for Key Decisions*, U.S. General Accounting Office, Washington, DC, 1998

against leaks. Newer reactors have secondary containment systems.

BNL's reactor will remain idle until improvements can be made in its operations. In the interim, engineers are draining a storage tank beneath the main reactor and redirecting the contaminated water 3,000 feet northward to an open basin. The water will then seep back into the ground, although after a total of 19 years, the water would have undetectable levels of tritium.

Crisis in the Industry

The long delay in providing disposal sites for nuclear wastes, coupled with the accelerated pace at which nuclear plants are being retired, has created a crisis in the industry. Several aging plants are being maintained (at a cost of $20 million a year for each reactor) simply because there is no place to send the waste once the plants are decom-

missioned. Under the Nuclear Waste Policy Act of 1982, the Energy Department was scheduled to begin picking up waste in January 1998, although that was not possible because no repository was ready. Although the 1987 waste amendment designated Yucca Mountain as the site, that site, if approved, is years away.

The DOE has a separate contract with each nuclear utility for disposal. Utilities have been paying a tenth of a cent per kilowatt-hour produced by the reactors to finance a repository. As of 1998, $13 billion in deposits and interest have accumulated in this Nuclear Waste Fund.

In 1996, in *Indiana Michigan Power Company v. Department of Energy* (88 F3d 1272), the U.S. Circuit Court of Appeals for the District of Columbia ruled that the federal government must begin accepting tons of used fuel from the nuclear industry by 1998, even though a permanent stor-

TABLE 7.5

Total U.S. Commercial Spent Nuclear Fuel Discharges, 1968-1994

Reactor Type	Number of Assemblies		
	Stored at Reactor Sites	Stored at Away-from-reactor Facilities	Total
Boiling-Water Reactor	57,187	2,957	60,144
Pressurized-Water Reactor	44,107	491	44,598
Total	101,294	3,448	104,742
	Metric Tons of Uranium		
Boiling-Water Reactor	10,347.3	554.0	10,901.3
Pressurized-Water Reactor	18,909.4	192.6	19,102.0
Total	29,256.7	746.6	30,003.3

Notes: A number of assemblies discharged prior to 1972 were reprocessed and are not included in this table. A total of 2,208 high-temperature, gas-cooled reactor (HTGR) fuel elements, with initial uranium content equal to 24.2 metric tons of uranium (MTU), were discharged. These HTGR fuel elements are not included in the above table. Totals may not equal sum of components because of independent rounding. Energy Information Administration, Form RW-859, "Nuclear Fuel Data" (1994).

Source: *Spent Nuclear Fuel Discharges from U.S. Reactors: 1994*, U.S. Department of Energy, Washington, DC, 1994

age site will not be ready until at least 2010. Because the DOE was unable to meet that deadline, the DOE's only option was essentially to open a temporary storage site, but this has not been approved.

In November 1998, the U.S. Court of Appeals for the District of Columbia, in *Northern States Power Company v. U.S. Department of Energy* (128 F3d 754) was unable to force the DOE to take possession of nuclear waste because there was no storage facility. The court ordered that utilities can postpone paying a portion of the fees owed to the Nuclear Waste Fund — an estimated $2.8 to $5 billion — and keep the earnings on the deferred fees. The utilities will be obligated to pay the withheld fees when the DOE begins to accept the spent fuel.

The Problem Is Now

At least 30,000 metric tons (Table 7.5) of nuclear uranium waste are sitting in what are called "spent fuel pools" at the 109 operating and 20 closed nuclear energy plants around the country. By the year 2000, the total waste is expected to reach 50,000 metric tons. According to the Nuclear Regulatory Commission (NRC), which licenses power plants, many of these plants will reach their capacity for storage by 2000.

In addition, many nuclear plants are shutting down well ahead of schedule because of skyrocketing maintenance and repair costs. Although the NRC licenses power plants to operate for 40 years, they do not last that long. The average life of the more than 20 reactors that have been shut down was approximately 13 years.

What happens when a nuclear plant closes down? Currently, the nuclear waste and the radioactive equipment generated stays on the premises since there is no place to put it. As a result, every nuclear power plant in the United States has become a temporary nuclear waste disposal site. Plants that close become mausoleums, largely untouched while they wait to be decommissioned or dismantled when a repository opens.

Other Problems Associated with Nuclear Waste

In 1993, then-Secretary of Energy Hazel O'Leary disclosed that over the past 45 years, the

United States conducted hundreds of unannounced atomic tests (from 1948 to 1952), experimented with human subjects on the effects of plutonium, often without their knowledge or approval, and dumped tons of toxic waste across the United States. Secretary O'Leary revealed that of 925 nuclear tests, 204 were secret, and that the government now stores 33.5 metric tons of plutonium in six U.S. locations. In 1996, the U.S. government announced that compensation agreements had been reached with many of the victims who sought damages for their injuries from radiation.

INTERNATIONAL APPROACH TO HIGH-LEVEL WASTE DISPOSAL

Governments around the world generally believe that deep geologic disposal offers the best option for isolating highly radioactive waste, although no country has yet built an operational facility. In fact, most do not plan to have a reposi-

tory until 2020 or later. (Table 7.6 shows estimates of repository opening dates in selected countries and the unique features of each nation's program.) The United States faces a serious challenge because it has, by far, the largest civilian nuclear power program in the world. Other countries are under less pressure because they have temporary storage facilities that will be adequate for decades or, as in France, the countries are reprocessing their spent fuel.

Growing Concern

In 1992, South Africa, Chile, Malaysia, and Indonesia barred Japanese ships from passing through their territories to transport plutonium from reprocessing centers in Europe to civilian reactors in Japan. Concerns have also developed over the smuggling of radioactive nuclear materials from the former Soviet Union countries into Western Europe. The arrests of suspected smugglers have

TABLE 7.6
Comparison of Waste Programs

Country	Number of reactors	Nuclear-generated electricity in 1992 (approx.)	Earliest repository date	Likely geologic medium	Status	Unique features
Canada	22	15%	2025	Granite	Reviewing concept	Province of Ontario has 20 of Canada's 22 reactors
France	56	73%	2020	Granite or clay	Developing concept	Public opposition significantly slowed program
Germany	21	30%	2008	Salt	Constructing test facility	Opposition from state may affect licensing
Japan	43	27%	2030	Not selected	Searching for site	Government plans to increase use of nuclear power
Sweden	12	43%	2020	Crystalline rock	Searching for site	Waste managers plan to use long-lived copper canister
Switzerland	5	40%	2020	Crystalline rock or clay	Searching for site	Government would prefer to use an international repository
United Kingdom	37	23%	2040	Not selected	Delaying decision	Government plans lower-level waste repository
United States	109	22%	2010	Tuff	Constructing test facility	Federal law designated candidate site

Developed by GAO from data provided primarily by foreign officials. Data are as of June 1993.

119

revealed the apparent failure of the Russian government to protect its radioactive materials.

Russian scientists have disclosed that, despite its denials, for the past three decades, the former USSR secretly pumped billions of gallons of atomic waste directly into the earth. They claim this practice of injecting the waste, which violates generally accepted global standards for waste disposal, continues today. The Russians report that about half of all nuclear waste the former Soviet Union ever generated has been pumped into the ground at three sites near several major rivers — the Volga, the Ob, and the Yenisei Rivers. Russian scientists contend the practice is safe because the wastes are pumped under layers of clay and shale to cut them off from the earth's surface. Nonetheless, the wastes at one site have already leaked beyond the expected range.

In 1994, the United States and Russia agreed to allow each other access to nuclear sites where weapons are being dismantled. The United States and several newly independent countries of the former Soviet Union also pledged to reduce their nuclear arsenals as part of post-cold-war agreements.

Scientific expeditions are underway in the Arctic fishing grounds near Norway to map illegal nuclear dumping by the Soviet Union. Russian authorities acknowledge that the area was used for three decades as a dumping ground for radioactive wastes. The radioactive wastes include 18 nuclear reactors and 80 nuclear submarines.

As recently as 1993, Russia also dumped hundreds of tons of nuclear waste into the Sea of Japan. Russian officials claim that their countries lack the technology and funds to safely remove spent uranium from the reactors or storage sites. Although radiation levels in area waters are currently within normal levels, Norway considers the region a time bomb and has committed $35 million since 1994 to Russian nuclear safety. The United States also continues to provide aid to Russia to upgrade its aging nuclear reactors to make them safer.

In 1998, with 30,000 German police guarding the route against protesters and threats of violence, 60 tons of atomic waste were moved to a temporary waste site in Ahaus, in southern Germany. Germany has no site for permanent storage of nuclear waste. Furthermore, Germany's new Chancellor Gerhard Schroeder and major power companies have agreed to close Germany's power plants within 20 years.

CHAPTER VIII

ELECTRICAL POWER AND SUPPLY

Then there is electricity, the demon, the angel, the almighty physical power, the all pervading intelligence! — Nathaniel Hawthorne, *The House of Seven Gables*

Since 1879, when Thomas Edison flipped the first switch to light Menlo Park, New Jersey, the use of electrical power has become nearly universal in the United States.

DEFINING ELECTRICITY

Electricity is a property of all matter. Electrons and protons can be separated by using energy caused by friction, induction, or chemical change, which produces electric current. In 1882, Sir W. Siemens proposed the name "watt" to indicate "the practical meter-kilogram-second (mks) unit of elec-trical power, equal to one joule per second, or equal to the power developed in a circuit by a current of one ampere flowing through a potential difference of one volt." The watt has become the standard measure of electricity. The term "wattage" refers to the amount of electrical power, expressed in watts or the amount of watts required to operate a particular appliance or device. A "kilowatt" is a unit of electrical power equal to 1,000 watts, while a "kilowatt-hour" is a unit of electrical energy or work equal to that done by one kilowatt acting for one hour.

FIGURE 8.1
Power Transmission Lines

ELECTRICAL CAPACITY

The generating capacity of an electrical plant, measured in watts, indicates its ability to produce electricity. For example, a 1,000-kilowatt generator running at full capacity for one hour supplies 1,000 kilowatt-hours. A generator that operates continuously for an entire year could produce 8,760,000 kilowatt-hours of electricity (1,000 kilowatts x 24 hours/day x 365 days a year). However, no generator can operate at 100 percent capacity during an entire year because of "down-time" for routine maintenance, partial outages, or legal restrictions. On the average, about one-fourth of the potential generating capacity of an electrical plant is not available at any given time.

Electricity demands vary daily and seasonally. Therefore, the continuous operation of electrical generators is not necessary. Utilities depend on steam, nuclear, and large hydroelectric plants to meet routine demand. Auxiliary gas, turbine, internal combustion, and smaller hydroelectric plants are normally used during short periods of high demand.

THE ELECTRIC POWER SYSTEM

An electric power system has several components: **generating units** that produce electricity; **transmission lines** that carry electricity over long distances (Figure 8.1); **distribution lines** that deliver the electricity to customers; **substations** that connect the pieces of the system together; and **energy control centers** that coordinate the operation of the different parts of the sys-

tem. Figure 8.2 illustrates a simple electric system with two power plants and three distribution systems connected by a transmission network of four transmission lines. Figure 8.3 shows the flow of electricity in the United States for 1997.

SOURCES OF ELECTRICAL ENERGY

Where does this electricity come from? In the United States, coal has been and continues to be the source for most electricity, accounting for over half the electricity generated in 1997. Nuclear power was second, followed by hydroelectric and petroleum and natural gas. (See Figure 8.4.)

A record 3.5 trillion kilowatt-hours of electricity was generated in 1997. Table 8.1 shows that electricity use in the United States has increased at an average annual rate of 5.6 percent every year since 1949. Conventional steam plants, run by fossil fuels, wood, and waste, were responsible for most of the growth. In 1997, they accounted for almost two-thirds of the total electricity generated.

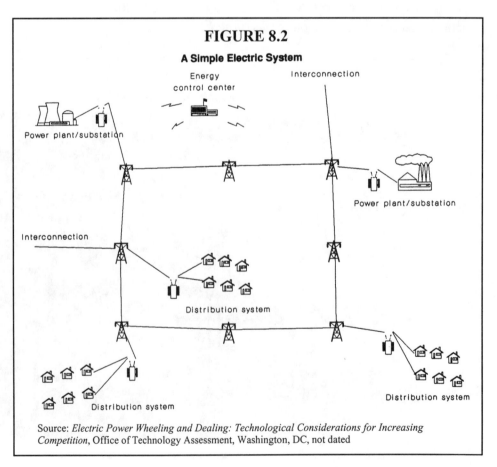

FIGURE 8.2

A Simple Electric System

Source: *Electric Power Wheeling and Dealing: Technological Considerations for Increasing Competition*, Office of Technology Assessment, Washington, DC, not dated

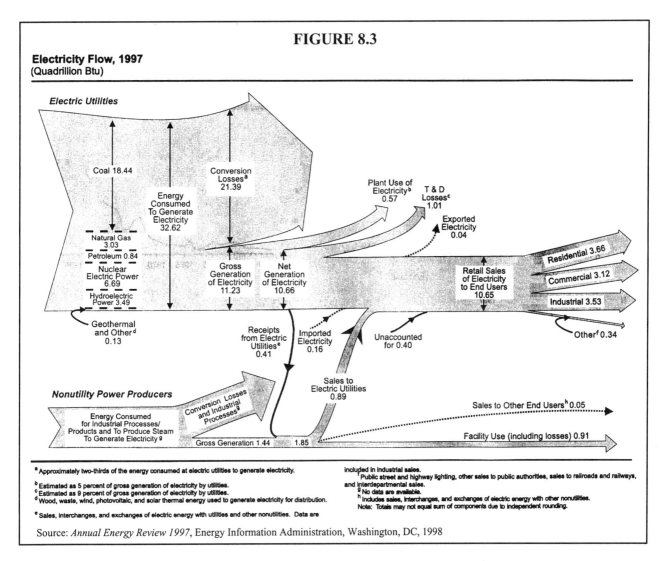

FIGURE 8.3

Electricity Flow, 1997
(Quadrillion Btu)

Electric Utilities

Coal 18.44

Energy Consumed To Generate Electricity 32.62

Natural Gas 3.03

Petroleum 0.84

Nuclear Electric Power 6.69

Hydroelectric Power 3.49

Conversion Losses[a] 21.39

Gross Generation of Electricity 11.23

Geothermal and Other[d] 0.13

Receipts from Electric Utilities[e] 0.41

Plant Use of Electricity[b] 0.57

T & D Losses[c] 1.01

Exported Electricity 0.04

Net Generation of Electricity 10.66

Imported Electricity 0.16

Unaccounted for 0.40

Retail Sales of Electricity to End Users 10.65

Residential 3.66

Commercial 3.12

Industrial 3.53

Other[f] 0.34

Nonutility Power Producers

Energy Consumed for Industrial Processes/Products and To Produce Steam To Generate Electricity [g]

Conversion Losses and Industrial Processes[g]

Gross Generation 1.44 1.85

Sales to Electric Utilities 0.89

Sales to Other End Users[h] 0.05

Facility Use (including losses) 0.91

[a] Approximately two-thirds of the energy consumed at electric utilities to generate electricity.

[b] Estimated as 5 percent of gross generation of electricity by utilities.

[c] Estimated as 9 percent of gross generation of electricity by utilities.

[d] Wood, waste, wind, photovoltaic, and solar thermal energy used to generate electricity for distribution.

[e] Sales, interchanges, and exchanges of electric energy with utilities and other nonutilities. Data are included in industrial sales.

[f] Public street and highway lighting, other sales to public authorities, sales to railroads and railways, and interdepartmental sales.

[g] No data are available.

[h] Includes sales, interchanges, and exchanges of electric energy with other nonutilities.

Note: Totals may not equal sum of components due to independent rounding.

Source: *Annual Energy Review 1997*, Energy Information Administration, Washington, DC, 1998

Coal accounted for a record 1.85 trillion kilowatt-hours, and petroleum/natural gas contributed to the production of 497 billion kilowatt-hours. Nuclear power accounted for 629 billion kilowatt-hours, while hydroelectric generation totaled 360 billion kilowatt-hours. (See Figure 8.4.) Geothermal, wood, municipal waste, wind, and solar energy produced only 6 billion kilowatt-hours in 1997.

The structure of the electric power industry is evolving, moving away from the traditional, highly regulated entities known as electric utilities and toward an environment marked by less regulation and increased competition from nonutility power producers. In 1997, 12 percent of the total net generation of electricity came from nonutility producers, such as independent power producers and cogenerators (Figure 8.5). (For more discussion of deregulation, see below.)

ELECTRICAL CONSUMPTION (END USE)

From 1949 through 1990, the industrial sector was the greatest user of electricity, but because of severe weather and economic factors, sales to the residential sector have since generally equaled those of industry. In 1997, 1,072 billion kilowatt-hours went to residential use, 1,036 billion kilowatt-hours to industrial customers, and 913 billion kilowatt-hours to commercial users. (See Table 8.2.)

THE ELECTRIC BILL

Electricity's assets are reflected in its cost to users. The price paid by a consumer includes the cost of converting the energy from its original form, such as coal, into electricity and the cost of deliv-

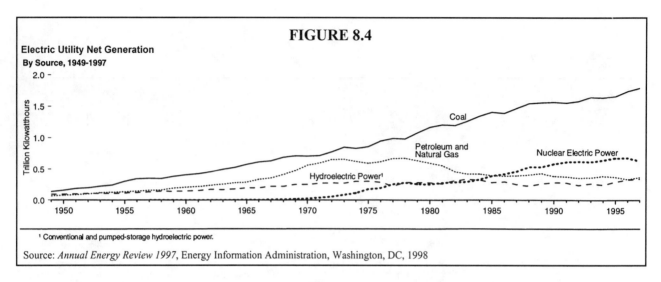

FIGURE 8.4

Electric Utility Net Generation
By Source, 1949-1997

Trillion Kilowatthours

Coal

Petroleum and Natural Gas

Hydroelectric Power¹

Nuclear Electric Power

¹ Conventional and pumped-storage hydroelectric power.

Source: *Annual Energy Review 1997*, Energy Information Administration, Washington, DC, 1998

ering it. In 1997, consumers paid an average of $24.91 per million Btu for the electric power delivered to their residences. Consumers paid an average of only $6.71 per million Btu for natural gas and an average of $10.32 per million Btu for motor gasoline for automobiles.

The unit cost of electricity is high because most of the energy purchased to generate it does not actually reach the end user but is expended in creating the electricity and moving it to the point of use. In 1997, for example, about 33 quadrillion Btu of energy were consumed to generate electricity in the United States, but only about 11 quadrillion were actually used. Most of the remaining 22 quadrillion Btu was lost as waste energy. In addition, some electricity is lost during the transmission and distribution process, when the voltage is lowered. In the end, for every three units of energy that are converted to create electricity, only about one unit actually reaches the end user.

Between 1935 and 1970, the price of electricity declined, but it began to increase during the 1970s due to the oil embargo (see Chapter II). Since 1985, the price of electricity has been dropping again because of the decline in energy resource prices (Figure 8.6). Prices vary considerably depending upon the location. In 1997, electricity was most expensive in the Middle Atlantic and New England states.

The average real price (adjusted for inflation) of electricity sold to the residential sector was 7.6

cents per kilowatt-hour in 1997, while the commercial sector paid 6.8 cents per kilowatt-hour. Industrial users pay less per kilowatt-hour (4.1 cents per kilowatt-hour in 1997) because they use huge amounts of electricity and receive volume discounts. Electricity remained, by far, the most expensive source of energy on a Btu basis.

HEALTH EFFECTS OF ELECTRICAL POWER FIELDS

Some scientists believe that exposure to electric and magnetic fields (EMFs) generated by electric power is responsible for certain cancers (particularly among children), reproductive dysfunction, birth defects, neurological disorders, and Alzheimer's disease. Some activist groups have alleged the hazards to be so great that they have called for closing schools and other public facilities near power lines and restructuring the entire power delivery system. EMFs are also cited as causing decreases in property values. Utility companies have countered that there is no proof of risk.

A 1979 Denver study found an increased incidence of leukemia among children who lived close to high-voltage lines. In 1996, the U.S. Public Health Service reviewed the scientific data on EMFs and determined that

In total, the epidemiological data on both residential and occupational exposures show a moderate risk of cancer, generally between 1.1 and 3.0, for adults and chil-

124

TABLE 8.1

Electricity Overview, 1949-1997
(Billion Kilowatthours)

Year	Net Generation			Imports [2]	Exports [2]	Losses and Unaccounted for [3]	Electric Utility Retail Sales	End Use		
	Electric Utilities	Nonutility Power Producers	Total					Nonutility Power Producers		Total
								Direct Use [4]	Sales to End Users	
1949	291	NA	NA	2	(s)	NA	255	NA	NA	NA
1950	329	NA	NA	2	(s)	NA	291	NA	NA	NA
1951	371	NA	NA	3	(s)	NA	330	NA	NA	NA
1952	399	NA	NA	2	(s)	NA	356	NA	NA	NA
1953	443	NA	NA	3	(s)	NA	396	NA	NA	NA
1954	472	NA	NA	3	(s)	NA	424	NA	NA	NA
1955	547	NA	NA	5	(s)	NA	497	NA	NA	NA
1956	601	NA	NA	5	(s)	NA	546	NA	NA	NA
1957	632	NA	NA	5	1	NA	576	NA	NA	NA
1958	645	NA	NA	4	1	NA	588	NA	NA	NA
1959	710	NA	NA	4	1	NA	647	NA	NA	NA
1960	756	NA	NA	5	1	NA	688	NA	NA	NA
1961	794	NA	NA	3	1	NA	722	NA	NA	NA
1962	855	NA	NA	3	2	NA	778	NA	NA	NA
1963	917	NA	NA	2	2	NA	833	NA	NA	NA
1964	984	NA	NA	6	4	NA	896	NA	NA	NA
1965	1,055	NA	NA	4	4	NA	954	NA	NA	NA
1966	1,144	NA	NA	4	3	NA	1,035	NA	NA	NA
1967	1,214	NA	NA	4	4	NA	1,099	NA	NA	NA
1968	1,329	NA	NA	5	4	NA	1,203	NA	NA	NA
1969	1,442	NA	NA	5	4	NA	1,314	NA	NA	NA
1970	1,532	NA	NA	6	4	NA	1,392	NA	NA	NA
1971	1,613	NA	NA	7	4	NA	1,470	NA	NA	NA
1972	1,750	NA	NA	10	3	NA	1,595	NA	NA	NA
1973	1,861	NA	NA	17	3	NA	1,713	NA	NA	NA
1974	1,867	NA	NA	15	3	NA	1,706	NA	NA	NA
1975	1,918	NA	NA	11	5	NA	1,747	NA	NA	NA
1976	2,038	NA	NA	11	2	NA	1,855	NA	NA	NA
1977	2,124	NA	NA	20	3	NA	1,948	NA	NA	NA
1978	2,206	NA	NA	21	1	NA	2,018	NA	NA	NA
1979	2,247	NA	NA	23	4	NA	2,071	NA	NA	NA
1980	2,286	NA	NA	25	4	NA	2,094	NA	NA	NA
1981	2,295	NA	NA	36	4	NA	2,147	NA	NA	NA
1982	2,241	NA	NA	33	4	NA	2,086	NA	NA	NA
1983	2,310	NA	NA	39	3	NA	2,151	NA	NA	NA
1984	2,416	NA	NA	42	3	NA	2,285	NA	NA	NA
1985	2,470	NA	NA	46	5	NA	2,324	NA	NA	NA
1986	2,487	NA	NA	41	5	NA	2,369	NA	NA	NA
1987	2,572	NA	NA	52	6	NA	2,457	NA	NA	NA
1988	2,704	NA	NA	39	7	NA	2,578	NA	NA	NA
1989	2,784	R184	2,968	26	15	232	2,647	83	18	2,747
1990	2,808	P213	3,021	23	21	206	2,713	84	20	2,817
1991	2,825	P244	3,069	31	9	218	2,762	100	11	2,873
1992	2,797	286	3,083	37	9	227	2,763	111	11	2,885
1993	2,863	314	3,197	39	11	237	2,861	111	16	2,988
1994	2,911	343	3,254	52	8	223	2,935	123	18	3,075
1995	2,995	P363	R3,358	47	9	R233	3,013	134	16	3,162
1996	R3,077	P370	R3,447	R47	R9	R238	R3,098	R135	R14	R3,247
1997	P3,126	P407	E3,533	P47	P10	E290	P3,120	E145	E14	E3,279

[2] Electricity transmitted across U.S. borders with Canada and Mexico.

[3] Energy losses that occur between the point of generation and delivery to the customer, and data collection frame differences and nonsampling error.

[4] Power generated and consumed onsite.

R=Revised. P=Preliminary. E=Estimated. NA=Not available. (s)=Less than 0.5 billion kilowatthours.

Notes: • Totals may not equal sum of components due to independent rounding.

Imports and Exports: • 1949-September 1977— unpublished Federal Power Commission data. • October 1977-1980— unpublished Economic Regulatory Administration (ERA) data. • 1981—Office of Energy Emergency Operations, "Report on Electric Energy Exchanges with Canada and Mexico for Calendar Year 1981," April 1982 (revised June 1982). • 1982 and 1983—ERA, *Electricity Exchanges Across International Borders*. • 1984-1986—ERA, *Electricity Transactions Across International Borders*. • 1987 and 1988—ERA, Form ERA-781R, "Annual Report of International Electrical Export/Import Data." • 1989-1996—Fossil Energy, Form FE-781R, "Annual Report of International Electrical Export/Import Data." • 1997—EIA estimates based on preliminary data from the National Energy Board of Canada and Department of Energy, Fossil Energy. **Losses and Unaccounted For:** Estimated as Total End Use and Exports minus Total Net Generation and Imports.

Source: *Annual Energy Review 1997*, Energy Information Administration, Washington, DC, 1998

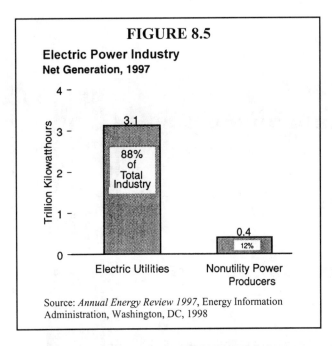

FIGURE 8.5

Electric Power Industry
Net Generation, 1997

Source: *Annual Energy Review 1997*, Energy Information
Administration, Washington, DC, 1998

dren exposed to magnetic fields. This is not extremely large relative to other known risks (for example, the smoking-related risk of approximately 10 or the asbestos-related risk of 5). However, what is unusual about magnetic field exposures is that they are universal. Virtually all of us are exposed.... This means that: (a) the observed risk may be underestimated because we cannot identify a truly unexposed comparison group; (b) because of the widespread exposure, even a small risk may result in a large number of individual cancers.

The Public Health Service concluded that "the cost of mitigation (remediation) already instituted far exceeds the health protection offered, and mitigation of other environmental risks is more important. From a cost-benefit view, only limited, low-cost mitigation should be considered."

The health effects are one of the most common concerns discussed by many people who live near existing or proposed transmission lines. If power frequency fields are human health hazards, the implications for the electric power industry could be great. It is important to remember, however, that exposure to high-voltage transmission lines is only one source of exposure to electrical fields. Exposure to appliances, lighting fixtures, home wiring, microwaves, televisions, electric blankets, and computers are more common and could play a more important role in determining public health risks relating to electricity.

OUTLOOK FOR THE ELECTRIC INDUSTRY

The Energy Information Administration of the U.S. Department of Energy forecasts continued electricity sales growth of between 2.1 and 2.6 percent annually. This means that more energy in the forms of fossil fuels and renewable sources will be needed by electricity producers. Electricity growth has been especially high in the western and southern United States, reflecting the higher population growth in those parts of the country.

Will Future Supply Meet Demand?

One reason for the growth in electric power is that electricity is increasingly taking over the tasks formerly done with coal, natural gas, or human muscle — manufacturing steel, assembling cars, or milking cows. Electricity is also being used extensively in growing technological fields that almost exclusively use electricity, such as the computer industry. Also, the use of air conditioning continues to increase. Many experts are unclear where the new electricity supplies will come from, given the public concern about environmental hazards from burning fossil fuel and the uncertainty among electric utility companies about the financial risk in building new power plants.

Electric Utility Planning for the Future

Electric industry officials warn that planning is not keeping pace with expected electric use. The Edison Electric Institute, the utility trade association, estimates that by 2000 the nation will need new electrical generating capacity equal to 72 large nuclear plants, but that only 37 percent of that amount is now under construction, most of it coal-fired. Coal, however, poses problems for the environment. "If we don't reconcile the demand for

126

TABLE 8.2

Electric Utility Retail Sales of Electricity by End-Use Sector, 1949-1997

(Billion Kilowatthours)

Year	Residential	Commercial	Industrial	Other [1]	Total
1949	67	45	123	20	255
1950	72	51	146	22	291
1951	83	57	166	24	330
1952	94	62	176	24	356
1953	104	67	199	26	396
1954	116	72	208	27	424
1955	128	79	260	29	497
1956	143	87	286	30	546
1957	157	94	294	31	576
1958	169	100	287	32	588
1959	185	112	315	36	647
1960	201	131	324	32	688
1961	214	138	337	32	722
1962	233	153	360	32	778
1963	251	171	377	34	833
1964	272	187	405	32	896
1965	291	200	429	34	954
1966	317	218	464	37	1,035
1967	340	234	485	40	1,099
1968	382	258	521	42	1,203
1969	427	282	559	46	1,314
1970	466	307	571	48	1,392
1971	500	329	589	51	1,470
1972	539	359	641	56	1,595
1973	579	388	686	59	1,713
1974	578	385	685	58	1,706
1975	588	403	688	68	1,747
1976	606	425	754	70	1,855
1977	645	447	786	71	1,948
1978	674	461	809	73	2,018
1979	683	473	842	73	2,071
1980	717	488	815	74	2,094
1981	722	514	826	85	2,147
1982	730	526	745	86	2,086
1983	751	544	776	80	2,151
1984	780	583	838	85	2,286
1985	794	606	837	87	2,324
1986	819	631	831	89	2,369
1987	850	660	858	88	2,457
1988	893	699	896	90	2,578
1989	906	726	926	90	2,647
1990	924	751	946	92	2,713
1991	955	766	947	94	2,762
1992	936	761	973	93	2,763
1993	995	795	977	95	2,861
1994	1,008	820	1,008	98	2,935
1995	1,043	863	1,013	95	3,013
1996	R1,082	R888	R1,030	R98	R3,098
1997P	1,072	913	1,036	99	P3,120

[1] "Other" is public street and highway lighting, other sales to public authorities, sales to railroads and railways, and interdepartmental sales.
R=Revised. P=Preliminary.

Notes: • Totals may not equal sum of components due to independent rounding.

Sources: • 1949-September 1977—Federal Power Commission, Form FPC-5, "Monthly Statement of Electric Operating Revenue and Income." • October 1977-February 1980—Federal Energy Regulatory Commission (FERC), Form FPC-5, "Monthly Statement of Electric Operating Revenue and Income." • March 1980-1982—FERC, Form FPC-5, "Electric Utility Company Monthly Statement." • 1983—Energy Information Administration (EIA), Form EIA-826, "Electric Utility Company Monthly Statement." • 1984-1996—EIA, Form EIA-861, "Annual Electric Utility Report." • 1997—EIA, Form EIA-826, "Monthly Electric Utility Sales and Revenue Report with State Distributions."

Source: *Annual Energy Review 1997*, Energy Information Administration, Washington, DC, 1998

electricity with our environment ... we'll be in deep trouble," claims a spokesperson for the Edison Institute.

The electric power industry intends to use several methods for meeting the growth in demand. Through the 1990s, most utility companies should be able to keep up with demand by already planned construction. The utility companies also plan to increase their use of renewable sources of power (see Chapter IX) and import more power from Canada and Mexico. However, electrical utility companies will have to construct about 234 gigawatts of capacity by 2010 beyond what is currently reported as planned. (A gigawatt is one billion watts of electrical energy.)

To do this, they will have to rely heavily on fossil fuels, such as natural gas and coal. However, growing concerns about acid rain and global warming could result in tightened environmental emission standards, which may well have an impact on electrical utility expansion decisions. Continued advances in solar and wind turbine technology could make renewable sources of electrical power not only more environmentally acceptable, but also more economical in the future.

Some energy experts think that increased electrical efficiency is an alternative to new construction or to burning more fossil fuels in existing plants. The now-defunct Office of Technological Assessment pointed out that pre-1988 electric water heaters used about 4,500 kilowatt-hours a year, while the average for those sold after 1988 was only 4,000 kilowatt-hours. The best heaters today

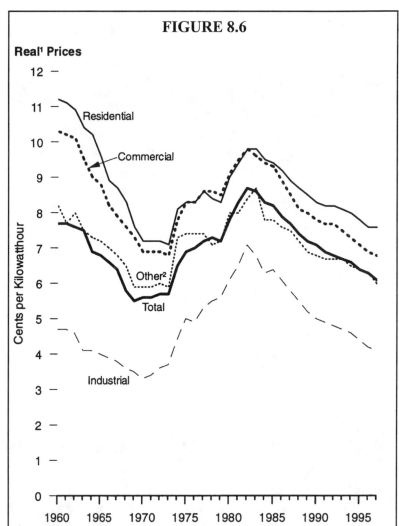

FIGURE 8.6

¹ In chained (1992) dollars, calculated by using gross domestic product implicit price deflators.

² Public street and highway lighting, other sales to public authorities, sales to railroads and railways, and interdepartmental sales.

Source: *Annual Energy Review 1997*, Energy Information Administration, Washington, DC, 1998

FIGURE 8.7

Population, gross domestic product, and electricity sales growth, 1960-2020 (index, 1960 = 1)

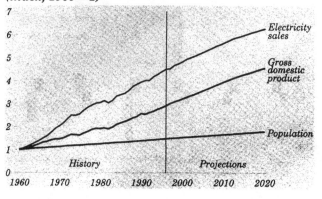

Source: *Annual Energy Outlook 1998*, Energy Information Administration, Washington, DC, 1997

128

use only about 2,000 kilowatt-hours, and further research and development could lower electric consumption to only 1,000 kilowatt-hours. If millions of American homes switched to more efficient water heaters and other types of large appliances, the global and regional environment would benefit, along with U.S. energy security. For more information on energy conservation, see Chapter X.

The issue of electric growth is important. If the industry underestimates the future needs for electricity, it could mean brownouts or blackouts (power shortages or losses). On the other hand, excessive projection of the nation's needs could mean billions of dollars spent on unneeded equipment.

However, the Energy Information Administration Agency of the U.S. Department of Energy predicts slower growth for U.S. electricity sales. Historically, the demand for electricity has been related to economic growth. This positive relationship will continue, but at a slower rate. During the 1960s, electricity demand grew by more than 7 percent per year. In the 1970s and 1980s, the ratio of electricity demand growth declined to 1.5 and 1.0, respectively. Several factors led to this occurrence, including increased market saturation of electric appliances and improvements in efficiency. (See Figure 8.7.)

DEREGULATION OF ELECTRIC UTILITIES

Regulated for decades as "natural monopolies," much like the railroad and telecommunications industries, electric utilities are in the midst of a radical shift toward increased competition. In 1978, Congress passed the Public Utilities Regulatory Policy Act (PURPA; PL 95-617), which required that utilities buy electricity from private companies when that was a lower cost alternative to building their own power plants. The federal Energy Policy Act of 1992 (PL 102-486) gave greater access to the market for other generators, resulting in a flurry of activity in state and federal legislatures as a host of interest groups debate regulatory, economic, energy, and environmental poli-

cies. More than half the state public utility commissions are conducting proceedings and designing rules related to competition in the electric utility industry.

In the past, utilities were assured a fair rate of return on investment. During the transition to competition, many electric utilities have been downsizing, consolidating, and merging to reduce costs.

The Energy Information Administration of the U.S. Department of Energy predicts that in most regions of the United States, competition in the electrical generation business could reduce average electricity prices for end-use consumers. Many states began allowing choice as of 1998. In California, the first state to offer options to consumers in March 1998, a cautious public was bombarded with aggressive sales pitches and confusing claims. Most residents have remained with their original utility provider. The move to competition may mean that at least 25 million customers around the country can choose their electric company. By 2002, at least three times that number will likely be selecting their electricity provider.

INTERNATIONAL ELECTRICITY SUPPLY AND CONSUMPTION

Electricity Supply

In 1996, almost 13 trillion kilowatt-hours of electricity were generated around the world. (See Table 8.3.) North America accounted for 32 percent; Western Europe, 20 percent; Eastern Europe and the former USSR, 12 percent; and the Far East and Oceania, 25 percent. In 1996, fossil fuel electricity (coal, gas, and oil) production accounted for 62 percent of all electricity generated; hydroelectric, 19 percent; nuclear, 18 percent; and geothermal and other sources, less than 1 percent of the world's total net electricity production.

Electricity Consumption

World total electricity consumption continued to increase, rising from 9,421 billion kilowatt-hours

TABLE 8.3

World Net Generation of Electricity by Type, 1994-1996
(Billion Kilowatthours)

Region and Country	Fossil Fuel 1994	Fossil Fuel 1995	Fossil Fuel 1996 P	Nuclear Electric Power 1994	Nuclear Electric Power 1995	Nuclear Electric Power 1996 P	Hydroelectric Power¹ 1994	Hydroelectric Power¹ 1995	Hydroelectric Power¹ 1996 P	Total² 1994	Total² 1995	Total² 1996 P
North America	R 2,497.6	2,515.0	2,570.5	R 747.0	774.4	770.3	R 601.4	666.2	724.7	R 3,932.6	4,039.7	4,151.4
Canada	111.1	112.5	111.7	R 102.4	93.0	88.1	324.7	330.7	349.2	R 538.4	536.2	549.2
Mexico	110.5	104.2	110.3	4.0	8.0	7.5	19.8	27.3	31.1	139.7	144.9	154.4
United States	R 2,275.2	2,297.5	2,347.7	640.5	673.4	674.7	R 256.8	308.3	344.4	R 3,253.8	3,357.8	3,447.1
Other	0.8	0.8	0.8	0.0	0.0	0.0	0.0	0.0	0.0	0.8	0.8	0.8
Central and South America	134.5	139.3	144.9	7.9	9.5	9.2	R 453.2	479.5	505.6	R 604.0	637.0	669.1
Argentina	28.7	28.9	29.1	7.8	7.1	6.9	33.3	33.4	33.4	R 69.8	69.4	64.7
Brazil	R 9.1	10.6	12.5	0.1	2.4	2.3	240.3	251.4	263.1	R 256.6	271.8	285.7
Colombia	10.4	10.4	10.4	0.0	0.0	0.0	32.0	33.9	43.4	42.4	44.3	53.7
Venezuela	R 20.4	18.1	15.0	0.0	0.0	0.0	50.9	55.0	58.0	71.3	73.2	73.0
Other	R 65.9	71.2	78.0	0.0	0.0	0.0	96.8	105.8	112.5	164.0	178.4	192.0
Western Europe	R 1,170.8	1,218.2	1,245.2	771.9	789.9	828.0	R 497.2	501.0	483.5	R 2,448.1	2,518.3	2,566.4
Austria	15.4	16.9	18.1	0.0	0.0	0.0	35.3	36.7	34.1	50.7	53.6	52.2
Finland	32.3	29.8	36.9	18.5	18.3	18.8	11.7	12.8	11.7	62.5	60.9	67.5
France	R 33.2	37.8	41.9	342.0	358.4	376.2	76.5	70.6	62.1	452.2	467.3	480.8
Germany	331.9	334.9	341.1	143.6	146.4	153.5	18.3	19.6	18.0	495.7	503.2	515.1
Italy	169.5	184.0	181.4	0.0	0.0	0.0	44.2	37.4	41.4	217.3	225.0	226.7
Netherlands	70.8	71.8	75.4	3.8	3.8	4.0	0.1	0.1	0.1	74.9	76.0	79.8
Norway	0.6	0.7	0.8	0.0	0.0	0.0	110.4	120.1	102.6	111.0	120.8	103.4
Spain	R 72.5	81.6	70.6	52.5	52.7	53.5	27.9	22.9	39.1	153.2	157.4	163.5
Sweden	9.7	9.4	13.2	69.5	66.4	71.1	58.5	66.3	50.7	137.8	142.2	135.2
Switzerland	2.0	2.1	2.2	23.1	23.7	23.7	38.7	34.8	28.9	63.8	60.6	54.8
Turkey	R 44.8	47.6	51.1	0.0	0.0	0.0	30.3	35.2	40.0	75.2	82.9	91.2
United Kingdom	R 216.4	224.0	223.8	76.0	76.6	81.5	5.0	5.2	4.0	297.7	306.1	309.7
Other	171.4	177.7	188.7	42.9	43.8	45.5	40.3	39.3	50.9	256.0	262.3	286.8
Eastern Europe and Former U.S.S.R.	R 1,124.9	1,113.6	1,091.3	217.7	224.3	249.8	R 272.4	270.5	247.8	R 1,615.0	1,608.4	1,589.1
Czech Republic	41.3	43.6	46.2	12.3	11.6	12.2	1.4	2.0	1.8	55.1	57.2	60.2
Kazakhstan	53.8	54.8	50.0	0.4	0.1	0.1	9.1	8.2	7.5	63.2	63.2	57.6
Poland	123.7	127.0	130.8	0.0	0.0	0.0	3.7	3.8	3.9	127.4	130.8	134.7
Romania	39.6	40.0	42.7	0.0	0.0	0.9	12.9	16.5	15.6	52.5	56.5	59.2
Russia	R 583.7	569.6	549.0	92.9	94.3	103.3	174.2	174.5	153.1	850.9	838.5	805.6
Ukraine	R 120.3	120.6	115.0	65.4	67.0	76.0	12.2	10.1	9.5	197.8	197.6	200.5
Other	162.5	158.0	157.6	46.8	51.2	57.3	58.8	55.4	56.4	268.1	264.6	271.3
Middle East	R 292.5	301.6	307.8	0.0	0.0	0.0	15.7	15.7	15.9	R 308.1	317.3	323.7
Iran	67.4	69.4	72.0	0.0	0.0	0.0	7.4	7.5	7.5	74.8	76.8	79.5
Saudi Arabia	91.0	93.9	95.0	0.0	0.0	0.0	0.0	0.0	0.0	91.0	93.9	95.0
Other	R 134.1	138.3	140.8	0.0	0.0	0.0	8.3	8.2	8.4	142.3	146.5	149.2
Africa	R 270.7	276.5	286.8	9.7	11.3	11.8	56.4	56.4	57.7	R 337.0	344.6	356.7
Egypt	R 36.4	35.8	35.0	0.0	0.0	0.0	10.6	10.7	11.0	47.1	46.5	46.0
South Africa	R 160.0	164.4	173.9	9.7	11.3	11.8	1.1	0.5	1.3	170.7	176.3	186.9
Other	74.3	76.3	78.0	0.0	0.0	0.0	44.6	45.1	45.4	119.2	121.8	123.7
Far East and Oceania	R 2,171.0	2,283.2	2,388.1	R 363.6	393.6	410.9	R 449.3	494.7	491.0	R 2,995.7	3,184.6	3,304.2
Australia	R 142.1	148.0	151.9	0.0	0.0	0.0	16.2	15.7	14.7	R 158.3	163.8	166.7
China	R 701.2	756.1	805.3	13.5	12.4	13.6	165.1	184.9	181.3	879.8	953.4	1,000.2
India	R 290.4	315.7	325.0	4.7	6.5	7.4	70.4	70.9	72.0	365.5	393.2	404.5
Indonesia	48.5	53.2	55.0	0.0	0.0	0.0	11.1	10.3	10.0	61.1	65.2	64.8
Japan	R 580.4	568.0	583.1	255.7	276.7	283.0	66.6	81.4	79.0	904.7	929.1	948.6
South Korea	96.1	105.4	118.8	R 55.7	63.7	70.2	4.1	5.4	5.1	155.9	174.5	194.2
Taiwan	76.6	84.2	89.6	R 33.5	33.9	36.3	8.8	8.8	8.9	118.8	126.9	134.9
Thailand	65.7	72.3	75.0	0.0	0.0	0.0	4.5	6.6	7.0	70.2	79.0	82.0
Other	170.0	180.3	184.9	0.6	0.5	0.3	102.7	110.5	112.9	281.5	299.6	306.5
World	R 7,661.8	7,847.4	8,035.2	2,117.8	2,203.0	2,280.0	R 2,345.5	2,484.0	2,526.2	12,240.6	12,649.9	12,960.7

¹ Excludes pumped storage, except for the United States.
² Geothermal, biofuels, wind, photovoltaic, solar thermal generation, hydrogen, sulfur, batteries, and chemicals are included in total.
R=Revised. P=Preliminary.
Notes: • Data include both electric utility and non-electric utility sources. • Totals may not equal sum of components due to independent rounding.

Source: *Annual Energy Review 1997*, Energy Information Administration, Washington, DC, 1998

TABLE 8.4

World Total Net Electricity Consumption, 1987 - 1996

(Billion Kilowatthours)

Region Country	1987	1988	1989	1990	1991	1992	1993	1994	1995	1996 [1]
North America										
Canada.....................................	404.0	424.8	438.8	435.1	438.3	443.4	449.8	457.0	462.1	473.1
Mexico.....................................	95.3	100.3	108.1	107.1	110.5	114.1	119.2	128.9	133.7	143.6
United States..[2]......................	2,457.3	2,578.1	2,646.8	2,712.6	2,762.0	2,885.4	2,988.5	3,075.6	3,163.3	3,242.7
Other.......................................	0.6	0.6	0.6	0.7	0.7	0.7	0.7	0.7	0.7	0.7
Total..................................	**2,957.2**	**3,103.8**	**3,194.4**	**3,255.4**	**3,311.5**	**3,443.6**	**3,558.2**	**3,662.2**	**3,759.8**	**3,860.2**
Central & South America										
Argentina................................	54.3	52.6	47.5	48.5	52.1	57.0	62.5	66.1	66.6	63.0
Bolivia.....................................	1.4	1.7	1.8	1.9	2.1	2.2	2.2	2.6	2.7	2.7
Brazil.......................................	203.8	214.9	225.1	228.6	242.1	246.3	259.4	271.7	288.4	303.2
Chile..	14.2	15.3	16.0	16.6	18.1	20.3	21.8	22.9	27.0	33.3
Colombia.................................	28.2	30.2	31.7	33.1	33.5	32.8	36.8	39.7	41.5	50.1
Costa Rica..............................	3.0	3.1	3.2	3.4	3.5	3.7	4.0	4.3	4.2	4.6
Cuba..	11.9	12.7	13.3	12.8	11.1	9.7	9.7	9.6	9.8	9.9
Dominican Republic.................	4.9	4.0	3.0	3.4	3.6	5.2	5.5	5.7	6.1	6.2
Ecuador...................................	4.9	5.1	5.2	5.8	6.3	6.5	6.8	7.4	7.6	7.9
El Salvador.............................	1.8	1.9	1.9	2.1	2.1	2.3	2.7	3.0	3.0	3.3
Guatemala...............................	1.8	2.0	2.1	2.1	2.3	2.5	2.8	2.9	2.9	2.9
Honduras.................................	1.2	1.8	1.9	2.1	2.1	2.1	2.3	2.5	2.5	2.5
Jamaica...................................	1.7	1.7	1.9	2.2	1.9	1.9	3.3	4.2	5.1	5.7
Nicaragua................................	1.3	1.3	1.4	1.4	1.4	1.4	1.4	1.5	1.5	1.5
Panama....................................	2.6	2.5	2.5	2.6	2.8	2.9	3.1	3.2	3.3	3.2
Peru..	12.8	12.3	12.4	12.6	13.2	12.0	13.5	14.5	14.7	15.1
Puerto Rico.............................	12.0	12.6	12.5	13.4	13.8	14.4	14.5	15.6	16.7	17.0
Suriname..................................	0.6	0.8	1.2	1.4	1.4	1.4	1.4	1.5	1.5	1.5
Trinidad and Tobago................	3.1	3.1	3.0	3.1	3.3	3.5	3.4	3.6	3.7	3.7
Uruguay...................................	4.0	4.3	4.1	5.6	4.6	4.8	5.1	5.3	7.5	7.6
Venezuela................................	48.8	52.5	52.0	53.7	54.5	59.6	64.3	66.0	67.9	67.7
Virgin Islands, U.S..................	0.8	0.8	0.8	0.9	0.9	0.9	0.9	0.9	0.9	0.9
Other.......................................	6.7	6.6	5.4	5.8	6.0	6.4	7.1	7.2	7.2	8.5
Total..................................	**426.0**	**443.8**	**450.1**	**463.3**	**482.7**	**499.9**	**534.4**	**561.8**	**592.4**	**622.3**
Western Europe										
Austria.....................................	30.0	40.8	42.1	44.2	46.9	46.6	45.8	46.4	47.4	49.3
Belgium....................................	52.7	54.7	56.3	58.1	60.8	63.0	63.9	66.9	68.8	70.3
Denmark...................................	28.1	28.2	29.2	29.4	29.8	30.7	30.7	30.2	31.4	31.7
Finland.....................................	52.9	48.3	56.5	59.0	58.8	59.7	61.8	64.7	63.7	66.4
France......................................	301.5	307.9	314.8	324.3	346.9	353.3	354.5	357.5	364.8	378.1
Germany...................................	--	--	--	--	469.9	463.3	459.8	463.3	472.8	473.4
Germany, East..........................	109.5	111.1	110.4	97.7	--	--	--	--	--	--
Germany, West.........................	388.7	397.0	379.8	386.9	--	--	--	--	--	--
Greece.....................................	26.4	28.0	29.6	31.2	32.0	33.1	34.2	35.7	37.0	38.6
Iceland.....................................	3.9	4.1	4.2	4.1	4.1	4.2	4.3	4.4	4.6	4.7
Ireland.....................................	11.0	11.1	11.8	12.5	13.1	13.8	14.2	14.8	15.4	16.5
Italy...	197.9	193.0	216.4	222.3	228.0	231.9	233.5	239.7	246.8	248.1
Luxembourg.............................	4.1	4.3	4.4	4.5	4.8	4.5	4.6	5.0	5.5	5.4
Netherlands..............................	63.5	66.7	68.8	71.1	74.1	76.3	77.7	80.3	82.1	84.8
Norway.....................................	95.3	95.2	94.7	96.0	99.0	99.1	102.4	103.1	105.6	105.1
Portugal...................................	21.0	21.3	23.8	25.2	26.5	27.5	27.7	28.8	30.4	31.7
Spain.......................................	117.3	119.3	128.1	133.4	136.4	139.0	138.8	144.3	150.9	153.1
Sweden....................................	127.7	128.2	128.8	129.5	130.8	129.5	130.4	128.5	130.6	131.9
Switzerland..............................	42.5	43.7	45.9	47.0	48.1	47.9	47.5	47.6	49.1	49.9
Turkey......................................	37.7	43.4	43.2	50.6	54.0	60.0	65.7	69.4	76.4	84.8
United Kingdom........................	273.9	280.5	285.9	286.2	293.5	293.2	291.7	293.8	301.0	304.6
Former Yugoslavia...................	72.2	72.9	73.0	72.8	65.5	--	--	--	--	--
Bosnia and Herzegovina.........	--	--	--	--	--	10.9	10.9	1.9	2.2	2.3
Croatia.....................................	--	--	--	--	--	10.9	10.7	11.1	11.5	13.9
Macedonia, TFYR....................	--	--	--	--	--	5.6	5.2	5.0	5.4	5.6
Serbia and Montenegro...........	--	--	--	--	--	33.0	29.6	30.7	33.0	33.5
Slovenia...................................	--	--	--	--	--	8.7	8.8	11.1	9.5	10.4
Other.......................................	1.1	1.2	1.2	1.3	1.4	1.5	1.5	1.6	1.6	1.6
Total..................................	**2,058.5**	**2,100.8**	**2,149.0**	**2,187.4**	**2,224.4**	**2,247.2**	**2,256.0**	**2,285.9**	**2,347.4**	**2,395.9**

See footnotes at end of table.

(continued)

131

TABLE 8.4 (Continued)

World Total Net Electricity Consumption, 1987 - 1996
(Billion Kilowatthours)

Region Country	1987	1988	1989	1990	1991	1992	1993	1994	1995	1996 [1]
Eastern Europe & Former U.S.S.R.										
Albania.................................	3.5	3.1	3.2	3.2	2.8	2.6	3.1	3.6	4.1	4.9
Bulgaria................................	42.4	43.8	44.4	40.5	36.3	33.9	33.6	33.5	36.7	38.2
Former Czechoslovakia..........	78.7	79.7	81.1	80.7	76.4	70.9	--	--	--	--
Czech Republic.....................	--	--	--	--	--	--	49.4	50.9	53.6	55.9
Slovakia...............................	--	--	--	--	--	--	23.9	24.2	23.9	24.5
Hungary...............................	36.7	36.9	37.0	36.2	33.7	31.1	31.7	31.5	32.3	33.0
Poland.................................	129.4	130.9	129.1	119.9	115.3	111.9	114.8	115.9	118.9	122.9
Romania...............................	70.4	73.5	74.7	66.2	55.5	52.1	51.0	49.6	52.9	55.9
Former U.S.S.R.....................	1,427.9	1,459.9	1,491.0	1,488.4	1,475.3	--	--	--	--	--
Armenia...............................	--	--	--	--	--	8.3	5.7	5.1	4.7	7.1
Azerbaijan............................	--	--	--	--	--	16.8	16.9	15.8	15.3	15.1
Belarus................................	--	--	--	--	--	39.3	35.2	31.4	29.1	29.0
Estonia................................	--	--	--	--	--	7.1	6.6	6.9	6.8	7.2
Georgia................................	--	--	--	--	--	11.3	9.9	7.1	7.0	6.5
Kazakhstan...........................	--	--	--	--	--	86.2	83.4	64.9	66.1	60.3
Kyrgyzstan............................	--	--	--	--	--	8.8	9.3	9.4	10.9	10.0
Latvia..................................	--	--	--	--	--	7.5	6.1	5.9	5.9	6.0
Lithuania..............................	--	--	--	--	--	11.2	10.3	9.8	8.8	8.6
Moldova...............................	--	--	--	--	--	9.8	6.9	7.8	7.8	6.2
Russia.................................	--	--	--	--	--	879.9	830.6	770.9	760.2	731.6
Tajikistan.............................	--	--	--	--	--	16.3	15.1	14.8	14.7	11.6
Turkmenistan.........................	--	--	--	--	--	8.6	7.9	6.6	6.7	6.5
Ukraine................................	--	--	--	--	--	216.7	200.6	183.5	181.9	186.9
Uzbekistan............................	--	--	--	--	--	44.2	40.4	43.7	42.1	40.9
Total..................................	1,789.1	1,827.7	1,860.5	1,835.1	1,795.3	1,674.4	1,592.3	1,492.8	1,490.5	1,468.7
Middle East										
Bahrain................................	2.9	3.0	3.1	3.1	3.1	3.1	3.8	4.0	4.2	4.4
Cyprus.................................	1.3	1.5	1.6	1.7	1.8	2.1	2.3	2.3	2.2	2.0
Iran....................................	33.4	41.2	42.6	51.9	56.4	60.4	66.9	69.5	71.4	73.9
Iraq....................................	21.2	24.0	25.3	25.5	18.2	22.1	23.0	24.5	25.4	25.7
Israel..................................	14.9	16.5	17.5	17.9	18.4	21.2	22.4	24.4	25.1	25.8
Jordan.................................	1.8	2.3	3.0	3.2	3.4	4.0	4.3	4.6	4.9	5.1
Kuwait.................................	16.1	17.5	18.8	16.5	9.5	14.9	15.9	20.2	21.1	21.4
Lebanon...............................	4.8	4.1	2.7	1.7	2.2	3.5	4.4	4.6	5.2	5.6
Oman..................................	3.4	3.9	4.1	4.7	4.8	5.5	6.4	6.9	7.2	7.4
Qatar..................................	3.9	3.9	4.1	4.2	4.1	4.5	4.9	5.1	5.0	4.8
Saudi Arabia.........................	47.1	53.2	57.3	60.4	64.4	68.8	76.4	84.6	87.3	88.3
Syria...................................	7.1	8.6	9.2	14.0	15.2	16.6	16.1	17.5	17.6	17.9
United Arab Emirates..............	11.9	13.0	13.6	14.9	15.1	15.3	15.4	16.5	16.7	16.7
Yemen.................................	1.1	1.5	1.5	1.5	1.5	1.6	1.7	1.7	1.7	1.8
Total..................................	170.9	194.2	204.4	221.3	218.2	243.8	263.8	286.5	295.1	301.0
Africa										
Algeria................................	12.1	13.1	13.4	14.0	14.5	15.1	15.8	16.3	16.8	16.8
Angola.................................	1.6	1.6	1.7	1.7	1.7	1.7	1.7	1.7	1.7	1.7
Cameroon.............................	2.2	2.4	2.5	2.5	2.5	2.5	2.5	2.5	2.5	2.5
Congo (Kinshasa)...................	4.8	4.8	6.3	5.0	4.7	5.4	4.1	4.1	4.6	5.8
Cote d'Ivoire (Ivory Coast)........	2.2	2.1	2.9	2.1	1.6	1.7	1.7	1.7	1.7	1.7
Egypt..................................	34.2	32.9	35.1	34.9	39.3	39.8	42.9	43.8	43.2	42.8
Ghana.................................	4.1	4.2	4.6	5.2	5.4	5.4	5.4	5.4	5.4	5.5
Kenya.................................	2.4	2.7	2.8	2.9	3.1	3.1	3.4	3.5	3.6	3.7
Libya..................................	13.6	14.0	14.1	14.7	14.8	14.8	14.9	15.6	15.7	15.8
Morocco...............................	7.2	7.9	8.0	8.1	8.7	9.5	10.0	10.6	11.2	11.7
Nigeria................................	9.9	10.3	11.3	13.5	12.7	13.1	12.7	12.7	12.7	12.8
South Africa..........................	132.1	137.8	142.7	143.8	146.1	144.6	149.4	156.2	161.0	168.3
Tunisia................................	4.0	4.3	4.4	5.1	5.3	5.7	5.8	6.1	6.7	7.1
Zambia................................	6.4	6.3	4.8	5.7	5.7	5.8	5.8	5.8	5.6	5.8
Zimbabwe.............................	8.1	8.3	8.4	10.2	9.6	9.7	9.0	9.4	9.5	10.2
Other..................................	13.4	13.7	14.4	16.0	16.8	17.1	18.7	18.2	18.4	19.4
Total..................................	258.2	266.4	277.1	285.4	292.6	294.9	303.5	313.5	320.4	331.7

See footnotes at end of table.

(continued)

TABLE 8.4 (Continued)

World Total Net Electricity Consumption, 1987 - 1996

(Billion Kilowatthours)

Region Country	1987	1988	1989	1990	1991	1992	1993	1994	1995	1996 [1]
Far East & Oceania										
Afghanistan	1.1	1.0	1.0	1.0	1.0	0.8	0.7	0.8	0.7	0.6
American Samoa	0.1	0.1	0.1	0.1	0.1	0.1	0.1	0.1	0.1	0.1
Australia	113.5	121.4	128.8	135.6	137.6	140.2	143.8	147.2	152.3	155.0
Bangladesh	5.2	6.0	6.5	7.1	7.8	8.4	8.7	9.3	10.2	10.5
Bhutan	(s)	0.1	(s)	(s)	0.1	0.1	0.1	0.1	0.1	0.1
Brunei	0.9	1.0	1.0	1.1	1.2	1.3	1.3	1.3	1.4	1.4
Burma	2.1	2.0	2.2	2.2	2.4	2.7	3.0	3.2	3.4	3.5
Cambodia	0.1	0.1	0.1	0.1	0.1	0.2	0.2	0.2	0.2	0.2
China	440.7	483.1	518.2	550.9	600.9	670.6	744.1	816.0	881.4	924.9
Fiji	0.4	0.4	0.4	0.4	0.4	0.4	0.4	0.5	0.5	0.5
French Polynesia	0.2	0.2	0.2	0.3	0.3	0.3	0.3	0.3	0.3	0.3
Guam	0.7	0.7	0.7	0.7	0.7	0.7	0.7	0.7	0.7	0.7
Hong Kong	19.4	20.9	22.2	23.5	24.8	25.7	27.3	25.4	28.8	29.5
India	194.5	214.4	238.1	257.1	280.6	295.1	316.9	341.3	367.2	377.7
Indonesia	32.7	36.4	35.9	43.2	45.5	48.6	52.1	56.8	60.6	62.1
Japan	635.8	664.2	697.9	749.8	775.8	782.4	790.8	841.3	864.0	882.2
Korea, North	45.2	47.8	48.2	48.2	48.2	34.3	34.3	33.4	32.5	31.6
Korea, South	64.9	75.0	83.2	94.9	104.5	115.2	127.1	145.0	162.3	180.6
Laos	0.2	0.1	0.2	0.3	0.2	0.2	0.3	0.2	0.2	0.2
Macau	0.6	0.6	0.7	0.8	0.9	1.0	1.1	1.2	1.5	1.4
Malaysia	15.3	17.1	19.2	22.3	25.0	28.1	31.4	35.4	41.1	44.6
Mongolia	2.8	3.0	3.3	3.1	2.9	2.7	2.3	2.5	2.7	2.5
Nepal	0.5	0.6	0.6	0.7	0.8	0.9	0.8	0.9	0.9	0.9
New Caledonia	0.9	1.1	1.1	1.0	1.0	1.0	1.0	1.0	1.0	1.1
New Zealand	26.5	27.2	28.1	28.8	29.7	28.4	30.2	32.1	32.9	33.0
Pakistan	30.0	34.5	36.0	39.2	42.3	46.2	49.1	50.9	53.7	55.2
Papua New Guinea	1.6	1.5	1.6	1.6	1.6	1.6	1.6	1.6	1.6	1.6
Philippines	19.3	21.1	22.9	22.7	22.8	23.0	23.1	27.0	29.6	29.9
Samoa	(s)	(s)	(s)	(s)	(s)	0.1	0.1	0.1	0.1	0.1
Singapore	10.3	11.4	12.3	13.7	14.5	15.3	16.5	18.0	19.3	19.5
Sri Lanka	2.5	2.6	2.6	2.9	3.1	2.9	3.7	4.0	4.4	4.7
Taiwan	60.9	66.6	74.6	80.1	87.7	93.5	102.2	110.5	118.0	125.5
Thailand	26.8	30.3	35.1	41.2	46.8	53.0	58.6	65.8	74.0	76.8
U.S. Pacific Islands	0.1	0.2	0.2	0.2	0.2	0.2	0.2	0.2	0.2	0.2
Vietnam	5.4	6.0	7.0	7.9	8.4	8.8	9.9	11.6	13.6	13.8
Other	0.1	0.1	0.1	0.1	0.1	0.1	0.2	0.2	0.2	0.2
Total	1,761.2	1,898.6	2,030.4	2,182.9	2,320.0	2,434.1	2,584.0	2,786.0	2,961.7	3,072.9
World Total	9,421.1	9,835.2	10,165.8	10,430.7	10,644.8	10,837.8	11,092.2	11,388.7	11,767.3	12,052.7

[1] Preliminary.

[2] There is a discontinuity in this time series between 1988 and 1990 due to the expanded coverage of non-electric utility use of renewable energy beginning in 1989 and biofuels electric power beginning in 1990.

-- Not applicable.

(s) = Value less than 50 million kilowatthours.

Notes: Sum of components may not equal total due to independent rounding.

Consumption equals generation plus imports minus exports minus distribution losses.

Source: *International Energy Annual 1996*, Energy Information Administration, Washington, DC, 1998

in 1987 to 12,052 billion kilowatt-hours in 1996. While all regions of the earth experienced increased consumption, Japan, China, and Canada had growth rates over 3 percent. North America accounted for 32 percent of the world's total consumption; the Far East and Oceania, 25.5 percent; Western Europe accounted for 20 percent of world energy use; while Eastern Europe and the former USSR used 12 percent in 1996. (See Table 8.4.)

CHAPTER IX

RENEWABLE ENERGY

Energy efficiency is America's largest least expensive energy resource, and we need to do more to tap it. The future is in using energy efficiently and getting it from alternative sources. — Robert K. Watson, energy specialist, Natural Resources Defense Council

WHAT IS RENEWABLE ENERGY?

Imagine an energy source that uses no oil, produces no pollution, cannot be affected by political events and cartels, creates no radioactive waste, and yet, is economical. Although that sounds impossible, some experts claim that technological advances could make a renewable-energy-based economy achievable within a few decades.

Renewable energy is a term used to describe energy from sources that are naturally regenerated and are, therefore, virtually unlimited. These energy sources include sun, wind, water, vegetation, and the heat of the earth.

Solar energy, wind energy, hydropower, and geothermal power are all renewable, cheap, and clean sources of energy. Each of these alternative energy sources has advantages and disadvantages, and many observers hope that one or more of them may provide a substantially better energy source than conventional, fossil-fuel-burning methods. As the United States and the rest of the world continue to expand their energy needs, putting a strain on the environment, alternative sources of energy continue to be explored in the hope that they might provide a higher percentage of America's energy requirements in the future.

AN HISTORICAL PERSPECTIVE

Before the nineteenth century, most energy used came from renewable sources. People burned wood for heat, used sails to harness the wind and propel boats, and installed water wheels on streams to grind grain. The large-scale shift to nonrenewable energy sources began in the 1700s with the Industrial Revolution, a period marked by the rise of factories first in Europe and then in North America. As the demand for energy grew, coal replaced wood as the main fuel source. Coal was the most efficient fuel for the steam engine, perhaps the most important invention of the Industrial Revolution.

Until the early 1970s, most Americans were unconcerned about the sources of the nation's energy. Supplies of coal and oil, which together provided more than 90 percent of U.S. energy, were believed to be plentiful. The decades preceding the 1970s were characterized by cheap gasoline and little public discussion of energy conservation.

That carefree approach to energy consumption ended in the 1970s. A fuel oil crisis made Americans more aware of the importance of developing alternative sources of energy to supplement and perhaps even replace fossil fuels. In major cities throughout the United States, gasoline rationing became commonplace, lower heat settings for offices and living quarters were encouraged, and people waited in line to fill their gas tanks. In a country where mobility and personal transportation are highly valued, the oil crisis was a shocking reality for many Americans. As a result, the administration of President Jimmy Carter (1977-1981) encouraged federal funding for research into alternative energy sources.

TABLE 9.1

Energy Consumption by Source, 1949-1997
(Quadrillion Btu)

Year	Coal	Coal Coke Net Imports[1]	Natural Gas[1]	Petroleum[2]	Total Fossil Fuels	Nuclear Electric Power	Hydroelectric Pumped Storage[3]	Conventional Hydroelectric Power[4]	Geothermal Energy[5]	Biofuels[6]	Solar Energy	Wind Energy	Total Renewable Energy	Total[7]
1949	11.981	-0.007	5.145	11.883	29.002	0	[8]	1.449	0	0.006	0	0	1.454	30.457
1950	12.347	0.001	5.968	13.315	31.632	0	[8]	1.440	0	0.005	0	0	1.446	33.078
1951	12.553	-0.021	7.049	14.428	34.008	0	[8]	1.454	0	0.005	0	0	1.459	35.467
1952	11.307	-0.012	7.550	14.956	33.800	0	[8]	1.496	0	0.006	0	0	1.503	35.302
1953	11.373	-0.009	7.907	15.556	34.826	0	[8]	1.439	0	0.005	0	0	1.444	36.270
1954	9.715	-0.007	8.330	15.839	33.877	0	[8]	1.388	0	0.003	0	0	1.391	35.269
1955	11.167	-0.010	8.998	17.255	37.410	0	[8]	1.407	0	0.003	0	0	1.411	38.821
1956	11.350	-0.013	9.614	17.937	38.888	0	[8]	1.487	0	0.002	0	0	1.489	40.377
1957	10.821	-0.017	10.191	17.932	38.926	(s)	[8]	1.557	0	0.002	0	0	1.559	40.484
1958	9.533	-0.007	10.663	18.527	38.717	0.002	[8]	1.629	0	0.002	0	0	1.631	40.349
1959	9.518	-0.008	11.717	19.323	40.550	0.002	[8]	1.587	0	0.002	0	0	1.589	42.141
1960	9.838	-0.006	12.385	19.919	42.137	0.006	[8]	1.657	0.001	0.002	0	0	1.659	43.802
1961	9.623	-0.008	12.926	20.216	42.758	0.020	[8]	1.680	0.002	0.001	0	0	1.684	44.462
1962	9.906	-0.006	13.731	21.049	44.681	0.026	[8]	1.822	0.002	0.001	0	0	1.825	46.533
1963	10.412	-0.007	14.403	21.701	46.509	0.038	[8]	1.772	0.004	0.001	0	0	1.777	48.325
1964	10.965	-0.010	15.288	22.301	48.543	0.040	[8]	1.907	0.005	0.002	0	0	1.913	50.496
1965	11.580	-0.018	15.769	23.246	50.576	0.043	[8]	2.058	0.004	0.003	0	0	2.065	52.684
1966	12.143	-0.025	16.995	24.401	53.514	0.064	[8]	2.073	0.004	0.003	0	0	2.081	55.659
1967	11.914	-0.015	17.945	25.284	55.127	0.088	[8]	2.344	0.007	0.003	0	0	2.354	57.569
1968	12.331	-0.017	19.210	26.979	58.502	0.142	[8]	2.342	0.009	0.004	0	0	2.355	60.999
1969	12.382	-0.036	20.678	28.338	61.362	0.154	[8]	2.659	0.013	0.003	0	0	2.676	64.191
1970	12.264	-0.058	21.795	29.521	63.522	0.239	[8]	2.654	0.011	0.004	0	0	2.669	66.431
1971	11.599	-0.033	22.469	30.561	64.596	0.413	[8]	2.861	0.012	0.003	0	0	2.876	67.885
1972	12.077	-0.026	22.698	32.947	67.696	0.584	[8]	2.944	0.031	0.003	0	0	2.979	71.258
1973	12.971	-0.007	22.512	34.840	70.316	0.910	[8]	3.010	0.043	0.003	0	0	3.056	74.282
1974	12.663	0.056	21.732	33.455	67.906	1.272	[8]	3.309	0.053	0.003	0	0	3.365	72.543
1975	12.663	0.014	19.948	32.731	65.355	1.900	[8]	3.219	0.070	0.002	0	0	3.291	70.546
1976	13.584	(s)	20.345	35.175	69.104	2.111	[8]	3.066	0.078	0.003	0	0	3.146	74.362
1977	13.922	0.015	19.931	37.122	70.989	2.702	[8]	2.515	0.077	0.005	0	0	2.597	76.288
1978	13.765	0.125	20.000	37.965	71.856	3.024	[8]	3.141	0.064	0.003	0	0	3.209	78.089
1979	15.040	0.063	20.666	37.123	72.892	2.776	[8]	3.141	0.084	0.005	0	0	3.230	78.898
1980	15.423	-0.035	20.394	34.202	69.985	2.739	[8]	3.118	0.110	0.005	0	0	3.232	75.956
1981	15.907	-0.016	19.928	31.931	67.750	3.008	[8]	3.105	0.123	0.004	0	0	3.232	73.990
1982	15.321	-0.022	18.505	30.232	64.037	3.131	[8]	3.572	0.105	0.003	0	0	3.680	70.848
1983	15.895	-0.011	17.357	30.054	63.290	3.203	[8]	3.899	0.129	0.003	0	0	4.032	70.525
1984	17.070	-0.011	18.507	31.051	66.617	3.553	[8]	3.800	0.165	0.009	0	0	3.974	74.144
1985	17.478	-0.013	17.834	30.922	66.221	4.149	[8]	3.398	0.198	0.012	0	0	3.611	73.980
1986	17.260	-0.017	16.708	32.196	66.148	4.471	[8]	3.446	0.219	0.012	0	0	3.678	74.297
1987	18.008	0.009	17.744	32.865	68.626	4.906	[8]	3.117	0.229	0.015	0	0	3.362	76.894
1988	18.846	0.040	18.552	34.222	71.660	5.661	[8]	2.662	0.217	0.017	0	0	2.897	80.218
1989	18.921	0.030	19.384	34.211	72.546	5.677	-0.036	2.912	0.197	0.020	(s)	(s)	3.130	81.353
1990	19.101	0.005	19.296	33.553	71.955	6.161	-0.047	R,3.123	R[10],0.355	[11],2.632	R[10],0.063	[10],0.023	R,6.197	R[9],84.118
1991	18.770	0.009	19.606	32.845	71.230	6.579	-0.043	3.205	R,0.365	2.642	0.066	0.027	6.304	R,84.026
1992	R,19.217	0.027	20.131	33.527	R,72.902	6.607	-0.042	R,2.863	R,0.379	2.788	0.068	0.030	R,6.128	R,85.554
1993	R,19.837	0.017	20.827	33.841	R,74.522	6.519	-0.043	R,3.147	R,0.393	2.784	0.071	0.031	R,6.426	R,87.368
1994	20.027	0.024	21.288	34.735	76.073	6.837	-0.028	2.969	0.395	2.838	0.072	0.036	6.309	89.250
1995	R,20.090	0.026	21.163	34.663	R,76.943	7.177	-0.028	3.472	R,0.339	R,2.846	0.073	0.033	R,6.763	R,90.864
1996	R,21.011	(s)	R,22.560	R,35.864	R,79.434	7.168	-0.032	3.914	0.352	R,2.938	0.075	0.035	R,7.315	R,93.871
1997P	21.439	0.018	22.588	36.314	80.360	6.686	-0.042	3.942	0.366	2.723	0.075	0.039	7.145	94.209

[1] Includes supplemental gaseous fuels.
[2] Petroleum products supplied, including natural gas plant liquids and crude oil burned as fuel.
[3] Represents total pumped storage facility production minus energy used for pumping.
[4] Through 1989, includes all net imports of electricity. From 1990, includes only the portion of net imports of electricity that is derived from hydroelectric power.
[5] Includes electricity imports from Mexico that are derived from geothermal energy.
[6] Includes wood, wood waste, peat, wood liquors, railroad ties, pitch, wood sludge, municipal solid waste, agricultural waste, straw, tires, landfill gases, fish oil, and/or other waste.
[7] From 1990, includes net imported electricity from nonrenewable sources and removes ethanol blended into motor gasoline, which would otherwise be double counted in both petroleum and renewable energy.
[8] Through 1989, pumped storage is included in conventional hydroelectric power.
[9] There is a discontinuity in this time series between 1989 and 1990; beginning in 1990, pumped storage is removed and expanded coverage of industrial use of hydroelectric power is included.
[10] There is a discontinuity in this time series between 1989 and 1990 due to the expanded coverage of nonutility use of renewable energy beginning in 1990.
[11] Independent power producers' use of coal is included beginning in 1992.
R=Revised. P=Preliminary. (s)=Less than 0.0005 quadrillion Btu.
Note: Totals may not equal sum of components due to independent rounding.
Web Page: http://www.eia.doe.gov/fueloverview.html#state.
Sources: Tables 5.1, 6.1, 7.1, 7.7, 8.1, 8.3, 10.1, Energy Information Administration estimates for industrial hydroelectric power, and conversion factors in Appendix A.

Source: *Annual Energy Review 1997*, Energy Information Administration, Washington, DC, 1998

In 1978, the U.S. Congress passed the Public Utilities Regulatory Policies Act (PURPA; PL 95-617), which was designed to help the struggling alternative energy industry. The act exempted small producers from state and federal utility regulations and required existing local utilities to buy electricity from them. PURPA encouraged the growth of small-scale electric power plants, especially those fueled by renewable sources. The renewable energy industries responded by growing rapidly, gaining experience, improving technologies, and lowering costs. This act was the single most important factor in the development of the commercial renewable energy market.

In the 1980s, President Ronald Reagan decided that private sector financing for the short-term development of alternative energy sources was best. As a result, he proposed the reduction or elimination of federal expenditures for alternative energy sources. Although funds were severely cut, the U.S. Department of Energy (DOE) continues to support some research and development to explore alternate sources of energy.

How Much of Today's Energy Is Renewable?

Renewable energy currently contributes only a small portion of the nation's energy supply, although its importance is expected to grow in the future. In 1997, the United States consumed an estimated 7.15 quadrillion Btu (British thermal unit — a standard unit of energy measurement) of renewable energy, 8 percent of the nation's total energy consumption. (See Table 9.1.) Hydroelectric power and biofuels (mainly wood) accounted for, by far, the largest shares (55 percent and 38 per-

cent, respectively) of renewable energy. Geothermal, solar, and wind energy accounted for the remainder. (See Figure 9.1.) Electric utilities and the industrial sector were the biggest consumers.

SOLAR ENERGY

Ancient Greek and Chinese civilizations used glass and mirrors to direct the sun's rays to start fires. Solar energy (energy from the sun) is a renewable, widely available energy source that generates neither greenhouse gases nor radioactive waste. Solar-powered cars have already competed in long-distance races, and solar energy has been used routinely for many

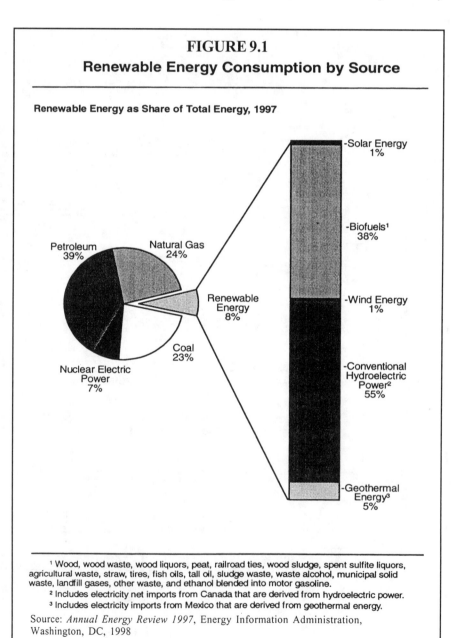

FIGURE 9.1
Renewable Energy Consumption by Source

Renewable Energy as Share of Total Energy, 1997

Petroleum 39%
Natural Gas 24%
Renewable Energy 8%
Coal 23%
Nuclear Electric Power 7%

-Solar Energy 1%
-Biofuels[1] 38%
-Wind Energy 1%
-Conventional Hydroelectric Power[2] 55%
-Geothermal Energy[3] 5%

[1] Wood, wood waste, wood liquors, peat, railroad ties, wood sludge, spent sulfite liquors, agricultural waste, straw, tires, fish oils, tall oil, sludge waste, waste alcohol, municipal solid waste, landfill gases, other waste, and ethanol blended into motor gasoline.
[2] Includes electricity net imports from Canada that are derived from hydroelectric power.
[3] Includes electricity imports from Mexico that are derived from geothermal energy.

Source: *Annual Energy Review 1997*, Energy Information Administration, Washington, DC, 1998

years to power spacecraft. Although many people consider solar energy a product of the space age, the Massachusetts Institute of Technology built the first solar house in 1939.

Solar radiation is nearly constant outside Earth's atmosphere, but the amount of solar energy, or *insolation*, reaching any point on Earth varies with changing atmospheric conditions, such as clouds and dust, and the changing position of Earth relative to the sun. In the United States, insolation is greatest in the West and Southwest regions. Nevertheless, almost all U.S. regions have solar resources that can be used.

Passive and Active Solar Energy Collection Systems

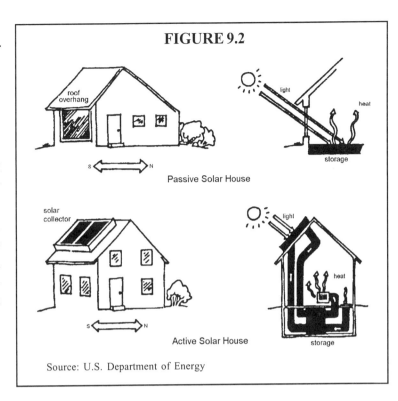

FIGURE 9.2

Passive Solar House

Active Solar House

Source: U.S. Department of Energy

Passive solar systems, such as greenhouses or windows with a southern exposure, use heat flow, evaporation, or other natural processes to collect and transfer heat. It is considered the least costly and least difficult system to implement. (See Figure 9.2.)

Active solar systems use mechanical methods to control the energy process. They require collectors and storage devices as well as motors, pumps, and valves to operate the systems that transfer heat. Collectors consist of an absorbing plate that transfers the sun's heat to a working fluid (liquid or gas), a translucent cover plate that prevents the heat from radiating back into the atmosphere, and insulation on the back of the collector panel to further reduce heat loss. (See Figure 9.2.) Excess solar energy is transferred to a storage facility so it may be used to provide power on cloudy days. In both active and passive systems, the conversion of solar energy into a form of power is made at the site where it is used. The most common and least expensive active solar systems are used for heating water.

Solar Thermal Energy Systems

A *solar thermal energy system* uses intensified sunlight to heat water or other fluids to more than 750

degrees. Mirrors or lenses constantly track the sun's position and focus its rays onto solar receivers that contain fluid. Solar heat (energy) is transferred to the water that, in turn, powers an electric generator. In a distributed solar thermal system, the collected energy powers irrigation pumps, providing electricity for small communities or capturing normally wasted heat from the sun in industrial areas. In a central solar thermal system, the energy is collected at a central location and used by utility networks for a large number of customers.

Other solar thermal energy systems include solar ponds and trough systems. Solar ponds are lined ponds filled with water and salt. Because salt water is denser than fresh water, the salt water on the bottom absorbs the heat, and the fresh water on top keeps the salt water contained and traps the heat. Trough systems use U-shaped mirrors to concentrate the sunshine on water or oil-filled tubes.

Photovoltaic Conversion Systems

The photovoltaic (PV) cell solar energy system converts sunlight directly into electricity without the use of mechanical generators. PV cells have no moving parts, are easy to install, require little maintenance, do not pollute the air, and usually last up to 20 years. PV cells are commonly used to power small devices, such as watches or calculators. They are also being used on a larger scale to provide electricity for rural households, recreational vehicles, and businesses. Solar panels using photovoltaic cells have generated electricity for space stations and satellites for many years. Solar panels have also provided electricity for a few major buildings in the United States.

Since PV systems produce electricity only when the sun is shining, a backup energy supply is needed. PV cells produce the most power around noon, when sunlight is the most intense. A photovoltaic system typically includes storage batteries that provide electricity during cloudy days and at night.

The use of photovoltaic technology is expanding both in the United States and abroad. Although PV systems have a higher initial cost than conventional power plants, they have a much lower operating cost.

Using Solar Energy

Because it is difficult to measure solar energy directly, shipments of equipment are often used as an indicator. From a high of 84 low-temperature collector manufacturers in 1979, the number dropped to only 22 in 1986, and in 1995, there were only 14. Total shipments of solar thermal collectors peaked in 1981 at over 21 million square feet and declined to approximately 7.6 million square feet by 1996 (Figure 9.3).

The market for solar energy space heating has virtually disappeared. Most of the solar thermal collector market is for residential purposes (mostly in the Sunbelt states), with only a small proportion for commercial purposes (Figure 9.4). In 1996, most of the solar-thermal collectors shipped were used for heating swimming pools, while virtually all the rest were used for domestic hot water (Figure 9.5). Some state

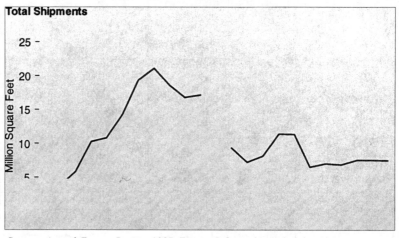

FIGURE 9.3
Solar Thermal Collector Shipments,
1974-1984 and 1986-1996

Source: *Annual Energy Review 1997*, Energy Information Administration, Washington, DC, 1998

and municipal power companies have added solar systems as adjuncts to their regular power sources during peak hours.

Advantages and Disadvantages of Solar Energy

The primary advantage of solar energy is its inexhaustible supply, while its primary disadvantage is its reliance on a consistently sunny climate to provide continuous electrical power. Very few areas of the country have enough constant sunshine to make this system an efficient alternative to conventional methods. In addition, a large amount of land area is necessary for the most efficient collection of solar energy for solar thermal units. Experts estimate that a new thermal energy plant would have a 60 percent higher cost of production than a conventional coal-fired plant.

A PV cell system is nonpolluting and silent and can be operated by computer. In addition, it is less expensive to operate because there are no turbines or other moving parts and maintenance is minimal. Above all, the fuel source (sunshine) is free and plentiful. The disadvantage of a photovoltaic cell energy system is the initial cost. Although the price has fallen considerably, PV cells are still too expensive for widespread use.

138

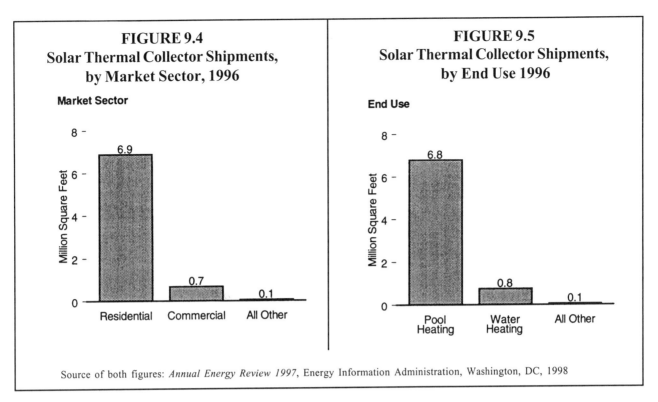

FIGURE 9.4
Solar Thermal Collector Shipments, by Market Sector, 1996

Market Sector

Million Square Feet

Residential 6.9 Commercial 0.7 All Other 0.1

FIGURE 9.5
Solar Thermal Collector Shipments, by End Use 1996

End Use

Million Square Feet

Pool Heating 6.8 Water Heating 0.8 All Other 0.1

Source of both figures: *Annual Energy Review 1997*, Energy Information Administration, Washington, DC, 1998

Future Development Trends

Interest in photovoltaic solar energy systems is particularly high in rural and remote areas where it is impractical to extend traditional electrical power lines. In some remote areas, PV cells are used as independent power sources for communications or for the operation of water pumps or refrigerators. The use of photovoltaic cells will likely increase where the traditional use of an electrical cord is a problem.

Although solar power still costs more than three times as much as fossil fuel energy, utilities could turn to solar energy to provide "peaking power" on extremely hot or cold days. In the long run, some people believe that building solar energy systems to provide peak power capacity would be cheaper than building new and expensive diesel fuel generators. Utility regulators may decide that the price of fossil-fuel power must include the hidden cost of fossil fuel damage to the environment through acid rain and the greenhouse effect.

WIND ENERGY

Wind energy is a form of solar energy. Winds are created by the uneven heating of the atmosphere by the sun, the irregularities of the earth's surface, and the rotation of Earth. As a result, winds are strongly influenced by local terrain, water bodies, weather patterns, vegetation, and other factors. This wind flow, when "harvested" by wind turbines, can be used to generate electricity.

Wind machines have changed dramatically from those that were common in the 1800s. Early windmills produced mechanical energy to pump water and run sawmills. In the late 1890s, Americans began experimenting with wind power to generate electricity. Their early efforts produced enough electricity to light one or two modern light bulbs.

Compared to the pinwheel-shaped farm windmills that can still be seen dotting the American rural landscape, today's state-of-the-art wind turbines look more like airplane propellers. Their sleek, high-tech fiberglass design and aerodynamics allow them to generate an abundance of electricity, while they also produce mechanical energy and heat. (Figures 9.6 and 9.7 show both the horizontal and vertical axis designs.) Unlike solar energy systems, they produce renewable energy at night as well as during the day. Over the past decade, industrial and developing countries alike have started using wind power as an adaptable source of

139

electricity to complement their existing power sources and to bring electricity to remote regions. Wind turbines cost less to install per unit of kilowatt capacity than either coal or nuclear facilities. After installing a windmill, there are few additional costs, as the fuel (wind) is free.

Wind speeds are generally highest and most consistent in mountain passes and along coastlines. Europe has the greatest coastal wind resources, and clusters of wind turbines, or wind farms, are being developed in much of Europe and Asia. Denmark, the Netherlands, China, and India are especially interested in fostering the development of domestic wind industries. In the United States, it is estimated that sufficient wind energy is available to provide more than one trillion kilowatt hours of electricity annually. Currently, electricity-producing wind turbines (not windmills used for mechanical energy) operate in 95 countries.

Energy Production by Wind Turbines

Wind is the world's fastest-growing energy source. Although wind power has not been adopted widely in the United States, U.S. companies export turbines to Spain, the Netherlands, Great Britain, India, and China. Following a slow period in the late 1980s, when the U.S. government discontinued tax credits for wind installations, the market for wind turbines has grown.

The wind industry in California began in 1981 with the erection of 144 relatively small turbines capable of generating a combined total of seven megawatts of electricity. Within a year, the number of turbines had increased 10 times, and by 1986 they had multiplied 100-fold. The 1980s saw an explosion of wind technology in California, where about 95 percent of the installed wind capacity in the United States is located.

The most recent wind installations have been in Texas and Minnesota. In 1995, wind energy generated 3.2 million kilowatts of power in the United States, comprising a tiny 0.04 percent of all electricity consumed. That year California produced enough wind power to supply all of San Francisco's residents. Other wind farm projects exist in Hawaii, Montana, New York, Oregon, and Wyoming.

FIGURE 9.6

**A Vertical Axis Wind Machine —
Darrieum Rotor**

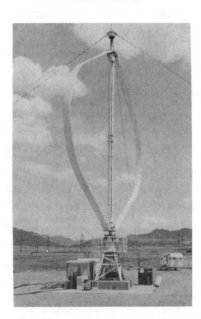

FIGURE 9.7

**A Windfarm —
Horizontal Axis Machines**

Source of both figures: "Renewable Energy: An Overview," *U.S. Department of Energy INFORMATION*, U.S. Department of Energy, FS175, 3rd Edition, March 1990

Experts point out that California's dominance has less to do with wind availability than tax incentives that were offered by the state until 1985. Developers are in the process of building wind energy farms in the Midwest. Studies show that several states, especially the plains states, have wind speeds sufficient to supply electricity to those states. Twelve states — North Dakota, South Dakota, Texas, Kansas, Montana, Nebraska, Wyoming, Oklahoma, Minnesota, Iowa, Colorado, and New Mexico — contain 90 percent of the U.S. wind energy potential. Refinements in wind-turbine technology may enable a substantial portion of the nation's electricity to be produced by wind energy.

Problems in the U.S. Wind Industry

For a number of reasons, growth in the wind industry has slowed. Crude oil prices have fallen drastically, making oil and gas the lowest-cost fuel sources. Concern over the federal budget has resulted in a change in federal policy toward renewable energies. Furthermore, some people are concerned about the uncertainty involving electric utility deregulation.

Development of Wind Energy Throughout the World

During the decade following the 1973 oil embargo, more than 10,000 wind machines were installed worldwide, ranging in size from portable units to multi-megawatt turbines. In third world villages, small wind turbines recharge batteries and provide essential services. In China, small wind turbines allow people to watch their favorite television shows, a major reason for the increased demand for turbines in China. In fact, five of the world's 10 largest manufacturers of small wind turbines are Chinese.

Global wind power generating capacity reached 5,000 megawatts in 1995, up from 2,976 in 1993, from more than 25,000 operating wind turbines. Most of the growth was in northern Europe. Although wind power supplies less than 0.1 percent of the world's electricity, it is one of the fastest-growing energy sources.

During the past few years, northern Europe and India have displaced California as the main user of wind power. European countries plan to install 4,000 megawatts of wind power capacity by the year 2000. The most ambitious wind energy program is planned for India, where the Ministry of Energy is promoting the installation of enough windmills to produce 5,000 megawatts by the year 2000 — enough electrical power to serve five million customers. India is expected to be the most rapidly growing market for wind turbines, and if the planned wind energy program is successful, wind may supply more energy for India than the country's nuclear program. Other countries planning to install wind turbines include Australia, Belgium, Israel, Italy, the United Kingdom, and Germany.

Interest in wind energy has been driven in part by the declining cost of capturing wind energy — from more than $.25 a kilowatt-hour in 1980 to $.05 per kilowatt-hour for new turbines today. At sites with especially strong winds, electricity is produced for $.05 per kilowatt-hour, which could make wind power nearly competitive with gas- and coal-powered plants, even before considering wind's environmental advantages.

Advantages and Disadvantages of Using Wind Energy

The main problem with wind energy is that the wind does not always blow. Some people object to the whirring noise of wind turbines or do not like to see wind turbines clustered in mountain passes and along shorelines because they interfere with scenic views. Some environmentalists have charged that the wind turbines are responsible for the loss of some species of endangered birds that fly into the blades.

On the other hand, generating electricity with wind offers many environmental advantages. Windfarms do not emit climate-altering carbon dioxide, acid rain-forming pollutants, respiratory irritants, or nuclear waste. Because windfarms do not require water to operate, they are especially well suited to semi-arid and arid regions. Windfarming also offers the added benefit of reducing soil loss on land prone to wind erosion because turbines capture the wind and decrease its potential for downwind destruction. Ironically, the winds that once created the Dust Bowl and contributed to the Great Depression may someday be harnessed to provide electricity.

141

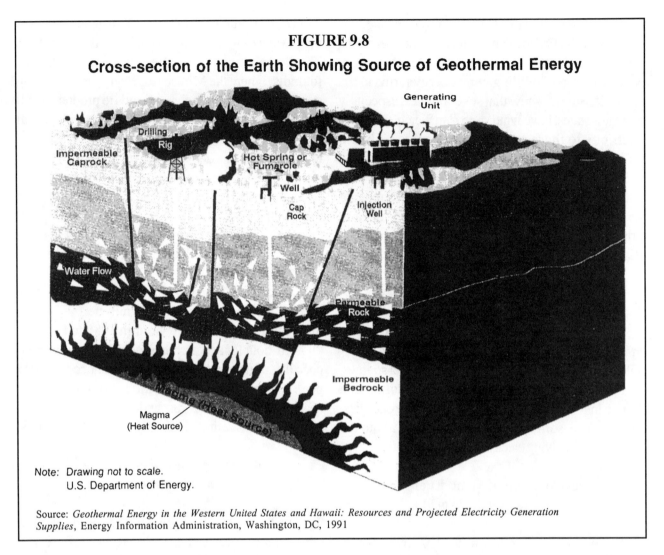

FIGURE 9.8

Cross-section of the Earth Showing Source of Geothermal Energy

Generating Unit

Drilling Rig

Impermeable Caprock

Hot Spring or Fumarole

Well

Cap Rock

Injection Well

Water Flow

Permeable Rock

Impermeable Bedrock

Magma (Heat Source)

Magma (Heat Source)

Note: Drawing not to scale.
U.S. Department of Energy.

Source: *Geothermal Energy in the Western United States and Hawaii: Resources and Projected Electricity Generation Supplies*, Energy Information Administration, Washington, DC, 1991

GEOTHERMAL ENERGY

Since ancient times, humans have exploited the earth's natural hot water sources. Although bubbling hot springs became public baths in ancient Rome, using hot water and underground steam to produce power is a relatively recent development. Electricity was first generated from natural steam in Italy in 1904. The world's first steam power plant was built in 1958 in a volcanic region of New Zealand. A field of 28 geothermal power plants covering 30 square miles in northern California was completed in 1960.

What Is Geothermal Energy?

Geothermal energy is the natural, internal heat of the earth trapped in rock formations deep within the earth. Only a fraction of this vast storehouse of energy can be extracted, usually through large fractures in the earth's crust. Hot springs, geysers, and fumaroles (holes in or near volcanoes from which vapor escapes) are the most easily exploitable sources of geothermal energy. (See Figure 9.8.) Geothermal reservoirs provide hot water or steam that can be used for heating buildings, processing food, and generating electricity.

To produce power from a geothermal energy source, pressurized steam or hot water is extracted from the earth and directed toward turbines. The electricity produced by turbines is then fed into a utility grid and distributed to residential and commercial customers. Today, electricity accounts for almost two-thirds of the world's geothermal energy use.

Types of Geothermal Energy

Like most natural energy sources, geothermal energy is usable only when it is concentrated in one spot in what is called a "thermal reservoir." The four basic categories of thermal reservoirs are hydrothermal (dry steam and hot, or wet, steam), dry rock, geopressurized, and magma reservoirs. Most of the known areas for geothermal power in the United States are located west of the Mississippi River (Figure 9.9).

Hydrothermal reservoirs consist of a heat source covered by a permeable formation through which water circulates. Dry steam is produced when hot water boils underground and some of the steam escapes to the surface under pressure. Once at the sur-

face, impurities and tiny rock particles are removed, and the steam is then piped directly to the electrical generating station. These systems are the cheapest and simplest form of geothermal energy. The Geysers, 90 miles north of San Francisco, California, are the most famous example of this type. The Geysers produce enough electricity to meet the needs of about 1.3 million people.

Hot steam systems are created when underground water is heated to more than 700 degrees Fahrenheit by the surrounding hot rock or magma (rock so hot it

FIGURE 9.9

Known Fields for Geothermal Resources

Temperature above 90°C (194°F)
Temperature below 90°C (194°F)
Geopressured Resources

Note: Hydrothermal reservoirs in the United States that offer potential for power generation with current or future technologies are located in the far western states. According to the U.S. Geological Survey, all of these western states, as well as others, have low-temperature reservoirs that are not suitable for power generation but could have the potential for direct-heat applications.

Source: U.S. Geological Survey.

Source: *Geothermal Energy: Outlook Limited for Some Uses but Promising for Geothermal Heat Pumps*, U.S. General Accounting Office, Washington, DC, 1994

has liquefied), but the water remains liquid because of the intense pressure. When the water is brought to the surface and the pressure is reduced, a small amount of water becomes steam that is then separated and used to power an electrical generating plant.

Dry rock formations are the most common geothermal source, especially in the West. To tap this source of energy, water is injected into rock formations that have been fractured, to produce steam or water for collection.

Geopressurized reservoirs are sedimentary formations containing hot water and methane gas. Supplies of geopressurized energy remain uncertain, and drilling is expensive. Scientists hope that advanced technology will eventually permit the commercial exploitation of the methane content in these reservoirs.

Magma resources are found where molten or partially liquefied rock is located from 10,000 to 33,000 feet below the earth's surface. Because magma is so hot, ranging from 1,650 degrees to 2,200 degrees Fahrenheit, it is a good geothermal resource. The process for extracting energy from magma is still in the experimental stages.

Disadvantages of Geothermal Energy

There are several disadvantages to using geothermal energy. Geothermal plants are expensive because they must be built near the source. Other drawbacks include low efficiency, bad odors from sulfur released in processing, noise, lack of access for most states, potentially harmful pollutants (hydrogen sulfide, ammonia, and radon), and poisonous arsenic or boron often found in geothermal waters. Serious environmental concerns have been raised over the release of chemical compounds, potential water contamination, the collapse of land surface around the area from which the water is being drained, and potential water shortages resulting from massive withdrawals of water.

American Production of Geothermal Energy

Geothermal energy ranks third in renewable energy production in the United States, after hydroelec-

tric and biomass energy. In the United States, public sector involvement in the geothermal industry began with the passage of the Geothermal Steam Act of 1970 (PL 91-581), which authorized the U.S. Department of Interior to lease geothermal resources on federal lands.

Although the United States is the greatest producer of geothermal power, with 44 percent of the world's capacity, the geothermal industry in the United States is currently static. In 1997, geothermal energy accounted for just 5 percent of renewable energy consumed in the United States (Figure 9.1). The energy market now has excess electrical generating capacity, and oil prices are low at a time when most of the easily exploited geothermal reserves have already been developed. In addition, utility companies and independent power producers are arguing over who should build additional generating capacity and what prices should be paid for the power. As a result, the rate of growth in U.S. geothermal capacity has slowed. Continued growth in the American market depends on the regulatory environment, oil price trends, and the success of unproven technologies for economically exploiting some of the presently inaccessible geothermal reserves.

World Production of Geothermal Energy

During the "oil crisis" days of the 1970s, when energy was at the forefront of the international agenda, governments scrambled to find domestic alternatives to imported oil. As public interest grew, research dollars became available, and a large number of geothermal energy plants were built. Although interest has since faded, geothermal power's commercial development has continued at a slow but steady pace.

Since 1979, worldwide geothermal electrical generating capacity has nearly tripled. Nonetheless, it is still little more than the energy output of 10 average-size, coal-fired power plants. World geothermal reserves are immense, but unevenly distributed. These reserves fall mostly in seismically active areas at the margins or borders of Earth's nine tectonic plates. Currently, exploited reserves represent only a small fraction of the overall potential — many countries are

144

believed to have in excess of 100,000 megawatts of geothermal energy available.

Geothermal energy makes only a tiny contribution to world electrical production — less than 1 percent. The United States is the largest geothermal power producer, followed by the Philippines. The Philippine government has committed itself to the development of geothermal power by providing tax incentives and cooperation with the private sector; geothermal energy currently provides about one-fourth of the nation's electricity. New Zealand and Iceland both use their rich steam reserves to provide significant amounts of power — Iceland now heats more than 80 percent of its buildings with geothermal energy. Italy, Japan, and Mexico are the other major geothermal powers.

A few nations in the developing world — El Salvador, Kenya, Bolivia, Costa Rica, Ethiopia, India, and Thailand — have considerable steam reserves available for power generation. Debt-ridden developing nations that have substantial unexploited geothermal reserves are especially eager to use them instead of relying on fossil fuel imports for their energy needs.

HYDROPOWER

Hydropower is the world's largest renewable energy source. Hydropower is the energy that comes from the natural flow of water. Usually, the power is harnessed by taking advantage of gravity when water falls from one level to another. The energy of falling water is converted into mechanical energy. In the past, it was harnessed by waterwheels to grind grain or turn saws, but today, water is used to turn modern turbines, which creates electricity. Hydropower is a renewable, nonpolluting, and reliable energy source. Hydroelectric power accounts for approximately half of all renewable energy production. In 1997, in the United States, hydroelectric power generated 3.9 quadrillion Btu of energy.

At present, hydropower is the only means of storing large quantities of electrical energy for almost instant use. This is done by holding water in a large reservoir behind a dam, with a hydroelectric power plant below. The dam creates a height from which water

flows. The fast-moving water pushes the turbine blades that turn the rotor part of the electric generator. When coils of wire on the rotor sweep past the generator's stationary coil, electricity is produced. Whenever power is needed at peak times, the valves are opened and, in a short amount of time, turbine generators produce power. (See Figure 9.10.)

Advantages and Disadvantages of Hydropower

Small hydropower plants in the United States are costly to build, but quickly become cost-efficient because of their low operating costs. One of the disadvantages of small hydropower generators is their reliance on rain and melting snow to fill reservoirs. (Some years bring drought conditions.) Other concerns include the difficult search for the proper terrain on which to build a hydroelectric power plant, the high cost of construction, and the ecological concern that dams could ruin streams, dry up waterfalls, and interfere with marine life habitats.

New Directions in Hydropower Energy

Since almost all power sites have already been developed, hydropower's contribution to energy generation should remain relatively constant, although existing sites can become more efficient as new generators are added.

Most of the new development in hydropower is occurring in the third world as developing nations see this as an effective method of supplying power to their growing populations. Most of these hydropower development programs are tremendous public works projects requiring huge amounts of money, most of it borrowed from the developed world. Third-world leaders believe that, in the long run, despite, in many cases, threats to the environment, the dams will pay for themselves by bringing cheap electric power to their people.

While the third world has developed only a small portion of its large-scale hydropower potential, the United States and Europe have developed a major proportion of their potential. Large-scale hydropower development has virtually stopped in the United States, with not one new dam being approved for federal funding in more than a decade. Hydroelectric power projects have been traditionally considered the prime example of "pork barrel" politics, in which politicians received payments for votes in the form of a power project in their district. Consequently, this was one of the areas that was cut back during the budget reductions of the 1980s and 1990s.

Until recently, in the United States, dams were usually funded entirely with federal monies. Since 1986, however, any new dam proposed in the United States must be built with at least half the money being put up by local governments. Any new major supplies of hydroelectric power for the United States will likely come from Canada.

OTHER ALTERNATIVES USING WATER

The potential power locked in the world's oceans is unknown. However, since the ocean is not as easily controlled as a river or water that is directed through canals into turbines, unlocking that potential power is far more challenging. Three ideas being considered are tidal plants, wave power, and ocean thermal energy conversion (OTEC).

Tidal Power

The tidal plant uses the power generated by the tidal flow of water as it ebbs (flows back out to sea). A minimum tidal range of three to five yards is generally considered necessary for an economically feasible plant. Canada, for example, has built a small 18-watt unit at the Bay of Fundy, with its 15-yard tidal range, the largest in the world, and is considering building a larger unit. The largest existing tidal facility is the 420-megawatt plant at the La Rance estuary in northern France. The People's Republic of China (PRC) has a tiny 10-watt plant.

Wave Energy

Norway has two operating wave power stations at Tostestallen on its Atlantic coast. The arrival of a wave forces water up the 65-foot tower, displacing

FIGURE 9.10

Grand Coulee Dam on the Columbia River. Franklin D. Roosevelt Lake holds nearly 2.8 cubic miles of water.

Source: *Water of the World*, U.S. Department of the Interior/Geological Survey, Washington, DC, no date

the air already in the tower. This air rushes out the top through a turbine. The rotors of that turbine then spin, generating electricity. When the wave falls back, and the water level falls, air is sucked back in through the turbine, again generating electricity.

The second type of ocean power plant uses the overflow of high waves. As the wave splashes against the top of a dam, some of the water goes over and is trapped in a reservoir on the other side. The water is then directed through a turbine as it flows back to the sea. These two kinds of plants are experimental. Several projects are underway in Japan and the Pacific region to determine a way to use the potential of the huge waves of the Pacific.

Ocean Thermal Energy Conversion (OTEC)

OTEC uses the temperature difference between the ocean's warm surface water and the cooler water in its depths to produce heat energy that can power a heat engine to produce electricity. OTEC systems can be installed on ships, barges, or offshore platforms with underwater cables that transmit electricity to shore.

146

BIOMASS ENERGY CONVERSION

The term *biomass* refers to organic material such as plant and animal waste, wood, seaweed and algae, and garbage. A *biofuel* is the product of biomass conversion. These raw materials can be converted into liquid or gaseous fuels or used directly to provide heat and electricity. The by-products of biomass conversion can be used for fertilizers and chemicals. Wood, the most commonly used biofuel, is used to heat millions of homes every year. Other than hydroelectric power, wood and other biomass resources provide the largest source of renewable electricity produced in the United States today.

When wood is widely used as a fuel in an area, deforestation can occur, resulting in the possibility of soil erosion and mudslides. Burning wood, like fossil fuels, also pollutes the environment.

Types of Biomass Conversion

There are two types of biofuel energy (bioenergy) conversion processes: thermochemical conversion and biochemical conversion. *Thermochemical conversion* uses heat to produce chemical reactions in biomass. Direct combustion is the easiest and most commonly used method. Materials such as dry wood or agricultural wastes are chopped and burned to produce steam, electricity, or heat for industries, utilities, and homes. Wood burning in stoves and fireplaces is one example. In the United States, the number of homes burning wood for fuel — 20 million — has remained relatively unchanged since 1980, although these homes are using less fuel.

Homes in the South consume far greater amounts of wood energy than in other parts of the country. Industrial-size wood boilers are operating throughout the country, and the U.S. Department of Energy (DOE) projects that many more will be built during the next decade. The burning of agricultural wastes is also becoming more widespread. In Florida, sugar cane producers use the residue from the cane to generate much of their energy.

Pyrolysis, also called gasification or carbonization, uses heat to break down biomass and yields liquid, gaseous, and solid substances. Charcoal is an example of this process.

The second type of conversion process, *biochemical conversion*, uses enzymes, fungi, or other microorganisms to convert high-moisture biomass into either liquid or gaseous fuels. Bacteria convert manure, agricultural wastes, paper, and algae into methane, which is used as fuel. Sewage treatment plants have used anaerobic (without oxygen) digestion for many years to generate methane gas. Small-scale digesters have been used on farms, primarily in Europe and Asia, for hundreds of years. The DOE estimates that many thousands of biofuel plants are in use today in Korea and perhaps half a million plants operate in China.

A second type of biochemical conversion process, fermentation, uses yeast to decompose carbohydrates to yield ethyl alcohol (ethanol) and carbon dioxide. Sugar crops, grains (corn, in particular), potatoes, and other starchy crops are common feedstocks that supply the sugar for ethanol production.

Biofuels accounted for 3 percent of total energy sources and 38 percent of renewable energy consumed in 1997 (Table 9.1 and Figure 9.1). Biofuel consumption totaled an estimated 2.7 quadrillion Btu, most (2.4 quadrillion Btu) of which was wood energy. Some industries, such as the paper and lumber industries, have ready access to wood and wood by-products and rely heavily on wood as an energy source.

Ethanol and Methanol — Important Agricultural By-Products

Ethanol (ethyl alcohol) is a colorless, nearly odorless, flammable liquid derived from fermenting plant material that contains carbohydrates in the form of sugar. Most of the ethanol manufactured for use as fuel is derived from corn, wood, and sugar. A mixture of 10 percent ethanol and 90 percent gasoline is usable in any internal combustion engine without the need to modify the motor. Although the DOE claims that the demand for alcohol/gasoline blends is increasing because alcohol can substitute for lead as an octane booster, there is little question that the development of ethanol depends more upon the continued support of farm state legislators than any economic benefit.

Ethanol is difficult and expensive to produce in bulk. Methanol-blend fuels have also been tested successfully. (Methanol is methyl alcohol.) Using methanol instead of diesel fuel virtually eliminates sulfur emissions and reduces other environmental pollutants usually emitted from trucks and buses. Burning biofuels in vehicle engines creates a "carbon cycle" in which the earth's vegetation can in turn make use of the products of combustion and, therefore, reduce net greenhouse gases (Figure 9.11). Producing methanol from biofuels, however, is costly.

Some scientists believe ethanol made from wood, sawdust, corncobs, or rice hulls could liberate the alcohol fuel industry from its dependence on food crops, such as corn and sugar cane. Worldwide, there are enough corncobs and rice hulls left over from annual crop production to produce more than 40 billion gallons of ethanol.

In just a decade, research has cut the cost of wood-derived ethanol from $4.00 per gallon to $1.35 per gallon. Advocates of wood-derived ethanol believe that the eventual result of wood-to-ethanol conversion research could be a sustainable liquid fuel industry that does not rely on pollution-generating fossil fuels. For instance, if new trees were planted to replace those that were cut for fuel, they would be available for later harvesting and, in the meantime, contribute to the prevention of global warming by continuing their carbon-dioxide processing function. Other scientists warn that a huge demand for transportation fuels could create a demand for wood that might accelerate the destruction of old-growth forests and endanger ecosystems. Without careful attention to forestry practices, ethanol production might aggravate rather than solve the fuel problem.

MUNICIPAL WASTE RECOVERY

Each year, millions of tons of garbage are buried in landfills and city dumps. This method of disposal is not only costly, it is also becoming increasingly difficult

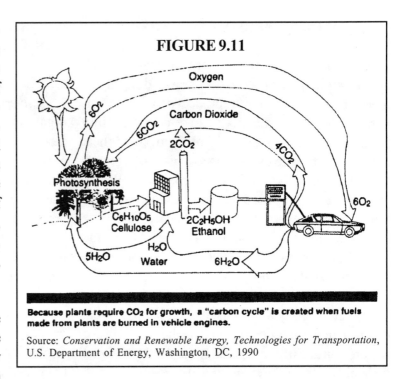

FIGURE 9.11

Because plants require CO₂ for growth, a "carbon cycle" is created when fuels made from plants are burned in vehicle engines.

Source: *Conservation and Renewable Energy, Technologies for Transportation,* U.S. Department of Energy, Washington, DC, 1990

as many landfills across the nation near capacity. Many communities discovered that they could solve both problems at once by constructing waste-to-energy plants. Not only was the garbage burned and reduced in volume by 90 percent, but energy in the form of steam or electricity was generated in a cost-effective way. The potential energy benefit is significant; solid waste generated by the nation's households is equal to more than 200 million barrels of oil per year.

Waste-To-Energy Plants

The two most common waste-to-energy plant designs are the *mass burn* (also called direct combustion) and the *refuse derived fuel* (RDF) systems.

Mass Burn System

Most waste-to-energy plants in the United States use the mass burn system. This system's advantage is that the waste does not have to be sorted or prepared before burning, except for removing obviously noncombustible, oversized objects. The mass burn eliminates expensive sorting, shredding, and transportation machinery that may be prone to break down.

Waste is carried to the plant in trash trucks and dropped into a storage pit. Large overhead cranes lift the garbage into a furnace feed hopper that controls the amount and rate of waste that is fed into the furnace. Next the garbage is moved through a combustion zone so that it burns to the greatest extent possible. The burning garbage produces heat, and that heat is used to produce steam. The steam can be used directly for industrial needs or heat or can be sent through a turbine to power a generator to produce electricity.

Refuse Derived Fuel (RDF)

RDF systems process waste to remove noncombustible objects and to create homogeneous and uniformly sized fuel. Large items such as bedsprings, dangerous materials, and flammable liquids are removed by hand. The trash is then shredded and carried to a screen to remove glass, rocks, and other material that cannot be burned. The remaining material is usually sifted a second time with an air separator to yield fluff. The fluff is sent to storage bins before being burned, or it can be compressed into pellets or briquettes for long-term storage. This fuel can be used as an energy source by itself in a variety of systems, or it can be used with other fuels, such as coal or wood.

Performance of Waste-To-Energy Systems

Most waste-to-energy systems can produce two to four pounds of steam for every pound of garbage burned. A 1,000-ton-per-day mass burn system will burn an average of 310,250 tons of trash each year and will recover 2 trillion Btu of energy. In addition, the plant will emit 96,000 tons of ash (32 percent of waste input) for landfill disposal. An RDF plant produces less ash but sends almost the same amount of waste to the landfill because of noncombustibles that accumulate in the separation process before burning. In 1995, there were 116 RDF facilities in 32 states, with a burning capacity of 100,969 tons per day

Disadvantages of Waste-To-Energy Plants

The major obstacle to increasing the use of municipal waste-to-energy plants is their effect on the environment. Noise from trucks, fans, and processing equipment at RDF plants can be unpleasant for nearby

residents. The emission of particles into the air is controlled by electrostatic precipitators, and most gases can be eliminated by proper combustion techniques. There is concern, however, about the amounts of dioxin (a very dangerous air pollutant) that is often emitted from these plants.

Landfill Gas Recovery

Landfills contain a large amount of biodegradable matter. Gas is created because of the lack of oxygen that helps the growth of methagens — types of bacteria that produce methane gas and carbon dioxide. In the past, as landfills aged, these gases built up and leaked out. This gas leakage prompted some communities to drill holes and burn off the dangerous methane.

The energy crisis of the 1970s made this methane gas an energy resource too valuable to waste, and efforts were made to find an inexpensive way to tap the gas. The first landfill gas-recovery site was finished in 1975 at the Palos Verdes Landfill in Rolling Hills Estates, California. Depending on the extraction rates, most existing sites can produce gas for about 20 years.

In a typical operation, garbage is allowed to decompose for several months. When a sufficient amount of methane gas has developed, it is piped out to a generating plant where it is turned into electricity. In its purest form, methane gas is equivalent to natural gas and can be used in exactly the same way.

The advantages of tapping gas from a landfill go beyond the energy provided by the methane. When internal pressure forces methane gas to seep into the air, it carries very unpleasant odors into the surrounding neighborhoods. The released methane can also be a danger because if it accumulates and is accidentally ignited, it can explode. Extracting the methane gas for energy eliminates both of these problems.

HYDROGEN — A FUEL OF THE FUTURE?

Hydrogen, the lightest and most abundant chemical element, is, from the environmental point of view, the ideal fuel. Its combustion produces only water vapor — it is entirely carbon-free. Three-quarters of the mass of the universe consists of hydrogen. However, the elemental, combustible form of hydrogen, a gas, is not found in nature. The many compounds of hydrogen cannot be converted into pure hydrogen without the expenditure of energy. The amount of energy that would be required is about the same as the amount of energy that would be obtained by the combustion of the hydrogen. Therefore, with today's technology, little or nothing could be gained from an energy point of view.

Hydrogen is not now economical to use as a fuel. It is useful, however, wherever weight is important, such as in rockets and domestic aircraft. A great amount of heat is released when hydrogen burns, and oxyhydrogen torches provide the high temperatures needed for many welding applications. However, hydrogen has considerable potential as a clean fuel and, because it is a gas, can be distributed with essentially the same technology as natural gas. Scientists are researching ways to economically produce hydrogen. Whether that will come from fusion, solar energy, or elsewhere, is not now possible to predict.

Scientists have considered the possibility of a transition to hydrogen for more than a century, and today, many see hydrogen as the logical "third-wave" fuel — hydrogen gas following oil, just as oil replaced coal decades earlier. While advocates note that the world's current energy needs could be met with less than 1 percent of today's fresh water supply and that hydrogen can be produced from seawater, hydrogen as an energy resource is still a long, long way in the future.

What Would a Solar-Hydrogen Energy System Look Like?

Christopher Flavin, vice-president for research of Worldwatch Institute (*Power Surge: Guide to the Coming Energy Revolution*, W. W. Norton, 1994), describes a vision of society fueled not by fossil fuels but by renewable power sources. One of the chief advantages of an energy system based upon solar power and hydrogen is that it would be largely invisible. Fuel cells and flywheels could be located in home basements. Solar rooftops would be nearly indistin-

guishable from conventional rooftops. Hydrogen pipelines would be buried underground, as are today's natural gas lines. Some rural farming areas would be sprinkled with wind turbines, but the larger wind and solar power plants would be located in remote areas.

THE NEXT ENERGY REVOLUTION? — THE FUTURE OF RENEWABLE ENERGY SOURCES

In 1997, renewable energy contributed 8 percent of the total energy consumed by the nation. The United States reversed a five-year decline in energy consumption in 1996, a boom year for the economy and energy use in the nation. The nation's fleet of automobiles has become less energy-efficient, and consumers are less interested in energy-saving technology. Many economists believe that only a return of higher energy prices will cause Americans to once again reduce their energy use and consider renewable energy sources. Despite their environmental advantage over fossil fuels, renewable energies have never attracted enough financial support from the government, the public, or energy companies to the point where they can be cost-competitive with fossil fuel power.

The Energy Information Administration (EIA) of the U.S. Department of Energy annually forecasts energy supply, demand, and prices for the coming two decades. Its projections are based upon business trends and federal, state, and local laws in effect at the time. These forecasts are used by government officials and planners and decision-makers in the public and private sectors. In its *Annual Energy Outlook 1998* (December 1997), the EIA predicted that electricity from renewable sources would barely increase, from 433 billion kilowatt-hours in 1996 to 436 billion in 2020 (Figure 9.12). A 34 percent increase in the generation of other renewables is expected to be offset by a decline in hydroelectricity. The largest growth will be in the use of biomass and recovery of methane from municipal solid waste (Figure 9.13). Improvements in wind energy technology, such as larger, more efficient turbines, could triple U.S. wind capacity from 1.4 gigawatts in 1996 to 4.1 gigawatts in 2020.

By the year 2010, the Energy Information Administration predicts that renewables *could* contribute about 10 percent of the nation's total energy consumption and as much as 50 to 70 percent of U.S. energy by 2030 *if* government supported the effort. Most experts believe that unlikely.

ABROAD — A GRASSROOTS MOVEMENT

While the use of renewable energy sources has stalled in the United States, other countries have shown more interest.

Wind Energy

Encouraged by improved technology, falling costs, and government incentives like tax credits and guaranteed prices, wind power is booming across Europe. With windmills springing up from the coasts of Sweden to the tip of Spain, Europe's wind industry already employs 20,000 people. Close to 100,000 Danes own shares in hundreds of small cooperatives that operate 4,700 windmills. Furthermore, they are making a profit. Wind power generates 6 percent of Denmark's electricity, the highest per capita output of wind energy in the world.

One reason for the growth in the industry is that the European Union wants to diversify its energy

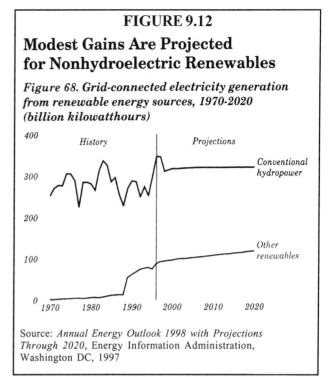

FIGURE 9.12

Modest Gains Are Projected for Nonhydroelectric Renewables

Figure 68. Grid-connected electricity generation from renewable energy sources, 1970-2020 (billion kilowatthours)

Source: *Annual Energy Outlook 1998 with Projections Through 2020*, Energy Information Administration, Washington DC, 1997

sources while clamping down on pollution. Almost no country supports the expansion of nuclear power, and in many areas, wind power is becoming economically viable. New wind turbines already generate electricity less expensively than solar panels, biomass, or other nontraditional sources. The International Energy Agency, a research organization based in Paris, reports that wind energy is now competitive with electricity from Europe's oil- and coal-fired power plants.

In wind power, Europe has already overtaken the United States, which led the drive to wind energy in the 1980s. Europe's capacity of 4,100 megawatts is two and one-half times that of the United States, with Germany alone surpassing the output of American wind farms.

Wind energy is produced under entirely different circumstances in the United States and in Europe. American entrepreneurs, seeing wind energy as a potentially profitable business, built large wind farms with huge numbers of turbines. When oil prices fell and tax credits were cut, growth stalled. In Northern Europe, wind power is a cottage industry. In Denmark, Germany, Sweden, and the Netherlands, wind energy began as a grass-roots movements with small groups of politically motivated investors installing one or a few machines at a time. In Spain, Britain, and Greece, the

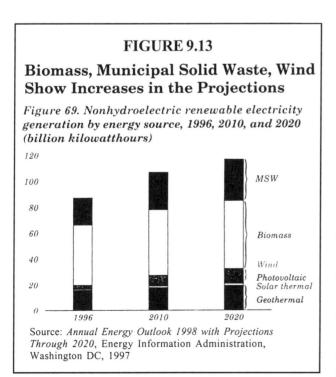

FIGURE 9.13

Biomass, Municipal Solid Waste, Wind Show Increases in the Projections

Figure 69. Nonhydroelectric renewable electricity generation by energy source, 1996, 2010, and 2020 (billion kilowatthours)

Source: *Annual Energy Outlook 1998 with Projections Through 2020*, Energy Information Administration, Washington DC, 1997

151

clusters were larger because money has been provided by local governments and utilities. The latest trend in Europe is to build wind farms offshore, where there is more wind and fewer complaints that they clutter the landscape. The Netherlands, which had approximately 11,000 windmills less than a century ago, has 1,120 modern turbines today, many of them standing beside the old-style windmills.

Solar Power

Rural areas are more expensive to serve than cities, and electrification has been slow to reach many people in rural areas of developing countries. In the United States, it was only after the Rural Electrification Administration in 1935 provided low-cost financing to rural electric cooperatives that most farmers received power. Many developing countries have similar programs, but as increasingly remote and mountainous areas have begun receiving electricity, the cost of hooking up new customers has grown greatly. The World Bank estimates that in places such as western China, the Himalayan foothills, or the Amazon basin, the cost of hooking up new rural customers is seven times that in cities. Furthermore, state-owned power systems have been badly managed in many countries, as well as riddled by graft and corruption. This has left many national power systems all but bankrupt and blackouts common.

In India, blackouts are so common that many factories and other businesses have, at great expense, set up their own private systems, based primarily on natural gas, propane, or fuel oil. Although rural families do not have access to those systems, they do have sunlight. In most tropical countries, considerable energy falls on rooftops in the form of sunlight. Electricity produced by solar photovoltaic cells (see above), semiconductor devices made of silicon, was initially too expensive, as much as a thousand times more than conventional plants. By 1996, the price had fallen to about $1.65 a killowatt-hour, opening up the global market. Solar energy advocates believe that solar cells eventually can be made so inexpensive that they can

provide economical power even for consumers already hooked up to conventional power.

During the 1990s, a different approach to solar electrification developed, driven less by government planners and more by the desire of individual families to meet their own need for electricity. In more than a dozen countries, solar power is now reaching thousands of families one by one, avoiding the delay for government planners to deliver. In Kenya, for example, where the state power company is on the verge of bankruptcy, eight domestic companies have merged to market, install, and maintain solar home systems. With little state or international assistance, those companies managed to electrify 20,000 rural households between 1987 and 1992, 3,000 more than the state power system.

The Problem — Lack of Credit

Despite those advances, only one of every thousand potential customers has yet been served. Part of the problem is lack of credit. Consumer credit is one of the most momentous financial advances of the twentieth century, leading to wide ownership of homes, automobiles, and appliances that the average person cannot afford outright. According to Neville Williams, president of Solar Electric Light Fund (SELF), a nonprofit U.S. energy agency, millions of families in the developing world could afford solar energy if credit were available.

To fill this gap, international agencies are working to set up revolving credit funds to finance solar energy systems in many countries, including Vietnam, India, Indonesia, Uganda, Swaziland, and the Dominican Republic. A number of nonprofit agencies, private foundations, investment firms, and the World Bank have been trying in recent years to satisfy this financial need. Many observers hope that newly developing nations can "leapfrog" many of the more damaging environmental practices, including a heavy dependence on fossil fuels that had characterized earlier modes of electrification.

CHAPTER X

ENERGY CONSERVATION

The United States has yet to fully unleash one if its most powerful weapons ... the aggressive promotion of energy conservation and efficiency.... It would be a mistake for us to begin to fight for energy independence by ignoring conservation — our most strategic weapon. — James L. Wolf, Executive Director, The Alliance to Save Energy (1990)

WHAT IS ENERGY CONSERVATION?

Energy conservation is the more efficient use of energy, not the curtailment of services that energy provides. Conservation occurs when societies adapt more efficient technologies that reduce energy use. Environmental concerns, such as acid rain and the potential for global warming, have increased public awareness about the importance of energy conservation.

Energy efficiency is measured by two indicators. The first is annual per capita (per person per year) consumption. Annual per person energy consumption topped 351 million Btu in 1973 and 1979, dropped to 301 million Btu in 1983, and rose to 352 million Btu per capita in 1997 (Figure 10.1).

The second indicator is energy consumption per dollar of gross domestic product (GDP: the total value of goods and services produced by a nation). In 1970, 19.6 thousand Btu of energy was consumed for each dollar of GDP, dropping to 13.1 thousand Btu per dollar in 1997 (Figure 10.2). Figure 10.3 shows U.S. energy use relative to GDP and population from 1950 and projected to the year 2010.

EFFICIENCY IN THE TRANSPORTATION SECTOR

The U.S. transportation system plays a central role in the economy. Highway transportation is dependent on internal combustion engine vehicles fueled almost exclusively by petroleum. The transportation sector accounted for 26 percent of energy consumed in the United States in 1997. That year, Americans used 24.8 quadrillion Btu, mostly from petroleum, for transportation. Despite im-

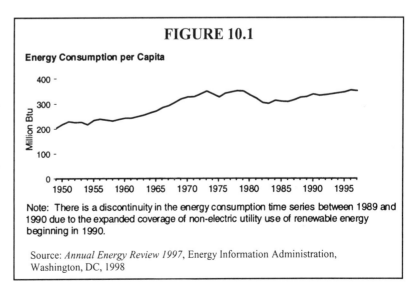

FIGURE 10.1

Energy Consumption per Capita

Note: There is a discontinuity in the energy consumption time series between 1989 and 1990 due to the expanded coverage of non-electric utility use of renewable energy beginning in 1990.

Source: *Annual Energy Review 1997*, Energy Information Administration, Washington, DC, 1998

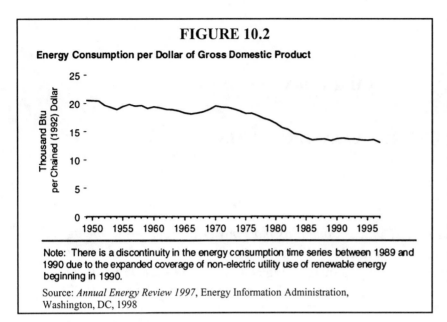

FIGURE 10.2

Energy Consumption per Dollar of Gross Domestic Product

Note: There is a discontinuity in the energy consumption time series between 1989 and 1990 due to the expanded coverage of non-electric utility use of renewable energy beginning in 1990.

Source: *Annual Energy Review 1997*, Energy Information Administration, Washington, DC, 1998

United States. The major growth over the past 10 years has been in fuel use by trucks. Meanwhile, automobile fuel use has remained nearly constant due to fuel efficiency increases that have offset the growth in car miles traveled. By the year 2000, the Energy Information Administration (EIA) of the U.S. Department of Energy predicts truck fuel use will be nearly equal to automobile fuel use. Boosting truck efficiency, therefore, will become increasingly important in holding down oil demand.

provements in U.S. transport energy efficiency in recent decades, the United States still consumes more than one-third of the world's transport energy. American dependence on oil not only makes the economy vulnerable to the supply and price volatility of the world oil market, but also exacerbates air quality problems.

Automotive Efficiency

Policy makers interested in transportation energy conservation are faced with an array of conservation options (Table 10.1). They do not have the freedom to pick and choose among conservation options because, even if not constrained by budgetary limits, some options may not be mutually supportive. For example, efforts to promote freer flow of automobile traffic, such as high-occupancy vehicle (HOV) lanes or free parking for carpools, may sabotage efforts to effect shifts to mass transit or to reduce trip lengths and frequency. Policy makers must consider how the implementation of one strategy will fit into an overall transportation plan.

Motor gasoline, which is divided among passenger cars, light and heavy-duty trucks, aircraft, and miscellaneous other, consumes approximately 45 percent of the oil used in the

The Corporate Average Fuel Economy (CAFE) Standards

The 1973 OPEC oil embargo painfully reminded America how dependent it had become on

FIGURE 10.3

Indices of U.S. Energy, Population, and Economic Growth, 1950-2010

Note: Total energy consumption excludes renewable sources of energy except for hydropower and geothermal sources used for electricity generation.

Source: *Improving Technology: Modeling Energy Futures for the National Energy Strategy*, Energy Information Administration, Washington, DC, 1991

154

foreign sources of fuel. Although the United States makes up only 5 percent of the world's population, it consumes 26 percent of the world's supply of oil, much of which is imported from the Middle East. The oil embargo prompted Congress to pass the 1975 Automobile Fuel Efficiency Act (PL 96-426), which set the initial Corporate Average Fuel Efficiency standards (commonly called the CAFE standards).

The CAFE standards required domestic automakers to increase the average mileage of the new cars sold every year, achieving 27.5 miles per gallon (mpg) by 1985. Under the CAFE rules, car

---

TABLE 10.1

Transportation Conservation Options

Improve the Technical Efficiency of Vehicles
1. Higher fuel economy requirements—CAFE standards (R).
2. Reducing congestion: smart highways (E,I), flextime (E,R), better signaling (I), improved maintenance of roadways (I), time of day charges (E), improved air traffic controls (I,R), plus options that reduce vehicular traffic.
3. Higher fuel taxes (E).
4. Gas guzzler taxes, or feebate schemes (E).
5. Support for increased R&D (E,I).
6. Inspection and maintenance programs (R).

Increase Load Factor
1. HOV lanes (I).
2. Forgiven tolls (E), free parking for carpools (E).
3. Higher fuel taxes (E).
4. Higher charges on other vmt trip-dependent factors (E): parking (taxes, restrictions, end of tax treatment as business cost), tolls, etc.

Change to More Efficient Modes
1. Improvements in transit service.
   a. New technologies—maglev, high speed trains (E,I).
   b. Rehabilitation of older systems (I).
   c. Expansion of service—more routes, higher frequency (I).
   d. Other service improvements (I)—dedicated busways, better security, more bus stop shelters, more comfortable vehicles.
2. Higher fuel taxes (E).
3. Reduced transit fares through higher U.S. transit subsidies (E).[a]
4. Higher charges on other vmt/trip-dependent factors for less efficient modes (E)—tolls, parking.
5. Shifting urban form to higher density, more mixed use, greater concentration through zoning changes (R), encouragement of "infill" development (E,R,I), public investment in infrastructure (I), etc.

Reduce Number or Length of Trips
1. Shifting urban form to higher density, more mixed use, greater concentration (E,R,I).
2. Promoting working at home or at decentralized facilities (E,I).
3. Higher fuel taxes (E).
4. Higher charges on other vmt/trip-dependent factors (E).

Shift to Alternative Fuels
1. Fleet requirements for alternative fuel-capable vehicles and actual use of alternative fuels (R).
2. Low-emission/zero emission vehicle (LEV/ZEV) requirements (R).
3. Various promotions (E): CAFE credits, emission credits, tax credits, etc.
4. Higher fuel taxes that do not apply to alternative fuels (E), or subsidies for the alternatives (E).
5. Support for increased R&D (E,I).
6. Public investment—government fleet investments (I).

Freight Options
1. RD&D of technology improvements (E,I).

[a] U.S. transit subsidies, already among the highest in the developed world, may merely promote inefficiencies.

KEY: CAFE = corporate average fuel economy; E = economic incentive; HOV = high-occupancy vehicle; I = public investment; maglev = trains supported by magnetic levitation; R = regulatory action; RD&D = research, development, and demonstration; vmt = vehicle-miles traveled.

Source: *Saving Energy in U.S. Transportation*, Office of Technology Assessment, Washington, DC, 1994

TABLE 10.2

Motor Vehicle Efficiency, 1960-1996

Year	Passenger Cars [1]						All Motor Vehicles [2]					
	Mileage		Fuel Consumption		Fuel Rate		Mileage		Fuel Consumption		Fuel Rate	
	Miles per Car	Index 1973 = 100.0	Gallons per Car	Index 1973 = 100.0	Miles per Gallon	Index 1973 = 100.0	Miles per Vehicle	Index 1973 = 100.0	Gallons per Vehicle	Index 1973 = 100.0	Miles per Gallon	Index 1973 = 100.0
1960	R9,518	R96.3	R668	R90.6	R14.3	R106.7	R9,732	R96.4	R784	R92.2	R12.4	R104.2
1961	R9,521	R96.3	R663	R90.0	R14.4	R107.5	R9,708	R96.1	R781	R91.9	R12.4	R104.2
1962	R9,494	R96.1	R662	R89.8	R14.3	R106.7	R9,687	R95.9	R779	R91.6	R12.4	R104.2
1963	R9,587	R97.0	R655	R88.9	R14.6	R109.0	R9,737	R96.4	R780	R91.8	R12.5	105.0
1964	R9,665	R97.8	R661	R89.7	R14.6	R109.0	R9,805	R97.1	R787	R92.6	R12.5	105.0
1965	R9,603	R97.2	R661	R89.7	R14.5	R108.2	R9,826	R97.3	R787	R92.6	R12.5	105.0
1966	R9,733	R98.5	R688	R93.4	R14.1	R105.2	9,675	95.8	780	91.8	R12.4	104.2
1967	R9,849	R99.6	R699	R94.8	R14.1	R105.2	9,751	96.6	786	92.5	R12.4	104.2
1968	R9,922	R100.4	R714	R96.9	R13.9	R103.7	R9,864	97.7	805	94.7	R12.2	R102.5
1969	R9,921	R100.4	R727	R98.6	R13.6	R101.5	9,885	97.9	821	96.6	R12.0	R100.8
1970	R9,989	R101.1	R737	R100.0	R13.5	R100.7	9,976	98.8	830	97.6	R12.0	R100.8
1971	R10,097	R102.2	R743	R100.8	R13.6	R101.5	R10,133	100.3	839	98.7	R12.1	R101.7
1972	R10,171	R102.9	R754	R102.3	R13.5	R100.7	10,279	101.8	857	100.8	R12.0	100.0
1973	R9,884	100.0	R737	100.0	R13.4	100.0	10,099	100.0	850	100.0	R11.9	100.0
1974	R9,221	R93.3	R677	R91.9	R13.6	R101.5	9,493	94.0	788	92.7	R12.0	R100.8
1975	R9,309	R94.2	R665	R90.2	R14.0	R104.5	9,627	95.3	790	92.9	R12.2	R102.5
1976	R9,418	R95.3	R681	R92.4	R13.8	R103.0	9,774	96.8	806	94.8	R12.1	R101.7
1977	R9,517	R96.3	R676	R91.7	R14.1	R105.2	9,978	98.8	814	95.8	R12.3	R103.4
1978	R9,500	R96.1	R665	R90.2	R14.3	R106.7	10,077	99.8	816	96.0	R12.4	R104.2
1979	R9,062	R91.7	R620	R84.1	R14.6	R109.0	9,722	96.3	776	91.3	R12.5	R105.0
1980	R8,813	R89.2	R551	R74.8	R16.0	R119.4	9,458	93.7	712	83.8	R13.3	111.8
1981	R8,873	R89.8	R538	R73.0	R16.5	R123.1	9,477	93.8	697	82.0	R13.6	R114.3
1982	R9,050	R91.6	R535	R72.6	R16.9	R126.1	9,644	95.5	686	80.7	R14.1	R118.5
1983	R9,118	R92.3	R534	R72.5	R17.1	R127.6	R9,760	96.6	686	80.7	R14.2	R119.3
1984	R9,248	R93.6	R530	R71.9	R17.4	R129.9	10,017	99.2	691	81.3	R14.5	R121.8
1985	R9,419	R95.3	R538	R73.0	R17.5	R130.6	R10,020	99.2	685	80.6	R14.6	R122.7
1986	R9,464	R95.8	R543	R73.7	R17.4	R129.9	R10,143	100.4	R692	R81.4	R14.7	R123.5
1987	R9,720	R98.3	R539	R73.1	R18.0	R134.3	R10,453	103.5	694	81.6	R15.1	R126.9
1988	R9,972	R100.9	R531	R72.0	R18.8	R140.3	R10,721	106.2	688	81.6	R15.6	R131.1
1989	R10,157	R102.8	R533	R72.3	R19.0	R141.8	R10,932	R108.2	688	80.9	R15.9	R133.6
1990	R10,277	R104.0	R506	R68.7	R20.3	R151.5	11,107	110.0	677	79.6	R16.4	R137.8
1991	R10,322	R104.4	R487	R66.1	R21.2	R158.2	11,294	111.8	R669	R78.7	R16.9	R142.0
1992	R10,571	R107.0	R502	R68.1	R21.0	R156.7	11,558	114.4	R683	80.4	R16.9	R142.0
1993	R10,545	R106.7	R512	R69.5	R20.8	R153.7	11,595	114.8	693	81.5	R16.7	R140.3
1994	R10,759	R108.9	R517	R70.1	R20.8	R155.2	11,683	115.7	698	82.1	R16.7	R140.3
1995	R11,203	R113.3	R530	R71.9	R21.1	R157.5	R11,793	R116.8	R700	R82.4	R16.8	R141.2
1996P	11,314	114.5	531	72.0	21.3	159.0	11,807	116.9	698	82.1	16.9	142.0

[1] From 1960 to 1965, passenger cars category also includes motorcycles.

[2] Passenger cars, motorcycles, buses, other 2-axle 4-tire vehicles (including vans, minivans, pickup trucks, and sport-utility vehicles), single-unit trucks with six or more tires, and combination trucks.

R=Revised. P=Preliminary.
• 1960-1994—Federal Highway Administration, *Highway Statistics Summary to 1995*, Table VM-201A. • 1995 forward—Federal Highway Administration, *Highway Statistics*, annual, Table VM-1.

Source: *Annual Energy Review 1997*, Energy Information Administration, Washington, DC, 1998

manufacturers could still sell the big, less efficient cars with powerful 8-cylinder engines, but to meet the *average* fuel efficiency rates, they also had to sell smaller, more efficient cars. Automakers that failed to meet each year's CAFE standards were fined. Those that managed to surpass the rates earned credits that they could use in years when they fell below the CAFE requirements. Faced with the CAFE standards, the car companies became more inventive and managed to keep their cars relatively large and roomy with such innovations as electronic fuel injection and front-wheel drive.

TABLE 10.3

Percentage of New Fleet Light Duty Purchases That Must Be AFVs

Year	Federal Government	State Government	Fuel Providers	Private/ Municipal✶
1993	7,500*	-	-	-
1994	11,250*	-	-	-
1995	15,000*	-	-	-
1996	25	-	-	-
1997	33	10	30	-
1998	50	15	50	-
1999	75	25	70	-
2000	75	50	90	-
2001	75	75	90	-
2002	75	75	90	20
2003	75	75	90	30
2004	75	75	90	40
2005	75	75	90	50
2006	75	75	90	60
2007	75	75	90	70

* Actual number of vehicles

✶ Dependent upon DOE final rulemaking in 2000

U.S. Department of Energy, March 1997.

Source: Kelly Hill, *Alternative Fuel Policies and Programs: A Legislator's Guide*, National Conference of State Legislators, Washington, DC, 1997

The contribution of increased automobile fuel efficiency has been significant. In the decades since the first oil shock in 1973, the fuel economy of passenger cars (all cars currently on the road) increased from 13 miles per gallon (mpg) to 21 mpg (Table 10.2). It has, however, remained constant since the early 1990s.

Greater gains have been made in the economy of new cars. In 1974, just after the oil embargo, vehicle miles per gallon averaged 14.2 (total fleet); today, the total new vehicle fleet fuel economy is 28 mpg, although it has remained virtually unchanged for several years. The introduction of new, more efficient models with more efficient engines, transmissions, and designs contributed to most of these gains. Consumer shifts to smaller cars have played a very small role (15 percent) in overall gains.

As a result, the total automobile fleet fuel economy has been expected to increase as more and more fuel-efficient cars enter the market and older, less fuel-efficient autos drop out of the nation's fleet as they wear out and can no longer be driven. However, the most vigorous new vehicle sales are of sport-utility vehicles (SUVs), vans, and light trucks, which are less fuel-efficient. In fact, November 1998 was the first month in which more SUVs, vans, and light trucks were sold than automobiles.

Generally, there is a trade-off between safety and energy conservation in automobiles. Weight reduction is the easiest way to increase car mileage. Weight reduction almost inevitably leads to reductions in strength and "crush space" that protect occupants during a collision. High mileage cars, therefore, tend to be more dangerous to their occupants in an accident. Safety may be increased, however, by the improved maneuverability of lighter vehicles, making it easier to avoid collisions. In addition, future automobiles will likely incor-

FIGURE 10.4

Alternative-Fueled Bus in Nebraska

Source: *Alternatives to Traditional Transportation Fuels*, Energy Information Administration, Washington, DC, 1997

porate lighter "space age" materials found in modern military aircraft, which will lighten automobiles while maintaining their strength.

The potential for savings from fuel economy in trucks is huge, since their current fuel economy is so much lower than that of automobiles. The EIA projects a small increase in fuel efficiency for the heavy truck fleet and a much larger increase for the small truck fleet. If the heavy truck fleet were to reach a fuel efficiency of 10 mpg through reduction of aerodynamic drag and improvements in engine and driving efficiency, projected oil demand would drop by 300,000 barrels per day. Over the past few years, more aerodynamically designed trucks have become common on American roads.

The Persian Gulf War (1991) was another strong reminder to the United States of its continuing heavy dependence on foreign oil, causing some members of Congress to want to raise the CAFE standards — 45 mpg for cars and 35 mpg for light trucks. Those in favor of raising CAFE standards claimed that this would save about 2.8 million barrels of oil a day. They also noted that if cars become even more fuel-efficient in the future,

emissions of carbon dioxide would be significantly reduced. Carbon dioxide has been identified as the main "greenhouse" gas contributing to global warming. Moreover, with better mileage, the nation's millions of drivers would save money in gas costs.

The domestic auto industry opposed the bill raising the CAFE standards, claiming

Ours is the most thoroughly regulated industry in America, but the U.S. motor vehicle market is the most wide open to foreign competition. We need to invest in new products and facilities to remain competitive, but the piling on of more and more regulations will drain ... the financial and human resources needed for that effort. — Thomas H. Hanna, president of the Motor Vehicle Manufacturers Association of the United States, *MVMA Motor Vehicle Facts and Figures '91*

Carmakers believe that the congressional fuel economy campaign saddled American motorists with car features they would not like and would

158

not buy. Although the required efficiency standard has been achieved consistently since, efficiency levels are not improving further due to America's preference for larger, less-efficient cars, minivans, and sport-utility vehicles and increased travel. The fall in the price of gasoline to less than $.90 a gallon has virtually eliminated any sense of urgency to the issue. In addition, when federal laws requiring 55-mph speed on interstate highways were repealed, states allowed increased speed limits, which also lower fuel efficiency.

Mandating of Alternative Fuel Vehicles

Over the past decade, several laws have been passed to encourage or mandate the use of vehicles powered by fuels other than gasoline. The Clean Air Act Amendments of 1990 (PL101-549) required certain businesses and local governments with fleets of 10 or more vehicles in 21 metropolitan areas nationwide to phase in alternative fuel vehicles (AFVs) over time. Twenty percent of those fleets were required to be AFVs by 1998. While great strides have been made in increasing the use of AFVs, there is currently no way to know if compliance has occurred because reporting and enforcement methods are inadequate.

The Energy Policy Act of 1992 (PL 102-486) was passed in the wake of the 1991 Persian Gulf War to conserve energy and increase the proportion of energy supplied domestically. It required the federal government to purchase 22,500 AFVs by 1995 and increase the percentage of such vehicles from 25 percent in 1996 to 75 percent in 1999 and thereafter (Table 10.3; budget cuts have slowed compliance with the schedule). Many municipal governments and the U.S. Postal Service have put into operation fleets of natural gas vehicles, such as garbage trucks, transit buses, and postal vans. Figure 10.4 shows an alternative-fueled bus.

Progress with Alternative Transportation Fuels and Vehicles

The market success of alternative fuels and AFVs hinges upon public acceptance.
— National Conference of State Legislatures, 1997

TABLE 10.4

Estimated Number of Alternative-Fueled Vehicles in Use in the United States, by Fuel, 1992-1998

Fuel	1992	1993	1994	1995	1996	1997	1998
Liquefied Petroleum Gases (LPG)[a]	221,000	269,000	264,000	259,000	263,000	271,000	*279,000*
Compressed Natural Gas (CNG)	23,191	32,714	41,227	50,218	60,144	73,773	*85,122*
Liquefied Natural Gas (LNG)	90	299	484	603	663	965	*1,136*
Methanol, 85 Percent[b] (M85)	4,850	10,263	15,484	18,319	20,265	20,656	*21,370*
Methanol, Neat (M100)	404	414	415	386	172	172	*172*
Ethanol, 85 Percent[b c] (E85)	172	441	605	1,527	4,536	9,389	*10,872*
Ethanol, 95 Percent[b] (E95)	38	27	33	136	361	357	*357*
Electricity	1,607	1,690	2,224	2,860	3,280	4,040	*4,761*
Non-LPG Subtotal	30,352	45,848	60,472	74,049	89,421	109,352	*123,790*
Total	**251,352**	**314,848**	**324,472**	**333,049**	**352,421**	**380,352**	***402,790***

[a] Values are rounded to thousands. Accordingly, these estimates are not equal to the sum of Federal fleet data (for which exact counts are available) and non-Federal fleet estimates (rounded to thousands).
[b]The remaining portion of 85-percent methanol and both ethanol fuels is gasoline.
[c]Does not include recently announced plans of some major automakers to make available large numbers of vehicles capable of operating on E85 fuel in the near future.
Notes: Estimates for 1996 have been revised. Estimates for 1997, which were based on company plans or projections, have been revised. Estimates for 1998, in italics, are based on plans or projections and may be revised.
     1992-1995: Science Applications International Corporation, "Alternative Transportation Fuels and Vehicles Data Development," unpublished final report prepared for the Energy Information Administration (McLean, VA, July 1996) and U.S. Department of Energy, Office of Energy Efficiency and Renewable Energy. **1996-1998:** Energy Information Administration, Office of Coal, Nuclear, Electric, and Alternate Fuels and U.S. Department of Energy, Office of Energy Efficiency and Renewable Energy.

Source: *Alternatives to Traditional Transportation Fuels*, Energy Information Administration, Washington, DC, 1997

TABLE 10.5

Estimated Number of Alternative-Fueled Vehicles In Use, by State and Fuel Type, 1996

	Liquefied Petroleum Gases	Natural Gas	Methanol	Ethanol	Electricity	Total
Alabama	2,887	456	0	0	19	3,362
Alaska	131	23	0	0	4	158
Arizona	2,807	2,005	10	0	157	4,979
Arkansas	1,301	448	0	1	4	1,754
California	31,258	11,075	14,660	348	1,326	58,667
Colorado	4,184	2,608	271	97	238	7,398
Connecticut	1,439	698	14	0	21	2,172
Delaware	261	241	30	0	1	533
District of Columbia	30	619	471	59	63	1,242
Florida	8,233	1,928	0	3	50	10,214
Georgia	7,748	2,118	135	0	46	10,047
Hawaii	443	0	13	0	70	526
Idaho	1,499	294	0	0	1	1,794
Illinois	15,896	1,360	254	862	19	18,391
Indiana	5,786	1,566	0	276	56	7,684
Iowa	4,753	248	42	481	1	5,525
Kansas	3,126	48	41	73	3	3,291
Kentucky	2,590	599	0	192	3	3,384
Louisiana	3,398	831	135	0	0	4,364
Maine	586	0	0	0	4	590
Maryland	2,671	1,272	538	26	9	4,516
Massachusetts	2,768	841	279	0	115	4,003
Michigan	13,365	1,180	316	214	230	15,305
Minnesota	1,801	385	0	401	9	2,596
Mississippi	4,356	93	0	0	3	4,452
Missouri	2,960	544	397	659	6	4,566
Montana	1,167	321	0	3	1	1,492
Nebraska	2,271	265	0	314	3	2,853
Nevada	1,063	1,456	3	0	20	2,542
New Hampshire	320	10	1	4	19	354
New Jersey	3,798	1,338	57	0	92	5,285
New Mexico	3,047	642	0	0	12	3,701
New York	7,672	4,519	445	1	45	12,682
North Carolina	7,795	122	0	9	13	7,939
North Dakota	731	422	0	14	9	1,176
Ohio	14,219	2,549	204	163	25	17,160
Oklahoma	16,012	1,555	2	3	59	17,631
Oregon	6,115	205	193	5	32	6,550
Pennsylvania	10,447	2,325	465	0	70	13,307
Rhode Island	469	196	0	0	5	670
South Carolina	4,293	93	0	1	18	4,405
South Dakota	808	49	2	63	0	922
Tennessee	7,461	317	0	3	31	7,812
Texas	30,024	5,759	530	4	67	36,384
Utah	1,786	2,006	5	47	31	3,875
Vermont	265	8	0	0	37	310
Virginia	3,556	1,351	3	28	43	4,981
Washington	5,004	1,327	773	0	158	7,262
West Virginia	642	988	3	0	2	1,635
Wisconsin	6,801	1,452	145	543	30	8,971
Wyoming	957	52	0	0	0	1,009
U.S. Total	**263,000**	**60,807**	**20,437**	**4,897**	**3,280**	**352,421**

Notes: Natural gas includes compressed natural gas (CNG) and liquefied natural gas (LNG). Methanol includes M85 and M100. Ethanol includes E85 and E95. Data for 1996 has been revised.

Office of Coal, Nuclear, Electric, and Alternative Fuels.

Source: *Alternatives to Traditional Transportation Fuels*, Energy Information Administration, Washington, DC, 1997

TABLE 10.6

Number of Alternative-Fueled Refueling Sites by State and Fuel Type, 1996

State	Methanol (M85)	Compressed Natural Gas (CNG)	Ethanol (E85)	Liquefied Petroleum Gas (LPG)	Electricity	Liquefied Natural Gas (LNG)	Total
Alabama		17		114		2	133
Alaska		1		9			10
Arizona	1	31		71	40	3	146
Arkansas		9		156			165
California	66	203		219	197	18	703
Colorado	2	45	1	48		3	99
Connecticut		22		18	1		41
Delaware		6		6			12
District of Columbia	1	8	1		2		12
Florida	3	60		222	4		289
Georgia	1	89		80		3	173
Hawaii					3		3
Idaho		7	1	20	1	1	30
Illinois	2	24	14	163			203
Indiana		47	2	125	1	3	178
Iowa		5	10	107	1		123
Kansas		18	2	38		1	59
Kentucky		13	3	35			51
Louisiana		21		44		2	67
Maine				12			12
Maryland	2	31		21		3	57
Massachusetts		18		42	4		64
Michigan	2	39	3	187	10	2	243
Minnesota		17	11	125		2	155
Mississippi		3		75			78
Missouri		11	3	83			97
Montana		13		48		1	62
Nebraska		11	6	47		1	66
Nevada		13		20			33
New Hampshire		1		31	1		33
New Jersey		24		37			61
New Mexico		18		46		1	65
New York	18	59		100	5		182
North Carolina		11		72	1		84
North Dakota		5	1	17			23
Ohio	2	70		98	1	1	172
Oklahoma		56		56			112
Oregon		9		21		1	31
Pennsylvania	1	61		141	1	1	205
Rhode Island		3		6			9
South Carolina		3		67	1		71
South Dakota		5	10	30			45
Tennessee	2	7		95	2		106
Texas		92		862		15	969
Utah		67		23		1	91
Vermont		1		40	9		50
Virginia		30		51	18	3	102
Washington	2	32		69	6	1	110
West Virginia	1	42		21	1		65
Wisconsin		29	3	190			222
Wyoming		19		47		2	68
U.S. Total	**106**	**1,426**	**71**	**4,255**	**310**	**71**	**6,240**

U.S. Department of Energy, National Renewable Energy Laboratory, Alternative Fuels Data Center Database (Extracted October 6, 1997).

Source: *Alternatives to Traditional Transportation Fuels*, Energy Information Administration, Washington, DC, 1997

TABLE 10.7

Estimated Consumption of Alternative Transportation Fuels in the United States, by Vehicle Ownership, 1994, 1996, and 1998
(Thousand Gasoline-Equivalent Gallons)

Fuel	1994				1996				1998			
	Federal	State and Local	Private	Total	Federal	State and Local	Private	Total	Federal	State and Local	Private	Total
Liquefied Petroleum Gases (LPG)	17	26,547	221,903	248,467	58	25,366	213,734	239,158	111	27,393	225,477	252,981
Compressed Natural Gas (CNG)	1,990	8,060	14,110	24,160	4,572	18,449	23,902	46,923	4,642	33,154	37,202	74,998
Liquefied Natural Gas (LNG)	7	2,289	49	2,345	88	2,735	424	3,247	135	4,256	699	5,090
Methanol, 85 Percent[a] (M85)	1,090	330	920	2,340	950	744	1,696	3,390	586	913	2,333	3,832
Methanol, Neat (M100)	0	3,190	*	3,190	0	347	0	347	0	347	0	347
Ethanol, 85 Percent[a] (E85)	20	50	10	80	217	284	193	694	513	636	465	1,614
Ethanol, 95 Percent[a] (E95)	0	130	10	140	0	2,628	71	2,699	0	2,628	0	2,628
Electricity	8	142	280	430	38	248	487	773	61	336	670	1,067
Total	3,132	40,738	237,282	281,152	5,923	50,801	240,507	297,231	6,048	69,663	266,846	342,557

[a]The remaining portion of 85-percent methanol and both ethanol fuels is gasoline. Consumption data include the gasoline portion of the fuel.

* Less than 0.5 thousand gasoline-equivalent gallons.

Notes: Fuel quantities are expressed in a common base unit of gasoline-equivalent gallons to allow comparisons of different fuel types. Gasoline-equivalent gallons do not represent gasoline displacement. Gasoline equivalent is computed by dividing the lower heating value of the alternative fuel by the lower heating value of gasoline and multiplying this result by the alternative fuel consumption value. Lower heating value refers to the Btu content per unit of fuel excluding the heat produced by condensation of water vapor in the fuel. Totals may not equal sum of components due to independent rounding. Estimates for historical years may be revised in future reports if new information becomes available. Estimates for 1998, in italics, are based on plans or projections. Data for 1994 and 1996 have been revised.

1994: Energy Information Administration, Office of Coal, Nuclear, Electric, and Alternate Fuels, and Science Applications International Corporation, "Alternative Transportation Fuels and Vehicles Data Development," unpublished final report prepared for the Energy Information Administration (McLean, VA, August 1995). **1996 and1998:** Energy Information Administration, Office of Coal, Nuclear, Electric, and Alternate Fuels.

Source: *Alternatives to Traditional Transportation Fuels*, Energy Information Administration, Washington, DC, 1997

In 1992, 251,352 AFVs were on U.S. roads. By 1996, more than 352,000 AFVs were in use in the United States, and the U.S. Department of Energy estimated that another 50,000 will be in use by the end of 1998. (See Table 10.4.) The total includes both vehicles originally manufactured to run on alternative fuels and vehicles converted from the use of gasoline or diesel. Each year, more and more AFVs are originally manufactured to run on the alternative fuels.

The fuels used in AFVs are liquefied petroleum gas (LPG — propane), compressed natural gas (CNG), liquified natural gas (LNG), methanol and ethanol blends, electricity, and biodiesel. LPG is a mixture of propane and butane. CNG is natural gas that is stored in pressurized tanks. CNG releases one-tenth the carbon monoxide, hydrocarbon, and nitrogen as gasoline. Methanol is a liquid fuel that can be produced from natural gas, coal, or biomass. Ethanol is ethyl alcohol, a grain alcohol mixed with gasoline and sold as gasohol. Three-fourths of the AFVs in use operate on LPG; two-thirds of the remainder use CNG.

The largest numbers of AFVs are located in the South, followed by the West, the Midwest, and the Northeast. California, Texas, Illinois, Oklahoma, and Ohio have the most AFVs — 42 percent of the total. (See Table 10.5.) Transit buses are one type of heavy-duty vehicle that have seen much AFV activity. In 1996, 1 of 5 new transit buses on order was an alternative-fuel-capable bus.

As of 1996, there were 6,240 refueling sites in the United States. Forty percent were in the South, 25 percent each in the Midwest and West, and 10 percent in the Northeast (Table 10.6). From 1992 to 1996, alternative fuel consumption increased 76 percent, while traditional highway fuel consumption increased only 10 percent. Alternative and replacement fuels now rep-resent 2 to 3 percent of onroad transportation fuel. Table 10.7 shows the consumption of alternative fuels in the United States by type of fuel and vehicle ownership. In 1998, 78 percent of alternative fuel was used by privately owned vehicles, 20 percent for state and local vehicles, and the remainder for federal vehicles.

Electric Cars — Promise and Reality

While technological dreams do not always come true, the electric car now seems to have more than a fighting chance. The major limitations of today's models are within sight of being overcome; indeed, a host of companies are betting billions of dollars on their ability to make that happen. And they cannot but be pleasantly surprised by the initial response to the EV1: according to Saturn dealers, the waiting list of several hundred hopeful lease-holders continues to grow. — Sean Dunn, *Worldwatch*, 1997

Instead of a more efficient gasoline-powered automobile, many observers are hoping that the development of the electric car will resolve much

FIGURE 10.5

The General Motors Impact — An Electric Car

Source: *Electric Vehicles: Likely Consequences of U.S. and Other Nations' Programs and Policies*, U.S. General Accounting Office, Washington, DC, 1994

of the nation's auto pollution problems. Electric cars (Figure 10.5) are the only vehicles that can meet zero emission standards.

The electric car is not a new invention. Popular during the 1890s, the quiet, clean, and simple vehicle was expected to dominate the automotive market of the twentieth century. Instead, it quietly disappeared as automobile companies chose to invest billions of dollars in the internal combustion engine. It has taken a century, but the electric car has returned.

Energy standards have created a clear market for alternative-energy cars. The combination of government mandates to reduce emissions and encouraging market opportunities has altered the automobile industry — most car manufacturers have an electric car either on the roads or in testing.

The primary difficulty with electric vehicles (EVs) lies in inadequate battery power. The cars must be recharged often. Currently, they use lead-acid or nickel-cadmium batteries and have a range of 50 to 100 miles on a single charge. The range is reduced by factors such as cold temperatures, the use of air conditioning, vehicle load, and steep terrain.

In addition, electric vehicles are expensive, although prices are coming down. In 1998, General Motors' EV1 leases for between $480 and $640 per month — less than the cost of luxury cars but more than the average mid-size American car. In California, some car rental companies are offering electric vehicles for rent at rates only slightly more than gas-powered vehicles.

Despite their current high price, electric cars have many advantages. They are relatively noiseless and simple in design and operation. They cost less to refuel and service and have fewer parts to break down. Their owners are likely to spend less

time on maintenance and, if they recharge at home, will rarely have to go to the service station. These time savings have real value in today's busy world. Over time, the cost gap between cars that pollute and electric cars that do not is not all that great. With another decade of battery development, the gap could close entirely. Car experts believe electric cars will assume a "second car" role for commuters and for short trips, much like the microwave oven has become not a replacement for, but an addition to, conventional ovens for cooking.

California had led the development of electric vehicles. In 1990, the California Air Resources Board (CARB), facing severe air pollution in Los Angeles and other cities, passed the toughest auto emissions standards in the world. Most notable was the requirement that 2 percent of cars sold in the

FIGURE 10.6
Charging Station

Source: *Electric Vehicles: Likely Consequences of U.S. and Other Nations' Programs and Policies*, U.S. General Accounting Office, Washington, DC, 1994

state by the seven major carmakers in 1998 be "zero-emission," and that proportion would rise to 10 percent by 2003. Auto-industry lobbyists protested and the 1998 mandate was lifted. But the big automakers are still required to achieve the 10 percent target in 2003. If the automakers actually achieve the goal — and this is a big if — approximately 800,000 zero-emission cars would be on California roads by 2010, up from 2,000 in use in the entire country in 1997.

In 1997, a federal judge ruled that the state of New York could order automobile manufacturers to sell thousands of electrically powered vehicles in New York in 1998, making New York the only state that mandates the sale of electric cars. Officials estimated that the mandate required the sale of 7,800 electric cars in 1998 alone.

In 1997, industry officials announced plans to produce hybrid vehicles by 2005 that operate on gasoline in conjunction with fuel cells. Such a vehicle would overcome the problem of fuel availability by use of conventional fuel and abundant refueling stops and yet burn fuel twice as efficiently as with current technology. For more information on alternative vehicles, see *Transportation — America's Lifeline*, Information Plus, Wylie, Texas, 1997.

Although most EVs will be recharged in personal residences during off-hours, cities are already installing public charging outlets in places such as grocery store parking lots and public parking garages. (See Figure 10.6.) In 1996, the Electric Vehicle Association of the Americas listed 295 public charging outlets at 43 sites in its directory, most in California, but a few in Virginia, Vermont, Washington, and Arizona. Residences can be equipped with EV recharging facilities for $200 to $2,000, depending on existing wiring.

Disadvantages of Electric Vehicles

Electric cars will likely produce far less carbon monoxide and hydrocarbon emissions, but the production of electricity to power them may well produce as much carbon dioxide and nitrous ox-

ide and may likely create more sulfur dioxide, which causes acid rain. In addition, the increased demand for electricity might lead to the building of more power plants. Many of these power plants will burn fossil fuels, mainly coal, adding to the nation's pollution.

In addition, researchers suggest that emissions from mining, smelting, and recycling the lead needed for batteries of a large fleet of electric vehicles could pose serious threats to public health. Safety is also an issue with current EV models, which surround the driver with about 1,000 pounds of lead acid batteries. Even if the liquid acid component could be isolated or put in a gel, accidents would still raise the possibility of exposing passengers or rescue workers to high levels of lead.

The primary difficulty with electric cars lies in inadequate battery power. Recharging the battery generally takes about eight hours, although recent technological developments will likely lower this to four to six hours. It is generally believed that such barriers must be overcome before EVs can become a viable transportation option.

Overcoming the Drawbacks

Despite these problems, Peugeot and Fiat have both introduced electric cars in Europe, where they have been embraced as city vehicles. European drivers, however, are more accustomed to lower-powered vehicles and have less need for air-conditioning, which is a major energy consumer.

A rapid improvement in fuel cells, which combine oxygen from air with hydrogen from oil or natural gas to make water and electricity, may help solve limitations of electric cars. Fuel cells would eliminate the need for massive batteries and increase the range of the vehicles. Henry Wedaa, chairman of the South Coast Air Quality Management District in Southern California, commented, "In the long run, batteries are dead, and fuel cells will carry the day. The problem is infrastructure: there aren't natural gas or hydrogen stations on every corner yet."

165

Tax breaks became available in 1993 for people who buy cars that run on alternative energy sources, especially electric cars. The law provides for a credit of 10 percent of the price of an electric vehicle. The law also permits a deduction of up to $2,000 for other clean-fuel vehicles. The tax breaks are intended to compensate for the price difference and to jump-start production of the vehicles.

Car manufacturers have agreed that beginning in 2001, they would make the gasoline models they sell in the 49 states other than California cleaner than required by federal regulation. Still, these cars will not run as cleanly as the least-polluting cars that California will require to be sold within its borders. California wants cleaner-running cars sold in other states because nearly 18 percent of the cars registered in California each year are bought elsewhere and brought into the state.

Lawn and Garden Equipment

In 1994, the EPA reported that as much as 10 percent of the nation's air pollution was generated by gasoline-powered lawn and garden equipment — lawn mowers, chain saws, even golf carts. EPA Administrator Carol Browner estimates that Americans use 89 million pieces of such equipment, with lawn mowers alone accounting for 5 percent of the nation's pollution.

The agency established engine label and warranty requirements, exhaust emissions standards, and test procedures, requiring that engine makers meet the new requirements by 1996. Effective that year, new products offered for sale were equipped with improved carburetion systems, and additional standards were scheduled for subsequent years. Agency officials predict the new regulations would reduce smog-forming hydrocarbon emissions by 32 percent and carbon monoxide by 14 percent by the year 2003.

Air Travel Efficiency

Airline travel is the fastest growing mode of passenger travel. Commercial aviation accounts for 76 percent of fuel use for air travel; general aviation, 4 percent; and Department of Defense military uses, 20 percent. Although more fuel-efficient jet aircraft are replacing older, less fuel-efficient planes, fuel savings in commercial and general aviation have been more than offset by increases in passenger travel and air freight.

Air travel in affluent nations is rising and causing a number of environmental problems. The average American now flies 1,739 miles a year. Europeans, though they fly fewer miles, have the world's most crowded skies. The most rapid growth in flying has been in Asia. Most air travel is done by a small portion of the world's people.

Flying carries an environmental price; it is the most energy-intensive form of transport. In much of the industrialized world, air travel is replacing more energy-efficient rail or bus travel. Despite the increased fuel efficiency of jet engines, jet fuel consumption has risen 65 percent since 1970. In addition, major airports frequently experience capacity problems and resulting delays, which waste significant amounts of fuel by idling aircraft on the runway and keeping arriving planes in holding patterns.

Another problem with air travel is its possible impact on global warming. Airplanes spew nearly 4 million tons of nitrogen oxide, much of it while cruising in the troposphere five to seven miles above the earth, where ozone is formed. Some experts estimate that air traffic accounts for 8 percent of all global greenhouse warming.

The EPA and the Federal Aviation Administration (FAA) counter that jet aircraft currently contribute a minor amount to pollution in the upper atmosphere, especially considering contributions from other sources, such as motor vehicles, industrial manufacturing, and public utilities. Nitrogen oxide emissions in the stratosphere (60,000 to 90,000 feet) currently have a small impact on upper-level ozone depletion. In 1995, the now-defunct Office of Technology Assessment (OTA) estimated that aircraft emissions represent about 5 percent of the 1.4 billion tons of air pollution produced annually from all sources. The OTA was, however, concerned that jet emissions of carbon dioxide and nitrogen oxides could be a concern in the future. Jet emissions could be a greater threat in the future if (1) manufacturer estimates of increases in supersonic aircraft hold true (this has not happened so far) and (2) technology developments cannot offset the increases.

Although each generation of airplane engines gets cleaner and more fuel-efficient, there seems to be little that can be done about the increased amount of flying. However, there is a movement toward doing something about the other engines — those on the trucks, cars, and carts that service airplane fleets. Electric utility companies, including the Edison Electric Institute and the Electric Power Research Institute, launched a program in 1993 to electrify airports. By converting terminal transport buses, food trucks, and baggage handling carts to electricity, airports hope to reduce air pollution.

CONSERVATION IN THE RESIDENTIAL AND COMMERCIAL SECTORS

Before the early 1970s, energy was not a very important consideration in building design or operation. Relatively little was known about building energy flows or effective policy plans. Two decades later, people know much more about which technologies work and which do not. Energy use in buildings has changed substantially over the past several decades.

TABLE 10.8

Research and Development Needs

Materials	Insulants, particularly transparent insulants such as aerogels. Electronically adjustable spectrally selective windows. Improved lighting controls for integrating daylighting and artificial lights. Improved and longer life gaskets and sealants. Phase-change materials. Desiccants for cooling systems. Selective surfaces. Improved catalysts for small-scale biomass combustion emissions control. Air-to-air heat exchanger materials.
Building physics	Passive cooling techniques, including radiant cooling. Perimeter daylighting systems, allowing deeper penetration of perimeter spaces. Atria design for better daylighting and thermal performance. Basic heat transfer and natural convection air-flow research to improve performance and comfort. Moisture absorption and desorption in building materials. Duct design.
Whole buildings	Testing advanced concepts in buildings. Performance monitoring of solar buildings. Model land-use controls to encourage proper subdivision/site design.
Human comfort research	Determining what makes people comfortable or uncomfortable with respect to temperature, humidity, lighting, and other factors within a building.
Design tools	Improved residential and commercial building design tools that perform integrated analysis, including daylighting and window design, space heating, space cooling, and utility demand-side management. Development of simplified design tools for the design and construction community. Validation of design tools.

Source: *Renewing Our Energy Future*, Office of Technology Assessment, Washington, DC, 1995

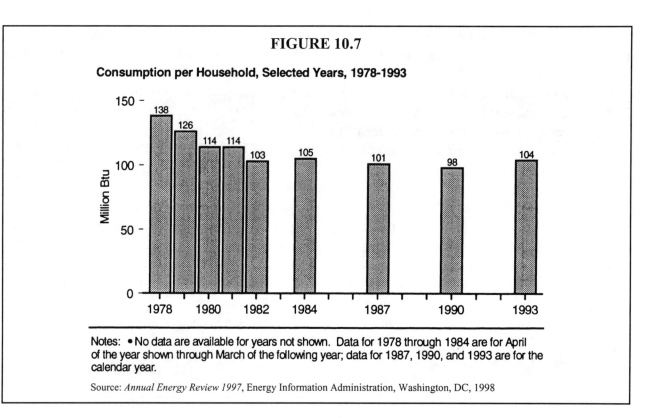

FIGURE 10.7

Consumption per Household, Selected Years, 1978-1993

Notes: • No data are available for years not shown. Data for 1978 through 1984 are for April of the year shown through March of the following year; data for 1987, 1990, and 1993 are for the calendar year.

Source: *Annual Energy Review 1997*, Energy Information Administration, Washington, DC, 1998

Total building energy use in the United States has increased — there are more people, more households, and more offices. Energy use per unit area (commercial) or per person (residential) has roughly stabilized over the past decade due to a variety of efficiency improvements. The sources of energy have changed dramatically. Use of fuel oil has dropped, and natural gas has largely made up the difference. At the same time, new "loads" have arisen. Electronic office equipment has sharply increased plug loads, caused by computers, fax machines, printers, and copiers, in commercial buildings. Energy use in buildings accounts for an increasing share of total U.S. energy consumption: 27 percent in 1950, 33 percent in 1970, and 36 percent in 1990. The residential and commercial sectors use roughly 35 percent of U.S. primary energy and 65 percent of U.S. electricity.

Building Efficiency

Table 10.8 summarizes the potential areas for research and development in energy conservation. Among the techniques useful in reducing energy loads are advanced window designs, daylighting (letting light in from the outside by using high windows, clerestories, skylights, atria in the center of large buildings), solar water heating, landscaping, and tree planting.

Energy conservation measures in the building sector have been substantial over the past 20 years. The now-defunct Office of Technology Assessment (OTA) claimed that the use of cost-effective, commercially available technologies could reduce total building energy use by about one-third by 2015. The use of those technologies would save energy and money and, in addition, would reduce the environmental damage associated with energy production.

One method of measuring the efficiency changes in buildings is to look at the amount of energy it takes to keep a building comfortably warm or cool. This gives an indication of the energy conservation and efficiency of the building shell (walls, windows, doors, and ceilings) and also of the heating and cooling equipment.

In the residential sector, the amount of energy used in newer homes is dramatically less than that of older homes. The houses built since 1980 use

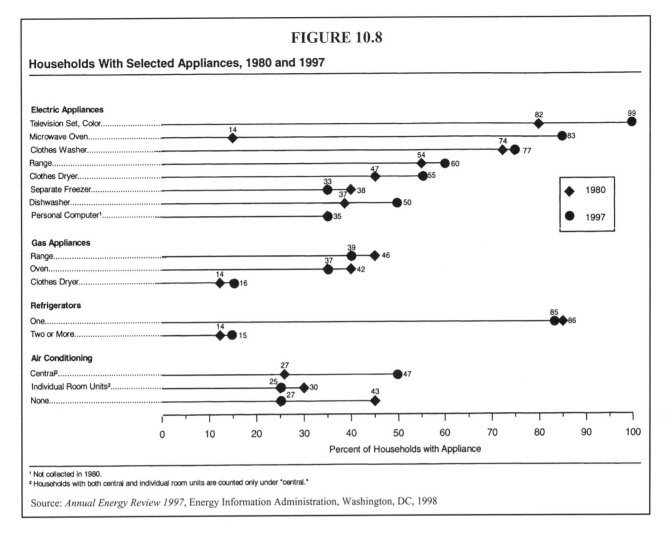

FIGURE 10.8

Households With Selected Appliances, 1980 and 1997

Electric Appliances
Television Set, Color............ 82 99
Microwave Oven............... 14 83
Clothes Washer................ 74 77
Range....................... 54 60
Clothes Dryer................ 47 55
Separate Freezer............. 33 37 38
Dishwasher.................. 37 50
Personal Computer[1]........... 35

Gas Appliances
Range....................... 39 46
Oven....................... 37 42
Clothes Dryer................ 14 16

Refrigerators
One......................... 85 86
Two or More................. 14 15

Air Conditioning
Central[2].................... 27 47
Individual Room Units[2]........ 25 30
None....................... 27 43

◆ 1980
● 1997

0   10   20   30   40   50   60   70   80   90   100

Percent of Households with Appliance

[1] Not collected in 1980.
[2] Households with both central and individual room units are counted only under "central."

Source: *Annual Energy Review 1997*, Energy Information Administration, Washington, DC, 1998

only slightly more than half of the energy consumed by older houses. The largest share of energy savings is due to better construction, higher quality insulation, and more energy-efficient windows and doors. (Figure 10.7 shows the energy consumption of households from 1978 to 1993.) However, although household size is declining, the number of households is increasing, thus increasing demand for energy-intensive services such as air conditioning.

As in the residential sector, improved technology has helped to lessen the growth in commercial building energy use. Commercial buildings constructed after 1980 use considerably less energy than those built in the early part of the 1900s.

This trend in commercial energy efficiency may be surprising since there has been a general perception that commercial building developers are less concerned about conservation of energy because someone else (usually the building tenants) will have to pay the energy bills. However, the majority of commercial buildings are actually owner-occupied. For this reason, the building owner/occupant has a definite incentive to have an energy-efficient commercial building. Whatever the motivation, it is clear that the conservation trend in commercial buildings has been strong and consistent with other sectors of the U.S. economy.

The OTA reported that roughly one-fourth the energy used to heat and cool buildings is lost through poor insulation and poorly insulated windows. Before the 1973 energy crisis, 70 percent of new windows sold were single-glazed. By 1990, due to changes in building codes and public interest, 80 percent of windows sold were double-glazed with double insulating ability, cutting energy loss in half.

169

TABLE 10.9

Major Factors Influencing Residential Energy Use

Factors causing an *increase* in consumption:
- Larger population—more households
- Fewer people per household—more households
- Increased demand for energy-intensive services

Factors causing a *decrease* in consumption:
- New housing more efficient than existing stock
- New appliances more efficient than existing stock
- Retrofits to existing housing
- Migration to the South and West
- More multifamily units

Factors causing fluctuations in consumption:
- Occupant behavior, changes in thermostat settings
- Fuel shifts—more electricity and less oil, changes in wood use
- Price changes

Source: Office of Technology Assessment, Washington, DC, 1992

In an interesting experiment to make buildings (and vehicles) more efficient and reduce energy consumption, researchers at Tufts University have developed a window that can regulate the amount of sunlight flowing into the building or car and the amount of heat flowing out. Called "Smart" windows, they could reduce a building's energy consumption by 50 percent. Still too expensive to be generally introduced, when they become available at lower prices, they may likely be incorporated in construction.

Home Appliance Efficiency

Home energy use accounts for 20 percent of the total national energy use. (Figure 10.8 shows the proportion of households with certain appliances in 1980 and 1997.) Like motor vehicles and jet aircraft, household appliances, including refrigerators, air conditioners, water heaters, and furnaces, have also adapted to conservation needs. (Table 10.9 shows the major factors influencing residential energy use.)

In 1987, Congress passed the National Appliance Energy Conservation Act (NAECA; PL 95-629), which gave the U.S. Department of Energy (DOE) the authority to formulate minimum efficiency requirements for 13 classes of consumer products. It could also revise and update those standards as technologies and economic conditions changed. Table 10.10 shows the products and years

TABLE 10.10

Effective dates of appliance efficiency standards, 1988-1995

Product	1988	1990	1992	1993	1994	1995
Clothes dryers	X				X	
Clothes washers	X				X	
Dishwashers	X				X	
Refrigerators and freezers		X		X		
Kitchen ranges and ovens		X				
Room air conditioners		X				
Direct heating equipment		X				
Fluorescent lamp ballasts		X				
Water heaters		X				
Pool heaters		X				
Central air conditioners and heat pumps			X			
Furnaces						
Central (45,000 Btu per hour)			X			
Small (-,000 Btu per hour)			X			
Mobile home		X				
Boilers			X			
Fluorescent lamps, 8 foot					X	
Fluorescent lamps, 2 and 4 foot (U tube)						X

Source: *Annual Energy Outlook 1998*, Energy Information Administration, Washington, DC, 1997

in which standards were established or revised. In 1997, the DOE established an advisory committee to review and revise the standards.

Energy efficiency has increased for all major household appliances but most dramatically for refrigerators and freezers. Since 1972, new refrigerators and freezers have almost doubled in energy conservation largely due to better insulation, motors, compressors, and accessories such as automatic defrost. These changes in efficiency have been accomplished at relatively low costs to manufacturers. In addition, consumers can now study required efficiency labels and comparison-shop.

A second major group of appliances, air conditioners and heat pumps (which are actually air conditioners running in reverse), has shown a 35 percent improvement over the past two decades.

Although this improvement in energy efficiency is less than the improvements in refrigerators and freezers, it is very important because these appliances are large energy users.

Water heaters and furnaces have improved efficiency between 5 percent and 20 percent. The technological improvements in water heaters and furnaces are relatively costly compared to the overall price of the product. This means that the more energy-conserving models have a higher retail price, thus discouraging many consumers from purchasing an efficient model, although more energy-efficient models will likely save money in the long run.

In addition, many of the purchases of water heaters and furnaces are made by builders, who have little incentive to pay more for the most effi-

TABLE 10.11

Oil Savings by Energy Efficiency Planning Unit

Dollars in thousands

Planning unit group/planning unit name	Initial funding year	Funds available FY 1996	2000 (mmby*)	2010 (mmby*)	2020 (mmby*)
IHEM/FEMP[a]					
IHEM	1977	$0	0	0.1	0.2
FEMP	1978	$17,100	0.8	2.5	4.2
Building Equipment and Materials					
Materials and Structures R&D	1977	$3,260	1.6	3.1	4.5
Space Conditioning R&D	1977	$15,257	1.0	3.1	6.0
Windows and Glazing R&D	1986	$6,106	0	0	0
Lighting and Appliance R&D	1980	$4,360	0.2	0.5	0.9
Building Systems Design					
Best Practices	1978	$4,571	0.7	2.4	5.2
Commercial Buildings	1985	$11,026	1.4	4.7	8.5
Residential Buildings	1989	$6,865	0	0.3	1.6
Codes and Standards					
Lighting and Appliance Codes and Standards	1979	$5,738	0.2	2.0	3.0
Building Codes and Standards	1984	$8,901	0.4	1.4	1.6
Industries of the Future					
Forest and Paper Products Vision	1995	$11,553	0	0.3	2.6
Glass Vision	1995	$1,414	0.2	0.5	1.2
Aluminum Vision	1985	$1,449	0.1	0.9	2.3
Chemicals Vision	1995	$13,840	1.0	24.8	50.1
Petroleum Refining Vision	1995	$6,726	35.7	89.7	64.9
Steel Vision	1986	$6,780	0	0.2	0.2
Metals Casting Vision	1990	$1,992	0	0	0
Cogeneration					
Cogeneration	1992	$22,125	4.3	4.3	0.1
Advanced Materials and CFCCs					

(continued)

TABLE 10.11 (Continued)

Dollars in thousands

Planning unit group/planning unit name	Initial funding year	Funds available FY 1996	2000 (mmby*)	2010 (mmby*)	2020 (mmby*)
Advanced Materials and CFCCs	1992	$17,476	0.1	1.1	3.5
Industrial Technology Assessment					
Climate Wise	1995	$2,000	5.9	0	0
IACs	1976	$8,679	0.1	0.1	0.1
Combustion Technologies	1977	$70	0	0.1	0.1
Motor Challenge	1995	$5,332	0	0	0
NICE-3	1991	$6,000	2.1	11.6	14.7
Inventions and Innovations					
Inventions and Innovations	1975	$5,504	0.6	2.1	0
Grants					
Weatherization Assistance Program	1977	$114,196	0.2	0.6	0.9
State Block Grants	1976	$26,500	5.9	13.8	14.1
Municipal Energy Management Program	1978	$1,843	0	0	0
Regional Biomass Program	1983	$3,940	0	0	0
Technology Access					
Commercialization Ventures	1994	$3,000	3.0	10.9	22.3
Information and Communications	1981	$2,940	0	0	0
International Market Development	1990	$2,907	0	0	0
Solar International	1990	$4,000	0	0	0
Biofuels					
Biofuels	1974	$27,200	5.0	150.0	219.0
Alternative Fuel Vehicles					
Alternative Fuel Vehicles R&D	1976	$29,303	12.1	46.6	24.1
PNGV					
Electric Vehicle R&D	1976	$17,692	4.0	46.0	37.0
Fuel Cell R&D	1987	$22,250	0	13.0	140.0
Hybrid Vehicle R&D	1993	$57,690	0	180.0	300.0
Lightweight Vehicle Materials R&D	1993	$13,360	0	32.0	35.0
Propulsion System Materials (Ceramics)	1983	$22,125	0	0	0
Conventional Vehicles					
Heavy Duty Engine R&D	1976	$5,454	1.0	73.0	237.0
Light Duty Engine R&D	1976	$4,649	0	39.0	43.0
Solar Technologies					
Biomass Power R&D	1992	$21,200	0.1	3.2	10.0
Photovoltaic Systems R&D	1974	$65,000	0	0.2	1.4
Solar Thermal Electric R&D	1976	$25,000	0	0.2	0.6

(continued)

cient models, or by homeowners in an emergency (for example, to replace a water heater that has flooded a home), when fast availability and installation seem much more important than energy efficiency.

Nonetheless, consumers are generally willing to purchase more expensive, energy-efficient models of air conditioners, refrigerators, and lights if the devices can save them enough money in the long run on their electricity bills to offset the higher purchase costs. According to a U.S. General Accounting Office study (*Energy Conservation: Efforts Promoting More Efficient Use*, Washington, DC, 1992), consumers will purchase such devices if the "payback period" is two years or less.

TABLE 10.11 (Continued)

Dollars in thousands

Planning unit group/planning unit name	Initial funding year	Funds available FY 1996	2000 (mmby*)	2010 (mmby*)	2020 (mmby*)
Wind Energy					
Wind Energy R&D	1974	$32,500	0.7	2.1	7.7
Geothermal Energy					
Geothermal Energy R&D	1973	$31,447	0.1	0.8	0.7
Hydrogen Research					
Hydrogen Research R&D	1979	$14,500	0	0	0
Electric Energy Systems					
Electric and Magnetic Fields R&D	1978	$9,924	0	0	0
Energy Storage R&D	1990	$2,000	0.1	0.3	0.3
High Temperature Superconductivity R&D	1989	$19,000	0	0.1	0.9
Utility Technology Access					
Climate Challenge	1995	$0	0	0	0
Total (mmby)			88.6	767.6	1,269.5
Total (mmbd)			0.2	2.1	3.5

Note: Oil savings are direct oil savings as reported and assumed to be 5 percent of electricity savings.

[a]The FEMP numbers in this table represent incremental oil savings resulting from fiscal year 1996 efforts in federal facilities only; they assume 20 percent energy savings in the year 2000 and 30 percent energy savings in the year 2005 (EPACT, Ex. Orders 12759 and 12902 goals).

* mmby = millions of barrels per year

Source: *Energy Security: Evaluating U.S. Vulnerability to Oil Supply Disruptions and Options for Mitigating Their Effects*, U.S. General Accounting Office, Washington, DC, 1996

In addition to concerns about efficiency, appliance makers, especially of refrigerators and air conditioning systems, are striving to develop alternative cooling techniques as substitutes for CFCs, which can no longer be sold legally in the United States. Current technology is replacing chlorofluorocarbons (CFCs) with somewhat less dangerous HCFCs (hydro-chlorofluorocarbons), which are temporary substitutes. In Europe, refrigeration units using other substances, such as propane ("Greenfreeze" technology), are rapidly replacing HCFCs.

ENERGY POLICIES AND PUBLIC HEALTH

The connection between energy policy and health has become clearer in recent years. People living in cities with high levels of pollution have a higher risk of mortality and of suffering from certain diseases than those living in less polluted cities. Energy-related emissions generate a vast majority of these polluting chemicals. In the past few years, a number of major studies have documented the growing body of evidence establishing the link between air pollution and public health. Clean energy technologies represent a cost-effective investment in public health.

Lung disease, which affects more than 10 percent of the population, is the third leading cause of death in the United States and among the fastest-growing. A 1996 Harvard School of Public Health study found that exposure to ozone was linked to 10,000 to 15,000 hospital admissions and between 30,000 and 50,000 emergency room visits during 1993 and 1994. Furthermore, ozone is linked to asthma attacks, above-average death rates, and allergies. Air pollution contributes to severe public health problems and expense, and the vast majority of air pollution is energy-related. For more information on environmental and health issues, see *The Environment — A Revolution in Attitudes*, Information Plus, Wylie, Texas, 1998.

CONSERVATION PROJECTIONS — WHERE TO GO FROM HERE?

The Energy Information Administration expects the United States to become substantially more energy-efficient over the next 20 years. Future gains in energy conservation, however, may be hampered or discouraged if the nation experiences continued low energy prices. Low prices for fuel reduce the motivation for introducing further, perhaps more difficult or expensive, measures. Nonetheless, the energy-saving trends of the past two decades are likely to continue as industries, homeowners, builders, businesses, and consumers replace older equipment and appliances with improved, energy-efficient models.

The prices of other energy supplies, natural gas, coal, and electricity can be affected by oil prices so that overall energy prices generally match oil prices. Higher energy prices would encourage the selection of more energy-efficient equipment, while lower prices would likely increase fuel consumption and result in less conservation. Nevertheless, whatever the price of energy, energy conservation is likely to play an increasingly greater role in the nation's energy use.

The National Energy Policy Plan (NEPP) of the Department of Energy (DOE) Organization Act of 1977 (PL 95-91) requires the president to periodically submit a national energy policy plan, which includes energy objectives, strategies to achieve those objectives, and projections of energy supply, demand, and prices. Table 10.11 shows the estimated oil savings attributable to the current NEPP by 2000, 2010, and 2020 by program. A savings of 89 million barrels per year (mmby) in consumption is estimated to be possible by 2000, 768 million barrels by 2010, and 1270 million barrels per year by 2020 by programs already planned.

The EIA projects that transportation fuel efficiency will grow more slowly from the present through 2020 than in the 1980s (Figure 10.9). The EIA predicts that light-duty vehicle efficiency will remain essentially steady. Low fuel prices and con-

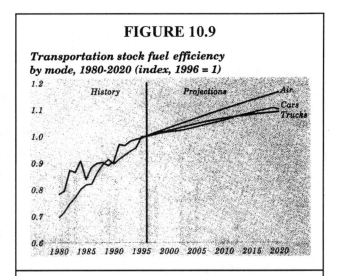

FIGURE 10.9

Transportation stock fuel efficiency by mode, 1980-2020 (index, 1996 = 1)

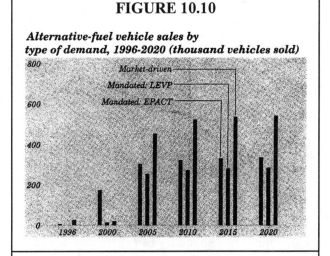

FIGURE 10.10

Alternative-fuel vehicle sales by type of demand, 1996-2020 (thousand vehicles sold)

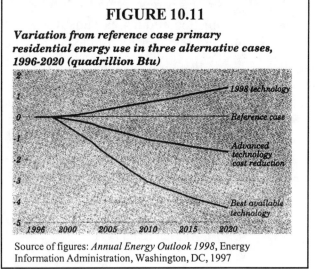

FIGURE 10.11

Variation from reference case primary residential energy use in three alternative cases, 1996-2020 (quadrillion Btu)

Source of figures: *Annual Energy Outlook 1998*, Energy Information Administration, Washington, DC, 1997

sumer preference for larger, more powerful vehicles will likely increase consumption overall, although the aging of the baby boomers will moderate the trend in later years.

The EIA predicts that the market for alternative-fuel vehicles will grow as a result of the Energy Policy Act of 1992 (EPACT) and Low Emission Vehicle Program (LEVP) to about 620,000 vehicles — about 8 percent of all vehicles — in 2020. (See Figure 10.10.) Roughly one-third each will be alcohol-fueled, electric-fueled, and gas-fueled.

In residential energy consumption, assuming the most efficient technology is always chosen in construction and operation, energy use could be 19 percent lower by 2020 (Figure 10.11).

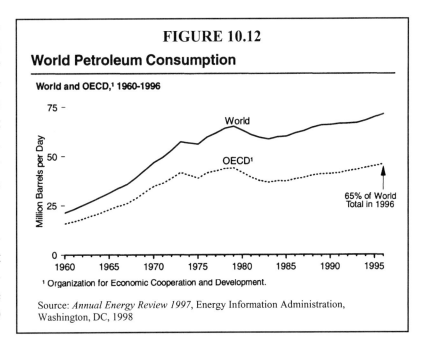

FIGURE 10.12

World Petroleum Consumption

World and OECD,¹ 1960-1996

65% of World Total in 1996

¹ Organization for Economic Cooperation and Development.

Source: *Annual Energy Review 1997*, Energy Information Administration, Washington, DC, 1998

The government predicted that a plentiful supply of energy will likely drive down prices. The average U.S. household could spend $170 less on energy in 2015 than it will in 2000 — a 16 percent drop in the price of natural gas, a 22 percent drop in the cost of fuel oil, and a 9 percent decline in the price of gasoline.

INTERNATIONAL COMPARISONS OF CONSERVATION EFFORTS

Domestic energy conservation trends can be evaluated by comparing the United States to other countries, especially other developed countries (those within the Organization for Economic Cooperation and Development or OECD). Figure 10.12 shows the total consumption of oil for both the world and OECD countries from 1960 through 1996. The patterns of usage for the United States and the other OECD countries are almost identi-

cal. The two major drops (early 1970s and early 1980s) reflected times when all nations were experiencing the effects of the international oil crises.

The changes in U.S. energy use over time are quite similar to changes in other countries. Meaningful comparisons are difficult because of geographic diversity and differences in culture, economics, and institutions. For example, the Japanese transportation sector is less energy-intensive than the transportation sector in the United States. The Japanese rely much more heavily on forms of transportation that are more energy-efficient, like rail, in contrast to America's reliance on cars. Also, the amount of floor space per capita (per person) in residential and commercial buildings in the United States is more than three times larger than in Japan.

IMPORTANT NAMES AND ADDRESSES

American Gas Institute
1515 Wilson Blvd.
Arlington, VA 22209
(703) 841-8647
FAX (703) 841-8697

American Petroleum Institute
1220 L St. NW
Washington, DC 20005
(202) 682-8495
FAX (202) 962-4730

American Wind Energy
Association
122 C St. NW, Fourth Floor
Washington, DC 20001
(202) 383-2500
FAX (202) 383-2505

Bureau of Land Management
Renewable Resources and
Planning
1849 C St. NW, #5650
Washington, DC 20240
(202) 208-4896
FAX (202) 208-5016

Council on Environmental
Quality
722 Jackson Pl. NW
Washington, DC 20503
(202) 456-6224
FAX (202) 456-2710

Edison Electric Institute
701 Pennsylvania Ave. NW
Washington, DC 20004
(202) 508-5000
FAX (202) 508-5759

Electric Power Research
Institute
2000 L St. NW, Suite 805
Washington, DC 20036
(202) 872-9222
FAX (202) 293-2697

Environmental Defense Fund
1875 Connecticut Ave., #1016
Washington, DC 20009
(202) 387-3500
FAX (202) 234-6049

Environmental Industry
Associations
4301 Connecticut Ave. NW,
#300
Washington, DC 20008
(202) 244-4700
FAX (202) 966-4818

Environmental Protection
Agency
401 M St. SW
Washington, DC 20460
(202) 260-4700
FAX (202) 260-0279

Friends of the Earth
1025 Vermont Ave. NW, #300
Washington, DC 20005
(202) 783-7400
FAX (202) 783-0444

Greenpeace USA
1436 U St. NW
Washington, DC 20009
(202) 462-1177
FAX (202) 462-4507

National Mining Association
1130 17th St. NW
Washington, DC 20036
(202) 463-2654
FAX (202) 833-9636

Natural Gas Supply
Association
805 15th St. NW, #510
Washington, DC 20005
(202) 326-9300
FAX (202) 326-9330

Natural Resources Defense
Council
1200 New York Ave. NW, #400
Washington, DC 20005
(202) 289-6868
FAX (202) 289-1060

Nuclear Energy Institute
1776 Eye St. NW, Suite 400
Washington, DC 20006
(202) 739-8000
FAX (202) 785-4019

Nuclear Regulatory Commission
11555 Rockville Pike
Rockville, MD 20852
(301) 415-2344
FAX (301) 415-2395

Public Citizen
1600 20th St. NW
Washington, DC 20009
(202) 588-1000
FAX (202) 588-7798

IMPORTANT NAMES AND ADDRESSES (Continued)

Sierra Club
408 C St. NE
Washington, DC 20002
(202) 547-1141
FAX (202) 547-6009

Solid Waste Association of
North America
P.O. Box 7219
Silver Spring, MD 20907
(301) 585-2898
FAX (301) 589-7068

Union of Concerned Scientists
1616 P St. NW, #310
Washington, DC 20036
(202) 332-0900
FAX (202) 332-0905

U.S. Department of Energy
1000 Independence Ave. SW
Washington, DC 20585
(202) 586-6151
FAX (202) 586-0956

U.S. House of Representatives
Subcommittee on Energy and
Mineral Resources
1337 Longworth Bldg.
Washington, DC 20515
(202) 225-9297

U.S. Senate Committee on
Energy and Natural Resources
364 Dirksen Bldg.
Washington, DC 20510
(202) 224-4971

Worldwatch Institute
1776 Massachusetts Ave. NW
Washington, DC 20036
(202) 452-1999
FAX (202) 296-7365

RESOURCES

The Energy Information Administration (EIA) of the Department of Energy (DOE) is the major source of energy statistics in the United States and publishes weekly, monthly, and yearly statistical collections on most phases of energy. The *Annual Energy Review 1997* (1998) provided a complete statistical overview, while *Annual Energy Outlook 1998: Long Term Projections* (1997) projected these findings into the future. The DOE's *International Energy Annual 1996* (1998) and *Coal Industry Annual 1996* (1997) presented a statistical overview of the world energy situation, while *U.S. Crude Oil, Natural Gas, and Natural Gas Liquid Reserves* (1997) discussed reserves of oil and gas. The DOE's *Yucca Mountain Studies* (1990) provided information on the Yucca Mountain repository, while *Conservation and Renewable Energy: Technologies for Transportation* (1990) discussed renewable energy use in U.S. transportation.

The DOE also provided *Spent Nuclear Fuel Discharges from U.S. Reactors, 1994* (1996), *Natural Gas Annual 1994* (1995), *Geothermal Energy in the Western United States and Hawaii* (1991), *Renewable Energy Annual 1997* (1998), *Petroleum: An Energy Profile* (1991), *Managing the Nation's Nuclear Waste* (1990), *Yucca Mountain Studies* (1990), *Alternatives to Traditional Transportation Fuels 1996* (1997), and *Estimates of U.S. Biomass Energy Conservation 1992* (1994).

The U.S. General Accounting Office (GAO) published numerous helpful reports, including *Department of Energy: Problems and Progress in Managing Plutonium* (1998), *Nuclear Waste: Understanding of Waste Migration at Hanford Is Inadequate for Key Decisions* (1998), *Nuclear Waste: Uncertainties About Opening Waste Isolation Pi-*lot Project* (1996), *Energy Security: Evaluating U.S. Vulnerability to Oil Supply Disruptions and Options for Mitigating Their Effects* (1996), and *Radioactive Waste: Status of Commercial Low-Level Waste Facilities* (1995). Also useful were *Air Pollution Allowance Trading Offers an Opportunity to Reduce Emissions at Less Cost* (1994), *Electric Vehicles: Likely Consequences of U.S. and Other Nations' Programs* (1994), *Geothermal Energy: Outlook Limited for Some Uses but Promising for Geothermal Heat Pumps* (1994), and *Nuclear Safety: International Assistance Efforts to Make Soviet-Designed Reactors Safer* (1994).

The Department of the Interior's Mineral Management Service publishes information directly bearing on the nation's energy resources. *Federal Offshore Statistics: 1993* (1994) and *Managing Oil and Gas Operations on the Outer Continental Shelf* (1986) provided information on offshore oil.

The now-defunct Office of Technology Assessment (OTA) published a variety of invaluable materials on conservation. Of particular use in the preparation of this book were *Electric Power Wheeling and Dealing: Technological Considerations for Increasing Competition* (not dated), *Building Energy Efficiency* (1992), *Renewing Our Energy Future* (1995), *Saving Energy in U.S. Transportation* (1994), and *Improving Automobile Fuel Economy* (1991).

Information Plus thanks the National Conference of State Legislatures for use of information on nuclear energy from *Farewell to Arms* (Denver, Colorado, 1993). Its *Alternative Fuel Policies and Programs: A Legislator's Guide* (1997) discussed the use of alternative energy sources.

INDEX

INDEX (Continued)